FOREWORD

The purpose of this collection of documents is to make easily accessible major sources of current Roman Catholic theology. Initiated by Pope John XXIII and followed up by conferences of local hierarchies, many new thrusts in Roman Catholic social theology have occurred. While the majority of these initiatives have been within the framework established by Vatican II, new orientations, concerns, and methodologies have surfaced and are of critical importance in understanding contemporary Roman Catholic social theology. Our hope, in presenting this volume, is that the easy accessibility of these major social documents will contribute to building a more lively, creative, and responsible Catholic community in the United States, a community whose members will enrich one another and together will enrich the country, to which Catholics owe so much and for whose future Catholics now share full responsibility.

College of the Holy Cross   DAVID J. O'BRIEN
Worcester Polytechnic Institute   THOMAS A. SHANNON
March 1977

ACKNOWLEDGMENT

Mr. John J. Delaney, now retired from Doubleday, initiated this project and won the undying gratitude of the editors by his unfailing hope and remarkable patience. Miss Patricia Kossmann has seen this project through to its completion and we are grateful for her efforts.

RENEWING THE EARTH

Catholic Documents on
Peace, Justice and Liberation

Edited by
David J. O'Brien
and
Thomas A. Shannon

IMAGE BOOKS

A DIVISION OF DOUBLEDAY & COMPANY, INC.

GARDEN CITY, NEW YORK

Acknowledgment is hereby made to the United States Catholic Conference, Washington, D.C., for permission to reprint the following documents:

Mater et Magistra
Pacem in Terris
Populorum Progressio
Octogesima Adveniens
Justice in the World
Human Life in Our Day
The Economy: Human Dimensions
Political Responsibility: Reflections on an Election Year

Excerpts from the Medellín Conference reprinted by permission of Division for Latin America—USCC, Washington, D.C.

The texts of *Gaudium et Spes* and *Dignitatis Humanae* are reprinted with permission of *America*, 1966, All Rights Reserved, © by America Press, 106 W. 56th Street, New York, N.Y. 10019

Excerpts from *The Jerusalem Bible*, copyright © 1966 by Darton, Longman & Todd, Ltd. and Doubleday & Company, Inc. Used by permission of the publisher.

Library of Congress Cataloging in Publication Data
Main entry under title:

Renewing the Earth.

Includes bibliographical references and index.
1. Church and social problems—United States—
Catholic Church. 2. Church and social problems—Latin
America—Catholic Church. 3. Church and social problems
—Catholic Church—Papal documents. I. O'Brien, David J.
II. Shannon, Thomas Anothony, 1940–
HN37.C3R397   261.8'3
ISBN 0-385-12954-8
Library of Congress Catalog Card Number 76–52008

To Jack Egan, Peggy Roach, and
the Catholic Committee on Urban Ministry;
to the Sisters, Priests, and Lay People of
the C.C.U.M. Network
and
to the People They Serve

CONTENTS

III. Latin American Documents

I. International Documents

INTRODUCTION:
ROMAN CATHOLIC SOCIAL
THEOLOGY

Not too many years ago, American Catholics who began to think seriously about economic and social problems looked to the papal encyclicals for guidance. Leo XIII's *Rerum Novarum*, published in 1891, the first of the modern papal statements on such matters, received scant attention in the United States largely because Catholics, like most Americans, found little fault with the structure or operation of the American economy. Only in the 1930s, when the Great Depression shook popular confidence in the American free enterprise system, did significant numbers of priests, sisters, and lay people begin to notice papal social doctrine, now supplemented by Pope Pius XI's *Quadragesimo Anno* (1931). While Catholics disagreed among themselves about the proper interpretation and application of the Church's social teachings, they did agree that papal teachings provided a basis for a distinctive Catholic approach to social issues. In the postwar years, the encyclicals, refined in the speeches and writings of Pope Pius XII, continued to provide assistance to Catholic social activists, many of whom found in them justification for their own instinctive welfare-state liberalism.

The earlier encyclicals of Leo XIII and Pius XI were too rigid in their theology and history and too European in their social, political, and economic analysis to be directly useful to Americans. While the contemporary statements have much in common with their predecessors, they are informed by new, more flexible approaches to Scripture and tradition. They take full account of the increasing sophistication of modern social science, and they leave behind that rejection of the modern world which was an outstanding feature of earlier Catholic social thought. The teachings of Leo XIII, Pius XI, and Pius XII were filled with charity and passion for justice, but these qualities were often smothered by a triumphalist ecclesiology and a conservative, even negative, understanding of natural law. The modern documents retain the philosophical perspectives of earlier teachings but they are liberated by a vision of the Church as servant to humanity, by a renewed concern for the individual person, and by an open, humble awareness of the historically conditioned character of all human life and consciousness. The social teachings of the modern Church also reflect the ideas and perspectives of the emerging Christian communities of the so-called "third world." If they remain somewhat European-centered, nevertheless they are now far more universal in origin, spirit, scope, and impact than previously.

These documents, in short, provide guidance for a Christian understanding of the dramatic events of the modern world. Insofar as American Catholics continue to acknowledge membership in a universal Church and to define their particular responsibilities as Americans from the perspective of a universal dedication to one human family shaped by divine creation, redeemed by the sacrifice of Jesus Christ, and destined for a Kingdom which is still to come, they should be familiar with the best and most authoritative expressions of the universal Church's attitude toward the problems of humanity in the last quarter of the twentieth century.

THE SOURCES OF CATHOLIC
SOCIAL THOUGHT

1. EARLY CHRISTIANITY

Jesus Christ was the son of a carpenter, yet in his public life as recorded by the Evangelists he seems not to have put in a day's work. Nonetheless, back in the 1920s, advertising executive Bruce Barton described Christ as history's greatest businessman, who took twelve men from the bottom rungs of society and forged them into an organization which changed the course of history. Scripture, however, credits this success directly to the Holy Spirit, who on Pentecost found the twelve in disarray, trying to figure out what they were to do. No executive worth his salt would have left town imparting only such vague instructions as "Feed my lambs" and "Teach all nations." No. As perceptive critics have long been aware, Jesus was no great organizer; he showed little talent for scheduling, delegating responsibility, fund raising, or public relations. It would be hard to find any solid evidence that he even provided very well for himself, much less that he fulfilled any serious economic function or that he made any substantial contribution to the theory or practice of business.

What Jesus Christ did do, and did very well, was preach a new and rather startling message, proclaiming the advent of the Kingdom of God and the redemption of people from sin. Those who listened learned that the world they knew, a world of toil and suffering, was not the all-sufficient and ultimate theater of human experience. There was another world, a world of grace and redemption, of joy and love, open to those who would but ask for admittance. Like his countrymen, Jesus knew pain, privation, and rejection; like them he suffered and died. But, unlike anyone before or since, he conquered death at Easter, and in doing so he revealed a whole new world. The good news of his life, death, and resurrection was so powerful a witness that word of it, carried in disorganized and haphazard fashion by a remnant of irritable, quarreling people, changed the history of the world, giving shape and substance to humanity's dreams and providing the basic inspiration of human thought and feeling for a considerable portion of humankind.

The turbulence and complexity of the life of Christ's followers over the last two thousand years offers eloquent testimony to the fact that, as known and experienced in this world, the legacy of Jesus is an ambiguous one. For those who could believe, the Kingdom of God had indeed arrived; they knew in their own day-to-day lives the joy and ecstasy of divine grace. Yet even those most profoundly committed could know that new life only imperfectly, could know it only within—and not beyond—their own world of ignorance, selfishness, and sin. The Kingdom of God was here; Christ's work was complete; his spirit carried forward his life among his people. Yet in some sense the Kingdom was not yet fully here; it existed as a promise, beckoning from that future time when the reality of the Resurrection would be ultimately and fully complete. Jesus himself had taught his followers to pray that God's will would be done on earth and to petition that God's Kingdom should come. At the same time he told them that his Kingdom was not of this world but somehow was apart from it. Nowhere is the ambiguity of the Christian story more apparent than in this vision of a Kingdom present "even now" but "not yet." Today, two thousand years removed from the world of Jesus Christ, people continue to live amid the mysteries of human history, in the "time between" his all-sufficient redemptive work and the final culmination of human destiny in the Kingdom of God.

Here lies the source of so much of the tension, even contradiction in Christian life and social thought. "It is the same God that said, 'Let there be light shining out of darkness,' who has shone in our minds to radiate the light of the knowledge of God's glory, the glory on the face of Christ. We are only the earthenware jars that hold this treasure, to make it clear that such an overwhelming power comes from God and not from us" (2 Cor. 4:6–7). Knowing God and his grace, but "through a glass darkly," the Christian's moral life is always torn between the demand to live Christ's teachings completely, here and now, and the need to do so in responsible relation to others and to society; between a perfectionism which can become irrelevant to the suffering of others and a responsibility which can just as easily become expediency or opportunism. This, then, is the enduring dilemma of Christian social ethics: to reconcile the demands of being faithful to God in Christ with the simultaneous exercise of responsibility to social institutions.

Over the course of two millennia the Apostles and their successors have preached the gospel of the Risen Savior and millions of men and women have acknowledged him as Lord and sought to shape their lives in accord with that decision. When people heard the message of Pentecost, they asked the

Apostles, "What must we do, brothers?" and Peter's answer was clear: "You must repent," said Peter, "and every one of you must be baptized." And to the crowd he repeated: "Save yourselves from this perverse generation." In its pristine form, the message was, and remained, a personal appeal to each person to "put on the new self." Throughout the ages since, all the Christian churches have recognized that, at a most profound level, the Christian appeal is personal and constitutes a call to a new life in and for the Lord.

The early community gradually formed a distinctive ethic based on its understanding of the gospel. Its core was the expectation of the imminent arrival of the Kingdom of God, around which the community was centered. While this community lived in the world, it knew for certain that it was not of the world and that the Lord was to return to bring his work to completion. Alongside this communitarian orientation was an emphasis on the individual and his or her personal sanctification through moral acts performed for God. This emphasis on personal sanctification led to a radical individualism in which eternal value was conferred on the individual because of his or her relation with God. Consequently all earthly differences were engulfed in a divine love which reduced all social or class distinctions to nothing. But this radical individualism was tempered by the universalism of the absoluteness of God's love for all. This universalism effected a strong community in which all individual differences merged into an unlimited and universal love which is God. These themes kept individuals and the community separated from worldly structures. The expectation of the Kingdom and the rejection of what was superfluous or what would distract from one's relationship with God kept the energies of the early Christians within their community. This sectarian orientation led to a heroic ethic which admitted of no compromise with the demands of life in the world.

However, Christianity did not remain static. It quickly spread beyond Jerusalem and Rome, and as it grew, new elements began to emerge. The first of these was the realization that the Kingdom of God would not be immediately established, which had a dramatic impact upon the community's understanding of theology and social action. This even-

tually led to a merging of the concept of the Kingdom into
that of the Church and to a closer identification of the life of
the Church with the world. By the mere fact of the community's prolonged existence and its increased membership,
closer connections with social institutions had to occur. A second element was the perception that the existing sociopoli-
tical conditions were static, and therefore the Church perceived that it had to work out its relationship to the world
within these fixed categories and within a static vision of the
future. A third key element in the transformation of the early
community was the increasing complexity of the social and
economic situation of the members of the Church. Even
though from the beginning, membership had been composed
of all different economic groups, rapid growth in membership
produced a much wider distribution of socioeconomic classes.
This brought about tension within the community because of
the needs and interests of each class. Also, as the community
grew both numerically and geographically, the members became more difficult to control. Authority had not yet been
centralized, and each community tended to work out its own
solutions for a variety of problems.

Yet, despite a larger membership, there remained an idealistic anarchism and a communism of love which combined
both indifference to the world with an effort to actualize the
love of God and neighbor within small groups. Emphasis on
the individual remained the focus of early Christianity, yet
this was always understood in a context of love lived within
community. Consequently, there was a conservatism based
on an attitude of submission to the will of God relative to
worldly affairs and a strong independence of the life of the
community based upon its religious claims. This meant that,
while the Church insisted on its own religious integrity and
identity, it still did not perceive itself as a force for social
change or social reorganization. The most that occurred came
through the Pauline teaching that Christians had to recognize and use social organizations and institutions. This, however, was tempered with a spirit of inner detachment and independence from these institutions since they would
eventually perish. Institutions were simply to be accepted and
used for the purposes they were meant to serve. God had

created these institutions, they served their purpose, and there was no thought of changing them, because in the end Christians knew they were to perish.

This understanding of the gospel and the community life led to a very distinctive perception of social responsibility. The main type of reform articulated in the Gospels and the early community was that of private charity whose purpose was not primarily to heal social wrongs or problems but rather to awaken a spirit of love in the giver. The purpose of charity, therefore, was to create a new spirit within the individual, not to create a new social order. The emphasis was on philanthropy, not social reform. Insofar as social reform may have been conceived of, it was relegated to the small Christian communities in which some change was possible and in which meaningful personal relationships would be the prime means through which change was effected.

At this period, the energies of the Church were focused on the individual and the Christian community, the sanctification of the individual and the expression of the love of God within the community. Insofar as it was necessary to deal with social organizations and institutions, Christians did so with a spirit of detachment. There was no strong perception that Christians either could or should attempt to make a contribution to the larger society. The emphasis was on living the life of God within the ecclesial community. Charity was practiced primarily to benefit the giver, although the needs of the community were taken care of through a communism of love. Thus social reform was seen as beginning and ending within the ecclesial community. The social structures were perceived as fixed, rigid, and ultimately insignificant. Although hope for the imminent arrival of the Kingdom faded toward the end of the fourth century, nonetheless anticipation of the Kingdom remained alive within the hearts of Christians and this led them to separate themselves from the world and its temptations.

2. Medieval Social Ethics

Christian social ethics, originally preoccupied with the question of the believer's responsibility to the Lord, took on

new tasks in the period following the Church's emergence as
the official religion of the West. New responsibilities in society encouraged modification of gospel norms and a new sense
of social obligation which encompassed all of society and not
simply the community of believers. Primitive communism
of property had been eloquent testimony to the equality of
all people in the sight of God, but continued stress on that
doctrine could breed explosive social discontent. In the absence of a coherent social theory which took account of prevailing inequalities and dominant social institutions, the
Christian vision of a world in which "there are no more
distinctions between Jew and Greek, slave and free, male and
female, but all of you are one in Christ Jesus," could have
revolutionary implications. The subjection of property to
religious authority in the early Church, the denunciation of
the rich and powerful in Scripture and among the early
Fathers, the vigorous charge of St. Ambrose—"It is greed
that has engendered the rights of poverty"—all made clear
that Christianity taken seriously contained dangers for the
social order. From St. Paul on, the Church's leaders sought
to contain discontent by counseling resignation for the poor,
benevolence for the rich, and charity for all. Later, as the
Church took on official responsibilities, such disciplinary exhortations were given the sanctions of natural law as well as
religious truth and enforced with ecclesiastical and even
political sanctions. Private property and coercive human
authority were recognized to derive from human sin, but
were at the same time taught to be required by God as a
consequence of sin. Gradually an organic, functional social
theory emerged which upheld the given social order as ordained by God and made clear the sinfulness of discontent
and the futility of efforts at social change. At the same time
this theoretical framework provided a firm foundation for the
specification and enforcement of rules governing social and
economic activity, rules well adapted to a society and economy oriented toward the efficient distribution of scarce resources.

The characteristic feature of medieval social theology was
reflected in the Church's move from the community focused
on its own expression of love to a community which became

coresponsible for the development of an organic understanding of civilization. Because of the many social, economic, and political changes that emerged in the formation
of the medieval era, the Church found itself moving closer to
the center. This was especially true as a result of its becoming
the official religion for Europe. The Church now became
aware that it might initiate social reform within the institutions of society. It might be possible now to promote the idea
of a unified Christian civilization whose spirit would penetrate and renew the whole fabric of the social enterprise.

The synthesis formed by Thomas Aquinas served as the
backbone of medieval social theology and the social structure
as a whole. While Aquinas borrowed from many traditions
and initiated many new ideas of his own, his lasting contribution was the masterful synthesis that he created. So successful
was the synthesis that in many respects it still provides a large
part of official Roman Catholic theology. The synthesis of
Aquinas comes from two main traditions, the Stoic and the
Aristotelian, with which he combined the common theology
of the Church, articulated in particular by Augustine.

From Aristotle, Aquinas took the idea of society as an
order existing for the mutual exchange of services for the
common good. This suggests that society, and implicitly government, is a part of the structure of nature. Within this
context law functions not simply as a regulatory agency but
as a part of the universal structure of creation, which derives
its rational character from the intelligent plan of the creator.
Aquinas accepts from Aristotle the concept of a hierarchically
ordered universe with definite structures ordained by the creator.

From the Stoics, Aquinas borrowed the concept of an absolute and a relative state of nature. From a theological perspective, Aquinas identified the absolute state of nature with
the human condition of innocence in the Garden of Eden. In
this state, harmony existed between persons, nature, and
God; no laws or government were necessary. Aquinas identified the relative state of nature with the human condition
after the fall of Adam and Eve, which brought a transition
from innocence to sinfulness and the consequent weakening
of human nature with its disastrous personal and social

implications. Thus it became necessary to introduce government and laws to regulate the community and to restrain evil.

Aquinas inserted these views of nature into a two-story
model of the universe. The first story is the created world,
which has passed from innocence to sin and corruption. Operative within this level are the two types of Stoic natural law
combined with the Aristotelian concept of nature and natural
law to provide the context for the regulation of the relative
state of nature. The second story is the supernatural, the
world of God and the heavenly court, which is the goal and
fulfillment of the natural world, the purpose for which it was
created. These two worlds are united by two major social
realities: law and the institutions of Church and state.

Eternal law for Aquinas is the plan or order of creation
which has existed in the mind of God from all eternity. It is
a divine reality, immutable and the locus of all truth and
values; consequently, it is the source of all morality. Parallel
to this is the natural law, the apprehension and articulation
of this eternal law by human reason. In its pure form, natural
law is the Stoic absolute law of nature; but given human
weakness and the clouding of the intellect due to sin, the natural law of Aquinas is the Stoic relative law of nature.
Aquinas defines two other types of law parallel to these: divine law, the law of the Church derived from revelation but
also having affinities to natural law and human law; and the
laws of states or governments, which regulate personal and
social interaction. This division of law forms the basic matrix
within which all persons and institutions act and provides the
norms to which they must conform.

The two major institutions for Aquinas are the Church and
the state. The state, which is natural to the human community, is coercive because of the consequences of sin. Thus, on
the one hand, the state provides a remedy for sin by holding evil in check and by regulating human behavior; on the
other hand, it can be a punishment for sin since the state,
through an evil ruler, can inflict harm on its citizens, which
must be endured as a way of atoning for sin. Thus while the
state is a natural institution and part of the fabric of the order
and plan of the universe, it does have a purpose wider than

that of simply providing for the common good—namely the active repression of evil. The Church is of divine origin; possesses revealed truth, and directs persons and institutions to their final end, the supernatural. The Church, therefore, is superior to the state in that it relates directly to the final end of the person's life, but it is similar to the state in that it has an interest in human affairs, in the production of good citizens, and in regulating the state. The Church, with its knowledge of revelation, also serves as a check which keeps the Aristotelian principle of rational self-determination and regulation from going to an extreme.

Thus in the Thomistic synthesis, the person stands in the center of two intersecting lines, the supernatural and the natural, which are united through eternal and natural law and through the Church and the state. As a consequence, Aquinas was able to construct a universe which was organically united politically and theologically and which had a transcendent norm, by which one could evaluate both political and religious behavior. The model of this universe produced an organic unity of civilization in which there was a proper ordering of all things and harmony not only within each separate order but also among the different orders.

One extremely important element in the social ethic of Aquinas is his definition and use of the concept that is now called the theory of rights. Given the feudal ordering of society which prevailed in medieval civilization, Aquinas elaborated a theory of social duties, not a theory of rights. Because of the theory of society and social obligations inherent in this understanding of society, individuals were bound to each other and to social institutions by duties which were inherent in their state of life. These social duties or obligations were not an inherent part of the person; rather they were attached to the social role which individuals fulfilled. Thus by virtue of being a serf, the individual acquired certain duties to his feudal lord. The lord, in turn, acquired certain responsibilities to the serfs of the manor. This understanding of social duties also applied to the Church. What held the society together was a theory of social obligation that sprang from the very nature of the society and was understood from a theological point of view as related to a hierarchically ordered universe ultimately ruled over by God. Consequently, Aquinas and other medieval philosophers and theologians did not have a theory of individual or social rights; they focused on the duties incumbent upon individuals because of their social obligations. This clearly implied that social obligations took priority over individual desires or wants. As a result, claims against society were made in terms of clearly specified social responsibilities that were proper to various roles within the society. This emphasis on social duties was another way in which the organic unity of the civilization was maintained. Each individual's fulfilling of the responsibilities of his or her place in society insured total domestic tranquility. It was only after the breakup of the medieval civilization that an emphasis on individual rights began to receive the attention that it now enjoys.

After 1100, the economy of Western Europe entered upon a period of significant expansion, and the tension between the ethic of the gospel and the demands of worldly concerns reappeared with renewed force. The money economy, the growing importance of trade, and the appearance of vigorous competition all challenged the ethical formulations of an earlier era. Gradually, as the conflict sharpened, alternative poles appeared. Radical exponents of primitive gospel simplicity denounced the luxury of the towns and the arrogance and pride of the rich. Religious apologists for the new class, on the other hand, bent the gospel injunctions to allow city merchants to enjoy religious security. The Middle Ages, then, was not a period of uniform adherence to a moderate gospel and integration of religion and life but a time of ferment and conflict occasioned by the growing chasm between Christian pretense and economic practice. Unfortunately, the Church was deeply involved in the economic developments of the era; it was an economic institution of prime importance, fostering and encouraging trade, acquiring enormous debts, engaging itself in trade, investment, and profit. Its theologians and religious leaders struggled to reconcile vigorous economic activity with the teachings of the founder, at times in creative ethical formulation, and at other times in expedient compromises or sheer hypocrisy.

3. The Reformation and the Christian Ethic

After 1350 the period of economic expansion ended and decline set in. The Black Death, the wars which punctuated the next century and a half, and the enormous burdens of indebtedness all inhibited economic growth and caused a recession of expectation. One result was the older disciplines' being restored with new force as the Church tried to protect itself from its creditors and to soften the burdens of scarcity upon the poor. The exaction of Church taxes and the scandal of the sale of indulgences were felt by a population struggling against extreme poverty and were vigorously resisted both by the rising national and semifeudal states seeking their own sources of revenue and by an urban bourgeoisie unwilling to surrender liberties and prerogatives gained in the earlier period. It was in this setting that the Renaissance, the Reformation, and new technological and geographic breakthroughs stimulated a new wave of economic expansion. When the Reformed churches advocated antipapal doctrines and moral positions apparently conducive to capitalist economic expansion, it was natural for later observers to correlate the two, and link Protestantism with the supposedly new spirit of capitalism. Yet, as in so many other respects, Protestantism's social ethic merely represented the reawakening of older tensions and contradictions within the broad Christian tradition.

There were several major themes associated with the Reformation which were consistently present in Christian history and which have exerted a major influence on modern Christian thought on economic problems. They bear brief examination.

1) *Asceticism.* While Jesus had shown great concern for the poor and the oppressed and deplored the selfishness frequently present among the well-to-do, he offered no systematic economic ethic. Instead he seemed supremely unconcerned with worldly goods, and at times he seemed to summon his followers to a complete break with the workaday world. From the start, many Christians took such teachings with the utmost seriousness, from the desert hermits, who literally ceased to make a living, through mendicant communi-

ties of the Middle Ages, who relied upon alms for support. Other religious orders devoted themselves to prayer and meditation, bearing witness to the ultimate importance of God and the ultimate insignificance of worldly possessions. Catholicism endorsed this position as a counsel of perfection, a fit style for those of saintly dedication, but it resisted efforts to define such a stance as the exclusive demand of the gospel. In particular it fought bitterly any effort to deny the right of individuals, and of the Church itself, to own property and to use that property wisely.

Protestantism—and Calvinism in particular—rejected completely the otherworldly stance and demanded that all, saints and sinners alike, were bound to live in the world, to struggle there with the realities of evil, suffering, and selfishness. At the same time, the Christian was to practice in the world the rigorous detachment and strict life for God characteristic of the monastic rule. No one individual was to live as hermit, monk, or contemplative, but all were to live a worldly life of disciplined self-control and mystical piety. The Christian was to live *in* but be not *of* the world. This was a worldly asceticism, carried into the marketplace, where one was to do one's duty to God, to family, and to community, but always with the inner life totally oriented toward God. Thus both Catholicism and Protestantism recognized the authenticity of the perfectionist demands of the gospel. But, whereas Catholicism confined such perfectionism to a special few in the monasteries, living an organized life oriented toward that end, Protestantism imposed the demand on everyone within and not apart from the workaday world.

2) *Vocation.* Catholics and Protestants shared a common Bible, and in that Bible they shared a common story of creation and fall. From that common foundation they drew some similar conclusions: that the earth was provided by God for the use of humans, and all were to appropriate the fruits of the earth for their satisfaction and enjoyment. The mode of appropriation, work, was a gift of God, but it was also part of one's obligation to God, a burden imposed by human sinful disposition. Further, the fruits of labor were not one's own alone: One owed sacrifice to God as an expression of dependence and gratitude, and that sacrifice was best made within

community, among those who also acknowledged God as creator and source of all things. With Christ, the need for sacrifice was eliminated: He was the one and perfect sacrifice to the Father, commemorated, or repeated, in the Eucharistic celebration. Nevertheless, the early Church demanded continued sacrifice of some portion of the fruits of labor, now in the form of alms. St. Paul expended enormous time and energy organizing collections in the Gentile churches for the poor of Jerusalem. Thereafter, the Catholic Church upheld the obligation of sharing and sacrifice, both as a bond of community and as an expression of dependence on and obligation to the Lord. The early reformers and their churches utterly rejected the manifold forms of ecclesiastical exactions which were justified in the name of this obligation, but they not only did not surrender the basic point, they renewed it with force.

Equally important, the Church never lost sight of the significance of labor itself. In an agricultural age, and one of economic stagnation, work's sinful sources were recognized; but with social and economic diversification came a new emphasis upon the manifold possibilities of human endeavor and the various forms which worldly work could take: that of the ecclesiastic or cleric, the scholar, the lawyer, the merchant, the warrior, the lord of the manor, and the serf. As these expressed themselves within the context of Christian civilization, they were all endowed with social significance. Medieval Catholic thought was thoroughly organic, conceiving society in terms of a body, or an organism, all the parts of which contributed to the life of the whole. Each person was called to a distinct task in the world, a task whose exactions were the result of sin but which was ennobled by the fact of its contribution to the whole community. This notion was a fundamental one in the moral discipline. The exercise of one's responsibilities was never simply a matter of personal gain or satisfaction but of social responsibility; the use of one's talents or one's property was always evaluated within community, subject to its discipline. Such doctrines were admirably suited to an age of relative scarcity of resources, when people took the existing distribution of power and wealth for granted, and when the Church enjoyed the support of the whole community, which acknowledged its legitimacy as judge and jury. Expansion, growth, and diversification undermined this organic model by raising the prospect of greater accumulation, challenging the ethical hegemony of the Church, and making more obvious the exploitation of some groups in society by others. Something of this sort happened in the expansion of the High Middle Ages, and it happened again during the Reformation.

The reformers redefined the doctrine of the calling. They confined the calling to the world, and urged individuals to the diligent and responsible exercise of their tasks. On the other hand, far from departing from the organic conception of society, some reformers sought to restore it to primacy, enforcing even more strongly than their medieval forebears the social responsibility of all and the primacy of the claims of the Church and the community over individual goals and satisfactions.

What had changed was the economic climate of the countries where Calvinism in particular enjoyed its greatest successes. In the Low Countries and in England a period of intense economic advance coincided with the Reformation. Diligence in one's calling could lead not only to the accumulation of wealth but even to the displacement of old elites and the ascendency of new ones. The merchant class in particular, with a dynamism associated with advances in trade and technology, gained wealth and power and demanded a new status. The new churches attracted them by a doctrine of calling which enjoined diligence in work, and celebrated success as a result of this virtue and a sign of God's blessing. The early ecclesiastical leaders attempted to contain these teachings within the context of medieval notions of community and social obligation; but as religious enthusiasm waned, these portions fell into disuse, and the notion of calling stood forth clearly, obscuring the social and religious context of its origins and its legitimation.

3) *Stewardship.* The paradoxes of the gospel are nowhere more apparent than in the contrast between Christ's instruction to the rich young man to sell his goods and distribute the proceeds to the poor, and the apparent teaching of the parable of the talents, where individuals are instructed to

nurture and guard that which is entrusted to them. As has been pointed out, the early Church held both the notion of actual poverty and the doctrine of stewardship, in practice allowing Christians to hold property in private and even accumulate wealth, while insisting that in particular circumstances Christian obligation might demand that that property be disposed of and its proceeds distributed among the poor. The notion of stewardship—the idea that all who possess talent or property are stewards, and that they hold their talent and their property as trustees; they are accountable to God—provided a foundation for accomodation to existing economic arrangements without surrendering control over the moral life of the individual. In medieval Catholicism and among the early reformers, these notions were usually held within a social theory which emphasized the mutual duties and obligations of all members of the social body, and within an ecclesiology which was also social, emphasizing the mediating role of the Church, either as community or in the form of its clerical leadership, in teaching and enforcing the individual's accountability for his or her wealth and talent. When in Acts St. Peter took it upon himself to demand of some Christians that they give over their wealth to the community, he was demonstrating the ability of the Church to act in God's name. The idea was given force in Scripture by the fact that when some particular Christians refused, they were struck dead. Many Catholic theologians endorsed private accumulation throughout the Middle Ages; indeed thirteenth-century Italy provides examples of such endorsement as clear and direct as any in Puritan literature. The Calvinist reformers re-emphasized the doctrine. But both groups did so with the firm conviction that individuals were responsible to God for the use of their talents and wealth, and that the obligation could and should be given practical expression in the life of the Christian community.

4) *Christian society*. Whether one considers the notion of calling, or stewardship, or any other doctrine related to the Christian moral life, one cannot but be struck by the importance of the community. While there no doubt were strong strands of individualist thought in Christian history, it seems clear that the major thinkers of medieval Catholicism and

Reformation Protestantism were at one in their conviction
that the whole community enjoyed a stature and importance
at least equal to that of the individual. Indeed few would
have conceived of the sharp distinction modern individuals
perceive between the claims of the individual person and the
claims of the community. To be a Christian was to be a
member of a people "sharing the common life." To be
human was to be in a community, in fact, to be in communities within a community. Any individual belonged to a variety of groups—family, working class, congregation—and all
of these were part of the larger community of Christian society with its twin pinnacles of Church and state.

While early Christianity had been content to construct
small enclaves of people living the Christian life removed
from the broader society, the Church of the Middle Ages and
the churches of the reformers sought an integration of
Christianity and society. They believed that social institutions should aid individuals in the attainment of their main
objective in life, salvation, and that they should manifest the
belief of the community in Christ and his message. Christian
teachings were not simply rules for those who wished to follow in his steps but rules for all which should guide society in
all phases of its life. The medieval Church held tenaciously
to the conviction that all worldly endeavors were subject to
the scrutiny of both Church and state on the basis of the
clear moral teachings of the gospel. Calvin in Geneva and
Luther in Germany had no argument at all with that point;
they simply wished to purge the Church of its own vested interests so that its role as judge and teacher could be more
fearlessly and honestly exercised. Puritans, too, desired to
bring the social order in line with the gospel teachings. Some
did this by imposing the Christian discipline on all society, a
reformed Christendom. Others, returning to the model of the
early Church by confining their holy community to the
collective life of believers alone, despaired of making sinful
humans abide by the radical demands of the gospel. In either
case, they believed in common with their predecessors that
the moral demands of Christianity were relatively clear, that
they were subject to specification in terms of the conditions
of the times, that they were to be enforced by the Church

upon its own members and upheld by society at large. At times Reformation teachings on economic life appeared to justify an intense, even antisocial individualism; they often appeared to do so only because the demands of social responsibility to Church and society were so clear they could be taken for granted. Almost without exception the reformers shared with their Catholic predecessors a desire to uphold the social order while reforming the Church and the morals of the community. Their doctrine of church and their desire to construct a truly holy, pious community were fundamental, and only when these ideas are borne in mind can a fair assessment be made of their economic and social teachings.

Contract theory. One of the major consequences of the breakup of the medieval unity of civilization was the perception that individuals now stood in an adversary relationship to the larger society. This was augmented by a new emphasis on the individual and his or her value. As a result of this new perception of the individual's place in society, a new theory of the proper relationship between the individual and society had to be articulated. This was done, over the course of several centuries, through the elaboration of a variety of contract theories of society, the most famous of which were those elaborated by Hobbes and Locke. While presenting diametrically opposed pictures of the individual and the society, both theories emphasized individual rights as claims against the larger society. Both theories hold that the individual is the bearer of certain rights which society cannot contravene. These were described, mainly by Locke, as rights to life, to property, and to religious freedom.

This articulation of a theory of rights created a major change in social ethics. On the one hand, there was continuity with the medieval tradition in that contract theories are related to natural law, understood as a permanent moral order. On the other hand, there was discontinuity with medieval philosophy in that this theory of natural law based itself on inalienable rights inherent in each individual. The implication of this is that forms of social organization become somewhat more arbitrary since they are not of necessity dictated by the content of natural law. On the other hand, the rights and values of the individual were enhanced because the individuals became a locus of natural law. One immediate consequence of this was that social obligations now had to be justified on new grounds. In the medieval tradition, social obligations were consequent upon one's state in life. In the contract framework, social obligations were a result of positive law which was agreed to by individuals. This gave rise to a situation in which there would be continual and inherent conflicts between the individual and society.

This shift from an emphasis on social duties in the medieval tradition to individual rights in the post-Reformation period gave rise to a variety of experiments in justifying the foundations of the particular social order and articulating the responsibilities of the individual to maintain this social order. Since rights now inhered in their individual, new means of justification for social obligation were necessary. Yet as new freedoms and rights were claimed by individuals, the unity of civilization began to crumble, nationalism arose, and individuals claimed a new role for themselves in the midst of social structures.

4. Modern Catholic Social Thought

Modern Catholic social thought emerged from an effort to confront the drift of events with a reaffirmation of divine purpose and human responsibility. During the eighteenth and nineteenth centuries basic social, economic, and political changes in Western Europe undermined the whole system of Christian culture and civilization on which traditional religious identification depended. Secularization was bound to influence most severely the Catholic Church, which in the aftermath of the Reformation linked its fortunes closely with the old order. As the growth of urban, industrial society created a new era, the Church was perceived as essentially irrelevant. By confusing faith with the forms of a particular culture, the Church helped transform the Enlightenment's basically healthy emancipation of the critical intellect from the tutelage of religion into an anti-Christian secularism.

The issues were clear during the French Revolution, when the Church, caught between a loyalty to the old order and an attraction to the new, decided in the end to become an ally of order and authority. Throughout the nineteenth century Catholics aligned themselves with the party of order, royalists emerged in positions of strength, and liberals were forced to defend both their religious and social orthodoxy. The predominantly negative character of Catholic thought in the nineteenth century did not imply that Catholics were not concerned about the problems raised by the industrial and political revolutions which gave the period its character, only that this concern was limited by ecclesiastical interest and doctrinal discipline. Catholic thinkers located the source of modern problems in secularism, particularly in the divorce of political authority from its divine foundations and the separation of economic life from moral and ethical influence. Excessive individualism had destroyed the rich group life of the Christian era and left individuals at the mercy of the absolute state and irresponsible capitalists. Catholic leaders, both liberal and reactionary, agreed that contemporary problems could be overcome by a restoration of organic unity and direction of modern life through the reconciliation of society and culture with the Church.

In France the work of de Maistre and Bonald provided a framework for the reactionary policies of the Restoration papacy and the Catholic monarchical party in France. Their clear recognition of the contrasts between the organic, hierarchical character of Catholic social philosophy and the egalitarian individualism of the Revolution, laid a foundation for antiliberal thought, a process in which Lamennais shared. But he and his followers emphasized with equal clarity the positive values of the Revolution and pointed to a solution of the Church's problems which would be based on freedom and consent. Only a few liberal Catholics like Frédéric Ozanam and Charles de Coux recognized the importance of changes in economic life and social structure. Ozanam anticipated much of later Catholic thought by his advocacy of a living wage and the right of workers to organize, but his major efforts were devoted to charitable activity aimed at the alleviation of misery and the easing of class hatreds, which was quite in keeping with the medieval model of social ethics.

Organized efforts by French Catholics to achieve specifically Christian reforms were to be politically conservative, dating from the advent of the Third Republic, when the Comte de La Tour du Pin and Comte Albert de Mun organized workers and employers in study clubs under aristocratic patronage. These "worker's circles" were designed to end antisocial and anti-Christian class division and overcome the divorce of social and economic life from Christian principles. The objective of the founders was a restoration of the medieval economic order with joint bodies of capital and labor eventually becoming constituents of government in a monarchical framework. A third figure in the movement, Léon Harmel, was unsympathetic with La Tour du Pin's legitimişm and paternalism and instead aimed to develop working-class leadership, cooperatives, and copartnership arrangements which would give the workers a sense of responsibility and a real participation in decision-making in industrial society. Another group of Catholics, led by economist Charles Perrin, accepted the basis of the prevailing order, opposed labor organization and all but the most minimal forms of social legislation, and, in particular, rejected any return to a guild arrangement similar to that advocated by La Tour du Pin through his workers' circles.

Such counterrevolutionary activity declined in France after the appearance of *Rerum Novarum* in 1891, but political preoccupations continued to plague Catholic social action. The idealistic efforts at social and political reform of the Christian Democrats of the nineties and the *Sillon* in the first decade of the new century came under strong criticism from conservative Catholics fearful of the influences of liberalism and modernism. Leo XIII warned against political activity and defined Christian Democracy as action inspired by a Christian desire to uplift the lower classes excluding political commitments. A more direct rebuke met Marc Sangnier's *Sillon* when it attempted to carry its mystical democracy into partisan politics.

More effective educational work was done in France by the *semaines sociales*, or study weeks, the teachings of which were reformist, encouraging the development of labor and professional groups rather than the mixed corporations. Similarly, new unions of study clubs and social journals promoted reform along the line of *Rerum Novarum*.

In Germany, the shift from a dogmatic and revolutionary corporatism to a more moderate, reformist participation in the liberal society anticipated rather than awaited *Rerum Novarum*. The pioneer of German social Catholicism was Bishop Emmanuel von Ketteler of Mainz. Ketteler believed that a new and revised guild order of joint organizations of workers and owners, inspired by Christian principles, would restore the institutions of function and status which liberalism had destroyed. He opposed state initiation of such a system both because of the consequences for state power and the necessity for a cooperative spirit and ethic as a prerequisite for the guild society. However, recognizing the impossibility of establishing a corporate social order in the near future, Ketteler, without abandoning his theoretical objective, gradually turned to state action to alleviate immediate economic abuses. Acutely aware of the responsibility of Christians to work for immediate alleviation of suffering and injustice, Ketteler eventually supported industrial legislation and trade unionism, the only methods by which the causes of poverty and insecurity could be eliminated in the reasonably near future.

Nineteenth-century Catholicism's rigid opposition to modern industrial civilization was very attractive to rural landowners, lower middle class artisans and shopkeepers, and alienated aristocrats. At the same time, the Church's determination to unify and discipline its organization, its nostalgia for the old order, and its self-righteous paternalism choked pastoral energies and insured the isolation of the Church from the working class. Having already defined the nature and mission of the Church in a way that emphasized its crucial importance to human salvation and identified its growth and power with the progress of the Kingdom of God, Catholic Church leaders tended to measure and judge social and political action in terms of the welfare of the institutional Church. The pioneers of Christian democracy from Félicité de Lamennais to Dom Luigi Sturzo could testify to the Church's willingness to use or discard their efforts in accord with prevailing political sentiment. In particular the Roman leaders of the Church and many bishops were vigilant against all movements for change that operated outside the control of Church officials. Even the relatively liberal Pope Leo XIII, in discussing the efforts for social reform that received his encouragement in *Rerum Novarum*, warned against official involvement in politics and held that even nonpolitical "Christian action in behalf of the people" in "whatever projects individuals or associations form . . . should be formed under episcopal authority." "Let your solicitude watch and let your authority be effective in controlling, compelling, and also in preventing, lest any under the pretext of good should cause the vigor of sacred discipline to be relaxed or the order which Christ has established in His Church to be disturbed," Leo instructed the bishops of the world. Such control easily led to manipulation. Always genuine concern for the poor and oppressed was subordinate to the presumed welfare and influence of the Church, not for its own sake but for the good of all men who, whether they knew it or not, needed the Church.

The overwhelming sentiment of Church leaders was that true social harmony and welfare was identical with Catholic influence and power. "Let it become more and more evident," Pope Leo wrote, "that the tranquillity of order and the true prosperity flourish especially among those people whom the Church controls and influences." At the end of the nineteenth century Pope Leo XIII, faced with the near catastrophic isolation of his Church from the main current of Western intellectual, cultural, and political life, attempted through a series of remarkable encyclicals to provide a foundation for reconquest. Convinced that the Church had once guided and shaped a unique, humane, and progressive civilization, Leo and his generation attributed modern social evils to "a spirit of innovation" unleashed by the Protestant Reformation and made demonic by the Enlightenment and the French Revolution. Leo's encyclicals were designed to demonstrate the happy union of reason and revelation, to show that the many modern dilemmas—of freedom and order, of progress and stability, of individual and society—were resolved by the proper understanding of God, man, and nature, knowledge accessible to reason and sanctioned by revelation.

Leo's great encyclicals on Christian philosophy, politics, and social order revived the classical teachings of St. Thomas. God had created man, endowed with reason and intended for salvation. State and Church were institutions designed to facilitate attainment of one's ultimate, spiritual, supernatural destiny. The Church had been divinely established to provide the means of salvation, and the state was bound both to profess the truths of Christianity and assist and support the Church in its high endeavors. Man was by nature both individual, possessing inherent rights and dignity, and social, requiring the fellowship of others for the realization of his highest goals. Because social life needed direction, the state was natural to man, divine in origin, and, when legitimate, possessed of divinely sanctioned authority. Leo, like his predecessors, believed that the Church preached obedience to subjects and justice to rulers. During his reign he began by doing a great deal of the latter, but in his last years he felt constrained to issue many warnings to his subjects to show due respect for the civil and ecclesiastical powers.

In the Leonine corpus, individual and social considerations blended happily together, but in the world things were quite different. In a remarkably evenhanded manner, the Pope laid anathemas on both liberal capitalism, which released the individual from social and moral constraints, and socialism, which subordinated individual liberty to social well-being without respect for human rights or religious welfare. Economic life, like political life, should reflect the dualistic nature of the person, Leo argued, providing for bodily needs and facilitating rather than obstructing the quest for salvation. It was a strong position from which to condemn wage slavery. Leo insisted that wages be determined not by economic considerations alone but by taking into account the basic needs of the individual. Property, too, was subject to social and moral restraints; while all had a right to possess private property, none had the right to use that property without reference to the needs of their neighbors and of the community. Into every economic system and indeed into every economic transaction Leo insisted that the moral law had to be inserted, a law based on a rational comprehension of human nature, supplemented by divine revelation. The

criteria given by that law were criteria of justice, demanding
equity in exchange and bargaining, balance between various
economic sectors, and organization of the constituent economic units. More generally, it demanded that the common
good of the community take precedence over individual gain
in determining economic policy without, however, necessarily
infringing on legitimate rights. This in turn suggested a wider
concept of economic organization and governance, implicit in
Leo's teaching and fully developed in Pius XI's *Quadragesimo
Anno,* published in 1931.

Drawing on the writings of numerous Central European
economists and theologians, Pius demanded the restoration
of structures of economic self-government in order to overcome the chaotic injustice of capitalism and the regimented
injustice of socialism. These structures were described as
vocational groups, patterned on the romantic vision of medieval guilds. Pius envisioned the full organization of workers
and managers together in joint organizations to determine
policy for the industry as a whole, with a council of industry
representatives determining overall national economic policy.
Based on the law of justice and infused with a sense of social
responsibility and Christian charity, taught and sanctioned by
the Church, such a system would be not simply another
method of social organization but, indeed, "the Christian social order." Papal social doctrine was a package, demanding
acceptance *in toto,* and demanding it in the name of faith.

Quadragesimo Anno, like *Rerum Novarum* before it, contained scathing denunciations of both liberal capitalism and
atheistic communism and socialism. Yet, the two encyclicals
differed in tone and general direction. Writing at the height
of the power of liberal capitalism, Leo attempted to divert
Catholics from a catastrophic stance of an almost utopian vision, which held out for the restoration of medieval guilds
and associations at a time when the power and success of
capitalism were at their height. Rather, he attempted to
nudge Catholics throughout Europe to join with the workers
in seeking to alleviate their plight through organized action
and social legislation, reforms which required some temporary
accommodation to modern society. Pius XI, writing forty
years later, confronted a liberal society and capitalist econ-

omy in the midst of its greatest crisis. World War I had shaken the confidence of Victorian liberalism to its foundations; the great Depression, reaching its lowest depths in 1931, threatened to overthrow both the economic and the political systems constructed in the nineteenth century. Pius was not alone; indeed he voiced a common opinion in foreseeing a titanic struggle between communism and a rampant materialism of wealth and power in the capitalist world. Like many Europeans of the day, especially those of a conservative bent who had never accepted the liberal era, he sought a middle way. Thus, rather than simply echoing Leo's pleas for reform, he went further, calling for the establishment of a full-fledged Christian social order as a middle way, indeed the only middle way, between a capitalism become oligarchic and a communism which, as he made clear in *Divini Redemptoris*, was the great enemy of the age.

The problem, in retrospect, was that the Christian social order envisioned by the Pope took little account of the historical experience of liberalism. In Austria, Portugal, and, to a lesser extent, Spain, some effort was made to implement the teaching of the encyclicals, but it could only be done through the instrumentality of an authoritarian party and a dictatorial state. Equally important, his mode of implementation reinforced the conviction, long sustained by Catholic isolation, that the Church possessed all the answers to the problems of the modern age, not just the answers of faith, but prescriptions for society, culture, and politics. The end result was that the magnificent effort to construct a body of Catholic social teaching produced thinkers and documents which were insightful and powerful in perceiving and denouncing the evils of liberalism, capitalism, and democracy, but which could never transcend that critique to formulate a positive, attractive, and compelling alternative. Because they distanced the Church from the worst features of the age, they could and did generate a pastoral approach which brought the Church closer to the suffering poor, particularly in the countryside, but they never succeeded in relating to the hopes and aspirations of the working class. For all its failings, liberalism had excited new hopes and aspirations among masses of ordinary people; the Church seemed only to offer a return to a former age which many knew instinctively had been neither secure nor happy for most people.

World War II brought another turning point in the history of the West. The Church, insulated from the structures of liberalism, skillfully present to both sides of the war, emerged from that terrible experience as one of the few transnational institutions left intact. Pope Pius XII began to offer a new affirmation of democratic political structures and of social reform, while Catholic anticommunism now corresponded with the stance of most leaders of Western governments. As a result, the papacy experienced a new prestige and Christian Democratic governments became major vehicles for the rebuilding of Western European society. That society, once perceived as threatening to the Church, now seemed the only available bulwark against a communist menace now even more dangerous as it turned viciously against the Church in Eastern Europe. Catholic social thought, under Pius XII's leadership, once again de-emphasized the call for total reorganization of society articulated by Pius XI, and returned to the reformism and moderation of Leo. Trade unionism, social insurance, and the welfare state, even mixed economic arrangements of government and private enterprise enjoyed the favor of the Church and the Catholic parties. Humanistic liberals like Jacques Maritain enjoyed prominence and importance and, while radical efforts such as that of the French worker priests were rejected, a liberal style of positive social action and liberal reformist politics became normative. And, below the surface and still laboring under the suspicion which had beset pioneers and critics since the ultramontane triumph of Vatican I, new seeds were being planted in movements for pastoral renewal in France and theological revision in Germany, France, and the English-speaking world. While liberal Catholics still chafed under ecclesiastical restrictions in the fifteen years following World War II, the climate had undoubtedly changed, new voices were being heard, the Church was beginning to look at itself through the lenses of new experience. The results would become clear only during the reign of Pope John XXIII and the Council that was his most significant achievement.

5. The Background of Contemporary Social Thought

In the last fifteen years, Catholic social doctrine has won wide attention in circles formerly far from interested in the Church. The encyclicals of Pope John XXIII and Pope Paul VI, the statement "The Church and the Modern World" of Vatican II, and the statement "Justice in the World" issued by the 1971 Synod of Bishops appeared to many to place the Church in a whole new stance in regard to the major social and economic questions confronting mankind. The fundamental flaws of the older Catholic social doctrine lay in its ecclesiology and its politics. Leo and Pius were very much spokesmen for and within the ultramontane Church, a Church whose centralization and cult of the papacy climaxed in Vatican I. That Council had defined both papal infallibility and papal primacy. While shying away from full endorsement of papal monarchy, the Council made clear that pastors and teachers in the Church owed full submission to Rome on matters of discipline as well as faith and morals. Concordats with Catholic states, Roman-based training of prominent ecclesiastics, and control of seminaries and universities following the condemnation of modernism in 1905 all strengthened the unity of the Church. Gradually the Church mobilized itself for entry into the chessboard of modern diplomacy. Just as the Church in practice tended to believe that the road to salvation led through the Vatican (and the Kingdom of God bore striking similarity to a very large Catholic Church), so acceptance of the papal social and economic teaching required, when the chips were down, acceptance of the Church. While Leo encouraged priests to go to the people, he had no idea that they would go there on their own. Pius XI went further, providing in Catholic Action an organized structure of Catholic efforts for social change, carefully defined as under episcopal supervision and control. The whole effort was aimed at reconquest of a lost world. Unfortunately, the Church became embroiled in the tragic events of the 1930s, discrediting old assumptions, forcing new alliances, and challenging the conscience of its members.

In recent Catholic social and economic thought the dream of a restored Christendom which fueled this stance has faded as Church leaders have internalized the realization that Catholicism is, and likely will remain, a minority faith in a secular world. This consciousness, which spread widely after World War II, deeply influenced postwar social action, particularly under the leadership of Emanuel Cardinal Suhard of Paris. Yves Congar, Henri de Lubac, and Karl Rahner all expressed in one form or another a sense of the Church as at least a semipermanent minority—"a minority in service to the majority," in Rahner's words. At the very least this entailed a recognition of the priority of home missions and pastoral care, seen in the worker priests' movement and the *mission de France*. Even more, it entailed a drastic reassessment of the restorationist mystique.

Vatican II replaced the juridicial, hierarchical definition of church with more biblical and symbolic images and clearly articulated a sense of the Church as taking its form and function from its relationship to the Kingdom of God. It remained for the postconciliar generation to carry the process further, questioning whether indeed the Church is the ordinary means of salvation and whether Christians should not discard at last a sense of human history which envisions the return of all people to the Church. This "Copernican revolution" in the notion of church, placing the Kingdom of God at the center of concern and locating the Church as one of a number of institutions related to Kingdom, has been carried furthest in Latin America, where liberation theology sees church not as institution but as movement in service to human liberation. The papal documents do not go this far, but they do express a new realization of church as servant to humanity in its struggle for peace, justice, and development.

A second shift marked by the Council resulted from the long, agonizing effort of Church leaders to come to terms with liberal, democratic principles. The nineteenth-century position that freedom of conscience, of the press, and of association were evils to be tolerated where necessary but never upheld as ideal, was continued in more subtle form by Leo XIII, Pius XI, and Pius XII. The opportunism of this position became evident in the Church's scandalous relation with fascist regimes and generated a determination to place human liberties on a solid foundation of principle within the Church. Most evident in the conciliar statement on religious freedom, this new stress on human rights occupied a central place with Pope John and Pope Paul. They have given considerable attention to the right to development, the notion that national self-determination and the rights of the poorer nations to have control over their resources and receive equity in international markets is simply a specification of the deeper right of all individuals to develop personally and to share in the riches of their culture and the fruits of their own economic endeavor.

On questions of justice and peace, the social documents of the Catholic Church retain many of the elements of the old: a modified scholastic approach, the stress upon the social responsibilities of property, the radical denial that any individual or nation has a right to superfluous possessions when others are in need. They retain, too, a powerful imperative of action and remove any doubt that such efforts are central elements of the Christian life. "Action on behalf of justice and participation in the transformation of the world fully appear to us as a constitutive dimension of the preaching of the Gospel, or in other words, of the Church's mission for the redemption of the human race and its liberation from every oppressive situation," the Synod Fathers stated. Whatever the direction the Church's renewal may take in the years to come, the struggle for justice and peace must be a central, perhaps even a determinative, element in the process.

Rather than attempting to order all human life and human relationships, the Church holds out its hand to people struggling for liberation with a strong endorsement of human rights and democratic participation. It no longer assumes that it possesses the answers, that it holds in its bag of tricks real knowledge of the way the world ought to be organized. Placing the Kingdom of God and a theory of individual and social rights at the center of its social ethic, the Church knows that in the Kingdom all power comes from the Lord, and that the power which some exercise over others is an evil to be struggled against, eliminated, or humanized through democratic participation. It knows, too, that the Kingdom is a

Kingdom of love and not of hate, of freedom and not of oppression, of justice and not of tyranny. But the Church does not know how the Kingdom will be organized, and it does not know with any assurance exactly how its values and ideals are to be realized. It is never possible simply to deduce from Christian principles any one single pattern of the world as it ought to be. This is a position which demands from Christians resistance to the obvious oppression and violence of our times and demands as well that they order their lives in relation to programs which effect their elimination. But this also induces a humility about possible solutions and forbids Christians or anyone else to endow their program with the sanctions of divine revelation. It is a stance which fully recognizes the ambiguities of freedom and necessity in a world which remains, as it was for our forebears, agonizing in the "even now–not yet" of the gospel.

In many ways the Vatican Council set the Church to recover not the social order of the medieval Church but the community of the pre-Constantinian period, when it was, and knew itself to be, a minority. Thus, Christians are encouraged to announce the good news of God's promise of liberation, to make of their Church a community of justice, freedom, equality, and love, a sign of that kingdom they know will come.

In our day, Church teachings celebrate the achievement of humanity's technology and the abundance which economic activity has produced. Like the Old Testament prophet who delighted in the milk and honey of the Promised Land, the popes recognize in the productive potential of modern industrial society the possibility of reducing human misery, eradicating the curse of poverty, and freeing all persons for a more responsible possession of their lives and history. At the same time that the Church welcomes the fruit of these tools and ingenuity, it recognizes the demonic potential of humanity's pride, the dehumanizing character of the productive process, and the glaring injustices of the maldistribution of the world's wealth and resources. As for Church members, they are more openly divided than in the past. Some, caught up in worldly success and achievement, lose their sense of the otherness of the Kingdom and the righteousness of God.

They can see no alternative to, or no need for an alternative to, the present system of economic life. Others, of equally strong faith, are overwhelmed by the gap between the promise of God and the potential of humans, and the actual, ugly realities of poverty, oppression, and exploitation. The former are apt to affirm the world as the best possible approximation of the Kingdom in our times; the latter, to reject a world so far removed from one in which good persons can live. The division is a perennial one in Christian history, and raises perennial questions. Is the Church to comfort or to challenge, to offer hope of release from the bondage of sin by personal salvation or to demand that individuals refashion their behavior and their social institutions on the basis of justice and love? Neither the Scriptures nor the history of Christianity offers a clear answer.

The paradox of "even now—not yet" remains. Christians must take their world with the utmost seriousness. While they must strive to serve others in the context of the social order in which they live, they know at the same time that their world is not, after all, the Kingdom of God; its spirit and structures, no matter how enlightened or elevated they may appear, are flawed by human sinfulness, selfishness, ignorance, and pride. They know that the world which God has made is good and they know that history is the arena in which God's purposes are revealed and ultimately fulfilled. They must affirm life, love all individuals made in God's image and celebrate the potential and the hopefulness of the community and history. But they also affirm the Cross, knowing that their reward in this life may not be life but death, not joy unallayed but suffering as well. Christians and their Church then will affirm their world but deny it ultimate significance; they will seek to live out the gospel in their lives and built a world fit for human habitation, but always with a sense of the otherness of God and the transiency of human life and experience.

CHRISTIANITY AND SOCIAL PROGRESS
(MATER ET MAGISTRA)

On December 30, 1960, Pope John announced during a public audience that he would issue a major encyclical letter on social questions. The new letter would review social changes since the earlier statements and attempt to evaluate them in the light of a changing world. Entitled *Mater et Magistra*, "Mother and Teacher," from the first three words of the text, its subtitle indicated its intent. "On recent developments of the social question in the light of Christian teaching."

"The social question" was the phrase used since the middle of the nineteenth century to denote the changes associated with the Industrial Revolution, particularly the appearance of new forms of work in the factory system, the consequent urbanization of society, and, most importantly, society's fragmentation into social classes defined by income, wealth, and roles in the productive process. The growing interest of Catholic leaders, and eventually of the popes, was occasioned by this almost total change of social values and organization. For some, a charitable impulse of human concern for the suffering stimulated intense interest in the social question. Political factors, particularly the manner in which the uprooted urban proletariat provided mass support for anticlerical and socialist movements, also forced church attention to the new problems. Finally, in much of Europe urban industrial society disturbed traditional religious loyalties, so that the European Church became preoccupied with "the loss of the working class." All these considerations found expression in the great encyclicals *Rerum Novarum* and *Quadragesimo Anno*, whose seventieth and thirtieth anniversaries respectively were the occasion of Pope John XXIII's *Mater et Magistra*.

Pope John's first encyclical faced a world sorely divided and deeply troubled, in which proletarian Communism threatened Western countries which had modified the liberal capitalism condemned by Leo but had not become fully socialistic. In that context, Pope John presented the Church as a friendly critic, pointing out problems and offering its aid in solving them. There was none of the ecclesiastical self-interest of the earlier documents, which had expressed the mind of a Church which felt itself surrounded by hostile forces. Instead the mood of the letter was one of participation and responsibility: The social order that exists and that will be built will be one in which all people must live. Pope John was saying that the Catholic Church had joined modern society.

The development of Catholic social teaching resulted from the intention of the popes to apply timeless principles of justice and truth to changing historical circumstances. In this encyclical, however, John attempted to develop the application of standards of social justice to the postwar world, where the social question had changed, it seemed, from one primarily related to the struggle of labor against capital to one which featured a complex effort to achieve balanced economic growth, providing sufficient profit to stimulate investment while insuring just remuneration for all the factors of production and providing a social balance among rural and urban, agricultural and industrial sectors of both the national and the international economy. Furthermore, the collapse of the imperialist systems of the nineteenth century and the awakening aspirations of new nations posed a problem of a balanced international order in a way that dramatically challenged the standards of social justice and even more dramatically threatened the precarious balance of the international political system.

Pope John went on to urge ever fuller organization of both workers and employers so that they might act as groups to ensure their own interests and promote the overall well-being of society. The demands of social justice, requiring all to give due consideration to the well-being of society, require effective instruments through which persons may act to fulfill that responsibility. These concerns led Pope John to focus on two specific areas: private property and the just wage. Although John recognizes the traditional teaching on the right to private property, he connects with this the duty of the effective distribution of goods throughout the whole society. Because of this, economic and social life are to be modified so that a more widespread private possession of a variety of durable goods is to be made easier. John recognizes and affirms the tendency to vest more ownership in the state and other public bodies because the common good demands this. However, this process should always be done in accord with the principle of subsidiarity. Public ownership should occur only when the common good requires it, and it should be accomplished in such a way that private ownership of property is not destroyed. John also goes a bit beyond the traditional teaching that the just wage must enable humans to lead a life of dignity and allow the possibility of fulfilling family responsibilities. The just wage, according to this encyclical, must take into account the contribution of individuals to the economic effort, the economic state of the enterprises within which they work, the requirements of each community, and what concerns the common good of all people. What Pope John hoped would occur from this is a breakdown of class differences and the distribution of goods according to the norms of justice so that everyone in the community can develop his or her self. The result would be a wider availability of employment and consequently a wider availability of goods and services for all. Through the just wage, economic benefits will be distributed to more and the foundation of a just society will be built.

Needs such as these led Pope John, in the most controversial section of the encyclical, to recognize and endorse the process of socialization—a word which seemed to describe the whole range of human action, including nationalization, by which individuals attempted to fulfill their tasks as members of social groups and as participants in religiously pluralistic and culturally diverse societies. The word seemed to suggest an endorsement of socialism. But while the Pope recognized the need for social ownership of firms or industries which could not be effectively and justly operated in private hands, he meant to imply less an endorsement of such moderate socialism than of the many economic, ethnic, social, and cultural organizations which mediated between individuals and society as a whole.

The imbalance between rich nations and poor drew the Pope's attention; he called it "the most difficult problem of the modern world," a statement given support by the growing preoccupation of Church leadership with these problems. Pope John warned against the dangers of neocolonialism, by which the outward trappings of political control are abandoned but many economic ties remain to perpetuate the state of dependency for the less developed nations. The problem of aid was not part of the discussion of social problems in the early social encyclicals. In discussing economic affairs and international relations, and the problem of effective aid for underdeveloped nations, John makes a first attempt in the encyclical to come to terms with this problem. First he points out the responsibility of the respective governments to bring about a just distribution of wealth and to minimize imbalances. The individual citizen should be brought into this process of economic and social reform as much as possible to deepen his own sense of dignity and to allow the widest possible application of the principle of subsidiarity. Also, the various imbalances in the nature of the world should naturally lead to a sense of cooperation and trade so that all may enjoy the riches of the world. The growing feeling of world brotherhood and the growing interdependence of countries present reasons for common development, as well as being a means to preserve peace and unity. *Mater et Magistra* also argues that on the basis of justice and humanity, nations with surpluses have an obligation to help those that are without them. It further recognizes that harm can come to some classes of the sharing nations and states that these economic inconveniences should be borne equally by all.

Specifically Pope John warns against a country's using aid as a means of turning political situations to its own advantage and of dominating underdeveloped countries. This is another form of colonialism which obstructs just international relations and endangers the orderly progress of all people. In giving aid, attention should be paid to helping the people in a country develop skills so that the country may eventually stand on its own.

The encyclical is also unique in that it contains a lengthy section on agriculture, which was not a feature of past social teaching. The first problem mentioned is the departure of large numbers of the rural population to nonrural areas. The reasons given for the shift of the population are summarized as the depression of the agricultural areas in terms of the labor force, productivity, and the standard of living. To help solve some of these problems and to answer questions raised by this situation, Pope John makes several suggestions.

First, improvements are to be made by public authorities in the services offered to people, such as highway construction, education, medical services, and marketing facilities. Second, a balance of growth must be established between the various sectors of the economy. Specifically, Pope John suggests making an immediate application of technical developments to agriculture. This will help agriculture absorb part of the industrial growth and will also help agriculture respond more productively to consumer needs. And because of this balance, agriculture will contribute to the stability of the purchasing power of money which is necessary for a stable development of the entire economic system. Third, the peculiar situation of agriculture should be kept in mind in setting up a program of taxation. A rural economy is subject to risk and there is often difficulty in finding capital to reinvest. For the same reasons, rural dwellers often cannot pay high interest rates. Therefore public authorities should make special provisions for this situation. Fourth, twofold insurance is suggested for agriculture: one form covering the actual output and another covering farmers and their families. Because their average wages are lower than those of urban workers, special consideration must be given to them to balance inequalities. This is also a means of helping to establish a just distribution of the national income to all citizens. Price protection is a fifth suggestion. A balance must be maintained between making produce available at prices that all can afford and allowing the farmer enough profit to enjoy a dignified life. With this is the suggestion that farmers organize farm co-operatives and professional associations, and that these groups function in public life to work for the development of agricultural areas.

These suggestions are meant to help rural dwellers increase their standard of living and also allow them to enter more effectively into the larger society. Pope John sees agriculture as a most dignified and necessary vocation and wants to ensure farmers their rights to a dignified life with protection because of their unique contribution to society.

As had happened so frequently in the past, the Pope's words became instruments in polemic controversy within the Catholic community. Liberal Catholics found in the encyclical general support for the social and economic policies of new deal-style liberalism. The conservative Catholic response was expressed in an editorial in William F. Buckley's *National Review* which quipped "Mater si, Magistra no." Although the debate continued for many months and even years, it did not detract from the spirit of optimism and hope which informed the encyclical, and the incarnationalist theology which called upon Catholics to abandon any "artificial opposition between the perfection of one's own being and one's personal, active presence in the world." That acceptance of full and personal participation in the world community, with a Christian spirit of optimism and confidence, inspired a new wave of ecumenical exchange in the churches of the West and laid a firm foundation for the gradual shifts of subsequent Church documents, leading to a more personal, practical, and person-oriented approach in Catholic social thought and action.

MATER ET MAGISTRA

ENCYCLICAL LETTER OF HIS HOLINESS,
JOHN XXIII BY DIVINE PROVIDENCE POPE

TO OUR VENERABLE BROTHERS, THE PATRIARCHS,
PRIMATES, ARCHBISHOPS, BISHOPS, AND OTHER
LOCAL ORDINARIES IN PEACE AND COMMUNION WITH THE
HOLY SEE, AND TO ALL THE CLERGY AND
FAITHFUL OF THE CATHOLIC WORLD:

New in Doc.

ON RECENT DEVELOPMENTS OF THE SOCIAL QUESTION
IN THE LIGHT OF THE CHRISTIAN TEACHING.

Before adressed to Bishops & Rulers.

POPE JOHN XXIII

Venerable Brothers and Dear Sons: Health and Apostolic Benediction

1. The Catholic Church has been established by Jesus Christ as MOTHER AND TEACHER of nations, so that all who in the course of centuries come to her loving embrace, may find salvation as well as the fullness of a more excellent life. To this Church, "the pillar and mainstay of the truth,"[1] her most holy Founder has entrusted the double task of begetting sons unto herself, and of educating and governing those whom she begets, guiding with maternal providence the life both of individuals and of peoples. The lofty dignity of this life, she has always held in the highest respect and guarded with watchful care.

2. For the teaching of Christ joins, as it were, earth with heaven, in that it embraces the whole man, namely, his soul and body, intellect and will, and bids him to lift up his mind from the changing conditions of human existence to that heavenly country where he will one day enjoy unending happiness and peace.

Holistic

3. Hence, although Holy Church has the special task of sanctifying souls and of making them sharers of heavenly blessings, she is also solicitous for the requirements of men in their daily lives, not merely those relating to food and sustenance, but also to their comfort and advancement in various kinds of goods and in varying circumstances of time.

4. Realizing all this, Holy Church implements the commands of her Founder, Christ, who refers primarily to man's eternal salvation when He says, "I am the Way, and the Truth, and the Life"[2] and elsewhere "I am the Light of the World."[3] On other occasions, however, seeing the hungry crowd, He was moved to exclaim sorrowfully, "I have compassion on the crowd,"[4] thereby indicating that He was also concerned about the earthly needs of mankind. The divine Redeemer shows this care not only by His words but also by the actions of His life, as when, to alleviate the hunger of the crowds, He more than once miraculously multiplied bread.

5. By this bread, given for the nourishment of the body, He wished to foreshadow that heavenly food of the soul which He was to give to men on *the day before He suffered*.

6. It is no wonder, then, that the Catholic Church, instructed by Christ and fulfilling His commands, has for two thousand years, from the ministry of the early deacons to the present time, tenaciously held aloft the torch of charity not only by her teaching but also by her widespread example—that charity which, by combining in a fitting manner the precepts and the practice of mutual love, puts into effect in a wonderful way this twofold commandment of *giving*, wherein is contained the full social teaching and action of the Church.

7. By far the most notable evidence of this social teaching and action, which the Church has set forth through the centuries, undoubtedly is the very distinguished Encyclical Letter *Rerum Novarum*,[5] issued seventy years ago by our predecessor of immortal memory, Leo XIII. Therein he put forward teachings whereby the question of the workers' condition would be resolved in conformity with Christian principles.

8. Seldom have the admonitions of a Pontiff been received

with such universal approbation, as was that Encyclical of
Leo XIII, rivaled by few in the depth and scope of its reasoning and in the forcefulness of its expression. Indeed, the
norms and recommendations contained therein were so mo-
mentous that their memory will never fall into oblivion. As a
result, the action of the Catholic Church became more
widely known. For its Supreme Pastor, making his own the
problems of weak and harassed men, their complaints and
aspirations had devoted himself especially to the defense and
restoration of their rights.

9. Even today, in spite of the long lapse of time since the
Letter was published, much of its effectiveness is still evident.
It is indeed evident in the documents of the Popes who succeeded Leo XIII, and who, when they discussed economic
and social affairs, have always borrowed something from it, either to clarify its application or to stimulate further activity
on the part of Catholics. The efficacy of the document also is
evident in the laws and institutions of many nations. Thus
does it become abundantly clear that the solidly grounded
principles, the norms of action, and the paternal admonitions
found in the masterly Letter of our predecessor, even today
retain their original worth. Moreover, from it can be drawn
new and vital criteria, whereby men may judge the nature
and extent of the social question, and determine what their
responsibilities are in this regard.

PART I

TEACHINGS OF THE ENCYCLICAL "RERUM NOVARUM" AND TIMELY DOCTRINAL DEVELOPMENTS DURING THE PONTIFICATES OF PIUS XI AND PIUS XII

THE PERIOD OF THE ENCYCLICAL, "RERUM NOVARUM"

10. The teachings addressed to mankind by this most wise
Pontiff undoubtedly shone with greater brilliance because
they were published when innumerable difficulties obscured

the issue. On the one hand, the economic and political situation was in process of radical change; on the other, numerous clashes were flaring up and civil strife had been provoked.

11. As is generally known, in those days an opinion widely prevailed and was commonly put into practice, according to which, in economic matters, everything was to be attributed to inescapable, natural forces. Hence, it was held that no connection existed between economic and moral laws. Wherefore, those engaged in economic activity need look no further than their own gain. Consequently, mutual relations between economic agents could be left to the play of free and unregulated competition. Interest on capital, prices of goods and services, profits and wages, were to be determined purely mechanically by the laws of the marketplace. Every precaution was to be taken lest the civil authority intervene in any way in economic affairs. During the era, trade unions, according to circumstances in different countries, were sometimes forbidden, sometimes tolerated, sometimes recognized in private law.

12. Thus, at that time, not only was the proud rule of the stronger regarded as legitimate, so far as economic affairs were concerned, but it also prevailed in concrete relations between men. Accordingly, the order of economic affairs was, in general, radically disturbed.

13. While a few accumulated excessive riches, large masses of workingmen daily labored in very acute need. Indeed, wages were insufficient for the necessities of life, and sometimes were at starvation level. For the most part, workers had to find employment under conditions wherein there were dangers to health, moral integrity, and religious faith. Especially inhuman were the working conditions to which children and women were subjected. The spectre of unemployment was ever present, and the family was exposed to a process of disorganization.

14. As a natural consequence, workers, indignant at their lot, decided that this state of affairs must be publicly protested. This explains why, among the working classes, extremist theories that propounded remedies worse than the evil to be cured, found widespread favor.

THE WAY TO RECONSTRUCTION

15. Such being the trend of the times, Leo XIII, in his Encyclical Letter *Rerum Novarum*, proclaimed a social message based on the requirements of human nature itself and conforming to the precepts of the Gospel and reason. We recall it as a message which, despite some expected opposition, evoked response on all sides and aroused widespread enthusiasm. However, this was not the first time the Apostolic See, in regard to the affairs of this life, undertook the defense of the needy, since that same predecessor of happy memory, Leo XIII, published other documents which to some extent paved the way for the document mentioned above. But this Letter so effected for the first time an organization of principles, and, as it were, set forth singlemindedly a future course of action, that we may regard it as a summary of Catholic teaching, so far as economic and social matters are concerned.

16. It can be said with considerable assurance that such proved to be the situation. For while some, confronted with the social question, unashamedly attacked the Church as if she did nothing except preach resignation to the poor and exhort the rich to generosity, Leo XIII did not hesitate to proclaim and defend quite openly the sacred rights of workers. In beginning his exposition of the principles and norms of the Church in social matters, he frankly stated: "We approach the subject with confidence and in the exercise of the rights that belong to us. For no satisfactory solution of this question will ever be found without the assistance of religion and the Church."[6]

17. Venerable Brothers, you are quite familiar with those basic principles expounded both clearly and authoritatively by the illustrious Pontiff, according to which human society should be renewed in so far as economic and social matters are concerned.

18. He first and foremost stated that work, inasmuch as it is an expression of the human person, can by no means be regarded as a mere commodity. For the great majority of

mankind, work is the only source from which the means of livelihood are drawn. Hence, its remuneration is not to be thought of in terms of merchandise, but rather according to the laws of justice and equity. Unless this is done, justice is violated in labor agreements, even though they are entered into freely on both sides.

19. Private property, including that of productive goods, is a natural right possessed by all, which the State may by no means suppress. However, as there is from nature a social aspect to private property, he who uses his right in this regard must take into account not merely his own welfare but that of others as well.

20. The State, whose purpose is the realization of the common good in the temporal order, can by no means disregard the economic activity of its citizens. Indeed, it should be present to promote in a suitable manner the production of a sufficient supply of material goods, "the use of which is necessary for the practice of virtue."[7] Moreover, it should safeguard the rights of all citizens, but especially the weaker, such as workers, women, and children. Nor may the state ever neglect its duty to contribute actively to the betterment of the living conditions of workers.

21. In addition, the State should see to it that labor agreements are entered into according to the norms of justice and equity, and that in the environment of work the dignity of the human being is not violated either in body or spirit. On this point, Leo XIII's Letter delineated the broad principles regarding a just and proper human existence. These principles, modern States have adopted in one way or another in their social legislation, and they have—as our predecessor of immortal memory, Pius XI, declared, in his Encyclical Letter *Quadragesimo Anno*[8]—contributed much to the establishment and promotion of that new section of legal science known as *labor law*.

22. In the same Letter, moreover, there is affirmed the natural right to enter corporately into associations, whether these be composed of workers only or of workers and management; and also the right to adopt that organizational structure judged more suitable to meet their professional needs.

And workers themselves have the right to act freely and on their own initiative within the above-mentioned associations, without hindrance and as their needs dictate.

23. Workers and employers should regulate their mutual relations in a spirit of human solidarity and in accordance with the bond of Christian brotherhood. For the unregulated competition which so-called *liberals* espouse, or the class struggle in the *Marxist sense*, are utterly opposed to Christian teaching and also to the very nature of man.

24. These, Venerable Brothers, are the fundamental principles on which a healthy socio-economic order can be built.

25. It is not surprising, therefore, that outstanding Catholic men inspired by these appeals began many activities in order to put these principles to action. Nor were there lacking other men of good will in various parts of the world who, impelled by the needs of human nature, followed a similar course.

26. For these reasons the Encyclical is known even to the present day as the *Magna Charta*[9] for the reconstruction of the economic and social order.

THE ENCYCLICAL "QUADRAGESIMO ANNO"

27. Furthermore, after a lapse of forty years since publication of that outstanding corpus, as it were, of directives, our predecessor of happy memory, Pius XI, in his turn decided to publish the Encyclical Letter *Quadragesimo Anno*.[10]

28. In it the Supreme Pontiff first of all confirmed the right and duty of the Catholic Church to make its special contribution in resolving the more serious problems of society which call for the full cooperation of all. Then he reaffirmed those principles and directives of Leo XIII's Letter related to the conditions of the times. Finally, he took this occasion not only to clarify certain points of doctrine on which even Catholics were in doubt, but he also showed how the principles and directives themselves regarding social affairs should be adapted to the changing times.

29. For at that time, some were in doubt as to what should be the judgment of Catholics regarding private prop-

erty, the wage system, and more especially, a type of moderate socialism.

30. Concerning private property, our predecessor reaffirmed its natural-law character. Furthermore, he set forth clearly and emphasized the social character and function of private ownership.

31. Turning to the wage system, after having rejected the view that would declare it unjust by its very nature, the Pontiff criticized the inhuman and unjust forms under which it was sometimes found. Moreover, he carefully indicated what norms and conditions were to be observed, lest the wage system stray from justice and equity.

32. In this connection, it is today advisable as our predecessor clearly pointed out, that work agreements be tempered in certain respects with partnership arrangements, so that "workers and officials become participants in ownership, or management, or share in some manner in profits."[11]

33. Of great theoretical and practical importance is the affirmation of Pius XI that "if the social and individual character of labor be overlooked, the efficiency of men can neither be justly appraised nor equitably recompensed."[12] Accordingly, in determining wages, justice definitely requires that, in addition to the needs of the individual worker and his family, regard be had on the one hand for conditions within the productive enterprises wherein the workers labor; on the other hand, for the "public economic good"[13] in general.

34. Furthermore, the Supreme Bishop emphasized that the views of *communists*, as they are called, and of Christians are radically opposed. Nor may Catholics, in any way, give approbation to the teachings of *socialists* who seemingly profess more moderate views. From their basic outlook it follows that, inasmuch as the order of social life is confined to time, it is directed solely to temporal welfare; that since the social relationships of men pertain merely to the production of goods, human liberty is excessively restricted and the true concept of social authority is overlooked.

35. Pius XI was not unaware that, in the forty years that had elapsed since the appearance of Leo XIII's letter, histori-

cal conditions had profoundly altered. In fact, unrestricted competition, because of its own inherent tendencies, had ended by almost destroying itself. It had caused a great accumulation of wealth and a corresponding concentration of power in the hands of a few who "are frequently not the owners, but only the trustees and directors of invested funds, who administer them at their good pleasure."[14]

36. Therefore, as the Supreme Pontiff noted, "economic power has been substituted for the free marketplace. Unbridled ambition for domination has replaced desire for gain; the whole economy has become harsh, cruel, and relentless in frightful measure."[15] Thus it happened that even public authorities were serving the interests of more wealthy men and that concentrations of wealth, to some extent, achieved power over all peoples.

37. In opposition to this trend, the Supreme Pontiff laid down the following fundamental principles: the organization of economic affairs must be conformable to practical morality; the interests of individuals or of societies especially must be harmonized with the requirements of the common good. This evidently requires, as the teaching of our predecessor indicated, the orderly reorganization of society with smaller professional and economic groups existing in their own right, and not prescribed by public authority. In the next place, civil authority should reassume its function and not overlook any of the community's interests. Finally, on a world-wide scale, governments should seek the economic good of all peoples.

38. The two fundamental points that especially characterize the Encyclical of Pius XI are these: First, one may not take as the ultimate criteria in economic life the interests of individuals or organized groups, nor unregulated competition, nor excessive power on the part of the wealthy, nor the vain honor of the nation or its desire for domination, nor anything of this sort.

39. Rather it is necessary that economic undertakings be governed by justice and charity as the principle laws of social life.

40. The second point that we consider to be basic to the Letter of Pius XI is that both within individual countries and

among nations there be established a juridical order, with appropriate public and private institutions, inspired by social justice, so that those who are involved in economic activities are enabled to carry out their tasks in conformity with the common good.

RADIO BROADCAST OF PENTECOST, 1941

41. In specifying social rights and obligations, our predecessor of immortal memory, Pius XII, made a significant contribution, when on the feast of Pentecost, June 1, 1941, he broadcast to the world community a message: "In order to call to the attention of the Catholic world the memory of an event worthy of being written in letters of gold on the Calendar of the Church: namely, the fiftieth anniversary of the publication of the epoch-making Encyclical of Leo XIII, *Rerum Novarum*."[16] He broadcast this message, moreover, "to render special thanks to Almighty God that His Vicar on earth, in a Letter such as this, gave to the Church so great a gift, and also to render praise to the eternal Spirit that through this same Letter, He enkindled a fire calculated to rouse the whole human race to new and better effort."[17]

42. In the message, the great Pontiff claimed for the Church "the indisputable competence" to "decide whether the bases of a given social system are in accord with the unchangeable order which God our Creator and Redeemer has fixed both in the natural law and revelation."[18] He noted that the Letter of Leo XIII is of permanent value and has rich and abiding usefulness. He takes the occasion "to explain in greater detail what the Catholic Church teaches regarding the three principal issues of social life in economic affairs, which are mutually related and connected one with the other, and thus interdependent: namely, the use of material goods, labor, and the family."[19]

43. Concerning the use of material goods, our predecessor declared that the right of every man to use them for his own sustenance is prior to all other rights in economic life, and hence is prior even to the right of private ownership. It is certain, however, as our predecessor noted, that the right of private property is from the natural law itself. Nevertheless, it is

the will of God the Creator that this right to own property should in no wise obstruct the flow of "material goods created by God to meet the needs of all men, to all equitably, as justice and charity require."[20]

44. As regards labor, Pius XII repeating what appeared in Leo XIII's Letter, declared it to be both a duty and a right of every human being. Consequently, it is in the first place the responsibility of men themselves to regulate mutual labor relations. Only in the event that the interested parties are unwilling or unable to fulfill their functions, does it "devolve upon the State to intervene and to assign labor equitably, safeguarding the standards and aims that the common good properly understood demands."[21]

45. Turning to the family, the Supreme Pontiff stresses that private ownership of material goods helps to safeguard and develop family life. Such goods are an apt means "to secure for the father of a family the healthy liberty he needs in order to fulfill the duties assigned him by the Creator, regarding the physical, spiritual, and religious welfare of the family."[22] From this arises the right of the family to migrate. Accordingly, our predecessor reminds governments, both those permitting emigration and those accepting immigrants, that "they never permit anything whereby mutual and sincere understanding between States is diminished or destroyed."[23] If this be mutually accomplished, it will come to pass that benefits are equalized and diffused widely among peoples, as the supply of goods and the arts and crafts are increased and fostered.

FURTHER CHANGES

46. But just as contemporary circumstances seemed to Pius XII quite dissimilar from those of the earlier period, so they have changed greatly over the past twenty years. This can be seen not only in the internal situation of each individual country, but also in the mutual relations of countries.

47. In the fields of science, technology, and economics, these developments are especially worthy of note: the discovery of atomic energy, employed first for military purposes and

later increasingly for peaceful ends; the almost limitless possibilities opened up by chemistry in synthetic products; the growth of automation in the sectors of industry and services; the modernization of agriculture; the nearly complete conquest, especially through radio and television, of the distance separating peoples; the greatly increased speed of all manner of transportation; the initial conquests of outer space.

48. Turning to the social field, the following contemporary trends are evident: development of systems for social insurance; the introduction of social security systems in some more affluent countries; greater awareness among workers, as members of unions, of the principal issues in economic and social life; a progressive improvement of basic education; wider diffusion among the citizenry of the conveniences of life; increased social mobility and a resulting decline in divisions among the classes; greater interest than heretofore in world affairs on the part of those with average education. Meanwhile, if one considers the social and economic advances made in a growing number of countries, he will quickly discern increasingly pronounced imbalances: first, between agriculture on the one hand and industry and the services on the other; between the more and the less developed regions within countries; and, finally, on a worldwide scale, between countries with differing economic resources and development.

49. Turning now to political affairs, it is evident that there, too, a number of innovations have occurred. Today, in many communities, citizens from almost all social strata participate in public life. Public authorities intervene more and more in economic and social affairs. The peoples of Asia and Africa, having set aside colonial systems, now govern themselves according to their own laws and institutions. As the mutual relationships of peoples increase, they become daily more dependent one upon the other. Throughout the world, assemblies and councils have become more common, which, being supranational in character, take into account the interests of all peoples. Such bodies are concerned with economic life, or with social affairs, or with culture and education, or, finally, with the mutual relationships of peoples.

REASONS FOR THE NEW ENCYCLICAL

50. Now, reflecting on all these things, we feel it our duty to keep alive the torch lighted by our great predecessors and to exhort all to draw from their writings light and inspiration, if they wish to resolve the social question in ways more in accord with the needs of the present time. Therefore, we are issuing this present Letter not merely to commemorate appropriately the Encyclical Letter of Leo XIII, but also, in the light of changed conditions, both to confirm and explain more fully what our predecessors taught, and to set forth the Church's teaching regarding the new and serious problems of our day.

PART II

EXPLANATION AND DEVELOPMENT OF THE TEACHINGS OF "RERUM NOVARUM"

PRIVATE INITIATIVE AND STATE INTERVENTION IN ECONOMIC LIFE

51. At the outset it should be affirmed that in economic affairs first place is to be given to the private initiative of individual men who, either working by themselves, or with others in one fashion or another, pursue their common interests.

52. But in this matter, for reasons pointed out by our predecessors, it is necessary that public authorities take active interest, the better to increase output of goods and to further social progress for the benefit of all citizens.

53. This intervention of public authorities that encourages, stimulates, regulates, supplements, and complements, is based on the *principle of subsidiarity*[24] as set forth by Pius XI in his Encyclical *Quadragesimo Anno*: "It is a fundamental principle of social philosophy, fixed and unchangeable, that one should not withdraw from individuals and commit to the community what they can accomplish by their

1 st to say that decision making a part of individual responsibility must happen to worker in work place.

own enterprise and industry. So, too, it is an injustice and at the same time a grave evil and a disturbance of right order, to transfer to the larger and higher collectivity functions which can be performed and provided for by lesser and subordinate bodies. Inasmuch as every social activity should, by its very nature, prove a help to members of the body social, it should never destroy or absorb them."[25]

54. Indeed, as is easily perceived, recent developments of science and technology provide additional reasons why, to a greater extent than heretofore, it is within the power of public authorities to reduce imbalances, whether these be between various sectors of economic life, or between different regions of the same nation, or even between different peoples of the world as a whole. These same developments make it possible to keep fluctuations in the economy within bounds, and to provide effective measures for avoiding mass unemployment. Consequently, it is requested again and again of public authorities responsible for the common good, that they intervene in a wide variety of economic affairs, and that, in a more extensive and organized way than heretofore, they adapt institutions, tasks, means, and procedures to this end.

55. Nevertheless, it remains true that precautionary activities of public authorities in the economic field, although widespread and penetrating, should be such that they not only avoid restricting the freedom of private citizens, but also increase it, so long as the basic rights of each individual person are preserved inviolate. Included among these is the right and duty of each individual normally to provide the necessities of life for himself and his dependents. This implies that whatever be the economic system, it allow and facilitate for every individual the opportunity to engage in productive activity.

56. Furthermore, the course of events thus far makes it clear that there cannot be a prosperous and well-ordered society unless both private citizens and public authorities work together in economic affairs. Their activity should be characterized by mutual and amicable efforts, so that the roles assigned to each fit in with requirements of the common good as changing times and customs suggest.

57. Experience, in fact, shows that where private initiative of individuals is lacking, political tyranny prevails. Moreover, much stagnation occurs in various sectors of the economy, and hence all sorts of consumer goods and services, closely connected with needs of the body and more especially of the spirit, are in short supply. Beyond doubt, the attainment of such goods and services provides remarkable opportunity and stimulus for individuals to exercise initiative and industry.

58. Where, on the other hand, appropriate activity of the State is lacking or defective, commonwealths are apt to experience incurable disorders, and there occurs exploitation of the weak by the unscrupulous strong, who flourish, unfortunately, like cockle among the wheat, in all times and places.

COMPLEXITY OF SOCIAL STRUCTURE

Direction of the Trend

59. One of the principal characteristics of our time is the multiplication of social relationships, that is, a daily more complex interdependence of citizens, introducing into their lives and activities many and varied forms of association, recognized for the most part in private and even in public law. This tendency seemingly stems from a number of factors operative in the present era, among which are technical and scientific progress, greater productive efficiency, and a higher standard of living among citizens.

60. These developments in social living are at once both a symptom and a cause of the growing intervention of public authorities in matters which, since they pertain to the more intimate aspects of personal life, are of serious moment and not without danger. Such, for example, are the care of health, the instruction and education of youth, the choice of a personal career, the ways and means of rehabilitating or assisting those handicapped mentally or physically. But this trend also indicates and in part follows from that human and natural inclination, scarcely resistible, whereby men are impelled voluntarily to enter into association in order to attain objectives which each one desires, but which exceed the capacity of single individuals. This tendency has given rise, es-

pecially in recent years, to organizations and institutes on both national and international levels which relate to economic and social goals, to cultural and recreational activities, to athletics, to various professions, and to political affairs.

Evaluation

61. Such an advance in social relationships definitely brings numerous services and advantages. It makes possible, in fact, the satisfaction of many personal rights, especially those of economic and social life; these relate, for example, to the minimum necessities of human life, to health services, to the broadening and deepening of elementary education, to a more fitting training in skills, to housing, to labor, to suitable leisure and recreation. In addition, through the ever more perfect organization of modern means for the diffusion of thought—press, cinema, radio, television—individuals are enabled to take part in human events on a world-wide scale.

62. But as these various forms of association are multiplied and daily extended, it also happens that in many areas of activity, rules and laws controlling and determining relationships of citizens are multiplied. As a consequence, opportunity for free action by individuals is restricted within narrower limits. Methods are often used, procedures are adopted, and such an atmosphere develops wherein it becomes difficult for one to make decisions independently of outside influences, to do anything on his own initiative, to carry out in a fitting way his rights and duties, and to fully develop and perfect his personality. Will men perhaps then become automatons, and cease to be personally responsible, as these social relationships multiply more and more? It is a question which must be answered negatively.

63. Actually, increased complexity of social life by no means results from a blind drive of natural forces. Indeed, as stated above, it is the creation of free men who are so disposed to act by nature as to be responsible for what they do. They must, of course, recognize the laws of human progress and the development of economic life and take these into account. Furthermore, men are not altogether free of their milieu.

64. Accordingly, advances in social organization can and should be so brought about that maximum advantages accrue to citizens while at the same time disadvantages are averted or at least minimized.

65. That these desired objectives be more readily obtained, it is necessary that public authorities have a correct understanding of the common good. This embraces the sum total of those conditions of social living, whereby men are enabled more fully and more readily to achieve their own perfection. Hence, we regard it as necessary that the various intermediary bodies and the numerous social undertakings wherein an expanded social structure primarily finds expression, be ruled by their own laws, and as the common good itself progresses, pursue this objective in a spirit of sincere concord among themselves. Nor is it less necessary that the above-mentioned groups present the form and substance of a true community. This they will do, only if individual members are considered and treated as persons, and are encouraged to participate in the affairs of the group.

66. Accordingly, as relationships multiply between men, binding them more closely together, commonwealths will more readily and appropriately order their affairs to the extent these two factors are kept in balance: (1) the freedom of individual citizens and groups of citizens to act autonomously, while cooperating one with the other; (2) the activity of the State whereby the undertakings of private individuals and groups are suitably regulated and fostered.

67. Now if social systems are organized in accordance with the above norms and moral laws, their extension does not necessarily mean that individual citizens will be gravely discriminated against or excessively burdened. Rather, we can hope that this will enable man not only to develop and perfect his natural talents, but also will lead to an appropriate structuring of the human community. Such a structure, as our predecessor of happy memory, Pius XI, warned in his Encyclical Letter *Quadragesimo Anno*,[26] is absolutely necessary for the adequate fulfillment of the rights and duties of social life.

REMUNERATION FOR WORK

Standards of Justice and Equity

68. Our heart is filled with profound sadness when we observe, as it were, with our own eyes a wretched spectacle indeed—great masses of workers who, in not a few nations, and even in whole continents, receive too small a return from their labor. Hence, they and their families must live in conditions completely out of accord with human dignity. This can be traced, for example, to the fact that in these regions, modern industrial techniques either have only recently been introduced or have made less than satisfactory progress.

69. It happens in some of these nations that, as compared with the extreme need of the majority, the wealth and conspicuous consumption of a few stand out, and are in open and bold contrast with the lot of the needy. It happens in other places that excessive burdens are placed upon men in order that the commonwealth may achieve within a brief span, an increase of wealth such as can by no means be achieved without violating the laws of justice and equity. Finally, it happens elsewhere that a disproportionate share of the revenue goes toward the building up of national prestige, and that large sums of money are devoted to armaments.

70. Moreover, in the economically developed countries, it frequently happens that great, or sometimes very great, remuneration is had for the performance of some task of lesser importance or doubtful utility. Meanwhile, the diligent and profitable work that whole classes of decent and hardworking citizens perform, receives too low a payment and one insufficient for the necessities of life, or else, one that does not correspond to the contribution made to the community, or to the revenues of the undertakings in which they are engaged, or to the national income.

71. Wherefore, we judge it to be our duty to reaffirm once again that just as remuneration for work cannot be left entirely to unregulated competition, neither may it be decided arbitrarily at the will of the more powerful. Rather, in this matter, the norms of justice and equity should be strictly ob-

served. This requires that workers receive a wage sufficient to lead a life worthy of man and to fulfill family responsibilities properly. But in determining what constitutes an appropriate wage, the following must necessarily be taken into account: first of all, the contribution of individuals to the economic effort; the economic state of the enterprises within which they work; the requirements of each community, especially as regards over-all employment; finally, what concerns the common good of all peoples, namely, of the various States associated among themselves, but differing in character and extent.

72. It is clear that the standards of judgment set forth above are binding always and everywhere. However, the measure in which they are to be applied in concrete cases cannot be established unless account is taken of the resources at hand. These resources can and in fact do vary in quantity and quality among different peoples, and may even change within the same country with the passing of time.

Balancing Economic Development and Social Progress

73. Whereas in our era the economies of various countries are evolving very rapidly, more especially since the last great war, we take this opportunity to draw the attention of all to a strict demand of social justice, which explicitly requires that, with the growth of the economy, there occur a corresponding social development. Thus, all classes of citizens will benefit equitably from an increase in national wealth. Toward this end vigilance should be exercised and effective steps taken that class differences arising from disparity of wealth not be increased, but lessened so far as possible.

74. "National wealth"—as our predecessor of happy memory, Pius XII, rightfully observed—"inasmuch as it is produced by the common efforts of the citizenry, has no other purpose than to secure without interruption those material conditions in which individuals are enabled to lead a full and perfect life. Where this is consistently the case, then such a people is to be judged truly rich. For the system whereby both the common prosperity is achieved and individuals exercise their right to use material goods, conforms fully to norms laid down by God the Creator."[27] From this it follows that

the economic prosperity of any people is to be assessed not so much from the sum total of goods and wealth possessed as from the distribution of goods according to norms of justice, so that everyone in the community can develop and perfect himself. For this, after all, is the end toward which all economic activity of a community is by nature ordered.

75. We must here call attention to the fact that in many countries today, the economic system is such that large and medium-size productive enterprises achieve rapid growth precisely because they finance replacement and plant expansion from their own revenues. Where this is the case, we believe that such companies should grant to workers some share in the enterprise, especially where they are paid no more than the minimum wage.

76. In this matter, the principle laid down by our predecessor of happy memory, Pius XI, in the Encyclical Letter *Quadragesimo Anno*, should be borne in mind: "It is totally false to ascribe to a single factor of production what is in fact produced by joint activity; and it is completely unjust for one factor to arrogate to itself what is produced, ignoring what has been contributed by other factors."[28]

77. The demands of justice referred to, can be met in various ways, as experience shows. Not to mention other ways, it is very desirable that workers gradually acquire some share in the enterprise by such methods as seem more appropriate. For today, more than in the times of our predecessor, "every effort should be made that, at least in the future, only an equitable share of the fruits of production accumulate in the hands of the wealthy, and a sufficient and ample portion go to the workingmen."[29]

78. But we should remember that adjustments between remuneration for work and revenues are to be brought about in conformity with the requirements of the common good, both of one's own community and of the entire human family.

79. Considering the common good on the national level, the following points are relevant and should not be overlooked: to provide employment for as many workers as possible; to take care lest privileged groups arise even among the workers themselves; to maintain a balance between wages and

prices; to make accessible the goods and services for a better life to as many persons as possible; either to eliminate or to keep within bounds the inequalities that exist between different sectors of the economy—that is, between agriculture, industry and services; to balance properly any increases in output with advances in services provided to citizens, especially by public authority; to adjust, as far as possible, the means of production to the progress of science and technology; finally, to ensure the advantages of a more humane way of existence not merely subserve the present generation but have regard for future generations as well.

80. As regards the common good of human society as a whole, the following condition should be fulfilled: that the competitive striving of peoples to increase output be free of bad faith; that harmony in economic affairs and a friendly and beneficial cooperation be fostered; and, finally, that effective aid be given in developing the economically underdeveloped nations.

81. It is evident from what has been said that these demands of the common good, on both the national and world levels, should be borne in mind, when there is question of determining the share of earnings assigned to those responsible for directing the productive enterprise, or as interest and dividends to those who have invested capital.

DEMANDS OF JUSTICE AS REGARDS PRODUCTIVE INSTITUTIONS

Institutions Conforming to the Dignity of Man

82. Justice is to be observed not merely in the distribution of wealth, but also in regard to the conditions under which men engaged in productive activity have an opportunity to assume responsibility and to perfect themselves by their efforts.

83. Consequently, if the organization and structure of economic life be such that the human dignity of workers is compromised, or their sense of responsibility is weakened, or their freedom of action is removed, then we judge such an economic order to be unjust, even though it produces a vast amount of goods whose distribution conforms to the norms of justice and equity.

Reaffirmation of a Directive

84. Nor is it possible in economic affairs to determine in one formula all the measures that are more conformable to the dignity of man, or are more suitable in developing in him a sense of responsibility. Nevertheless, our predecessor of happy memory, Pius XII, appropriately laid down certain norms of action: "Small and medium-sized holdings in agriculture, in the arts and crafts, in commerce and industry, should be safeguarded and fostered. Such enterprises should join together in mutual-aid societies in order that the services and benefits of large-scale enterprises will be available to them. So far as these larger enterprises are concerned, work agreements should in some way be modified by partnership arrangements."[30]

Artisan Enterprises and Cooperative Associations

85. Wherefore, conformable to requirements of the common good and the state of technology, artisan and farm enterprises of family type should be safeguarded and fostered, as should also cooperatives that aim to complement and perfect such enterprises.

86. We shall return shortly to the subject of farm enterprises. Here, we think it appropriate to say something about artisan enterprises and cooperative associations.

87. Above all, it must be emphasized that enterprises and bodies of this sort, in order that they may survive and flourish, should be continuously adapted—both in their productive structure and in their operating methods—to new conditions of the times. These new conditions constantly arise from advances in science and technology, or from changing consumer needs and preferences. It is especially appropriate that all this can be done by the craftsmen themselves and by the associates in the cooperatives.

88. Hence, it is more fitting not only that both these groups be suitably formed in technical and in spiritual and intellectual matters, but also that they be joined together professionally. Nor is it less fitting that the State make special provision for them in regard to instruction, taxes, credit facilities, social security and insurance.

89. Moreover, the measures taken by the State on behalf of the craftsmen and members of cooperatives are also justified by the fact that these two categories of citizens are producers of genuine wealth, and contribute to the advance of civilization.

90. Accordingly, we paternally exhort our beloved sons, craftsmen and members of cooperatives throughout the world, that they fully realize the dignity of their role in society, since, by their work, the sense of responsibility and spirit of mutual aid can be daily more intensified among the citizenry, and the desire to work with dedication and originality be kept alive.

Participation of Workers in Medium-size and Large Enterprises

91. Furthermore, as did our predecessors, we regard as justifiable the desire of employees to be partners in enterprises with which they are associated and wherein they work. We do not think it possible, however, to decide with certain and explicit norms the manner and degree of such partnership, since this must be determined according to the state of the individual productive enterprises. For the situation is not everywhere the same, and, in fact, it can change suddenly within one and the same enterprise. Nevertheless, we do not doubt that employees should have an active part in the affairs of the enterprise wherein they work, whether these be private or public. But it is of utmost importance that productive enterprises assume the character of a true human fellowship whose spirit suffuses the dealings, activities, and standing of all its members.

92. This requires that mutual relations between employers and directors on the one hand and the employees of the enterprise on the other, be marked by mutual respect, esteem, and good will. It also demands that all collaborate sincerely and harmoniously in their joint undertaking, and that they perform their work not merely with the objective of deriving an income, but also of carrying out the role assigned them and of performing a service that results in benefit to others. This means that the workers may have a say in, and may make a contribution toward, the efficient running and devel-

opment of the enterprise. Thus, our predecessor of happy memory, Pius XII, clearly indicated: "The economic and social functions of individuals be not wholly subjected to the will of others."[31] Beyond doubt, an enterprise truly in accord with human dignity should safeguard the necessary and efficient unity of administration. But it by no means follows that those who work daily in such an enterprise are to be considered merely as servants, whose sole function is to execute orders silently, and who are not allowed to interject their desires and interests, but must conduct themselves as idle standbys when it comes to assignment and direction of their tasks.

93. Finally, attention is drawn to the fact that the greater amount of responsibility desired today by workers in productive enterprises, not merely accords with the nature of man, but also is in conformity with historical developments in the economic, social, and political fields.

94. Unfortunately, in our day, there occur in economic and social affairs many imbalances that militate against justice and humanity. Meanwhile, throughout all of economic life, errors are spread that seriously impair its operation, purposes, organization, and the fulfillment of responsibilities. Nevertheless, it is an undeniable fact that the more recent productive systems, thanks to the impulse deriving from advances in technology and science, are becoming more modern and efficient, and are expanding at a faster rate than in the past. This demands of workers greater abilities and professional qualifications. Accordingly, workers should be provided with additional aids and time to achieve a suitable and more rounded formation, and to carry out more fittingly their duties as regards studies, morals, and religion.

95. Thus it happens that in our day youths can be allotted additional years to acquire a basic education and necessary skills.

96. Now if these things be done, a situation will emerge wherein workers are enabled to assume greater responsibilities even within their own enterprises. As regards the commonwealth as such, it is of great importance that all ranks of citizens feel themselves daily more obligated to safeguard the common good.

Participation of Workers at All Levels

97. Now, as is evident to all, in our day associations of workers have become widespread, and for the most part have been given legal status within individual countries and even across national boundaries. These bodies no longer recruit workers for purposes of strife, but rather for pursuing a common aim. And this is achieved especially by collective bargaining between associations of workers and those of management. But it should be emphasized how necessary, or at least very appropriate, it is to give workers an opportunity to exert influence outside the limits of the individual productive unit, and indeed within all ranks of the commonwealth.

98. The reason is that individual productive units, whatever their size, efficiency, or importance within the commonwealth, are closely connected with the over-all economic and social situation in each country, whereon their own prosperity ultimately depends.

99. Nevertheless, to decide what is more helpful to the over-all economic situation is not the prerogative of individual productive enterprises, but pertains to the public authorities and to those institutions which, established either nationally or among a number of countries, function in various sectors of economic life. From this is evident the propriety or necessity of ensuring that not only managers or agents of management are represented before such authorities and institutions, but also workers or those who have the responsibility of safeguarding the rights, needs, and aspirations of workers.

100. It is fitting, therefore, that our thoughts and paternal affection be directed toward the various professional groups and associations of workers which, in accord with principles of Christian teaching, carry on their activities on several continents. We are aware of the many and great difficulties experienced by these beloved sons of ours, as they effectively worked in the past and continue to strive, both within their national boundaries and throughout the world, to vindicate the rights of workingmen and to improve their lot and conduct.

101. Furthermore, we wish to give deserved praise to the

work of these our sons. Their accomplishments are not always immediately evident, but nevertheless permeate practically the entire field of labor, spreading correct norms of action and thought, and the beneficial influence of the Christian religion.

102. And we wish also to praise paternally those dear sons of ours who, imbued with Christian principles, give their special attention to other labor associations and those groups of workingmen that follow the laws of nature and respect the religious and moral liberty of individuals.

103. Nor can we at this point neglect to congratulate and to express our esteem for the International Labor Organization—variously signified popularly by the letters O.I.L. or I.L.O. or O.I.T.—which, for many years, has done effective and valuable work in adapting the economic and social order everywhere to the norms of justice and humanity. In such an order, the legitimate rights of workers are recognized and preserved.

PRIVATE PROPERTY

Changed Conditions

104. In recent years, as we are well aware, the role played by the owners of capital in very large productive enterprises has been separated more and more from the role of management. This has occasioned great difficulties for governments, whose duty it is to make certain that directors of the principal enterprises, especially those of greatest influence in the economic life of the entire country, do not depart from the requirements of the common good. These difficulties, as we know from experience, are by no means less, whether it be private citizens or public bodies that make the capital investments requisite for large-scale enterprises.

105. It is also quite clear that today the number of persons is increasing who, because of recent advances in insurance programs and various systems of social security, are able to look to the future with tranquillity. This sort of tranquillity once was rooted in the ownership of property, albeit modest.

106. It sometimes happens in our day that men are more

inclined to seek some professional skill than possession of goods. Moreover, such men have greater esteem for income from labor or rights arising from labor, than for that deriving from capital investment or rights associated therewith.

107. This clearly accords with the inherent characteristics of labor, inasmuch as this proceeds directly from the human person, and hence is to be thought more of than wealth in external goods. These latter, by their very nature, must be regarded as instruments. This trend indicates an advance in civilization.

108. Economic conditions of this kind have occasioned popular doubt as to whether, under present circumstances, a principle of economic and social life, firmly enunciated and defended by our predecessors, has lost its force or is to be regarded as of lesser moment; namely, the principle whereby it is established that men have from nature a right of privately owning goods, including those of a productive kind.

Confirmation of the Right of Private Property

109. Such a doubt has no foundation. For the right of private property, including that pertaining to goods devoted to productive enterprises, is permanently valid. Indeed, it is rooted in the very nature of things, whereby we learn that individual men are prior to civil society, and hence, that civil society is to be directed toward man as its end. Indeed, the right of private individuals to act freely in economic affairs is recognized in vain, unless they are at the same time given an opportunity of freely selecting and using things necessary for the exercise of this right. Moreover, experience and history testify that where political regimes do not allow to private individuals the possession also of productive goods, the exercise of human liberty is violated or completely destroyed in matters of primary importance. Thus it becomes clear that in the right of property, the exercise of liberty finds both a safeguard and a stimulus.

110. This explains the fact that socio-political groups and associations which endeavor to reconcile freedom with justice within society, and which until recently did not uphold the right of private property in productive goods, have now,

enlightened by the course of social events, modified their views and are disposed actually to approve this right.

111. Accordingly, we make our own the insistence of our predecessor of happy memory, Pius XII: "In defending the right of private property, the Church has in mind a very important ethical aim in social matters. She does not, of course, strive to uphold the present state of affairs as if it were an expression of the divine will. And even less does she accept the patronage of the affluent and wealthy, while neglecting the rights of the poor and needy. . . . The Church rather does intend that the institution of private property be such as is required by the plan of divine wisdom and the law of nature."[32] Private ownership should safeguard the rights of the human person, and at the same time make its necessary contribution to the establishment of right order in society.

112. While recent developments in economic life progress rapidly in a number of countries, as we have noted, and produce goods ever more efficiently, justice and equity require that remuneration for work also be increased within limits allowed by the common good. This enables workers to save more readily and hence to achieve some property status of their own. Wherefore, it is indeed surprising that some reject the natural role of private ownership. For it is a right which continually draws its force and vigor from the fruitfulness of labor, and which, accordingly, is an effective aid in safeguarding the dignity of the human person and the free exercise of responsibility in all fields of endeavor. Finally, it strengthens the stability and tranquillity of family life, thus contributing to the peace and prosperity of the commonwealth.

Effective Distribution

113. It is not enough, then, to assert that man has from nature the right of privately possessing goods as his own, including those of productive character, unless, at the same time, a continuing effort is made to spread the use of this right through all ranks of the citizenry.

114. Our predecessor of happy memory, Pius XII, clearly reminded us that on the one hand the dignity of the human person necessarily "requires the right of using external goods

in order to live according to the right norm of nature. And to this right corresponds a most serious obligation, which requires that, so far as possible, there be given to all an opportunity of possessing private property."[33] On the other hand, the nobility inherent in work, besides other requirements, demands "the conservation and perfection of a social order that makes possible a secure, although modest, property to all classes of the people."[34]

115. It is especially appropriate that today, more than heretofore, widespread private ownership should prevail, since, as noted above, the number of nations increases wherein the economic systems experience daily growth. Therefore, by prudent use of various devices already proven effective, it will not be difficult for the body politic to modify economic and social life so that the way is made easier for widespread private possession of such things as durable goods, homes, gardens, tools requisite for artisan enterprises and family-type farms, investments in enterprises of medium or large size. All of this has occurred satisfactorily in some nations with developed social and economic systems.

Public Property

116. Obviously, what we have said above does not preclude ownership of goods pertaining to production of wealth by States and public agencies, especially "if these carry with them power too great to be left in private hands, without injury to the community at large."[35]

117. It seems characteristic of our times to vest more and more ownership of goods in the State and in other public bodies. This is partially explained by the fact that the common good requires public authorities to exercise ever greater responsibilities. However, in this matter, the *principle of subsidiarity*, already mentioned above, is to be strictly observed. For it is lawful for States and public corporations to expand their domain of ownership only when manifest and genuine requirements of the common good so require, and then with safeguards, lest the possession of private citizens be diminished beyond measure, or, what is worse, destroyed.

118. Finally, we cannot pass over in silence the fact that

economic enterprises undertaken by the State or by public corporations should be entrusted to citizens outstanding in skill and integrity, who will carry out their responsibilities to the commonwealth with a deep sense of devotion. Moreover, the activity of these men should be subjected to careful and continuing supervision, lest, in the administration of the State itself, there develop an economic imperialism in the hands of a few. For such a development is in conflict with the highest good of the commonwealth.

Social Function of Property

119. Our predecessors have always taught that in the right of private property there is rooted a social responsibility. Indeed, in the wisdom of God the Creator, the over-all supply of goods is assigned, first of all, that all men may lead a decent life. As our predecessor of happy memory, Leo XIII, clearly reminded us in the Encyclical Letter *Rerum Novarum*, "This is the heart of the matter: whoever has received from the divine bounty a larger share of blessings, whether these be corporal or external or gifts of mind, has received them to use for his own perfection, and, at the same time, as the minister of God's providence, for the benefit of others. 'He who has a talent' [says St. Gregory the Great], 'let him take care that he hides it not; he who has abundance, let him arouse himself to mercy and generosity; he who has skill in managing affairs, let him make special effort to share the use and utility thereof with his neighbor.'"[36]

120. Although in our day, the role assigned the State and public bodies has increased more and more, it by no means follows that the social function of private ownership is obsolescent, as some seem to think. For social responsibility in this matter derives its force from the very right of private property. Furthermore, it is quite clear that there always will be a wide range of difficult situations, as well as hidden and grave needs, which the manifold providence of the State leaves untouched, and of which it can in no way take account. Wherefore, there is always wide scope for humane action by private citizens and for Christian charity. Finally, it is evident that in stimulating efforts relating to spiritual wel-

fare, the work done by individual men or by private civic groups has more value than what is done by public authorities.

121. Moreover, it is well to recall here that the right of private ownership is clearly evident in the Gospels, which reveal Jesus Christ ordering the rich to share their goods with the poor so as to turn them into spiritual possessions: "Do not lay up for yourselves treasures on earth, where rust and moth consume, and where thieves break in and steal; but lay up for yourselves treasures in heaven, where neither rust nor moth consumes nor thieves break in and steal."[37] And the divine Master states that whatever is done for the poor is done for Him: "Amen I say to you, as long as you did it for one of these, the least of My brethren, you did it for Me."[38]

PART III

NEW ASPECTS OF THE SOCIAL QUESTION

122. The progress of events and of time have made it increasingly evident that the relationships between workers and management in productive enterprises must be readjusted according to norms of justice and charity. But the same is also true of the systems whereby various types of economic activity and the differently endowed regions within a country ought to be linked together. Meanwhile, within the over-all human community, many nations with varied endowments have not made identical progress in their economic and social affairs.

JUST REQUIREMENTS IN THE MATTER OF INTERRELATED PRODUCTIVE SECTORS

Agriculture: A Depressed Sector

123. First of all, to lay down some norms in regard to agriculture, we would note that the over-all number of rural dwellers seemingly has not diminished. Beyond doubt, however, many farmers have abandoned their rural birthplace,

and seek out either the more populous centers or the cities themselves. Now since this is the case in almost all countries, and since it affects large numbers of human beings, problems concerning life and dignity of citizens arise, which are indeed difficult to overcome.

124. Thus, as economic life progresses and expands, the percentage of rural dwellers diminishes, while the great number of industrial and service workers increases. Yet, we feel that those who transfer from rural activities to other productive enterprises often are motivated by reasons arising from the very evolution of economic affairs. Very often, however, they are caught up by various enticements of which the following are noteworthy: a desire to escape from a confined environment offering no prospect of a more comfortable life; the wish, so common in our age, to undertake new activities and to acquire new experiences; the attraction of quickly acquired goods and fortunes; a longing after a freer life, with the advantages that larger towns and cities usually provide. But there is no doubt about this point: rural dwellers leave the fields because nearly everywhere they see their affairs in a state of depression, both as regards labor productivity and the level of living of farm populations.

125. Accordingly, in this grave matter, about which enquiries are made in nearly all countries, we should first of all ask what is to be done to prevent so great imbalances between agriculture, industry, and the services in the matter of productive efficiency? Likewise, what can be done to minimize differences between the rural standard of living and that of city dwellers whose money income is derived from industry or some service or other? Finally, how can it be brought about that those engaged in agricultural pursuits no longer regard themselves as inferior to others? Indeed, rural dwellers should be convinced not only that they can strengthen and develop their personalities by their toil, but also that they can look forward to the future vicissitudes with confidence.

126. Accordingly, we judge it opportune in this connection to lay down some norms of permanent validity; although, as is evident, these must be adapted as various circumstances of time and place permit, or suggest, or absolutely require.

Provision for Essential Public Services

127. First, it is necessary that everyone, and especially public authorities, strive to effect improvements in rural areas as regards the principal services needed by all. Such are, for example: highway construction; transport services; marketing facilities; pure drinking water; housing; medical services; elementary, trade, and professional schools; things requisite for religion and for recreation; finally, furnishings and equipment needed in the modern farm home. Where these requirements for a dignified farm life are lacking to rural dwellers, economic and social progress does not occur at all, or else very slowly. Under such conditions, nothing can be done to keep men from deserting the fields, nor can anyone readily estimate their number.

Gradual and Orderly Development of the Economic System

128. It is desirable, moreover, that economic development of commonwealths proceed in orderly fashion, meanwhile preserving appropriate balance between the various sectors of the economy. In particular, care must be had that within the agricultural sector innovations are introduced as regards productive technology, whether these relate to productive methods, or to cultivation of the fields, or to equipment for the rural enterprise, as far as the over-all economy allows or requires. And all this should be done, as far as possible, in accordance with technical advances in industry and in the various services.

129. In this way, agriculture not only absorbs a larger share of industrial output, but also demands a higher quality of services. In its turn, agriculture offers to the industrial and service sectors of the economy, as well as to the community as a whole, those products which in kind and in quantity better meet consumer needs. Thus, agriculture contributes to stability of the purchasing power of money, a very positive factor for the orderly development of the entire economic system.

130. By proceeding in this manner, the following advan-

tages, among other, arise: first of all, it is easier to know the origins and destinations of rural dwellers displaced by modernization of agriculture. Thereupon, they can be instructed in skills needed for other types of work. Finally, economic aids and helps will not be lacking for their intellectual and cultural development, so that they can fit into new social groups.

Appropriate Economic Policy

131. To achieve orderly progress in various sectors of economic life, it is absolutely necessary that as regards agriculture, public authorities give heed and take action in the following matters: taxes and duties, credit, insurance, prices, the fostering of requisite skills, and, finally, improved equipment for rural enterprises.

Taxation

132. As regards taxation, assessment according to ability to pay is fundamental to a just and equitable system.

133. But in determining taxes for rural dwellers, the general welfare requires public authorities to bear in mind that income in a rural economy is both delayed and subject to greater risk. Moreover, there is difficulty in finding capital so as to increase returns.

Capital at Suitable Interest

134. Accordingly, those with money to invest are more inclined to invest it in enterprises other than in the rural economy. And for the same reason, rural dwellers cannot pay high rates of interest. Nor are they generally able to pay prevailing market rates for capital wherewith to carry on and expand their operations. Wherefore, the general welfare requires that public authorities not merely make special provision for agricultural financing, but also for establishment of banks that provide capital to farmers at reasonable rates of interest.

Social Insurance and Social Security

135. It also seems necessary to make provision for a twofold insurance, one covering agricultural output, the other

covering farmers and their families. Because, as experience shows, the income of individual farmers is, on the average, less than that of workers in industry and the services, it does not seem to be fully in accord with the norms of social justice and equity to provide farmers with insurance or social security benefits that are inferior to those of other classes of citizens. For those insurance plans or provisions that are established generally should not differ markedly one from the other, whatever be the economic sector wherein the citizens work or from which they derive their income.

136. Moreover, since social security and insurance can help appreciably in distributing national income among the citizens according to justice and equity, these systems can be regarded as means whereby imbalances among various classes of citizens are reduced.

Price Protection

137. Since agricultural products have special characteristics, it is fitting that their price be protected by methods worked out by economic experts. In this matter, although it is quite helpful that those whose interests are involved take steps to safeguard themselves, setting up, as it were, appropriate goals, public authorities cannot stand entirely aloof from the stabilization procedure.

138. Nor should this be overlooked, that, generally speaking, the price of rural products is more a recompense for farmers' labor than for capital investment.

139. Thus, our predecessor of happy memory, Pius XI, touching on the welfare of the human community, appropriately notes in his Encyclical Letter *Quadragesimo Anno*, that "a reasonable relationship between different wages here enters into consideration." But he immediately adds, "Intimately connected with this is a reasonable relationship between the prices obtained for the products of the various economic groups: agrarian, industrial, and so forth."[39]

140. Inasmuch as agricultural products are destined especially to satisfy the basic needs of men, it is necessary that their price be such that all can afford to buy them. Nevertheless, there is manifest injustice in placing a whole group of

citizens, namely, the farmers, in an inferior economic and social status, with less purchasing power than required for a decent livelihood. This, indeed, is clearly contrary to the common good of the country.

Strengthening Farm Income

141. In rural areas it is fitting that industries be fostered and common services be developed that are useful in preserving, processing, and finally, in transporting farm products. There is need, moreover, to establish councils and activities relating to various sectors of economic and professional affairs. By such means, suitable opportunity is given farm families to supplement their incomes, and that within the milieu wherein they live and work.

Appropriate Organization of Farming Enterprises

142. Finally, no one person can lay down a universal rule regarding the way in which rural affairs should be definitely organized, since in these matters there exists considerable variation within each country, and the difference is even greater when we consider the various regions of the world. However, those who hold man and the family in proper esteem, whether this be based upon nature alone, or also upon Christian principles, surely look toward some form of agricultural enterprise, and particularly of the family type, which is modeled upon the community of men wherein mutual relationships of members and the organization of the enterprise itself are conformed to norms of justice and Christian teaching. And these men strive mightily that such organization of rural life be realized as far as circumstances permit.

143. The family farm will be firm and stable only when it yields money income sufficient for decent and humane family living. To bring this about, it is very necessary that farmers generally receive instruction, be kept informed of new developments, and be technically assisted by trained men. It is also necessary that farmers form among themselves mutual-aid societies; that they establish professional associations; that they function efficiently in public life, that is, in various administrative bodies and in political affairs.

RURAL WORKERS: PARTICIPANTS IN IMPROVING CONDITIONS

144. We are of the opinion that in rural affairs, the principal agents and protagonists of economic improvement, of cultural betterment, or of social advance, should be the men personally involved, namely, the farmers themselves. To them it should be quite evident that their work is most noble, because it is undertaken, as it were, in the majestic temple of creation; because it often concerns the life of plants and animals, a life inexhaustible in its expression, inflexible in its laws, rich in allusions to God, Creator and Provider. Moreover, labor in the fields not only produces various foodstuffs wherewith humankind is nourished, but also furnishes an increasing supply of raw materials for industry.

145. Furthermore, this is a work endowed with a dignity of its own, for it bears a manifold relationship to the mechanical arts, chemistry, and biology: these must be continually adapted to the requirements of emerging situations because scientific and technological advance is of great importance in rural life. Work of this kind, moreover, possesses a special nobility because it requires farmers to understand well the course of the seasons and to adapt themselves to the same; that they await patiently what the future will bring; that they appreciate the importance and seriousness of their duties; that they constantly remain alert and ready for new developments.

Solidarity and Cooperation

146. Nor may it be overlooked that in rural areas, as indeed in every productive sector, farmers should join together in fellowships, especially when the family itself works the farm. Indeed, it is proper for rural workers to have a sense of solidarity. They should strive jointly to set up mutual-aid societies and professional associations. All these are very necessary either to keep rural dwellers abreast of scientific and technical progress, or to protect the prices of goods produced by their labor. Besides, acting in this manner, farmers are put on the same footing as other classes of workers who, for the

most part, join together in such fellowships. Finally, by acting thus, farmers will achieve an importance and influence in public affairs proportionate to their own role. For today it is unquestionably true that the solitary voice speaks, as they say, to the winds.

Recognizing Demands of the Common Good

147. But when rural dwellers, just as other classes of workers, wish to make their influence and importance felt, they should never disregard moral duties or civil law. Rather they should strive to bring their rights and interests into line with the rights and needs of other classes, and to refer the same to the common good. In this connection, farmers who strive vigorously to improve the yield of their farm may rightly demand that their efforts be aided and complemented by public authorities, provided they themselves keep in mind the common needs of all and also relate their own efforts to the fulfillment of these needs.

148. Wherefore, we wish to honor appropriately those sons of ours who everywhere in the world, either by founding and fostering mutual-aid societies or some other type of association, watchfully strive that in all civic affairs farmers enjoy not merely economic prosperity but also a status in keeping with justice.

Vocation and Mission

149. Since everything that makes for man's dignity, perfection, and development seems to be invoked in agricultural labor, it is proper that man regard such work as an assignment from God with a sublime purpose. It is fitting, therefore, that man dedicate work of this kind to the most provident God who directs all events for the salvation of men. Finally, the farmer should take upon himself, in some measure, the task of educating himself and others for the advancement of civilization.

AID TO LESS DEVELOPED AREAS

150. It often happens that in one and the same country citizens enjoy different degrees of wealth and social advance-

ment. This especially happens because they dwell in areas which, economically speaking, have grown at different rates. Where such is the case, justice and equity demand that the government make efforts either to remove or to minimize imbalances of this sort. Toward this end, efforts should be made, in areas where there has been less economic progress, to supply the principal public services, as indicated by circumstances of time and place and in accord with the general level of living. But in bringing this about, it is necessary to have very competent administration and organization to take careful account of the following: labor supply, internal migration, wages, taxes, interest rates, and investments in industries that foster other skills and developments—all of which will further not merely the useful employment of workers and the stimulation of initiative, but also the exploitation of resources locally available.

151. But it is precisely the measures for advancement of the general welfare which civil authorities must undertake. Hence, they should take steps, having regard for the needs of the whole community, that progress in agriculture, industry, and services be made at the same time and in a balanced manner so far as possible. They should have this goal in mind, that citizens in less developed countries—in giving attention to economic and social affairs, as well as to cultural matters—feel themselves to be the ones chiefly responsible for their own progress. For a citizen has a sense of his own dignity when he contributes the major share to progress in his own affairs.

152. Hence, those also who rely on their own resources and initiative should contribute as best they can to the equitable adjustment of economic life in their own community. Nay, more, those in authority should favor and help private enterprise in accordance with the *principle of subsidiarity*, in order to allow private citizens themselves to accomplish as much as is feasible.

Imbalances Between Land and Population

153. It is appropriate to recall at this point that in a number of nations there exists a discrepancy between available agricultural land and the number of rural dwellers. Some na-

tions experience a shortage of citizens, but have rich land resources; others have many citizens but an insufficiency of agricultural land.

154. Nor are there lacking nations wherein, despite their great resource potential, farmers use such primitive and obsolete methods of cultivation that they are unable to produce what is needed for the entire population. On the other hand, in certain countries, agriculture has so adapted itself to recent advances that farmers produce surpluses which to some extent harm the economy of the entire nation.

155. It is evident that both the solidarity of the human race and the sense of brotherhood which accords with Christian principles, require that some peoples lend others energetic help in many ways. Not merely would this result in a freer movement of goods, of capital, and of men, but it also would lessen imbalances between nations. We shall treat of this point in more detail below.

156. Here, however, we cannot fail to express our approval of the efforts of the Institute known as F.A.O. which concerns itself with the feeding of peoples and the improvement of agriculture. This Institute has the special goal of promoting mutual accord among peoples, of bringing it about that rural life is modernized in less developed nations, and finally, that help is brought to people experiencing food shortages.

REQUIREMENTS OF JUSTICE AS BETWEEN NATIONS DIFFERING IN ECONOMIC DEVELOPMENT

Problem of the Modern World

157. Perhaps the most pressing question of our day concerns the relationship between economically advanced commonwealths and those that are in process of development. The former enjoy the conveniences of life; the latter experience dire poverty. Yet, today men are so intimately associated in all parts of the world that they feel, as it were, as if they are members of one and the same household. Therefore, the nations that enjoy a sufficiency and abundance of everything may not overlook the plight of other nations whose citizens experience such domestic problems that they are all but over-

come by poverty and hunger, and are not able to enjoy basic human rights. This is all the more so inasmuch as countries each day seem to become more dependent on each other. Consequently, it is not easy for them to keep the peace advantageously if excessive imbalances exist in their economic and social conditions.

158. Mindful of our role of universal father, we think it opportune to stress here what we have stated in another connection: "We all share responsibility for the fact that populations are undernourished.[40] [Therefore], it is necessary to arouse a sense of responsibility in individuals and generally, especially among those more blessed with this world's goods."[41]

159. As can be readily deduced, and as the Church has always seriously warned, it is proper that the duty of helping the poor and unfortunate should especially stir Catholics, since they are members of the Mystical Body of Christ. "In this we have come to know the love of God," said John the Apostle, "that He laid down His life for us; and we likewise ought to lay down our life for the brethren. He who has the goods of this world and sees his brother in need and closes his heart to him, how does the love of God abide in him?"[42]

160. Wherefore, we note with pleasure that countries with advanced productive systems are lending aid to less priviledged countries, so that these latter may the more readily improve their condition.

Emergency Assistance

161. It is clear to everyone that some nations have surpluses in foodstuffs, particularly of farm products, while elsewhere large masses of people experience want and hunger. Now justice and humanity require that these richer countries come to the aid of those in need. Accordingly, to destroy entirely or to waste goods necessary for the lives of men, runs counter to our obligations in justice and humanity.

162. We are quite well aware that to produce surpluses, especially of farm products, in excess of the needs of a country, can occasion harm to various classes of citizens. Nevertheless, it does not therefore follow that nations with surpluses have no obligation to aid the poor and hungry where some particu-

lar emergency arises. Rather, diligent efforts should be made
that inconveniences arising from surplus goods be minimized
and borne by every citizen on a fair basis.

Scientific, Technical, and Financial Cooperation

163. However, the underlying causes of poverty and hunger will not be removed in a number of countries by these
means alone. For the most part, the causes are to be found in
the primitive state of the economy. To effect a remedy, all
available avenues should be explored with a view, on the one
hand, to instruct citizens fully in necessary skills and in carrying out their responsibilities, and, on the other hand, to enable them to acquire the capital wherewith to promote economic growth by ways and means adapted to our times.

164. It has not escaped our attention that in recent years
there has grown in many minds a deep awareness of their
duty to aid poorer countries still lacking suitable economic
development, in order that these may more readily make economic and social progress.

165. Toward this end, we look to councils, either of a
number of nations, or within individual nations; we look to
private enterprises and societies to exert daily more generous
efforts on behalf of such countries, transmitting to them requisite productive skills. For the same reason help is given to
as many youths as possible that they may study in the great
universities of more developed countries, thus acquiring a
knowledge of the arts and sciences in line with the standards
of our time. Moreover, international banks, single nations, or
private citizens often make loans to these countries that they
may initiate various programs calculated to increase production. We gladly take this opportunity to give due praise to
such generous activity. It is hoped that in the future the
richer countries will make greater and greater efforts to provide developing countries with aid designed to promote sciences, technology, and economic life.

Avoidance of Past Errors

166. In this matter we consider it our duty to offer some
warnings.

167. First of all, it seems only prudent for nations which

thus far have made little or no progress, to weigh well the principal factor in the advance of nations that enjoy abundance.

168. Prudent foresight and common need demand that not only more goods be produced, but that this be done more efficiently. Likewise, necessity and justice require that wealth produced be distributed equitably among all citizens of the commonwealth. Accordingly, efforts should be made to ensure that improved social conditions accompany economic advancement. And it is very important that such advances occur simultaneously in the agricultural, industrial, and various service sectors.

Respect for Individual Characteristics of Countries

169. It is indeed clear to all that countries in process of development often have their own individual characteristics, and that these arise from the nature of the locale, or from cultural tradition, or from some special trait of the citizens.

170. Now when economically developed countries assist the poorer ones, they not only should have regard for these characteristics and respect them, but also should take special care lest, in aiding these nations, they seek to impose their own way of life upon them.

Disinterested Aid

171. Moreover, economically developed countries should take particular care lest, in giving aid to poorer countries, they endeavor to turn the prevailing political situation to their own advantage, and seek to dominate them.

172. Should perchance such attempts be made, this clearly would be but another form of colonialism, which, although disguised in name, merely reflects their earlier but outdated dominion, now abandoned by many countries. When international relations are thus obstructed, the orderly progress of all peoples is endangered.

173. Genuine necessity, as well as justice, requires that whenever countries give attention to the fostering of skills or commerce, they should aid the less developed nations without thought of domination, so that these latter eventually

will be in a position to progress economically and socially on their own initiative.

174. If this be done, it will help much toward shaping a community of all nations, wherein each one, aware of its rights and duties, will have regard for the prosperity of all.

Respect for a Hierarchy of Values

175. There is no doubt that when a nation makes progress in science, technology, economic life, and the prosperity of its citizens, a great contribution is made to civilization. But all should realize that these things are not the highest goods.

176. Accordingly, we note with sorrow that in some nations economic life indeed progresses, but that not a few men are there to be found, who have no concern at all for the just ordering of goods. No doubt, these men either completely ignore spiritual values, or put these out of their minds, or else deny they exist. Nevertheless, while they pursue progress in science, technology, and economic life, they make so much of external benefits that for the most part they regard these as the highest goods of life. Accordingly, there are not lacking grave dangers in the help provided by more affluent nations for development of the poorer ones. For among the citizens of these latter nations, there is operative a general awareness of the higher values on which moral teachings rests—an awareness derived from ancient traditional custom which provides them with motivation.

177. Thus, those who seek to undermine in some measure the right instincts of these peoples, assuredly do something immoral. Rather, those attitudes, besides being held in honor, should be perfected and refined, since upon them true civilization depends.

CONTRIBUTION OF THE CHURCH

178. Moreover, the Church by divine right pertains to all nations. This is confirmed by the fact that she already is everywhere on earth and strives to embrace all peoples.

179. Now, those peoples whom the Church has joined to Christ have always reaped some benefits, whether in economic affairs or in social organization, as history and contem-

porary events clearly record. For everyone who professes Christianity promises and gives assurance that he will contribute as far as he can to the advancement of civil institutions. He must also strive with all his might not only that human dignity suffer no dishonor, but also, by the removal of every kind of obstacle, that all those forces be promoted which are conducive to moral living and contribute to it.

180. Moreover, when the Church infuses her energy into the life of a people, she neither is, nor feels herself to be, an alien institution imposed upon that people from without. This follows from the fact that wherever the Church is present, there individual men are reborn or resurrected in Christ. Those who are thus reborn or who have risen again in Christ feel themselves oppressed by no external force. Rather, realizing they have achieved perfect liberty, they freely move toward God. Hence, whatever is seen by them as good and morally right, that they approve and put into effect.

181. "The Church of Jesus Christ," as our predecessor Pius XII clearly stated, "is the faithful guardian of God's gracious wisdom. Hence, she makes no effort to discourage or belittle those characteristics and traits which are proper to particular nations, and which peoples religiously and tenaciously guard, quite justly, as a sacred heritage. She aims indeed at a unity which is profound and in conformity with that heavenly love whereby all are moved in their innermost being. She does not seek a uniformity which is merely external in its effects and calculated to weaken the fibre of the peoples concerned. And all careful rules that contribute to the wise development and growth within bounds of these capacities and forces, which indeed have their deeply rooted ethnic traits, have the Church's approval and maternal prayers, provided they are not in opposition to those duties which spring from the common origin and destiny of all mortal men."[43]

182. We note with deep satisfaction that Catholic men, citizens of the less developed nations, are for the most part second to no other citizens in furthering efforts of their countries to make progress economically and socially according to their capacity.

183. Furthermore, we note that Catholic citizens of the

richer nations are making extensive efforts to ensure that aid given by their own countries to needy countries is directed increasingly toward economic and social progress. In this connection, it seems specially praiseworthy that appreciable aid in various forms is provided increasingly each year to young people from Africa and Asia, so that they may pursue literary and professional studies in the great universities of Europe and America. The same applies to the great care that has been taken in training for every responsibility of their office men prepared to go to less developed areas, there to carry out their profession and duties.

184. To those sons of ours who, by promoting solicitously the progress of peoples and by spreading, as it were, a wholesome civilizing influence, everywhere demonstrate the perennial vitality of Holy Church and her effectiveness, we wish to express our paternal praise and gratitude.

POPULATION INCREASE AND ECONOMIC DEVELOPMENT

185. More recently, the question often is raised how economic organization and the means of subsistence can be balanced with population increase, whether in the world as a whole or within the needy nations.

Imbalance Between Population and Means of Subsistence

186. As regards the world as a whole, some, consequent to statistical reasoning, observe that within a matter of decades mankind will become very numerous, whereas economic growth will proceed much more slowly. From this some conclude that unless procreation is kept within limits, there subsequently will develop an even greater imbalance between the number of inhabitants and the necessities of life.

187. It is clearly evident from statistical records of less developed countries that, because recent advances in public health and in medicine are there widely diffused, the citizens have a longer life expectancy consequent to lowered rates of infant mortality. The birth rate, where it has traditionally been high, tends to remain at such levels, at least for the im-

mediate future. Thus the birth rate in a given year exceeds the death rate. Meanwhile the productive systems in such countries do not expand as rapidly as the number of inhabitants. Hence, in poorer countries of this sort, the standard of living does not advance and may even deteriorate. Wherefore, lest a serious crisis occur, some are of the opinion that the conception of birth of humans should be avoided or curbed by every possible means.

The Terms of the Problem

188. Now to tell the truth, the interrelationships on a global scale between the number of births and available resources are such that we can infer grave difficulties in this matter do not arise at present, nor will in the immediate future. The arguments advanced in this connection are so inconclusive and controversial that nothing certain can be drawn from them.

189. Besides, God in His goodness and wisdom has, on the one hand, provided nature with almost inexhaustible productive capacity; and, on the other hand, has endowed man with such ingenuity that, by using suitable means, he can apply nature's resources to the needs and requirements of existence. Accordingly, that the question posed may be clearly resolved, a course of action is not indeed to be followed whereby, contrary to the moral law laid down by God, procreative function also is violated. Rather, man should, by the use of his skills and science of every kind, acquire an intimate knowledge of the forces of nature and control them ever more extensively. Moreover, the advances hitherto made in science and technology give almost limitless promise for the future in this matter.

190. When it comes to questions of this kind, we are not unaware that in certain locales and also in poorer countries, it is often argued that in such an economic and social order, difficulties arise because citizens, each year more numerous, are unable to acquire sufficient food or sustenance where they live, and peoples do not show amicable cooperation to the extent they should.

191. But whatever be the situation, we clearly affirm these

problems should be posed and resolved in such a way that man does not have recourse to methods and means contrary to his dignity, which are proposed by those persons who think of man and his life solely in material terms.

192. We judge that this question can be resolved only if economic and social advances preserve and augment the genuine welfare of individual citizens and of human society as a whole. Indeed, in a matter of this kind, first place must be accorded everything that pertains to the dignity of man as such, or to the life of individual men, than which nothing can be more precious. Moreover, in this matter, international cooperation is necessary, so that, conformably with the welfare of all, information, capital, and men themselves may move about among the peoples in orderly fashion.

Respect for the Laws of Life

193. In this connection, we strongly affirm that human life is transmitted and propagated through the instrumentality of the family, which rests on marriage, one and indissoluble, and, so far as Christians are concerned, elevated to the dignity of a sacrament. Because the life of man is passed on to other men deliberately and knowingly, it therefore follows that this should be done in accord with the most sacred, permanent, inviolate prescriptions of God. Everyone without exception is bound to recognize and observe these laws. Wherefore, in this matter, no one is permitted to use methods and procedures which may indeed be permissible to check the life of plants and animals.

194. Indeed, all must regard the life of man as sacred, since, from its inception, it requires the action of God the Creator. Those who depart from this plan of God not only offend His divine majesty and dishonor themselves and the human race, but they also weaken the inner fibre of the commonwealth.

Education Toward a Sense of Responsibility

195. In these matters it is of great importance that new offspring, in addition to being very carefully educated in human culture and in religion—which indeed is the right

and duty of parents—should also show themselves very conscious of their duties in every action of life. This is especially true when it is a question of establishing a family and of procreating and educating children. Such children should be imbued not only with a firm confidence in the providence of God, but also with a strong and ready will to bear the labors and inconveniences which cannot be lawfully avoided by anyone who undertakes the worthy and serious obligation of associating his own activity with God in transmitting life and in educating offspring. In this most important matter certainly nothing is more relevant than the teachings of and supernatural aids provided by the Church. We refer to the Church whose right of freely carrying out her function must be recognized also in this connection.

Creation for Man's Benefit

196. When God, as we read in the book of Genesis, imparted human nature to our first parents, He assigned them two tasks, one of which complements the other. For He first directed: "Be fruitful and multiply,"[44] and then immediately added: "Fill the earth and subdue it."[45]

197. The second of these tasks, far from anticipating a destruction of goods, rather assigns them to the service of human life.

198. Accordingly, with great sadness we note two conflicting trends: on the one hand, the scarcity of goods is vaguely described as such that the life of men reportedly is in danger of perishing from misery and hunger; on the other hand, the recent discoveries of science, technical advances and economic productivity are transformed into means whereby the human race is led toward ruin and a horrible death.

199. Now the provident God has bestowed upon humanity sufficient goods wherewith to bear with dignity the burdens associated with procreation of children. But this task will be difficult or even impossible if men, straying from the right road and with a perverse outlook, use the means mentioned above in a manner contrary to human reason or to their social nature, and hence, contrary to the directives of God Himself.

INTERNATIONAL COOPERATION

World Dimensions of Important Human Problems

200. Since the relationships between countries today are closer in every region of the world, by reason of science and technology, it is proper that peoples become more and more interdependent.

201. Accordingly, contemporary problems of moment—whether in the fields of science and technology, or of economic and social affairs, or of public administration, or of cultural advancement—these, because they may exceed the capacities of individual States, very often affect a number of nations and at times all the nations of the earth.

202. As a result, individual countries, although advanced in culture and civilization, in number and industry of citizens, in wealth, in geographical extent, are not able by themselves to resolve satisfactorily their basic problems. Accordingly, because States must on occasion complement or perfect one another, they really consult their own interests only when they take into account at the same time the interests of others. Hence, dire necessity warns commonwealths to cooperate among themselves and provide mutual assistance.

Mutual Distrust

203. Although this becomes more and more evident each day to individuals and even to all peoples, men, and especially those with high responsibility in public life, for the most part seem unable to accomplish the two things toward which peoples aspire. This does not happen because peoples lack scientific, technical, or economic means, but rather because they distrust one another. Indeed, men, and hence States, stand in fear of one another. One country fears lest another is contemplating aggression and lest the other seize an opportunity to put such plans in effect. Accordingly, countries customarily prepare defenses for their cities and homeland, namely, armaments designed to deter other countries from aggression.

204. Consequently, the energies of man and the resources

of nature are very widely directed by peoples to destruction rather than to the advantage of the human family, and both individual men and entire peoples become so deeply solicitous that they are prevented from undertaking more important works.

Failure to Acknowledge the Moral Order

205. The cause of this state of affairs seems to be that men, more especially leaders of States, have differing philosophies of life. Some even dare to assert that there exists no law of truth and right which transcends external affairs and man himself, which of necessity pertains to everyone, and, finally, which is equitable for all men. Hence, men can agree fully and surely about nothing, since one and the same law of justice is not accepted by all.

206. Although the word *justice* and the related term *demands of justice* are on everyone's lips, such verbalizations do not have the same meaning for all. Indeed, the opposite frequently is the case. Hence, when leaders invoke *justice* or the *demands of justice*, not only do they disagree as to the meaning of the words, but frequently find in them an occasion of serious contention. And so they conclude that there is no way of achieving their rights or advantages, unless they resort to force, the root of very serious evils.

God, the Foundation of the Moral Order

207. That mutual faith may develop among rulers and nations and may abide more deeply in their minds, the laws of truth and justice first must be acknowledged and preserved on all sides.

208. However, the guiding principles of morality and virtue can be based only on God; apart from Him, they necessarily collapse. For man is composed not merely of body, but of soul as well, and is endowed with reason and freedom. Now such a composite being absolutely requires a moral law rooted in religion, which, far better than any external force or advantage, can contribute to the resolution of problems affecting the lives of individual citizens or groups of citizens, or with a bearing upon single States or all States together.

209. Yet, there are today those who assert that, in view of the flourishing state of science and technology, men can achieve the highest civilization even apart from God and by their own unaided powers. Nevertheless, it is because of this very progress in science and technology that men often find themselves involved in difficulties which affect all peoples, and which can be overcome only if they duly recognize the authority of God, author and ruler of man and of all nature.

210. That this is true, the advances of science seem to indicate, opening up, as they do, almost limitless horizons. Thus, an opinion is implanted in many minds that inasmuch as mathematical sciences are unable to discern the innermost nature of things and their changes, or express them in suitable terms, they can scarcely draw inferences about them. And when terrified men see with their own eyes that the vast forces deriving from technology and machines can be used for destruction as well as for the advantage of peoples, they rightly conclude that things pertaining to the spirit and to moral life are to be preferred to all else, so that progress in science and technology do not result in destruction of the human race, but prove useful as instruments of civilization.

211. Meanwhile it comes to pass that in more affluent countries men, less and less satisfied with external goods, put out of their minds the deceptive image of a happy life to be lived here forever. Likewise, not only do men grow daily more conscious that they are fully endowed with all the rights of the human person, but they also strive mightily that relations among themselves become more equitable and more conformed to human dignity. Consequently, men are beginning to recognize that their own capacities are limited, and they seek spiritual things more intensively than heretofore. All of which seems to give some promise that not only individuals, but even peoples may come to an understanding for extensive and extremely useful collaboration.

PART IV

RECONSTRUCTION OF SOCIAL RELATIONSHIPS IN TRUTH, JUSTICE AND LOVE

INCOMPLETE AND ERRONEOUS PHILOSOPHIES OF LIFE

212. As in the past, so too in our day, advances in science and technology have greatly multiplied relationships between citizens; it seems necessary, therefore, that the relationships themselves, whether within a single country or between all countries, be brought into more humane balance.

213. In this connection many systems of thought have been developed and committed to writing: some of these already have been dissipated as mist by the sun; others remain basically unchanged today; still others now elicit less and less response from men. The reason for this is that these popularized fancies neither encompass man, whole and entire, nor do they affect his inner being. Moreover, they fail to take into account the weaknesses of human nature, such as sickness and suffering: weaknesses that no economic or social system, no matter how advanced, can completely eliminate. Besides, men everywhere are moved by a profound and unconquerable sense of religion, which no force can ever destroy nor shrewdness suppress.

214. In our day, a very false opinion is popularized which holds that the sense of religion implanted in men by nature is to be regarded as something adventitious or imaginary, and hence, is to be rooted completely from the mind as altogether inconsistent with the spirit of our age and the progress of civilization. Yet, this inward proclivity of man to religion confirms the fact that man himself was created by God, and irrevocably tends to Him. Thus we read in Augustine: "Thou hast made us for Thyself, O Lord, and our hearts are restless until they rest in Thee."[46]

215. Wherefore, whatever the progress in technology and economic life, there can be neither justice nor peace in the

world, so long as men fail to realize how great is their dignity; for they have been created by God and are His children. We speak of God, who must be regarded as the first and final cause of all things He has created. Separated from God, man becomes monstrous to himself and others. Consequently, mutual relationship between men absolutely require a right ordering of the human conscience in relation to God, the source of all truth, justice, and love.

216. It is well known and recognized by everyone that in a number of countries, some of ancient Christian culture, many of our very dear brothers and sons have been savagely persecuted for a number of years. Now this situation, since it reveals the great dignity of the persecuted, and the refined cruelty of their persecutors, leads many to reflect on the matter, though it has not yet healed the wounds of the persecuted.

217. However, no folly seems more characteristic of our time than the desire to establish a firm and meaningful temporal order, but without God, its necessary foundation. Likewise, some wish to proclaim the greatness of man, but with the source dried up from which such greatness flows and receives nourishment: that is, by impeding and, if it were possible, stopping the yearning of souls for God. But the turn of events in our times, whereby the hopes of many are shattered and not a few have come to grief, unquestionably confirm the words of Scripture: "Unless the Lord build the house, they labor in vain who built it."[47]

THE CHURCH'S TRADITIONAL TEACHING REGARDING MAN'S SOCIAL LIFE

218. What the Catholic Church teaches and declares regarding the social life and relationships of men is beyond question for all time valid.

219. The cardinal point of this teaching is that individual men are necessarily the foundation, cause, and end of all social institutions. We are referring to human beings, insofar as they are social by nature, and raised to an order of existence that transcends and subdues nature.

220. Beginning with this very basic principle whereby the

dignity of the human person is affirmed and defended, Holy Church—especially during the last century and with the assistance of learned priests and laymen, specialists in the field—has arrived at clear social teachings whereby the mutual relationships of men are ordered. Taking general norms into account, these principles are in accord with the nature of things and the changed conditions of man's social life, or with the special genius of our day. Moreover, these norms can be approved by all.

221. But today, more than ever, principles of this kind must not only be known and understood, but also applied to those systems and methods which the various situations of time or place either suggest or require. This is indeed a difficult, though lofty, task. Toward its fulfillment we exhort not only our brothers and sons everywhere, but all men of good will.

Study of Social Matters

222. Above all, we affirm that the social teaching proclaimed by the Catholic Church cannot be separated from her traditional teaching regarding man's life.

223. Wherefore, it is our earnest wish that more and more attention be given to this branch of learning. First of all, we urge that attention be given to such studies in Catholic schools on all levels, and especially in seminaries, although we are not unaware that in some of these latter institutions this is already being done admirably. Moreover, we desire that social study of this sort be included among the religious materials used to instruct and inspire the lay apostolate, either in parishes or in associations. Let this diffusion of knowledge be accomplished by every modern means: that is, in journals, whether daily or periodical; in doctrinal books, both for the learned and the general reader; and finally, by means of radio and television.

224. We judge that our sons among the laity have much to contribute through their work and effort, that this teaching of the Catholic Church regarding the social question be more and more widely diffused. This they can do, not merely by learning it themselves and governing their actions accord-

ingly, but also by taking special care that others also come to know its relevance.

225. Let them be fully persuaded that in no better way can they show this teaching to be correct and effective, than by demonstrating that present day social difficulties will yield to its application. In this way they will win minds today antagonistic to the teaching because they do not know it. Perhaps it will also happen that such men will find some enlightenment in the teaching.

APPLICATION OF SOCIAL TEACHING

226. But social norms of whatever kind are not only to be explained but also applied. This is especially true of the Church's teaching on social matters, which has truth as its guide, justice as its end, and love as its driving force.

227. We consider it, therefore, of the greatest importance that our sons, in addition to knowing these social norms, be reared according to them.

228. To be complete, the education of Christians must relate to the duties of every class. It is therefore necessary that Christians thus inspired, conform their behavior in economic and social affairs to the teachings of the Church.

229. If it is indeed difficult to apply teaching of any sort to concrete situations, it is even more so when one tries to put into practice the teachings of the Catholic Church regarding social affairs. This is especially true for the following reasons: there is deeply rooted in each man an instinctive and immoderate love of his own interests; today there is widely diffused in society a materialistic philosophy of life; it is difficult at times to discern the demands of justice in a given situation.

230. Consequently, it is not enough for men to be instructed, according to the teachings of the Church, on their obligation to act in a Christian manner in economic and social affairs. They must also be shown ways in which they can properly fulfill their duty in this regard.

231. We do not regard such instructions as sufficient, unless there be added to the work of instruction that of the formation of man, and unless some action follow upon the teachings, by way of experience.

232. Just as, proverbially, no one really enjoys liberty unless he uses it, so no one really knows how to act according to Catholic teaching in the economic and social fields, unless he acts according to this teaching in the same area.

A Task for Lay Apostolate

233. Accordingly, in popular instruction of this kind, it seems proper that considerable attention be paid to groups promoting the lay apostolate, especially those whose aim is to ensure that efforts in our present concern draw their inspiration wholly from Christian law. Seeing that members of such groups can first train themselves by daily practice in these matters, they subsequently will be able the better to instruct young people in fulfilling obligations of this kind.

234. It is not inappropriate in this connection to remind all, the great no less than the lowly, that the will to preserve moderation and to bear difficulties, by God's grace, can in no wise be separated from the meaning of life handed down to us by Christian wisdom.

235. But today, unfortunately, very many souls are preoccupied with an inordinate desire for pleasure. Such persons see nothing more important in the whole of life than to seek pleasure, to quench the thirst for pleasure. Beyond doubt, grave ills to both soul and body proceed therefrom. Now in this matter, it must be admitted that one who judges even with the aid of human nature alone, concludes that it is the part of the wise and prudent man to preserve balance and moderation in everything, and to restrain the lower appetites. He who judges matter in the light of divine revelation, assuredly will not overlook the fact that the Gospel of Christ and the Catholic Church, as well as the ascetical tradition handed down to us, all demand that Christians steadfastly mortify themselves and bear the inconveniences of life with singular patience. These virtues, in addition to fostering a firm and moderate rule of mind over body, also present an opportunity of satisfying the punishment due to sin, from which, except for Jesus Christ and His Immaculate Mother, no one is exempt.

Practical Suggestions

236. The teachings in regard to social matters for the most part are put into effect in the following three stages: first, the actual situation is examined; then, the situation is evaluated carefully in relation to these teachings; then only is it decided what can and should be done in order that the traditional norms may be adapted to circumstances of time and place. These three steps are at times expressed by the three words: *observe, judge, act.*

237. Hence, it seems particularly fitting that youth not merely reflect upon this order of procedure, but also, in the present connection, follow it to the extent feasible, lest what they have learned be regarded merely as something to be thought about but not acted upon.

238. However, when it comes to reducing these teachings to action, it sometimes happens that even sincere Catholic men have differing views. When this occurs they should take care to have and to show mutual esteem and regard, and to explore the extent to which they can work in cooperation among themselves. Thus they can in good time accomplish what necessity requires. Let them also take great care not to weaken their efforts in constant controversies. Nor should they, under pretext of seeking what they think best, meanwhile, fail to do what they can and hence should do.

239. But in the exercise of economic and social functions, Catholics often come in contact with men who do not share their view of life. On such occasions, those who profess Catholicism must take special care to be consistent and not compromise in matters wherein the integrity of religion or morals would suffer harm. Likewise, in their conduct they should weigh the opinions of others with fitting courtesy and not measure everything in the light of their own interests. They should be prepared to join sincerely in doing whatever is naturally good or conducive to good. If, indeed, it happens that in these matters sacred authorities have prescribed or decreed anything, it is evident that this judgment is to be obeyed promptly by Catholics. For it is the Church's right and duty not only to safeguard principles relating to the

integrity of religion and morals, but also to pronounce authoritatively when it is a matter of putting these principles into effect.

Manifold Action and Responsibility

240. But what we have said about the norms of instruction should indeed be put into practice. This has special relevance for those beloved sons of ours who are in the ranks of the laity, inasmuch as their activity ordinarily centers around temporal affairs and making plans for the same.

241. To carry out this noble task, it is necessary that laymen not only should be qualified, each in his own profession, and direct their energies in accordance with rules suited to the objective aimed at, but also should conform their activity to the teachings and norms of the Church in social matters. Let them put sincere trust in her wisdom; let them accept her admonitions as sons. Let them reflect that, when in the conduct of life they do not carefully observe principles and norms laid down by the Church in social matters, and which we ourselves reaffirm, then they are negligent in their duty and often injure the rights of others. At times, matters can come to a point where confidence in this teaching is diminished, as if it were indeed excellent but really lacks the force which the conduct of life requires.

A GRAVE DANGER

242. As we have already noted, in this present age men have searched widely and deeply into the laws of nature. Then they invented instruments whereby they can control the forces of nature; they have perfected and continue to perfect remarkable works worthy of deep admiration. Nevertheless, while they endeavor to master and transform the external world, they are also in danger, lest they become neglectful and weaken the powers of body and mind. This is what our predecessor of happy memory, Pius XI, noted with sorrow of spirit in his Encyclical Letter *Quadragesimo Anno*: "And so bodily labor, which was decreed by divine providence for the good of man's body and soul even after original

sin, has too often been changed into an instrument of perversion: for dead matter leaves the factory ennobled and transformed whereas men are there corrupted and degraded."[48]

243. And our predecessor of happy memory, Pius XII, rightly asserted that our age is distinguished from others precisely by the fact that science and technology have made incalculable progress, while men themselves have departed correspondingly from a sense of dignity. It is a "monstrous masterpiece" of this age "to have transformed man, as it were, into a giant as regards the order of nature, yet in the order of the supernatural and the eternal, to have changed him into a pygmy."[49]

244. Too often in our day is verified the testimony of the Psalmist concerning worshipers of false gods, namely, human beings in their activity very frequently neglect themselves, but admire their own works as if these were gods: "Their idols are silver and gold; the handiwork of men."[50]

Respect for the Hierarchy of Values

245. Wherefore, aroused by the pastoral zeal wherewith we embrace all men, we strongly urge our sons that, in fulfilling their duties and in pursuing their goals, they do not allow their consciousness of responsibilities to grow cool, nor neglect the order of the more important goods.

246. For it is indeed clear that the Church has always taught and continues to teach that advances in science and technology and the prosperity resulting therefrom, are truly to be counted as good things and regarded as signs of the progress of civilization. But the Church likewise teaches that goods of this kind are to be judged properly in accordance with their natures: they are always to be considered as instruments for man's use, the better to achieve his highest end: that he can the more easily improve himself, in both the natural and supernatural orders.

247. Wherefore, we ardently desire that our sons should at all times heed the words of the divine Master: "For what does it profit a man, if he gain the whole world, but suffer the loss of his own soul? Or what will a man give in exchange for his soul?"[51]

Sanctification of Holy Days

248. Not unrelated to the above admonitions is the one having to do with rest to be taken on feast days.

249. In order that the Church may defend the dignity with which man in endowed, because he is created by God and because God has breathed into him a soul to His own image, she has never failed to insist that the third commandment: "Remember to keep holy the Sabbath day,"[52] be carefully observed by all. It is the right of God, and within His power, to order that man put aside a day each week for proper and due worship of the divinity. He should direct his mind to heavenly things, setting aside daily business. He should explore the depths of his conscience in order to know how necessary and inviolable are his relations with God.

250. In addition, it is right and necessary for man to cease for a time from labor, not merely to relax his body from daily hard work and likewise to refresh himself with decent recreation, but also to foster family unity, for this requires that all its members preserve a community of life and peaceful harmony.

251. Accordingly, religion, moral teaching, and care of health in turn require that relaxation be had at regular times. The Catholic Church has decreed for many centuries that Christians observe this day of rest on Sunday, and that they be present on the same day at the Eucharistic Sacrifice because it renews the memory of the divine Redemption and at the same time imparts its fruits to the souls of men.

252. But we note with deep sorrow, and we cannot but reprove the many who, though they perhaps do not deliberately despise this holy law, yet more and more frequently disregard it. Whence it is that our very dear workingmen almost necessarily suffer harm, both as to the salvation of their souls and to the health of their bodies.

253. And so, taking into account the needs of soul and body, we exhort, as it were, with the words of God Himself, all men, whether public officials or representatives of management and labor, that they observe this command of God Himself and of the Catholic Church, and judge in their souls

that they have a responsibility to God and society in this regard.

RENEWED DEDICATION

254. From what we have briefly touched upon above, let none of our sons conclude, and especially the laity, that they act prudently if, in regard to the transitory affairs of this life, they become quite remiss in their specific Christian contributions. On the contrary, we reaffirm that they should be daily more zealous in carrying out this role.

255. Indeed, when Christ our Lord made that solemn prayer for the unity of His Church, He asked this from the Father on behalf of His disciples: "I do not pray that Thou take them out of the world, but that Thou keep them from evil."[53] Let no one imagine that there is any opposition between these two things so that they cannot be properly reconciled: namely, the perfection of one's own soul and the business of this life, as if one had no chance but to abandon the activities of this world in order to strive for Christian perfection, or as if one could not attend to these pursuits without endangering his own dignity as a man and as a Christian.

256. However, it is in full accord with the designs of God's providence that men develop and perfect themselves by exercise of their daily tasks, for this is the lot of practically everyone in the affairs of this mortal life. Accordingly, the role of the Church in our day is very difficult: to reconcile a man's modern respect for progress with the norms of humanity and of the Gospel teaching. Yet, the times call the Church to this role; indeed, we may say, earnestly beseech her, not merely to pursue the higher goals, but also to safeguard her accomplishments without harm to herself. To achieve this, as we have already said, the Church especially asks the cooperation of the laity. For this reason, in their dealings with men, they are bound to exert effort in such a way that while fulfilling their duties to others, they do so in union with God through Christ, for the increase of God's glory. Thus the Apostle Paul asserts: "Whether you eat or drink, or do any-

thing else, do all for the glory of God."[54] And elsewhere: "Whatever you do in word or in work, do all in the name of the Lord Jesus Christ, giving thanks to God the Father through Him."[55]

Greater Effectiveness in Temporal Affairs

257. As often, therefore, as human activity and institutions having to do with the affairs of this life help toward spiritual perfection and everlasting beatitude, the more they are to be regarded as an efficacious way of obtaining the immediate end to which they are directed by their very nature. Thus, valid for all times is that noteworthy sentence of the divine Master: "Seek first the kingdom of God and His justice, and all these things shall be given you besides."[56] For he who is, as it were, a *light in the Lord*,[57] and walks as a *son of light*,[58] perceives more clearly what the requirements of justice are, in the various sectors of human zeal, even in those that involve greater difficulties because of the excessive love which many have for their own interests, or those of their country, or race. It must be added that when one is motivated by Christian charity, he cannot but love others, and regard the needs, sufferings and joys of others as his own. His work, wherever it be, is constant, adaptable, humane, and has concern for the needs of others: For "Charity is patient, is kind; charity does not envy, is not pretentious, is not puffed up, is not ambitious, is not self-seeking, is not provoked; thinks no evil, does not rejoice over wickedness, but rejoices with the truth; bears with all things, believes all things, hopes all things, endures all things."[59]

LIVING MEMBERS OF THE MYSTICAL BODY OF CHRIST

258. But we do not wish to bring this letter of ours to a close, Venerable Brothers, without recalling to your minds that most fundamental and true element of Catholic teaching, whereby we learn that we are living members of His Mystical Body, which is the Church: "For as the body is one and has many members, and all the members of the body, many as they are, form one body, so also is it with Christ."[60]

259. Wherefore, we urgently exhort all our sons in every part of the world, whether clergy or laity, that they fully understand how great is the nobility and dignity they derive from being joined to Christ, as branches to the vine, as He Himself said: "I am the vine, you are the branches,"[61] and that they are sharers of His divine life. Whence it is, that if Christians are also joined in mind and heart with the most Holy Redeemer, when they apply themselves to temporal affairs, their work in a way is a continuation of the labor of Jesus Christ Himself, drawing from it strength and redemptive power: "He who abides in Me, and I in him, he bears much fruit."[62] Human labor of this kind is so exalted and ennobled that it leads men engaged in it to spiritual perfection, and can likewise contribute to the diffusion and propagation of the fruits of the Redemption to others. So also it results in the flow of that Gospel leaven, as it were, through the veins of civil society wherein we live and work.

260. Although it must be admitted that the times in which we live are torn by increasingly serious errors, and are troubled by violent disturbances, yet, it happens that the Church's laborers in this age of ours have access to enormous fields of apostolic endeavor. This inspires us with uncommon hope.

261. Venerable Brothers and beloved sons, beginning with that marvelous letter of Leo, we have thus far considered with you the varied and serious issues which pertain to the social conditions of our time. From them we have drawn norms and teachings, upon which we especially exhort you not merely to meditate deeply, but also to do what you can to put them into effect. If each one of you does his best courageously, it will necessarily help in no small measure to establish the kingdom of Christ on earth. This is indeed: "A kingdom of truth and of life; a kingdom of holiness and grace; a kingdom of justice, of love and of peace."[63] And this we shall some day leave to go to that heavenly beatitude, for which we were made by God, and which we ask for with most ardent prayers.

262. For it is a question here of the teaching of the Catholic and Apostolic Church, mother and teacher of all nations, whose light illumines, sets on fire, inflames. Her warning

voice, filled with heavenly wisdom, reaches out to every age. Her power always provides efficacious and appropriate remedies for the growing needs of men, for the cares and solicitudes of this mortal life. With this voice, the age-old song of the Psalmist is in marvelous accord, to strengthen at all times and to uplift our souls: "I will hear what God proclaims; the Lord—for He proclaims peace to His people, and to His faithful ones, and to those who put in Him their hope. Near indeed is His salvation to those who fear Him, glory dwelling in our land. Kindness and truth shall meet; justice and peace shall kiss. Truth shall spring out of the earth, and justice shall look down from heaven. The Lord Himself will give His benefits; our land shall yield its increase. Justice shall walk before Him, and salvation, along the way of His steps."[64]

263. This is the plea, Venerable Brothers, we make at the close of this Letter, to which we have for a considerable time directed our concern about the Universal Church. We desire that the divine Redeemer of mankind, "who has become for us God-given wisdom, and justice, and sanctification, and redemption,[65] may reign and triumph gloriously in all things and over all things, for centuries on end. We desire that, in a properly organized order of social affairs, all nations will at last enjoy prosperity, and happiness, and peace.

264. As an evidence of these wishes, and a pledge of our paternal good will, we affectionately bestow in the Lord our apostolic blessing upon you, Venerable Brothers, and upon all the faithful committed to your care, and especially upon those who will reply with generosity to our appeals.

265. Given at Rome, at Saint Peter's, the fifteenth day of May, in the year 1961, the third year of our Pontificate.

JOHN XXIII, Pope

NOTES

1. Cf. 1 Tim. 3, 15.
2. John 14, 6.
3. John 8, 12.
4. Mark 8, 2.

5. *Acta Leonis XIII*, XI (1891), p. 97–144.
6. *Ibid.*, p. 107.
7. St. Thomas, *De regimine principum*, I, 15.
8. Cf. *Acta Apostolicae Sedis*, XXIII (1931), p. 185.
9. Cf. *Ibid.*, p. 189.
10. *Ibid.*, p. 177–228.
11. Cf. *Ibid.*, p. 190.
12. Cf. *Ibid.*, p. 200.
13. Cf. *Ibid.*, p. 201.
14. Cf. *Ibid.*, p. 210f.
15. Cf. *Ibid.*, p. 211.
16. Cf. *Acta Apostolicae Sedis*, XXXIII (1941), p. 196.
17. Cf. *Ibid.*, p. 197.
18. Cf. *Ibid.*, p. 196.
19. Cf. *Ibid.*, p. 198f.
20. Cf. *Ibid.*, p. 199.
21. Cf. *Ibid.*, p. 201.
22. Cf. *Ibid.*, p. 202.
23. Cf. *Ibid.*, p. 203.
24. *Acta Apostolicae Sedis*, XXIII (1931), p. 203.
25. *Ibid.*, p. 203.
26. Cf. *Ibid.*, p. 222f.
27. Cf. *Acta Apostolicae Sedis*, XXXIII (1941), p. 200.
28. *Acta Apostolicae Sedis*, XXIII (1931), p. 195.
29. *Ibid.*, p. 198.
30. Radio Broadcast, September 1, 1944; cf. A.A.S., XXXVI (1944), p. 254.
31. *Allocution*, October 8, 1956; cf. A.A.S., XLVIII (1956), pp. 799–800.
32. Radio Broadcast, September 1, 1944; cf. A.A.S., XXXVI (1944), p. 253.
33. Radio Broadcast, December 24, 1942; cf. A.A.S., XXXV (1943), p. 17.
34. Cf. *Ibid.*, p. 20.
35. Encyclical Letter *Quadragesimo Anno*; A.A.S., XXIII (1931), p. 214.
36. *Acta Leonis XIII*, XI (1891), p. 114.
37. Matt. 6, 19–20.
38. Matt. 25, 40.
39. Cf. *Acta Apostolicae Sedis*, XXIII (1931), p. 202.
40. *Allocution*, May 3, 1960; cf. A.A.S., LII (1960), p. 465.
41. Cf. *Ibid.*
42. 1 John 3, 16–17.
43. Encyclical Letter *Summi Pontificatus*; A.A.S., XXXI (1939), pp. 428–29.
44. Gen. 1, 28.
45. *Ibid.*
46. *Confessions* I, 1.
47. Ps. 126, 1.

48. *Acta Apostolicae Sedis*, XXIII (1931), p. 221f.
49. Radio Broadcast, Christmas Eve, 1953; cf. A.A.S., XLVI (1954), p. 10.
50. Ps. 113, 4.
51. Matt. 16, 26.
52. Exod. 20, 8.
53. John 17, 15.
54. 1 Cor. 10, 31.
55. Col. 3, 17.
56. Matt. 6, 33.
57. Eph. 5, 8.
58. Cf. *Ibid*.
59. 1 Cor. 13, 4-7.
60. 1 Cor. 12, 12.
61. John 15, 5.
62. *Ibid*.
63. *Preface of Jesus Christ the King*.
64. Ps. 84, 9ff.
65. 1 Cor. 1, 30.

PEACE ON EARTH
(PACEM IN TERRIS)

Mater et Magistra stood solidly within the tradition of Catholic social teachings. It attracted considerable attention in secular circles as commentators around the world welcomed its liberal tone and even suggested that the Pope had been converted to socialism. Yet *Mater et Magistra* remained very much a Catholic document, written to and for Catholics, discussed vigorously by them, drawn upon by liberal and conservative Catholics to support already firm positions on questions of public policy. Few non-Catholics were intrigued by the significance of socialization, few would argue with the Pope's general demands for great justice and equity in social and economic policy. But, when it appeared in 1961, few had yet caught the significance of the changes which by then were already sweeping the Catholic world.

Pacem in Terris was different. Issued only a few months before Pope John's death, the new encyclical came at an appropriate time. The Vatican Council had already begun, and the world watched with new interest this dramatic effort of the world's most conservative institution to reform itself. Pope John had already become a world figure. His personality touched some vital nerve in Western society; he seemed that rarest of public men: humble, wise, and in touch with the deepest aspirations of humanity in the simplest acts of life. Somehow this pope had become a leader of all people; his words and actions were of as much interest to non-Catholics as Catholics, his disinterestedness beyond question, his charity and fairness unchallenged and deeply valued. By the time *Pacem in Terris* appeared, the audience for a major papal announcement was immensely larger than it had been a few years before. When Pope John for the first time addressed a papal encyclical to "all men of good will," many listened. The year after its publication, John Cogley wrote that *Pacem in Terris* has had much more universal appeal and general impact than any other of this century's remarkable papal documents.

Equally important, the dangers of nuclear war were more apparent than ever before. The world had been "to the brink" twice—over Berlin and Cuba—and people everywhere had been forced to confront the awesome prospect that the weapons of mass destruction in the hands of America and the Soviet Union might, someday, be used. Pope John's eloquent statement of the urgency of peace thus struck a receptive world. The values of freedom and justice, the potential of reason in human affairs, the enthusiastic endorsement of the United Nations, the powerful statement that a just war in a nuclear age was nearly impossible—all these features of the encyclical found a responsive audience not only in the Church but in the world community.

Pacem in Terris was even more optimistic and open than *Mater et Magistra*. The incredibly tortured language of papal monarchy was gone, replaced by a language of fraternity, shared concern, and mutual responsibility. Addressed to Catholics and to "men of good will," it spoke of a world that belonged not to Catholics but to all people everywhere. It took the principles of traditional social doctrine and made them truly universal, awakening their long-hidden potential to speak directly to humanity, united not simply by common creation in God's image but by shared responsibility for the earth and common interest in avoiding nuclear annihilation. Most dramatic was the manner in which, without in the least surrendering the Church's longstanding opposition to liberalism, Pope John was able to accept and endorse that most cherished of modern values, freedom.

The encyclical had the tone of Pope John's pontificate: service to all humans as they are found—diverse, conflicting, often caught up in conditions and ideologies with which Catholics disagree, but still people, to be cherished, loved, and served. And finally, freedom, that ideal of liberalism, long resisted and reinterpreted by the Church but now validated in its simplest and most radical form: freedom of individuals and social groups to define their destinies and to pursue them within the framework of human community. The emphasis on freedom was new in Catholic teaching, and it constituted a major break with the past.

The natural-law framework of the document also represented a break from the past. Natural law was not used as a means of attempting a restoration of the medieval social framework that had long been the ideal of modern papal social teaching. Rather natural law was interpreted in almost a secular way as a means of creating a basic order within the world. Even though references to natural law were reinforced with reference to Catholic teaching, nonetheless the encyclical attempted to argue on the basis of reason that it was possible to discover a natural order and use it as the foundation for a new sense of international harmony and order. In doing this, the Pope placed the human person at the center of the encyclical. John developed in the first section the various rights and duties that were proper to the human person. While the references to duties were part of a standard Catholic orientation toward natural law and the hierarchal order in which persons existed, nonetheless Pope John attempted to surpass this tradition by his development of the rights of the individual vis-à-vis the larger society. In many ways this is an attempt to have it both ways at once. On the one hand he implicitly acknowledges the tradition which states that individuals by reason of their place in society have certain duties to society; on the other hand he validates the modern claim that individuals by virtue of their personhood have legitimate moral claims over and against a society. While many would argue that the introduction of the philosophy of rights is a major improvement in papal social teaching, nonetheless it is not clear how one can systematically reconcile the philosophy of both rights and duties within the encyclical. Beginning with this encyclical, this problem is part of an ongoing dilemma within Roman Catholic social teaching: How does one reconcile both the concepts of rights and of duties, in particular since each of these concepts comes from a different philosophic tradition?

A partial answer, although not clearly developed within the

encyclical, is the natural-law framework that John uses as the major outline in the encyclical. This framework begins with an understanding of the person and his or her role within society. Then the individual is placed in relationship to the state, and the rights and duties of each are elaborated. The encyclical next moves to a discussion of rights and duties that are proper in the relations between states. Finally, Pope John moves to his highest level, that of the rights and duties of individuals and political communities within a world community. In setting forth this traditional hierarchal framework, Pope John assumes that the weight and validity of his ongoing natural-law argument will guarantee the explication of the duties that he sees as inherent in the variety of relationships at different levels within the organization of the world community. He also attempts to draw from these relationships the series of rights or moral claims that individuals and communities always have over and against the next higher form of social organization. In doing this, the Pope hopes to have both stability within the community from its own natural ordering and the guarantee that individuals may argue against the communities to which they belong to protect their own rights.

There are many themes in this encyclical which are quite significant. Four, however, stand out as having a great importance: the rights proper to each individual, the relation between authority and conscience, disarmament, and the development of the common good.

The rights that the Pope argues are proper to all individuals are not in themselves that unique or constitutive of a major departure from traditional Catholic social thought. What is important is the encyclical's grouping of them together and listing them in an explicit manner. Many of them, such as the right to live in a dignified manner, the right to respect for one's person, and the right to religious freedom, are traditional rights which most people would accept without too much argument. But the Pope also argues for rights that might not be accepted as easily: the right to freedom in searching for the truth and in expressing one's opinions, the right to choose freely one's state of life, the right to free initiative in economics, the right to work, the right of freedom of assembly and association, and the right to emigrate and immigrate. This listing of rights sets out a major social agenda and also provides an initial orientation to many issues of concern to the Pope in this encyclical. It also provides the basis for an evaluation of the societies in which individuals live and a foundation for arguing for and claiming these various rights that the Pope lists.

These rights also form a general background for the document's teaching on the relation between conscience and authority. John begins with the traditional doctrine that authority is derived from God, but it also must derive its obligatory force from the moral order. A traditional orientation of this section is shown by John's arguing that authority "must appeal primarily to the conscience of individual citizens, that is, to each one's duty to collaborate readily for the common good of all." This is the traditional doctrine that social positions imply social duties that are binding on all by the natural order. Then John continues that the state can oblige individuals in conscience only if its authority is intrinsically related to the authority which stands behind the moral order, that is, God. This helps establish that individuals may make claims against the society based upon an order which is also to regulate society. Therefore, if civil authorities legislate anything contrary to the natural order and therefore contrary to the will of God, these laws cannot be binding on the consciences of individuals. Again, this is arguing for two things at once: a natural order of the universe which is the foundation of authority and its legitimation, and the basis for claims over and against the authority when it deviates from the natural order that is in the universe. Although the teaching on conscience and authority is traditional, nonetheless John does emphasize that individuals can make claims against governments and that these claims are recognized by the natural law.

The problem of the arms race also is a central concern of the encyclical. John argues that the arms race deprives individuals and nations of the economic goods necessary for social progress. It also causes individuals to live in constant fear not only from the fact of nuclear war but also from the hazards that come from nuclear testing. The Pope therefore argues that justice, reason, and humanity demand that the arms race should cease, that nuclear weapons be banned, and that progressive disarmament begin. In addition to the cooperation and trust that will be necessary for such disarmament, Pope John also introduces a strong statement as to why the arms race, especially with its emphasis on nuclear weapons, should be terminated. The Pope argues that, because of the terrible destructive force of such weapons and the horror that their use would bring, "it is contrary to reason to hold that war is now a suitable way to restore rights which have been violated."

The concept of the common good has been a traditional feature of Roman Catholic social thought. What is unique about the concept here is the way in which Pope John uses it as a principle of integration. Part of the common good is the totality of the rights which the Pope argues for in the first part of the encyclical. These are to be shared by all members of the political community, and it is the responsibility of the civil authority to ensure that these rights are promoted. What is also important is Pope John's argument that each political community also has a common good which transcends the individual person's good, but which cannot be divorced from the common good of the entire human community. Such a realization of a variety of goods demands international cooperation and planning so that each individual entity—whether this be a person or a political community— can realize the goods proper to it. This finds its fulfillment in what Pope John refers to as the universal common good, or the common good of the entire human family. The Pope argues that unrestrained nationalism and economic competition have created almost insurmountable barriers to realizing this universal common good. Therefore a new principle of authority operating on a worldwide basis must be established. Pope John argues that the United Nations may be one viable way of achieving such a universal common good. Although recognizing that as it presently exists it is not completely fulfilling this task, he hopes that it may become more nearly equal to the needs that are manifest by individuals and communities and so serve as a proper vehicle for achieving a state of harmony and cohesion within the world.

Pacem in Terris had far more impact on the world community than any previous encyclical letter. Robert Hutchins and the Fund for the Republic sponsored a series of remarkable conferences of world leaders to examine the themes of the encyclical. At one session, Hutchins stated that the encyclical was one of the most profound and significant documents of our age. While some commentators, including American theologians Reinhold Niebuhr and John Courtney Murray, found it too idealistic and impractical, the encyclical still received wide acclaim. One reason was its strong affirmation of human rights, which had universal appeal. Another was the drama of such affirmations, and such strong language on questions of war and peace, emanating from the papacy. As Michael Novak noted, many non-Catholics regarded the American Catholic community as politically and socially selfish and unenlightened; for the Pope, the symbol of Catholic conservatism, to utter words of such evident goodness and sincerity seemed dramatic and compelling. Catholic liberals were delighted; for Justus George Lawler, one of the few to give serious attention to moral problems of war in the nuclear age, the encyclical marked the end of the Catholic ghetto, of that period of history when Catholics had cut themselves off from the rest of the world as a beseiged fortress. With *Pacem in Terris* and the Vatican Council, Catholicism was finally emerging into full participation in the human community. It was a fitting climax to Pope John's reign, offering a standard of human rights and world peace against which to measure the pastoral effectiveness of the changes initiated by the Council. The standard of Catholic life could never again be simply the power and strength of the Church, for the Church itself would now be judged by the standards of truth, justice, charity, and freedom Pope John had set forth.

PACEM IN TERRIS

ENCYCLICAL LETTER ON ESTABLISHING
UNIVERSAL PEACE IN TRUTH, JUSTICE,
CHARITY AND LIBERTY

TO OUR VENERABLE BROTHERS THE PATRIARCHS,
PRIMATES, ARCHBISHOPS, BISHOPS AND OTHER
LOCAL ORDINARIES IN PEACE AND COMMUNION WITH THE
APOSTOLIC SEE, TO THE CLERGY AND FAITHFUL OF THE
WHOLE WORLD AND TO ALL MEN OF GOOD WILL

POPE JOHN XXIII

VENERABLE BROTHERS AND BELOVED CHILDREN,
HEALTH AND APOSTOLIC BENEDICTION

INTRODUCTION

ORDER IN THE UNIVERSE

1. Peace on earth, which all men of every era have most eagerly yearned for, can be firmly established only if the order laid down by God be dutifully observed.

2. The progress of learning and the inventions of technology clearly show that, both in living things and in the forces of nature, an astonishing order reigns, and they also bear witness to the greatness of man, who can understand that order and create suitable instruments to harness those forces of nature and use them to his benefit.

3. But the progress of science and the inventions of technology show above all the infinite greatness of God, Who created the universe and man himself. He created all things out of nothing, pouring into them the abundance of His wisdom and goodness, so that the holy psalmist praises God in these words: "O Lord our master, the majesty of thy name

fills all the earth."[1] Elsewhere he says: "What diversity, Lord, in thy creatures! What wisdom has designed them all!"[2] God also created man in His own "image and likeness,"[3] endowed him with intelligence and freedom, and made him lord of creation, as the same psalmist declares in the words: "Thou hast placed him only a little below the angels, crowning him with glory and honor and bidding him rule over the works of thy hands. Thou hast put all under his dominion."[4]

ORDER IN HUMAN BEINGS

4. How strongly does the turmoil of individual men and peoples contrast with the perfect order of the universe! It is as if the relationships which bind them together could be controlled only by force.

5. But the Creator of the world has imprinted in man's heart an order which his conscience reveals to him and enjoins him to obey: "This shows that the obligations of the law are written in their hearts; their conscience utters its own testimony."[5] And how could it be otherwise? For whatever God has made shows forth His infinite wisdom, and it is manifested more clearly in the things which have greater perfection.[6]

6. But fickleness of opinion often produces this error, that many think that the relationships between men and States can be governed by the same laws as the forces and irrational elements of the universe, whereas the laws governing them are of quite a different kind and are to be sought elsewhere, namely, where the Father of all things wrote them, that is, in the nature of man.

7. By these laws men are most admirably taught, first of all how they should conduct their mutual dealings among themselves, then how the relationships between the citizens and the public authorities of each State should be regulated, then how States should deal with one another, and finally how, on the one hand individual men and States, and on the other hand the community of all peoples, should act towards each other, the establishment of such a community being urgently

demanded today by the requirements of universal common good.

PART I

ORDER BETWEEN MEN

EVERY MAN IS A PERSON WITH RIGHTS AND DUTIES

First of all, it is necessary to speak of the order which should exist between men.

9. Any human society, if it is to be well-ordered and productive, must lay down as a foundation this principle, namely, that every human being is a person; that is, his nature is endowed with intelligence and free will. Indeed, precisely because he is a person he has rights and obligations flowing directly and simultaneously from his very nature.[7] And as these rights and obligations are universal and inviolable, so they cannot in any way be surrendered.

10. If we look upon the dignity of the human person in the light of divinely revealed truth, we cannot help but esteem it far more highly; for men are redeemed by the blood of Jesus Christ, they are by grace the children and friends of God and heirs of eternal glory.

RIGHTS

The Right to Life and a Worthy Standard of Living

11. Beginning our discussion of the rights of man, we see that every man has the right to life, to bodily integrity, and to the means which are suitable for the proper development of life; these are primarily food, clothing, shelter, rest, medical care, and finally the necessary social services. Therefore a human being also has the right to security in cases of sickness, inability to work, widowhood, old age, unemployment, or in any other case in which he is deprived of the means of subsistence through no fault of his own.[8]

Rights Pertaining to Moral and Cultural Values

12. By the natural law every human being has the right to respect for his person, to his good reputation; the right to freedom in searching for truth and in expressing and communicating his opinions, and in pursuit of art, within the limits laid down by the moral order and the common good; and he has the right to be informed truthfully about public events.

13. The natural law also gives man the right to share in the benefits of culture, and therefore the right to a basic education and to technical and professional training in keeping with the stage of educational development in the country to which he belongs. Every effort should be made to ensure that persons be enabled, on the basis of merit, to go on to higher studies, so that, as far as possible, they may occupy posts and take on responsibilities in human society in accordance with their natural gifts and the skills they have acquired.[9]

The Right to Worship God According to One's Conscience

14. This too must be listed among the rights of a human being, to honor God according to the sincere dictates of his own conscience, and therefore the right to practice his religion privately and publicly. For as Lactantius so clearly taught: "We were created for the purpose of showing to the God Who bore us the submission we owe Him, of recognizing Him alone, and of serving Him. We are obliged and bound by this duty to God; from this religion itself receives its name."[10] And on this point Our Predecessor of immortal memory, Leo XIII, declared: "This genuine, this honorable freedom of the sons of God, which most nobly protects the dignity of the human person, is greater than any violence or injustice; it has always been sought by the Church, and always most dear to her. This was the freedom which the Apostles claimed with intrepid constancy, which the apologists defended with their writings, and which the martyrs in such numbers consecrated with their blood."[11]

The Right to Choose Freely One's State of Life

15. Human beings have the right to choose freely the state of life which they prefer, and therefore the right to set up a family, with equal rights and duties for man and woman, and also the right to follow a vocation to the priesthood or the religious life.[12]

16. The family, grounded on marriage freely contracted, monogamous and indissoluble, is and must be considered the first and essential cell of human society. From this it follows that most careful provision must be made for the family both in economic and social matters as well as in those which are of a cultural and moral nature, all of which look to the strengthening of the family and helping it carry out its function.

17. Parents, however, have a prior right in the support and education of their children.[13]

Economic Rights

18. If we turn our attention to the economic sphere, it is clear that man has a right by the natural law not only to an opportunity to work, but also to go about his work without coercion.[14]

19. To these rights is certainly joined the right to demand working conditions in which physical health is not endangered, morals are safeguarded, and young people's normal development is not impaired. Women have the right to working conditions in accordance with their requirements and their duties as wives and mothers.[15]

20. From the dignity of the human person, there also arises the right to carry on economic activities according to the degree of responsibility of which one is capable.[16] Furthermore—and this must be specially emphasized—the worker has a right to a wage determined according to criterions of justice, and sufficient, therefore, in proportion to the available resources, to give the worker and his family a standard of living in keeping with the dignity of the human person. In this regard, Our Predecessor Pius XII said: "To the personal duty to work imposed by nature, there corresponds and follows the natural right of each individual to make of

his work the means to provide for his own life and the lives of his children; so fundamental is the law of nature which commands man to preserve his life."[17]

21. The right to private property, even of productive goods, also derives from the nature of man. This right, as We have elsewhere declared, "is an effective means for safeguarding the dignity of the human person and for the exercise of responsibility in all fields; it strengthens and gives serenity to family life, thereby increasing the peace and prosperity of the state."[18]

22. However, it is opportune to point out that there is a social duty essentially inherent in the right of private property.[19]

The Right of Meeting and Association

23. From the fact that human beings are by nature social, there arises the right of assembly and association. They have also the right to give the societies of which they are members the form they consider most suitable for the aim they have in view, and to act within such societies on their own initiative and on their own responsibility in order to achieve their desired objectives.[20]

24. And, as We Ourselves in the encyclical *Mater et Magistra* have strongly urged, it is by all means necessary that a great variety of organizations and intermediate groups be established which are capable of achieving a goal which an individual cannot effectively attain by himself. These societies and organizations must be considered the indispensable means to safeguard the dignity of the human person and freedom while leaving intact a sense of responsibility.[21]

The Right to Emigrate and Immigrate

25. Every human being has the right to freedom of movement and of residence within the confines of his own country; and, when there are just reasons for it, the right to emigrate to other countries and take up residence there.[22] The fact that one is a citizen of a particular state does not detract in any way from his membership in the human family as a whole, nor from his citizenship in the world community.

Political Rights

26. The dignity of the human person involves the right to take an active part in public affairs and to contribute one's part to the common good of the citizens. For, as Our Predecessor of happy memory, Pius XII, pointed out: "The human individual, far from being an object and, as it were, a merely passive element in the social order, is in fact, must be and must continue to be, its subject, its foundation and its end."[23]

27. The human person is also entitled to a juridical protection of his rights, a protection that should be efficacious, impartial, and inspired by the true norms of justice. As Our Predecessor Pius XII teaches: "That perpetual privilege proper to man, by which every individual has a claim to the protection of his rights, and by which there is assigned to each a definite and particular sphere of rights, immune from all arbitrary attacks, is the logical consequence of the order of justice willed by God."[24]

DUTIES

Rights and Duties Necessarily Linked in the One Person

28. The natural rights with which We have been dealing are, however, inseparably connected, in the very person who is their subject, with just as many respective duties; and rights as well as duties find their source, their sustenance and their inviolability in the natural law which grants or enjoins them.

29. Therefore, to cite a few examples, the right of every man to life is correlative with the duty to preserve it; his right to a decent standard of living with the duty of living it becomingly; and his right to investigate the truth freely, with the duty of seeking it ever more completely and profoundly.

Reciprocity of Rights and Duties Between Persons

30. Once this is admitted, it also follows that in human society to one man's right there corresponds a duty in all other

persons: the duty, namely, of acknowledging and respecting the right in question. For every fundamental human right draws its indestructible moral force from the natural law, which in granting it imposes a corresponding obligation. Those, therefore, who claim their own rights, yet altogether forget or neglect to carry out their respective duties, are people who build with one hand and destroy with the other.

Mutual Collaboration

31. Since men are social by nature they are meant to live with others and to work for one another's welfare. A well-ordered human society requires that men recognize and observe their mutual rights and duties. It also demands that each contribute generously to the establishment of a civic order in which rights and duties are more sincerely and effectively acknowledged and fulfilled.

32. It is not enough, for example, to acknowledge and respect every man's right to the means of subsistence if we do not strive to the best of our ability for a sufficient supply of what is necessary for his sustenance.

33. The society of men must not only be organized but must also provide them with abundant resources. This certainly requires that they observe and recognize their mutual rights and duties; it also requires that they collaborate in the many enterprises that modern civilization either allows or encourages or even demands.

An Attitude of Responsibility

34. The dignity of the human person also requires that every man enjoy the right to act freely and responsibly. For this reason, therefore, in social relations man should exercise his rights, fulfill his obligations and, in the countless forms of collaboration with others, act chiefly on his own responsibility and initiative. This is to be done in such a way that each one acts on his own decision, of set purpose and from a consciousness of his obligation, without being moved by force or pressure brought to bear on him externally. For any human society that is established on relations of force must be regarded as inhuman, inasmuch as the personality of its

members is repressed or restricted, when in fact they should be provided with appropriate incentives and means for developing and perfecting themselves.

Social Life in Truth, Justice, Charity, and Freedom

35. A civic society is to be considered well-ordered, beneficial and in keeping with human dignity if it is grounded on truth. As the Apostle Paul exhorts us: "Away with falsehood then; let everyone speak out the truth to his neighbor; membership of the body binds us to one another."[25] This will be accomplished when each one duly recognizes both his rights and his obligations towards others. Furthermore, human society will be such as We have just described it, if the citizens, guided by justice, apply themselves seriously to respecting the rights of others and discharging their own duties; if they are moved by such fervor of charity as to make their own the needs of others and share with others their own goods; if, finally, they work for a closer fellowship in the world of spiritual values. Yet this is not sufficient; for human society is bound together by freedom, that is to say, in ways and means in keeping with the dignity of its citizens, who accept the responsibility of their actions, precisely because they are by nature rational beings.

36. Therefore, venerable brothers and beloved children, human society must primarily be considered something pertaining to the spiritual. Through it, in the bright light of truth men should share their knowledge, be able to exercise their rights and fulfill their obligations, be inspired to seek spiritual values, mutually derive genuine pleasure from the beautiful of whatever order it be, always be readily disposed to pass on to others the best of their own cultural heritage and eagerly strive to make their own the spiritual achievements of others. These benefits not only influence, but at the same time give aim and scope to all that has bearing on cultural expressions, economic and social institutions, political movements and forms, laws, and all other structures by which society is outwardly established and constantly developed.

God and the Moral Order

37. The order which prevails in society is by nature moral. Grounded as it is in truth, it must function according to the norms of justice, it should be inspired and perfected by mutual love, and finally it should be brought to an ever more refined and human balance in freedom.

38. Now an order of this kind, whose principles are universal, absolute and unchangeable, has its ultimate source in the one true God, Who is personal and transcends human nature. Inasmuch as God is the first Truth and the highest Good, He alone is that deepest source from which human society can draw its vitality, if that society is to be well ordered, beneficial, and in keeping with human dignity.[26] As St. Thomas Aquinas says: "Human reason is the norm of the human will, according to which its goodness is measured, because reason derives from the eternal law which is the divine reason itself. It is evident then that the goodness of the human will depends much more on the eternal law than on human reason."[27]

CHARACTERISTICS OF THE PRESENT DAY

39. Our age has three distinctive characteristics.

40. First of all, the working classes have gradually gained ground in economic and public affairs. They began by claiming their rights in the socio-economic sphere; they extended their action then to claims on the political level, and finally applied themselves to the acquisition of the benefits of a more refined culture. Today, therefore, workers all over the world refuse to be treated as if they were irrational objects without freedom, to be used at the arbitrary disposition of others. They insist that they be always regarded as men with a share in every sector of human society: in the social and economic sphere, in the fields of learning and culture, and in public life.

41. Secondly, it is obvious to everyone that women are now taking part in public life. This is happening more rapidly perhaps in nations of Christian civilization, and, more

slowly, but broadly, among peoples who have inherited other traditions or cultures. Since women are becoming ever more conscious of their human dignity, they will not tolerate being treated as mere material instruments, but demand rights befitting a human person both in domestic and in public life.

42. Finally, in the modern world human society has taken on an entirely new appearance in the field of social and political life. For since all nations have either achieved or are on the way to achieving independence, there will soon no longer exist a world divided into nations that rule others and nations that are subject to others.

43. Men all over the world have today—or will soon have —the rank of citizens in independent nations. No one wants to feel subject to political powers located outside his own country or ethnical group. Thus in very many human beings the inferiority complex which endured for hundreds and thousands of years is disappearing, while in others there is an attenuation and gradual fading of the corresponding superiority complex which had its roots in social-economic privileges, sex or political standing.

44. On the contrary, the conviction that all men are equal by reason of their natural dignity has been generally accepted. Hence racial discrimination can in no way be justified, at least doctrinally or in theory. And this is of fundamental importance and significance for the formation of human society according to those principles which We have outlined above. For, if a man becomes conscious of his rights, he must become equally aware of his duties. Thus he who possesses certain rights has likewise the duty to claim those rights as marks of his dignity, while all others have the obligation to acknowledge those rights and respect them.

45. When the relations of human society are expressed in terms of rights and duties, men become conscious of spiritual values, understand the meaning and significance of truth, justice, charity and freedom, and become deeply aware that they belong to this world of values. Moreover, when moved by such concerns, they are brought to a better knowledge of the true God Who is personal and transcendent, and thus they make the ties that bind them to God the solid foundation and supreme criterion of their lives, both of that life which

they live interiorly in the depths of their own souls and of
that in which they are united to other men in society.

PART II

RELATIONS BETWEEN INDIVIDUALS AND THE
PUBLIC AUTHORITIES WITHIN A SINGLE STATE

NECESSITY AND DIVINE ORIGIN OF AUTHORITY

46. Human society can be neither well ordered nor prosperous unless it has some people invested with legitimate authority to preserve its institutions and to devote themselves as
far as is necessary to work and care for the good of all. These,
however, derive their authority from God, as St. Paul teaches
in the words: "Authority comes from God alone."[28] These
words of St. Paul are explained thus by St. John Chrysostom:
"What are you saying? Is every ruler appointed by God? I do
not say that, he replies, for I am not dealing now with individual rulers, but with authority itself. What I say is, that it
is the divine wisdom and not mere chance, that has ordained
that there should be government, that some should command and others obey."[29] Moreover, since God made men
social by nature, and since no society "can hold together unless some one be over all, directing all to strive earnestly for
the common good, every civilized community must have a
ruling authority, and this authority, no less than society itself, has its source in nature, and has, consequently, God for
its author."[30]

47. But authority is not to be thought of as a force lacking
all control. Indeed, since it is the power to command according to right reason, authority must derive its obligatory force
from the moral order, which in turn has God for its first
source and final end. Wherefore Our Predecessor of happy
memory, Pius XII, said: "The absolute order of living beings
and man's very destiny (We are speaking of man who is free,
bound by obligations and endowed with inalienable rights,
and at once the basis of society and the purpose for which it
exists) also includes the state as a necessary society invested

with the authority without which it could not come into being or live. . . . And since this absolute order, as we learn from sound reason, and especially from the Christian faith, can have no origin save in God Who is our Creator, it follows that the dignity of the state's authority is due to its sharing to some extent in the authority of God Himself."[31]

48. Wherefore, a civil authority which uses as its only or its chief means either threats and fear of punishment or promises of rewards cannot effectively move men to promote the common good of all. Even if it did so move them, this would be altogether opposed to their dignity as men, endowed with reason and free will. As authority rests chiefly on moral force, it follows that civil authority must appeal primarily to the conscience of individual citizens, that is, to each one's duty to collaborate readily for the common good of all. But since by nature all men are equal in human dignity, it follows that no one may be coerced to perform interior acts. That is in the power of God alone, Who sees and judges the hidden designs of men's hearts.

49. Those therefore who have authority in the State may oblige men in conscience only if their authority is intrinsically related with the authority of God and shares in it.[32]

50. By this principle the dignity of the citizens is protected. When, in fact, men obey their rulers, it is not at all as men that they obey them, but through their obedience it is God, the provident Creator of all things, Whom they reverence, since He has decreed that men's dealings with one another should be regulated by an order which He Himself has established. Moreover, in showing this due reverence to God, men not only do not debase themselves but rather perfect and ennoble themselves. "For to serve God is to rule."[33]

51. Since the right to command is required by the moral order and has its source in God, it follows that, if civil authorities pass laws or command anything opposed to the moral order and consequently contrary to the will of God, neither the laws made nor the authorizations granted can be binding on the consciences of the citizens, since "God has more right to be obeyed than men."[34] Otherwise, authority breaks down completely and results in shameful abuse. As St.

Thomas Aquinas teaches: "Human law has the true nature of law only in so far as it corresponds to right reason, and in this respect it is evident that it is derived from the eternal law. In so far as it falls short of right reason, a law is said to be a wicked law; and so, lacking the true nature of law, it is rather a kind of violence."[35]

52. It must not be concluded, however, because authority comes from God, that therefore men have no right to choose those who are to rule the state, to decide the form of government, and to determine both the way in which authority is to be exercised and its limits. It is thus clear that the doctrine which We have set forth can be fully consonant with any truly democratic regime.[36]

ATTAINMENT OF THE COMMON GOOD IS THE PURPOSE OF THE PUBLIC AUTHORITY

53. Individual citizens and intermediate groups are obliged to make their specific contributions to the common welfare. One of the chief consequences of this is that they must bring their own interests into harmony with the needs of the community, and must contribute their goods and their services as civil authorities have prescribed, in accord with the norms of justice and within the limits of their competence. Clearly then those who wield power in the state must do this by such acts which not only have been justly carried out, but which also either have the common welfare primarily in view or which can lead to it.

54. Indeed since the whole reason for the existence of civil authorities is the realization of the common good, it is clearly necessary that, in pursuing this objective, they should respect its essential elements, and at the same time conform their laws to the circumstances of the day.[37]

Essentials of the Common Good

55. Assuredly, the ethnic characteristics of the various human groups are to be respected as constituent elements of the common good,[38] but these values and characteristics by no means exhaust the content of the common good. For the

common good since it is intimately bound up with human nature cannot therefore exist fully and completely unless the human person is taken into consideration and the essential nature and realization of the common good be kept in mind.[39]

56. In the second place, the very nature of the common good requires that all members of the state be entitled to share in it, although in different ways according to each one's tasks, merits and circumstances. For this reason, every civil authority must take pains to promote the common good of all, without preference for any single citizen or civic group. As Our Predecessor of immortal memory, Leo XIII, has said: "The civil power must not serve the advantage of any one individual, or of some few persons, inasmuch as it was established for the common good of all."[40] Considerations of justice and equity, however, can at times demand that those involved in civil government give more attention to the less fortunate members of the community, since they are less able to defend their rights and to assert their legitimate claims.[41]

57. In this context, We judge that attention should be called to the fact that the common good touches the whole man, the needs both of his body and of his soul. Hence it follows that the civil authorities must undertake to effect the common goods by ways and means that are proper to them; that is, while respecting the hierarchy of values, they should promote simultaneously both the material and the spiritual welfare of the citizens.[42]

58. These principles are clearly contained in the doctrine stated in Our Encyclical *Mater et Magistra*, where We emphasized that the common good of all "embraces the sum total of those conditions of social living whereby men are enabled to achieve their own integral perfection more fully and more easily."[43]

59. Men, however, composed as they are of bodies and immortal souls, can never in this mortal life succeed in satisfying all their needs or in attaining perfect happiness. Therefore the common good is to be procured by such ways and means which not only are not detrimental to man's eternal salvation but which positively contribute to it.[44]

Responsibilities of the Public Authority, and
Rights and Duties of Individuals

60. It is agreed that in our time the common good is chiefly guaranteed when personal rights and duties are maintained. The chief concern of civil authorities must therefore be to ensure that these rights are acknowledged, respected, coordinated with other rights, defended and promoted, so that in this way each one may more easily carry out his duties. For "to safeguard the inviolable rights of the human person, and to facilitate the fulfillment of his duties, should be the chief duty of every public authority."[45]

61. This means that, if any government does not acknowledge the rights of man or violates them, it not only fails in its duty, but its orders completely lack juridical force.[46]

Reconciliation and Protection of Rights and
Duties of Individuals

62. One of the fundamental duties of civil authorities, therefore, is to coordinate social relations in such fashion that the exercise of one man's rights does not threaten others in the exercise of their own rights nor hinder them in the fulfillment of their duties. Finally, the rights of all should be effectively safeguarded and, if they have been violated, completely restored.[47]

Duty of Promoting the Rights of Individuals

63. It is also demanded by the common good that civil authorities should make earnest efforts to bring about a situation in which individual citizens can easily exercise their rights and fulfill their duties as well. For experience has taught us that, unless these authorities take suitable action with regard to economic, political and cultural matters, inequalities between the citizens tend to become more and more widespread, especially in the modern world, and as a result human rights are rendered totally ineffective and the fulfillment of duties is compromised.

64. It is therefore necessary that the administration give wholehearted and careful attention to the social as well as to

the economic progress of the citizens, and to the development, in keeping with the development of the productive system, of such essential services as the building of roads, transportation, communications, water supply, housing, public health, education, facilitation of the practice of religion, and recreational facilities. It is necessary also that governments make efforts to see that insurance systems are made available to the citizens, so that, in case of misfortune or increased family responsibilities, no person will be without the necessary means to maintain a decent standard of living. The government should make similarly effective efforts to see that those who are able to work can find employment in keeping with their aptitudes, and that each worker receives a wage in keeping with the laws of justice and equity. It should be equally the concern of civil authorities to ensure that workers be allowed their proper responsibility in the work undertaken in industrial organization, and to facilitate the establishment of intermediate groups which will make social life richer and more effective. Finally, it should be possible for all the citizens to share as far as they are able in their country's cultural advantages.

Harmonious Relation Between Public Authority's Two Forms of Intervention

65. The common good requires that civil authorities maintain a careful balance between coordinating and protecting the rights of the citizens, on the one hand, and promoting them, on the other. It should not happen that certain individuals or social groups derive special advantage from the fact that their rights have received preferential protection. Nor should it happen that governments, in seeking to protect these rights, become obstacles to their full expression and free use. "For this principle must always be retained: that State activity in the economic field, no matter what its breadth or depth may be, ought not to be exercised in such a way as to curtail an individual's freedom of personal initiative. Rather it should work to expand that freedom as much as possible by the effective protection of the essential personal rights of each and every individual."[48]

66. The same principle should inspire the various steps which governments take in order to make it possible for the citizens more easily to exercise their rights and fulfill their duties in every sector of social life.

STRUCTURE AND OPERATION OF THE PUBLIC AUTHORITY

67. It is impossible to determine, in all cases, what is the most suitable form of government, or how civil authorities can most effectively fulfill their respective functions, i.e., the legislative, judicial and executive functions of the state.

68. In determining the structure and operation of government which a state is to have, great weight has to be given to the circumstances of a given people, circumstances which will vary at different times and in different places. We consider, however, that it is in keeping with the innate demands of human nature that the state should take a form which embodies the threefold division of powers corresponding to the three principal functions of public authority. In that type of state, not only the official functions of government but also the mutual relations between citizens and public officials are set down according to law, which in itself affords protection to the citizens both in the enjoyment of their rights and in the fulfillment of their duties.

69. If, however, this political and juridical structure is to produce the advantages which may be expected of it, public officials must strive to meet the problems which arise in a way that conforms both to the complexities of the situation and the proper exercise of their function. This requires that, in constantly changing conditions, legislators never forget the norms of morality, or constitutional provisions, or the common good. Moreover, executive authorities must coordinate the activities of society with discretion, with a full knowledge of the law and after a careful consideration of circumstances, and the courts must administer justice impartially and without being influenced by favoritism or pressure. The good order of society also demands that individual citizens and intermediate organizations should be effectively pro-

tected by law whenever they have rights to be exercised or obligations to be fulfilled. This protection should be granted to citizens both in their dealings with each other and in their relations with government agencies.[49]

Law and Conscience

70. It is unquestionable that a legal structure in conformity with the moral order and corresponding to the level of development of the state is of great advantage to achievement of the common good.

71. And yet, social life in the modern world is so varied, complex and dynamic that even a juridical structure which has been prudently and thoughtfully established often seems inadequate for the needs of society.

72. It is also true that the relations of the citizens with each other, of citizens and intermediate groups with public authorities, and finally of the public authorities with one another are often so complex and so sensitive that they cannot be regulated by inflexible legal provisions. Such a situation therefore demands that the civil authorities have clear ideas about the nature and extent of their official duties if they wish to maintain the existing juridical structure in its basic elements and principles, and at the same time meet the exigencies of social life, adapting their legislation to the changing social scene and solving new problems. They must be men of great equilibrium and integrity, competent and courageous enough to see at once what the situation requires and to take necessary action quickly and effectively.[50]

Citizens' Participation in Public Life

73. It is in keeping with their dignity as persons that human beings should take an active part in government, although the manner in which they share in it will depend on the level of development of the country to which they belong.

74. Men will find new and extensive advantages in the fact that they are allowed to participate in government. In this situation, those who administer the government come into frequent contact with the citizens, and it is thus easier for

them to learn what is really needed for the common good. And since public officials hold office only for a specified period of time their authority, far from withering, rather takes on a new vigor in a measure proportionate to the development of human society.[51]

CHARACTERISTICS OF THE PRESENT DAY

75. From these considerations it becomes clear that in the juridical organization of states in our times the first requisite is that a charter of fundamental human rights be drawn up in clear and precise terms and that it be incorporated in its entirety in the constitution.

76. The second requisite is that the constitution of each state be drawn up, phrased in correct juridical terminology, which prescribes the manner of designating the public officials along with their mutual relations, the spheres of their competence, the forms and systems they are obliged to follow in the performance of their office.

77. The last requisite is that the relations between the government and the governed are then set forth in terms of rights and duties; and it is clearly laid down that the paramount task assigned to government officials is that of recognizing, respecting, reconciling, protecting and promoting the rights and duties of citizens.

78. It is of course impossible to accept the theory which professes to find the original and single source of civic rights and duties, of the binding force of the constitution, and of a government's right to command, in the mere will of human beings, individually or collectively.[52]

79. The tendencies to which We have referred, however, do clearly show that the men of our time are becoming increasingly conscious of their dignity as human persons. This awareness prompts them to claim a share in the public administration of their country, while it also accounts for the demand that their own inalienable and inviolable rights be protected by law. It also requires that government officials be chosen in conformity with constitutional procedures, and perform their specific functions within the limits of law.

PART III

RELATIONS BETWEEN STATES

Subjects of Rights and Duties

80. Our Predecessors have constantly maintained, and We join them in reasserting, that nations are reciprocally subjects of rights and duties. This means that their relationships also must be harmonized in truth, in justice, in a working solidarity, in liberty. The same natural law, which governs relations between individual human beings, serves also to regulate the relations of nations with one another.

81. This is readily clear to anyone if he would consider that the heads of states can in no way put aside their natural dignity while they represent their country and provide for its welfare, and that they were never allowed to depart from the natural law by which they are bound and which is the norm of their conduct.

82. Moreover, it is inconceivable that men because they are heads of government are forced to put aside their human endowments. On the contrary, they occupy this place of eminence for the very reason that they have earned a reputation as outstanding members of the body politic in view of their excellent intellectual endowments and accomplishments.

83. Indeed it follows from the moral order itself that authority is necessary for civil society, for civil society is ruled by authority; and that authority cannot be used to thwart the moral order without instantly collapsing because its foundation has been destroyed. This is the warning of God Himself: "A word, then, for the kings' ears to hear, kings' hearts to heed: a message for you, rulers, wherever you be! Listen well, all you that have multitudes at your command, foreign hordes to do your bidding. Power is none but comes to you from the Lord, nor any royalty but from One who is above all. He it is that will call you to account for your doings with a scrutiny that reads your inmost thoughts."[53]

84. Lastly it is to be borne in mind that also in the regulating of relations between states, authority is to be exer-

cised for the achievement of the common good which constitutes the reason for its existence.

85. But a fundamental factor of the common good is acknowledgment of the moral order and exact observance of its commands. "A well established order among nations must be built upon the unshakable and unchangeable rock of the moral law, made manifest in the order of nature by the Creator Himself and by Him engraved on the hearts of men with letters that can never be effaced. . . . Like the rays of a gleaming beacon, its principles must guide the plans and policies of men and nations. From its signals, which give warning and point out the safe and sure course, they must get their norms and guidance if they would not see all their laborious efforts to establish a new order condemned to tempest and shipwreck."[54]

IN TRUTH

86. First among the rules governing the relations between states is that of truth. This calls, above all, for the elimination of every trace of racism, and the consequent recognition of the principle that all states are by nature equal in dignity. Each of them accordingly is vested with the right to existence, to self-development, to the means fitting to its attainment, and to be the one primarily responsible for this self-development. Add to that the right of each to its good name, and to the respect which is its due.

87. Very often, experience has taught us, individuals will be found to differ enormously, in knowledge, power, talent and wealth. From this, however, no justification is ever found for those who surpass the rest to subject others to their control in any way. Rather they have a more serious obligation which binds each and everyone to lend mutual assistance to others in their efforts for improvement.

88. Likewise it can happen that one country surpasses another in scientific progress, culture and economic development. But this superiority, far from permitting it to rule others unjustly, imposes the obligation to make a greater contribution to the general development of the people.

89. In fact, men cannot by nature be superior to others

since all enjoy an equal natural dignity. From this it follows
that countries too do not differ at all from one another in the
dignity which they derive from nature. Individual states are
like a body whose members are human beings. Furthermore,
we know from experience that nations are wont to be very
sensitive in all matters which in any way concern their dignity and honor, and rightly so.

90. Truth further demands that the various media of social
communications made available by modern progress, which
enable the nations to know each other better, be used with
serene objectivity. That need not, of course, rule out any legitimate emphasis on the positive aspects of their way of life.
But methods of information which fall short of the truth,
and by the same token impair the reputation of this people
or that, must be discarded.[55]

IN JUSTICE

91. Relations between nations are to be further regulated
by justice. This implies, over and above recognition of their
mutual rights, the fulfillment of their respective duties.

92. Since nations have a right to exist, to develop themselves, to acquire a supply of the resources necessary for their
development, to defend their good name and the honor due
to them, it follows that they are likewise bound by the obligation of effectively guarding each of these rights and of
avoiding those actions by which these rights can be jeopardized. As men in their private enterprises cannot pursue their
own interests to the detriment of others, so too states cannot
lawfully seek that development of their own resources which
brings harm to other states and unjustly oppresses them. This
statement of St. Augustine seems to be very apt in this
regard: "What are kingdoms without justice but large bands
of robbers."[56]

93. Not only can it happen, but it actually does happen
that the advantages and conveniences which nations strive to
acquire for themselves become objects of contention; nevertheless, the resulting disagreements must be settled, not by
force, nor by deceit or trickery, but rather in the only manner
which is worthy of the dignity of man, i.e., by a mutual

assessment of the reasons on both sides of the dispute, by a
mature and objective investigation of the situation, and by an
equitable reconciliation of differences of opinion.

The Treatment of Minorities

94. Closely related to this point is the political trend which
since the nineteenth century has gathered momentum and
gained ground everywhere, namely, the striving of people of
the same ethnic group to become independent and to form
one nation. Since this cannot always be accomplished for
various reasons, the result is that minorities often dwell within the territory of a people of another ethnic group, and this
is the source of serious problems.

95. In the first place, it must be made clear that justice is
seriously violated by whatever is done to limit the strength
and numerical increase of these lesser peoples; the injustice is
even more serious if vicious attempts of this kind are aimed
at the very extinction of these groups.

96. It is especially in keeping with the principles of justice
that effective measures be taken by the civil authorities to improve the lot of the citizens of an ethnic minority, particularly when that betterment concerns their language, the development of their natural gifts, their ancestral customs, and
their accomplishments and endeavors in the economic
order.[57]

97. It should be noted, however, that these minority
groups, either because of their present situation which they
are forced to endure, or because of past experiences, are often
inclined to exalt beyond due measure anything proper to
their own people, and to such a degree as to look down on
things common to all mankind, as if the welfare of the
human family must yield to the good of their own ethnic
group. Reason rather demands that these very people recognize also the advantages that accrue to them from their peculiar circumstances; for instance, no small contribution is
made toward the development of their particular talents and
spirit by their daily dealings with people who have grown up
in a different culture since from this association they can
gradually make their own the excellence which belongs to the
other ethnic group. But this will happen only if the minori-

ties through association with the people who live around them make an effort to share in their customs and institutions. Such, however, will not be the case if they sow discord, which causes great damage and hinders progress.

ACTIVE SOLIDARITY

98. Since the mutual relations among nations must be regulated by the norm of truth and justice, they must also derive great advantage from an energetic union of mind, heart and resources. This can be effected at various levels by mutual cooperation in many ways, as is happening in our own time with beneficial results in the economic, social, political, educational, public health and sports spheres. We must remember that, of its very nature, civil authority exists, not to confine its people within the boundaries of their nation, but rather to protect, above all else, the common good of the entire human family.

99. So it happens that civil societies in pursuing their interests not only must not harm others, but must join their plans and forces whenever the efforts of an individual government cannot achieve its desired goals; but in the execution of such common efforts, great care must be taken lest what helps some nations should injure others.

100. Furthermore, the universal common good requires that in every nation friendly relations be fostered in all fields between the citizens and their intermediate societies. Since in many parts of the world there are groups of people of varying ethnic backgrounds, we must be on our guard against isolating one ethnic group from its fellow men. This is clearly inconsistent with modern conditions since distances which separate people from each other have been almost wiped out. Neither are we to overlook the fact that men of every ethnic group, in addition to their own characteristic endowments by which they are distinguished from the rest of men, have other important gifts of nature in common with their fellow men by which they can make more and more progress and perfect themselves, particularly in matters that pertain to the spirit. They have the right and duty therefore to live in communion with one another.

The Proper Balance Between Population, Land, and Capital

101. Everyone certainly knows that in some parts of the world there is an imbalance between the amount of arable land and the size of the population, and in other parts between the fertility of the soil and available farm implements. Consequently, necessity demands a cooperative effort on the part of the people to bring about a quicker exchange of goods, or of capital, or the migration of people themselves.[58]

102. In this case We think it most opportune that as far as possible employment should seek the worker, not vice versa. For then most citizens have an opportunity to increase their holdings without being forced to leave their native environment and seek a new home with many a heartache, and adopt a new state of affairs and make new social contacts with other citizens.

The Problem of Political Refugees

103. The sentiment of universal fatherhood which the Lord has placed in Our heart makes Us feel profound sadness in considering the phenomenon of political refugees: a phenomenon which has assumed large proportions and which always hides numberless and acute sufferings.

104. Such expatriations show that there are some political regimes which do not guarantee for individual citizens a sufficient sphere of freedom within which their souls are allowed to breathe humanly; in fact, under those regimes even the lawful existence of such a sphere of freedom is either called into question or denied. This undoubtedly is a radical inversion of the order of human society, because the reason for the existence of public authority is to promote the common good, a fundamental element of which is the recognition of that sphere of freedom and the safeguarding of it.

105. At this point it will not be superfluous to recall that such exiles are persons, and that all their rights as persons must be recognized, since they do not lose those rights on losing the citizenship of the states of which they are former members.

106. Now among the rights of a human person there must

be included that by which a man may enter a political community where he hopes he can more fittingly provide a future for himself and his dependents. Wherefore, as far as the common good rightly understood permits, it is the duty of that state to accept such immigrants and to help to integrate them into itself as new members.

107. Wherefore, on this occasion, We publicly approve and commend every undertaking, founded on the principles of human solidarity and Christian charity, which aims at making migration of persons from one country to another less painful.

108. And We will be permitted to signal for the attention and gratitude of all right-minded persons the manifold work which specialized international agencies are carrying out in this very delicate field.

Disarmament

109. On the other hand, it is with deep sorrow that We note the enormous stocks of armaments that have been and still are being made in more economically developed countries, with a vast outlay of intellectual and economic resources. And so it happens that, while the people of these countries are loaded with heavy burdens, other countries as a result are deprived of the collaboration they need in order to make economic and social progress.

110. The production of arms is allegedly justified on the grounds that in present-day conditions peace cannot be preserved without an equal balance of armaments. And so, if one country increases its armaments, others feel the need to do the same; and if one country is equipped with nuclear weapons, other countries must produce their own, equally destructive.

111. Consequently, people live in constant fear lest the storm that every moment threatens should break upon them with dreadful violence. And with good reason, for the arms of war are ready at hand. Even though it is difficult to believe that anyone would dare bring upon himself the appalling destruction and sorrow that war would bring in its train, it cannot be denied that the conflagration can be set off by some

unexpected and unpremeditated act. And one must bear in mind that, even though the monstrous power of modern weapons acts as a deterrent, there is nevertheless reason to fear that the mere continuance of nuclear tests, undertaken with war in mind, can seriously jeopardize various kinds of life on earth.

112. Justice, then, right reason and consideration for human dignity and life urgently demand that the arms race should cease, that the stockpiles which exist in various countries should be reduced equally and simultaneously by the parties concerned, that nuclear weapons should be banned, and finally that all come to an agreement on a fitting program of disarmament, employing mutual and effective controls. In the words of Pius XII, Our Predecessor of happy memory: "The calamity of a world war, with the economic and social ruin and the moral excesses and dissolution that accompany it, must not be permitted to envelop the human race for a third time."[59]

113. All must realize that there is no hope of putting an end to the building up of armaments, nor of reducing the present stocks, nor, still less—and this is the main point—of abolishing them altogether, unless the process is complete and thorough and unless it proceeds from inner conviction: unless, that is, everyone sincerely cooperates to banish the fear and anxious expectation of war with which men are oppressed. If this is to come about, the fundamental principle on which our present peace depends must be replaced by another, which declares that the true and solid peace of nations consists not in equality of arms but in mutual trust alone. We believe that this can be brought to pass, and we consider that, since it concerns a matter not only demanded by right reason but also eminently desirable in itself, it will prove to be the source of many benefits.

114. In the first place, it is an objective demanded by reason. There can be, or at least there should be, no doubt that relations between states, as between individuals, should be regulated not by the force of arms but by the light of reason, by the rule, that is, of truth, of justice and of active and sincere cooperation.

115. Secondly, We say that it is an objective earnestly to be desired in itself. Is there anyone who does not ardently yearn to see dangers of war banished, to see peace preserved and daily more firmly established?

116. And finally, it is an objective which will be a fruitful source of many benefits, for its advantages will be felt everywhere, by individuals, by families, by nations, by the whole human family. The warning of Pius XII still rings in our ears: "Nothing is lost by peace; everything may be lost by war."[60]

117. Since this is so, We, the Vicar on earth of Jesus Christ, Savior of the World and Author of Peace, and as interpreter of the very profound longing of the entire human family, following the impulse of Our heart, seized by anxiety for the good of all, feel it Our duty to beseech men, especially those who have the responsibility of public affairs, to spare no pain or effort until world events follow a course in keeping with man's destiny and dignity.

118. In the highest and most authoritative assemblies, let men give serious thought to the problem of a peaceful adjustment of relations between political communities on a world level: an adjustment founded on mutual trust, on sincerity in negotiations, on faithful fulfillment of obligations assumed. Let them study the problem until they find that point of agreement from which it will be possible to commence to go forward towards accords that will be sincere, lasting and fruitful.

119. We, for Our part, will not cease to pray God to bless these labors so that they may lead to fruitful results.

IN LIBERTY

120. It has also to be borne in mind that relations between states should be based on freedom, that is to say, that no country may unjustly oppress others or unduly meddle in their affairs. On the contrary, all should help to develop in others a sense of responsibility, a spirit of enterprise, and an earnest desire to be the first to promote their own advancement in every field.

The Evolution of Economically Underdeveloped Countries

121. Because all men are joined together by reason of their common origin, their redemption by Christ, and their supernatural destiny, and are called to form one Christian family, We appealed in the Encyclical *Mater et Magistra* to economically developed nations to come to the aid of those which were in the process of development.[61]

122. We are greatly consoled to see how widely that appeal has been favorably received; and We are confident that even more so in the future it will contribute to the end that the poorer countries, in as short a time as possible, will arrive at that degree of economic development which will enable every citizen to live in conditions more in keeping with his human dignity.

123. But it is never sufficiently repeated that the cooperation to which reference has been made should be effected with the greatest respect for the liberty of the countries being developed, for these must realize that they are primarily responsible, and that they are the principal artisans in the promotion of their own economic development and social progress.

124. Our Predecessor Pius XII already proclaimed that "in the field of a new order founded on moral principles, there is no room for violation of freedom, integrity and security of other nations, no matter what may be their territorial extension or their capacity for defense. It is inevitable that the powerful states, by reason of their greater potential and their power, should pave the way in the establishment of economic groups comprising not only themselves but also smaller and weaker states as well. It is nevertheless indispensable that in the interests of the common good they, as all others, should respect the rights of those smaller states to political freedom, to economic development and to the adequate protection, in the case of conflicts between nations, of that neutrality which is theirs according to the natural, as well as international, law. In this way, and in this way only, will they be able to obtain a fitting share of the common good, and assure the material and spiritual welfare of their people."[62]

125. It is vitally important, therefore, that the wealthier states, in providing varied forms of assistance to the poorer, should respect the moral values and ethnic characteristics peculiar to each, and also that they should avoid any intention of political domination. If this is done, "a precious contribution will be made towards the formation of a world community, a community in which each member, whilst conscious of its own individual rights and duties, will work in a relationship of equality towards the attainment of the universal common good."[63]

SIGNS OF THE TIME

126. Men are becoming more and more convinced that disputes which arise between states should not be resolved by recourse to arms, but rather by negotiation.

127. We grant indeed that this conviction is chiefly based on the terrible destructive force of modern weapons and a fear of the calamities and frightful destruction which such weapons would cause. Therefore, in an age such as ours which prides itself on its atomic energy it is contrary to reason to hold that war is now a suitable way to restore rights which have been violated.

128. Nevertheless, unfortunately, the law of fear still reigns among peoples, and it forces them to spend fabulous sums for armaments, not for aggression they affirm—and there is no reason for not believing them—but to dissuade others from aggression.

129. There is reason to hope, however, that by meeting and negotiating, men may come to discover better the bonds that unite them together, deriving from the human nature which they have in common; and that they may also come to discover that one of the most profound requirements of their common nature is this: that between them and their respective peoples it is not fear which should reign but love, a love which tends to express itself in a collaboration that is loyal, manifold in form and productive of many benefits.

PART IV

RELATIONSHIP OF MEN AND OF POLITICAL
COMMUNITIES WITH THE WORLD COMMUNITY

INTERDEPENDENCE BETWEEN POLITICAL COMMUNITIES

130. The recent progress of science and technology, since it has profoundly influenced human conduct, is rousing men everywhere in the world to more and more cooperation and association with one another. Today the exchange of goods and ideas, travel from one country to another have greatly increased. Consequently, the close relations of individuals, families, intermediate associations belonging to different countries have become vastly more frequent and conferences between heads of states are held at shorter intervals. At the same time the interdependence of national economies has grown deeper, one becoming progressively more closely related to the other, so that they become, as it were, integral parts of the one world economy. Finally, the social progress, order, security and peace of each country are necessarily connected with the social progress, order, security and peace of all other countries.

131. Given these conditions, it is obvious that individual countries cannot rightly seek their own interests and develop themselves in isolation from the rest, for the prosperity and development of one country follows partly in the train of the prosperity and progress of all the rest and partly produces that prosperity and progress.

Insufficiency of Modern States to Ensure the Universal Common Good

132. No era will destroy the unity of the human family since it is made up of human beings sharing with equal right their natural dignity. For this reason, necessity, rooted in man's very nature, will always demand that the common

good be sought in sufficient measure because it concerns the entire human family.

133. In times past, it seemed that the leaders of nations might be in a position to provide for the universal common good, either through normal diplomatic channels, or through top-level meetings, or through conventions or treaties, by making use of methods and instruments suggested by natural law, the law of nations, or international law.

134. In our time, however, relationships between states have changed greatly. On the one hand, the universal common good poses very serious questions which are difficult and which demand immediate solution especially because they are concerned with safeguarding the security and peace of the whole world. On the other hand, the heads of individual states, inasmuch as they are juridically equal, are not entirely successful no matter how often they meet or how hard they try to find more fitting juridical instruments. This is due not to lack of good will and initiative but to lack of adequate power to back up their authority.

135. Therefore, under the present circumstances of human society, both the structure and form of governments as well as the power which public authority wields in all the nations of the world must be considered inadequate to promote the universal common good.

Connection Between the Common Good and Political Authority

136. Moreover, if we carefully consider the essential nature of the common good on the one hand, and the nature and function of public authority on the other, everyone sees that there is an intrinsic connection between the two. And, indeed, just as the moral order needs public authority to promote the common good in civil society, it likewise demands that public authority actually be able to attain it. From this it follows that the governmental institutions, on which public authority depends and through which it functions and pursues its end, should be provided with such structure and efficacy that they can lead to the common good by ways and methods which are suitably adapted to various contingencies.

137. Today the universal common good poses problems of

world-wide dimensions, which cannot be adequately tackled or solved except by the efforts of public authority endowed with a wideness of powers, structure and means of the same proportions: that is, of public authority which is in a position to operate in an effective manner on a world-wide basis. The moral order itself, therefore, demands that such a form of public authority be established.

Public Authority Instituted by Common Consent and Not Imposed by Force

138. This public authority, having world-wide power and endowed with the proper means for the efficacious pursuit of its objective, which is the universal common good in concrete form, must be set up by common accord and not imposed by force. The reason is that such an authority must be in a position to operate effectively; yet, at the same time, its action must be inspired by sincere and real impartiality: it must be an action aimed at satisfying the universal common good. The difficulty is that there would be reason to fear that a supra-national or world-wide public authority, imposed by force by the more powerful nations might be an instrument of one-sided interests; and even should this not happen, it would be difficult for it to avoid all suspicion of partiality in its actions, and this would take from the force and effectiveness of its activity. Even though there may be pronounced differences between nations as regards the degree of their economic development and their military power, they are all very sensitive as regards their juridical equality and the excellence of their way of life. For that reason, they are right in not easily yielding obedience to an authority imposed by force, or to an authority in whose creation they had no part, or to which they themselves did not decide to submit by their own free choice.

The Universal Common Good and Personal Rights

139. Like the common good of individual states, so too the universal common good cannot be determined except by having regard for the human person. Therefore, the public and universal authority, too, must have as its fundamental objective the recognition, respect, safeguarding and promotion

of the rights of the human person; this can be done by direct action when required, or by creating on a world scale an environment in which leaders of the individual countries can suitably maintain their own functions.

The Principle of Subsidiarity

140. Moreover, just as it is necessary in each state that relations which the public authority has with its citizens, families and intermediate associations be controlled and regulated by the principle of subsidiarity, it is equally necessary that the relationships which exist between the world-wide public authority and the public authorities of individual nations be governed by the same principle. This means that the world-wide public authority and the public authorities must tackle and solve problems of an economic, social, political or cultural character which are posed by the universal common good. For, because of the vastness, complexity and urgency of those problems, the public authorities of the individual states are not in a position to tackle them with any hope of a positive solution.

141. The world-wide public authority is not intended to limit the sphere of action of the public authority of the individual state, much less to take its place. On the contrary, its purpose is to create, on a world basis, an environment in which the public authorities of each state, its citizens and intermediate associations, can carry out their tasks, fulfill their duties and exercise their rights with greater security.[64]

Modern Developments

142. As is known, the United Nations Organization (U.N.O.) was established on June 26, 1945, and to it there were subsequently added specialized agencies consisting of members designated by the public authority of the various countries with important international tasks in the economic, social, cultural, educational and health fields. The United Nations Organization had as its essential purpose the maintenance and consolidation of peace between peoples, fostering between them friendly relations, based on the principles of equality, mutual respect, and varied forms of cooperation in every sector of human endeavor.

143. An act of the highest importance performed by the United Nations Organization was the Universal Declaration of Human Rights, approved in the General Assembly on December 10, 1948. In the preamble of that Declaration, the recognition and respect of those rights and respective liberties is proclaimed as a goal to be achieved by all peoples and all countries.

144. We are fully aware that some objections and reservations were raised regarding certain points in the Declaration, and rightly so. There is no doubt, however, that the document represents an important step on the path towards the juridical-political organization of all the peoples of the world. For in it, in most solemn form, the dignity of a human person is acknowledged to all human beings; and as a consequence there is proclaimed, as a fundamental right, the right of every man freely to investigate the truth and to follow the norms of moral good and justice, and also the right to a life worthy of man's dignity, while other rights connected with those mentioned are likewise proclaimed.

145. It is therefore our ardent desire that the United Nations Organization—in its structure and in its means—may become ever more equal to the magnitude and nobility of its tasks, and may the time come as quickly as possible when every human being will find therein an effective safeguard for the rights which derive directly from his dignity as a person, and which are therefore universal, inviolable and inalienable rights. This is all the more to be hoped for since all human beings, as they take an ever more active part in the public life of their own country, are showing an increasing interest in the affairs of all peoples, and are becoming more consciously aware that they are living members of the whole human family.

PART V

PASTORAL EXHORTATIONS

Duty of Taking Part in Public Life

Once again We exhort Our children to take an active part in public life, and to contribute towards the attainment of

the common good of the entire human family as well as to
that of their own country. They should endeavor, therefore,
in the light of the Faith and with the strength of love, to ensure that the various institutions—whether economic, social,
cultural or political in purpose—should be such as not to
create obstacles, but rather to facilitate or render less arduous
man's perfecting of himself both in the natural order as well
as in the supernatural.

Scientific Competence, Technical Capacity and Professional Experience

147. Nevertheless, in order to imbue civilization with right
norms and Christian principles, it is not enough to be
illumined with the gift of faith and enkindled with the desire
of forwarding a good cause. For this end it is necessary to
take an active part in the various organizations and influence
them from within.

148. And since our present age is one of outstanding
scientific and technical progress and excellence, one will not
be able to enter these organizations and work effectively from
within unless he is scientifically competent, technically capable and skilled in the practice of his own profession.

Apostolate of a Trained Laity

149. We desire to call attention to the fact that scientific
competence, technical capacity and professional experience,
although necessary, are not of themselves sufficient to elevate
the relationships of society to an order that is genuinely
human: that is, to an order whose foundation is truth, whose
measure and objective is justice, whose driving force is love,
and whose method of attainment is freedom.

150. For this end it is certainly necessary that human
beings carry on their own temporal activities in accordance
with the laws governing them and following the methods corresponding to their nature. But at the same time it is also
necessary that they should carry on those activities as acts
within the moral order: therefore, as the exercise or vindication of a right, as the fulfillment of a duty or the performance of a service, as a positive answer to the providential

design of God directed to our salvation. In other words, it is necessary that human beings, in the intimacy of their own consciences, should so live and act in their temporal lives as to create a synthesis between scientific, technical and professional elements on the one hand, and spiritual values on the other.

Integration of Faith and Action

151. It is no less clear that today, in traditionally Christian nations, secular institutions, although demonstrating a high degree of scientific and technical perfection, and efficiency in achieving their respective ends, not infrequently are but slightly affected by Christian motivation or inspiration.

152. It is beyond question that in the creation of those institutions many contributed and continue to contribute who were believed to be and who consider themselves Christians; and without doubt, in part at least, they were and are. How does one explain this? It is Our opinion that the explanation is to be found in an inconsistency in their minds between religious belief and their action in the temporal sphere. It is necessary, therefore, that their interior unity be re-established, and that in their temporal activity faith should be present as a beacon to give light, and charity as a force to give life.

Integral Education

153. It is Our opinion, too, that the above-mentioned inconsistency between the religious faith in those who believe and their activities in the temporal sphere, results—in great part—from the lack of a solid Christian education. Indeed, it happens in many quarters and too often that there is no proportion between scientific training and religious instruction: the former continues and is extended until it reaches higher degrees, while the latter remains at elementary level. It is indispensable, therefore, that in the training of youth, education should be complete and without interruption, namely, that in the minds of the young religious values should be cultivated and the moral conscience refined in a manner to keep pace with the continuous and ever more abundant assimila-

tion of scientific and technical knowledge. And it is indispensable, too, that they be instructed regarding the proper way to carry out their actual task.[65]

Constant Endeavor

154. We deem it opportune to point out how difficult it is to understand clearly the relation between the objective requirements of justice and concrete situations, namely to define the degrees and forms in which doctrinal principles and directives ought to be applied to reality.

155. And the definition of those degrees and forms is all the more difficult in our times, which are marked by a pronounced dynamism. For this reason, the problem of bringing social reality into line with the objective requirements of justice is a problem which will never admit of a definitive solution. Meanwhile, Our children must watch over themselves lest they relax and feel satisfied with objectives already achieved.

156. In fact, all human beings ought rather to reckon that what has been accomplished is but little in comparison with what remains to be done in regard to organs of production, trade unions, associations, professional organizations, insurance systems, legal systems, political regimes, institutions for cultural, health, recreational or sporting purposes. These must all be adjusted to the era of the atom and of the conquest of space: an era which the human family has already entered, wherein it has commenced its new advance towards limitless horizons.

Relations Between Catholics and Non-Catholics in Social and Economic Affairs

157. The doctrinal principles outlined in this document derive from both nature itself and the natural law. In putting these principles into practice it frequently happens that Catholics in many ways cooperate either with Christians separated from this Apostolic See, or with men of no Christian faith whatever, but who are endowed with reason and adorned with a natural uprightness of conduct. "In such relations let the faithful be careful to be always consistent in

their actions, so that they may never come to any compromise in matters of religion and morals. At the same time, however, let them be, and show themselves to be, animated by a spirit of understanding and detachment, and disposed to work loyally in the pursuit of objectives which are of their nature good, or conducive to good."[66]

158. However, one must never confuse error and the person who errs, not even when there is question of error or inadequate knowledge of truth in the moral or religious field. The person who errs is always and above all a human being, and he retains in every case his dignity as a human person; and he must be always regarded and treated in accordance with that lofty dignity. Besides, in every human being, there is a need that is congenital to his nature and never becomes extinguished, compelling him to break through the web of error and open his mind to the knowledge of truth. And God will never fail to act on his interior being, with the result that a person, who at a given moment of his life lacks the clarity of faith or even adheres to erroneous doctrines, can at a future date be enlightened and believe the truth. For Catholics, if for the sake of promoting the temporal welfare they cooperate with men who either do not believe in Christ or whose belief is faulty because they are involved in error, can provide them either the occasion or the inducement to turn to truth.

159. It is, therefore, especially to the point to make a clear distinction between false philosophical teachings regarding the nature, origin, and destiny of the universe and of man, and movements which have a direct bearing either on economic and social questions, or cultural matters or on the organization of the state, even if these movements owe their origin and inspiration to these false tenets. While the teaching once it has been clearly set forth is no longer subject to change, the movements, precisely because they take place in the midst of changing conditions, are readily susceptible of change. Besides, who can deny that those movements, in so far as they conform to the dictates of right reason and are interpreters of the lawful aspirations of the human person, contain elements that are positive and deserving of approval?

160. For these reasons it can at times happen that meetings for the attainment of some practical results which previously seemed completely useless now are either actually useful or may be looked upon as profitable for the future. But to decide whether this moment has arrived, and also to lay down the ways and degrees in which work in common might be possible for the achievement of economic, social, cultural, and political ends which are honorable and useful, these are the problems which can only be solved with the virtue of prudence, which is the guiding light of the virtues that regulate the moral life, both individual and social. Therefore, as far as Catholics are concerned, this decision rests primarily with those who live and work in the specific sectors of human society in which those problems arise, always, however, in accordance with the principles of the natural law, with the social doctrine of the church, and with the directives of ecclesiastical authorities. For it must not be forgotten that the Church has the right and the duty not only to safeguard the principles of ethics and religion, but also to intervene authoritatively with Her children in the temporal sphere when there is a question of judging the application of those principles to concrete cases.[67]

Little by Little

161. There are some souls, particularly endowed with generosity, who, on finding situations where the requirements of justice are not satisfied or not satisfied in full, feel enkindled with the desire to change the state of things, as if they wished to have recourse to something like a revolution.

162. It must be borne in mind that to proceed gradually is the law of life in all its expressions; therefore in human institutions, too, it is not possible to renovate for the better except by working from within them gradually. Pius XII proclaimed: "Salvation and justice are not to be found in revolution, but in evolution through concord. Violence has always achieved only destruction, not construction; the kindling of passions, not their pacification; the accumulation of hate and ruin, not the reconciliation of the contending parties. And it has reduced men and parties to the difficult task of rebuilding, after sad experience, on the ruins of discord."[68]

An Immense Task

163. We must therefore consider this point most closely joined to the great tasks of magnanimous men, namely, to establish with truth, justice, charity, and liberty new methods of relationships in human society: the relations among individual citizens, among citizens and their own countries, among nations themselves, among individuals, families, intermediate associations and individual states on the one hand, and with the community of all mankind on the other. This is a most exalted task, for it is the task of bringing about true peace in the order established by God.

164. These men, necessarily few in number, but deserving recognition for their contributions in the field of human relations, We publicly praise and at the same time We earnestly invite them to persevere in their work with ever greater zeal. And We are comforted by the hope that their number will increase, especially among those who believe. For it is an imperative duty; it is a requirement of Love. Every believer in this world of ours must be a spark of light, a center of love, a vivifying leaven amidst his fellowmen; and he will be this all the more perfectly the more closely he lives in communion with God and in the intimacy of his own soul.

165. In fact, there can be no peace between men unless there is peace within each one of them, unless, that is, each one builds up within himself the order wished by God. Hence St. Augustine asks: "Does your soul desire to overcome your lower inclinations? Let it be subject to Him Who is on high and it will conquer the lower self: there will be peace in you; true, secure and well-ordered peace. In what does that order consist? God commands the soul; the soul commands the body; and there is nothing more orderly than this."[69]

The Prince of Peace

166. These words of Ours, which We have wished to dedicate to the problems that most beset the human family today and on the just solution of which the ordered progress of society depends, are dictated by a profound aspiration which

We know is shared by all men of good will: the consolidation of peace in the world.

167. As the humble and unworthy Vicar of Him Whom the Prophet announced as the *Prince of Peace*,[70] We have the duty to expend all Our energies in an effort to protect and strengthen this gift. However, peace will be but an empty-sounding word unless it is founded on the order which this present document has outlined in confident hope: an order founded on truth, built according to justice, vivified and integrated by charity, and put into practice in freedom.

168. This is such a noble and elevated task that human resources, even though inspired by the most praiseworthy good will, cannot bring it to realization alone. In order that human society may reflect as faithfully as possible the Kingdom of God, help from on high is absolutely necessary.

169. For this reason, during these sacred days Our supplication is raised with greater fervor towards Him Who by His painful Passion and death overcame sin—the root of discord and the source of sorrows and inequalities—and by His Blood reconciled mankind to the Eternal Father; "For he himself is our peace, he it is that hath made both one. . . . And coming he announced the good tidings of peace to you who were afar off, and of peace to those who were near."[71]

170. And in the Liturgy of these days we hear the announcement: "Our Lord Jesus Christ, after His resurrection, stood in the midst of His disciples and said 'Peace be to you,' allelulia: The disciples rejoiced seeing the Lord."[72] He leaves us peace, He brings us peace: "Peace I leave with you, my peace I give to you; not as the world gives do I give to you."[73]

171. This is the peace which We implore of Him with the ardent yearning of Our prayer. May He banish from the hearts of men whatever might endanger peace. May He transform them into witnesses of truth, justice and brotherly love. May He enlighten the rulers of peoples so that in addition to their solicitude for the proper welfare of their citizens, they may guarantee and defend the great gift of peace; may He enkindle the wills of all, so that they may overcome the barriers that divide, cherish the bonds of mutual charity, understand others, and pardon those who have done them wrong;

by virtue of His action, may all peoples of the earth become as brothers, and may the most longed-for peace blossom forth and reign always among them.

172. As a pledge of this peace, and with the ardent wish that it may shine forth on the Christian communities entrusted to your care, especially for the benefit of those who are most lowly and in the greatest need of help and defense, We are glad to impart to you, venerable brothers, to the priests both secular and religious, to the religious men and women and to the faithful of your dioceses, particularly to those who make every effort to put these exhortations of Ours into practice, Our Apostolic Blessing. Finally, upon all men of good will, to whom this encyclical letter is also addressed, We implore from Almighty God health and prosperity.

173. Given at Rome at St. Peter's, on Holy Thursday, the eleventh day of April, in the year 1963, the fifth of Our Pontificate.

JOHN XXIII

NOTES

1. Ps. 8, 1.
2. Ps. 103, 24.
3. Cf. Gen. 1, 26.
4. Ps. 8, 6–8.
5. Rom. 2, 15.
6. Cf. Ps. 18, 8–11.
7. Cf. Radio Message of Pius XII, Christmas Eve, 1942, A.A.S. XXXV, 1943, pp. 9–24; and Discourse of John XXIII, Jan. 4, 1963, A.A.S. LV, 1963, pp. 89–91.
8. Cf. Encycl. *Divini Redemptoris* of Pius XI, A.A.S. XXIX, 1937, p. 78; and Radio Message of Pius XII, Pentecost, June 1, 1941, A.A.S. XXXIII, 1941, pp. 195–205.
9. Cf. Radio Message of Pius XII, Christmas Eve, 1942, A.A.S. XXXV, 1943, pp. 9–24.
10. *Divinae Institutiones*, Book IV, ch. 28, 2; Patrologia Latina, 6, 535.
11. Encycl. *Libertas Praestantissimum, Acta Leonis XIII*, VIII, 1888, pp. 237–238.

12. Cf. Radio Message of Pius XII, Christmas Eve, 1942, A.A.S. XXXV, 1943, pp. 9–24.

13. Cf. Encycl. *Casti Connubii* of Pius XI, A.A.S. XXII, 1930, pp. 539–592; and Radio Message of Pius XII, Christmas Eve, 1942, A.A.S. XXXV, 1943, pp. 9–24.

14. Cf. Radio Message of Pius XII, Pentecost, June 1, 1941, A.A.S. XXXIII, 1941, p. 201.

15. Cf. Encycl. *Rerum Novarum* of Leo XIII, Acta Leonis XIII, XI, 1891, pp. 128–129.

16. Cf. Encycl. *Mater et Magistra* of John XXIII, A.A.S. LIII, 1961, p. 422.

17. Cf. Radio Message, Pentecost, June 1, 1941, A.A.S. XXXIII, 1941, p. 201.

18. Encycl. *Mater et Magistra*, A.A.S. LIII, 1961, p. 428.

19. Cf. *Ibid.*, p. 430.

20. Cf. Encycl. *Rerum Novarum* of Leo XIII, Acta Leonis XIII, XI, 1891, pp. 134–142; Encycl. *Quadragesimo Anno* of Pius XI, A.A.S. XXIII, 1931, pp. 199–200; Encycl. *Sertum Laetitiae* of Pius XII, A.A.S. XXXI, 1939, pp. 635–644.

21. Cf. A.A.S. LIII, 1961, p. 430.

22. Cf. Radio Message of Pius XII, Christmas Eve, 1952, A.A.S. XLV, 1953, pp. 33–46.

23. Cf. Radio Message, Christmas Eve, 1944, A.A.S. XXXVII, 1945, p. 12.

24. Cf. Radio Message, Christmas Eve, 1942, A.A.S. XXXV, 1943, p. 21.

25. Eph. 4, 25.

26. Radio Message of Pius XII, Christmas Eve, 1942, A.A.S. XXXV, 1943, p. 14.

27. *Summa Theol.*, Ia–IIae, q. 19, a. 4; cf. a. 9.

28. Rom. 13, 1–6.

29. *In Epist. ad Rom.* c. 13, vv. 1–2, homil. XXIII; Patrologia Graeca, 60, 615.

30. Encycl. *Immortale Dei* of Leo XIII, Acta Leonis XIII, V, 1885, p. 120.

31. Cf. Radio Message, Christmas Eve, 1944, A.A.S. XXXVII, 1945, p. 15.

32. Cf. Encycl. *Diuturnum illud* of Leo XIII, Acta Leonis XIII, II, 1881, p. 274.

33. Cf. *Ibid.*, p. 278; and Encycl. *Immortale Dei* of Leo XIII, Acta Leonis XIII, V, 1885, p. 130.

34. Acts 5, 29.

35. *Summa Theol.*, Ia–IIae, q. 93, a. 3 ad 2um; cf. Radio Message of Pius XII, Christmas Eve, 1944, A.A.S. XXXVII, 1945, pp. 5–23.

36. Cf. Encycl. *Diuturnum illud* of Leo XIII, Acta Leonis XIII, II, 1881, pp. 271–272; and Radio Message of Pius XII, Christmas Eve, 1944, A.A.S. XXXVII, 1945, pp. 5–23.

37. Cf. Radio Message of Pius XII, Christmas Eve, 1942, A.A.S. XXXV, 1943, p. 13; and Encycl. *Immortale Dei* of Leo XIII, *Acta Leonis XIII*, V, 1885, p. 120.

38. Cf. Encycl. *Summi Pontificatus* of Pius XII, A.A.S. XXXI, 1939, pp. 412–453.

39. Cf. Encycl. *Mit brennender Sorge* of Pius XI, A.A.S. XXIX, 1937, p. 159; and Encycl. *Divini Redemptoris*, A.A.S. XXIX, 1937, pp. 65–106.

40. Encycl. *Immortale Dei, Acta Leonis XIII*, V, 1885, p. 121.

41. Cf. Encycl. *Rerum Novarum* of Leo XIII, *Acta Leonis XIII*, XI, 1891, pp. 133–134.

42. Cf. Encycl. *Summi Pontificatus* of Pius XII, A.A.S. XXXI, 1939, p. 433.

43. A.A.S. LIII, 1961, p. 19.

44. Cf. Encycl. *Quadragesimo Anno* of Pius XI, A.A.S. XXIII, 1931, p. 215.

45. Cf. Radio Message of Pius XII, Pentecost, June 1, 1941, A.A.S. XXXIII, 1941, p. 200.

46. Cf. Encycl. *Mit brennender Sorge* of Pius XI, A.A.S. XXIX, 1937, p. 159; and Encycl. *Divini Redemptoris*, A.A.S. XXIX, 1937, p. 79; and Radio Message of Pius XII, Christmas Eve, 1942, A.A.S. XXXV, 1943, pp. 9–24.

47. Cf. Encycl. *Divini Redemptoris* of Pius XI, A.A.S. XXIX, 1937, p. 81; and Radio Message of Pius XII, Christmas Eve, 1942, A.A.S. XXXV, 1943, pp. 9–24.

48. Encycl. *Mater et Magistra* of John XXIII, A.A.S. LIII, 1961, p. 415.

49. Cf. Radio Message of Pius XII, Christmas Eve, 1942, A.A.S. XXXV, 1943, p. 21.

50. Cf. Radio Message of Pius XII, Christmas Eve, 1944, A.A.S. XXXVII, 1945, pp. 15–16.

51. Cf. Radio Message of Pius XII, Christmas Eve, 1942, A.A.S. XXXV, 1943, p. 12.

52. Cf. Apostolic letter *Annum ingressi* of Leo XIII, *Acta Leonis XIII*, XXII, 1902–1903, pp. 52–80.

53. Wis. 6, 1–4.

54. Cf. Radio Message of Pius XII, Christmas Eve, 1941, A.A.S. XXXIV, 1942, p. 16.

55. Cf. Radio Message of Pius XII, Christmas Eve, 1940, A.A.S. XXXIII, 1941, pp. 5–14.

56. *De civitate Dei*, Book IV, ch. 4; Patrologia Latina, 41, 115; cf. Radio Message of Pius XII, Christmas Eve, 1939, A.A.S. XXXII, 1940, pp. 5–13.

57. Cf. Radio Message of Pius XII, Christmas Eve, 1941, A.A.S. XXXIV, 1942, pp. 10–21.

58. Cf. Encycl. *Mater et Magistra* of John XXIII, A.A.S. LIII, 1961, p. 439.

59. Cf. Radio Message, Christmas Eve, 1941, A.A.S. XXXIV,

1942, p. 17; and Exhortation of Benedict XV to the rulers of peoples at war, Aug. 1, 1917, A.A.S. IX, 1917, p. 418.

60. Cf. Radio Message, Aug. 24, 1939, A.A.S. XXXI, 1939, p. 334.

61. A.A.S. LIII, 1961, pp. 440–441.

62. Cf. Radio Message, Christmas Eve, 1941, A.A.S. XXIV, 1942, pp. 16–17.

63. Encycl. *Mater et Magistra* of John XXIII, A.A.S. LIII, 1961, p. 443.

64. Cf. Address of Pius XII to youths of Catholic Action from the dioceses of Italy gathered in Rome, Sept. 12, 1948, A.A.S. XL, p. 412.

65. Cf. Encycl. *Mater et Magistra* of John XXIII, A.A.S. LIII, 1961, p. 454.

66. *Ibid.*, p. 456.

67. *Ibid.*, p. 456; cf. Encycl. *Immortale Dei* of Leo XIII, *Acta Leonis XIII*, V, 1885, p. 128; Encycl. *Ubi Arcano* of Pius XI, A.A.S. XIV, 1922, p. 698; and Address of Pius XII to Delegates of the International Union of Catholic Women's Leagues gathered in Rome for a joint convention, Sept. 11, 1947, A.A.S. XXXIX, 1947, p. 486.

68. Cf. Address to workers from the dioceses of Italy gathered in Rome, Pentecost, June 13, 1943, A.A.S. XXXV, 1943, p. 175.

69. *Miscellanea Augustiniana . . . Sermones post Maurinos reperti* of St. Augustine, Rome, 1930, p. 633.

70. Cf. Is. 9, 5.

71. Eph. 2, 14–17.

72. Responsory at Matins on the Friday after Easter.

73. Jn. 14, 27.

PASTORAL CONSTITUTION ON THE CHURCH IN THE MODERN WORLD (GAUDIUM ET SPES)

The Second Vatican Council was Pope John XXIII's most significant achievement. His decision to call the first Ecumenical Council in a century began as a private inspiration; when he broached the idea with his advisors, he received little encouragement. Yet he persisted, convinced that the time had come to gather the universal Church to reflect on the state of the Church and the world and to open the windows of the Vatican to the fresh air of the contemporary world. It was a bold and courageous decision. No great heresies which needed to be condemned threatened the Church. Most Catholics felt that the major enemy of the day was Communism and no council was needed to reaffirm the Church's hostility to that ideology or to the states which professed to uphold it. In much of Europe and North America, and even in the still European-dominated Churches of the emerging world, the mood was one of general satisfaction with the prosperity and prestige Catholicism enjoyed in the postwar world. Yet for two decades the voices of reform had been growing. In France, theologians like Yves Congar and Henri de Lubac had already given voice to a new sense of the Church's service to the world; in Germany, Karl Rahner had already begun his reconstruction of theology, emphasizing the dynamics of interplay between traditional faith and currents of modern thought long kept outside Catholic consciousness. Pope John was familiar with the pastoral revival of France; he had himself experienced the agonizing dilemmas which confronted the Church in the secularized environment of an industrial city. Certainly no radical, Pope John was only vaguely a liberal. His spirituality, his commitment to the institutional Church, even his reverence for Church practices regarded by many as antiquated, all indicated the presence of a profoundly conservative nature. Yet he was a sensitive, loving man who, despite his long lack of pastoral experience, had an acute awareness of the difficulties faced by priests and laity who tried to live fully Christian lives in the modern age. So the Council he called was not to be doctrinal but pastoral, not to preoccupy itself with new theological definitions or condemnations of modern eras but to reform the Church's practice in order more effectively to evoke a religious and moral response from contemporary humans.

"The greatest concern of the Ecumenical Council is this: that the sacred deposit of Christian doctrine should be guarded and taught more efficaciously," Pope John stated in his opening speech to the Council. "In order that this doctrine may influence the numerous fields of human activity," the Church "should never depart from the sacred patrimony of truth revealed from the fathers." This was familiar enough, but such protection did not require a Council. Pope John went further, arguing that influence on human activity also required the Church to "look to the present, to the new conditions and new forms of life introduced into the modern world which have opened new avenues to the Catholic apostolate." While "the substance of the ancient deposit of faith is one thing, the way in which it is presented is another." It was this, the way the Church preached the gospel, bore witness to the gospel in its internal life, and gave flesh to that gospel in its work with and for the world that was to be the center of the Council's attention.

The Roman Congregations planned to control the Council as they have long controlled the universal Church, but early in the first session the leading Council fathers seized control, reorganized the commissions that were assigned the task of preparing documents, and set to work dealing with major outstanding questions. Open debate, excellent press relations, the presence of lay and non-Catholic observers, all gave the Council an atmosphere of freedom and open dialogue, that startled those who had grown accustomed to the monolithic, authoritarian images of post-Reformation Catholicism.

The document itself is a pastoral constitution, which indicates immediately that its purpose is to declare that the Church is interested primarily in stating how it may be of service to humanity rather than in hurling condemnations from behind the walls of a fortress. The emphasis is not on proclaiming revealed truth or asserting the creed. The purpose of the document is to attempt to read the signs of the times so the Church can articulate its best hopes for humanity and to evaluate what is happening in the world of today. The basic characteristic of the document is its feeling of openness to the world and to our contemporary situation The document emphasizes that the Church can learn from this world. It also emphasizes that the Church must help in the process of the evaluation of what the world has to offer. What is critical, therefore, is that this critique must also occur from within—that is, from a positive understanding and appreciation of the values under discussion.

There are a variety of things in this document which merit special attention: personalism, the social nature of the person, the relation between the Church and the world, justice, and development.

Although many of the references in the document are to traditional Church teaching or doctrine, to natural law, or to the teachings of the gospel, a new focus of attention is brought to bear in the category of the person. While on the one hand this is a way concretizing the Council's teaching and a point of reference for testing both positions and teachings, it also represents a major shift of emphasis. Rather than focus on a traditional theory of duties articulated within the context of a hierarchically ordered universe, the Council centers on a doctrine of individual rights which focuses on the person and which validates the claims of the person over and against society. The Council sees the person as the center and crown of all things on earth. This is a way of expressing the uniqueness of the person. It also suggests that reality is to be interpreted in terms of the person; i.e., created reality finds its meaning and fulfillment in terms of the person. In this context the person is also seen as a center of freedom. This emphasizes on the one hand a capacity for self-determination, and on the other hand gives a central role to conscience, for according to the person's conscience will he or she be judged.

But while the Council emphasized the centrality of the category of the person, it also recognized the social nature of the person. Individuals are not seen as solitary beings, for by their inmost nature persons are social beings, and unless they are related to others, they can neither live nor attain their full potential. Therefore interdependence is a characteristic of our modern age. While initiated and encouraged by technologies such as the mass media and scientific cooperation, interdependence nonetheless reaches its fulfillment only on an interpersonal level. This implies that at the center of the social nature of the person must be a mutual respect for the equal dignity of every person. Within this context, the Council emphasizes that God calls persons to salvation not as individuals but as members of communities. This means that salvation is achieved not in solitude or through personal, private piety, but rather through life in the community and the living out of one's religious belief. It is the destiny of persons to become one people united in love and justice.

In articulating the relation between the Church and the world, the document opens with the words: "The joys and the hopes, the griefs and the anxieties of the men of this age . . . are [those] of the followers of Christ." This means that the Church is composed of human persons, and nothing that is human should fail to raise an echo in their hearts. This is a strong affirmation that the Christian community is truly and internally linked with humanity and its history. Consequently the document affirms that human activity which betters the world accords with God's mandate to persons to subject to themselves the world and all that it contains and to govern the world with justice and holiness. This subjugation of all things to persons, the Council says, is a form of worship which glorifies God. This, then, is the norm of human activity: that in accordance with the divine will and plan, it should harmonize with the genuine good of the human race and allow persons as individuals and as members of society to pursue their total vocation and to fulfill it.

In this context the Church is to serve as a leaven in society and as a sign of the promise of God's future for humanity. Because of this the Church rightly understands that it has no proper mission in the political, social, or economic order. But although its main mission is a religious one, it does have an indirect mission to society, based on its religious mission, which is to help examine the values of life. The document says that we are to avoid the errors of thinking that since we are destined for heaven we may safely ignore earthly realities and of thinking that religion would consist only of worship. The expectation of a new heaven and a new earth must not weaken but rather must stimulate our concern for this earth. For on this earth grows the body of a new human family, a body which is to give a foreshadowing of the new age. While earthly progress must indeed be distinguished from the growth of Christ's kingdom, nonetheless to the extent that earthly progress contributes to the better ordering of human society, it is of concern to the kingdom of God. Therefore, after we have nurtured on the earth the values of human dignity, brother- and sisterhood, freedom, and all the goods of our nature, we will at the coming of the kingdom find these again—but transformed and present in purification.

This document related its teaching on justice to the dignity of the person which implies that all must be treated equally. This implies first of all that more humane and just conditions of life must be brought about and that human institutions must minister to the dignity of persons. These obligations of justice are fulfilled only if each person, contributing to the common good according to his or her abilities and the needs of others, promotes and assists public and private institutions which are dedicated to improving the social life of all. This rejects a purely private ethic and insists that there must be a social ethic which evaluates common goals, problems, and the institutions that help actualize the values of dignity, equality, and freedom.

To make this teaching concrete the document says that to satisfy justice and equality, presently existing economic inequalities must be removed. Also productivity must not be a mere multiplication of products but rather must be oriented toward the service of the whole person. Consequently, economic power and development must not be left in the hands of a few but must be distributed as widely as possible so that all can exercise their rights. The basis for this is that God has intended that the earth and all that it contains is for the use of all people. Therefore, in justice, created goods should abound for all on a reasonable basis. Whatever the forms of ownership may be, attention must be paid to the universal purpose for which they are intended. Even private property, which provides a necessary arena of independence and is a form of freedom has a social nature derived from the communal purpose of earthly goods.

The quest for peace is also related to justice. Peace results from harmony built into society by God and actualized by persons as they search for justice; but it is also the fruit of love which goes beyond what strict justice can provide. This search demands a safeguarding of personal rights and values and a determination to respect other persons and their dignity. The document therefore praises those who renounce the use of violence in the vindication of their rights. It also, in one of its few condemnations, denounces those actions destined for the methodological extermination of an entire people, nation, or ethnic minority. Similarly, the Council condemned any act of war aimed indiscriminately at the destruction of entire cities or of extensive areas along with their populations. This, in the Council's perspective, is a crime against God and humanity, and it merits unequivocal and unhesitating condemnation.

The document also begins an initial discussion of the theme of development. The explicit and fixed goal of progress should be the complete human fulfillment of all citizens. The advanced nations have the obligation to help developing nations achieve this goal. Also, the international community should help in the coordination and stimulation of economic growth which is necessary to obtain such a level of development. To ensure equity, however, the Council emphasizes that there is a pressing need to reform economic and social structures to make this goal possible. Although the Council does not go into detail, these general orientations set a framework for a discussion of development in which justice is an important element. Consequently, the Council engaged in an analysis of the structures of international trade and of national economic assistance which perpetuate serious divisions between rich and poor.

Gaudium et Spes, despite all the compromises it embodied, was a powerful document, more powerful perhaps than the encyclicals precisely because it represented the opinion of the overwhelming majority of the world's bishops. It embodied the incarnationalist theology which brought the Church into the heart of human life; it spoke in humble and sincere terms to Catholics and non-Catholics alike; it offered a systematic and synthetic ethical framework for dealing with world problems; and it urged pastoral action to make its commitments real in Christian life and work. Reflecting the more dynamic and humble understanding of the Church in *Lumen Gentium*, it brought Catholicism into a new stance in regard to contemporary humans and their world. The servant Church, seeking to fulfill its gospel mandate in service to all people, everywhere, as they struggled to realize the age-old dream of peace on earth, would never again be able to deal with any phase of its life apart from the struggles of the poor and the oppressed, the victims of war and injustice. In that sense, by giving strong and forceful voice to Pope John's vision of a Church in service to real people in the concrete circumstances of human history, *Gaudium et Spes* represented the culmination of the changes begun with *Mater et Magistra* and set new directions for Catholic social thought for the future.

GAUDIUM ET SPES

PASTORAL CONSTITUTION ON THE
CHURCH IN THE MODERN WORLD[1]

PAUL, BISHOP,
SERVANT OF THE SERVANTS OF GOD,
TOGETHER WITH THE FATHERS OF
THE SACRED COUNCIL,
FOR EVERLASTING MEMORY

PREFACE

The Intimate Bond Between the Church and Mankind

1. The joys and the hopes, the griefs and the anxieties of the men of this age, especially those who are poor or in any way afflicted, these too are the joys and hopes, the griefs and anxieties of the followers of Christ. Indeed, nothing genuinely human fails to raise an echo in their hearts. For theirs is a community composed of men. United in Christ, they are led by the Holy Spirit in their journey to the Kingdom of their Father and they have welcomed the news of salvation which is meant for every man. That is why this community realizes that it is truly and intimately linked with mankind and its history.

For Whom This Message Is Intended

2. Hence this Second Vatican Council, having probed more profoundly into the mystery of the Church, now addresses itself without hesitation, not only to the sons of the Church and to all who invoke the name of Christ, but to the whole of humanity. For the Council yearns to explain to everyone how it conceives of the presence and activity of the Church in the world of today.

Therefore, the Council focuses its attention on the world

of men, the whole human family along with the sum of those realities in the midst of which that family lives. It gazes upon that world which is the theater of man's history, and carries the marks of his energies, his tragedies, and his triumphs; that world which the Christian sees as created and sustained by its Maker's love, fallen indeed into the bondage of sin, yet emancipated now by Christ. He was crucified and rose again to break the stranglehold of personified Evil, so that this world might be fashioned anew according to God's design and reach its fulfillment.

The Service to Be Offered to Humanity

3. Though mankind today is struck with wonder at its own discoveries and its power, it often raises anxious questions about the current trend of the world, about the place and role of man in the universe, about the meaning of his individual and collective strivings, and about the ultimate destiny of reality and of humanity. Hence, giving witness and voice to the faith of the whole People of God gathered together by Christ, this Council can provide no more eloquent proof of its solidarity with the entire human family with which it is bound up, as well as its respect and love for that family, than by engaging with it in conversation about these various problems.

The Council brings to mankind light kindled from the gospel, and puts at its disposal those saving resources which the Church herself, under the guidance of the Holy Spirit, receives from her Founder. For the human person deserves to be preserved; human society deserves to be renewed. Hence the pivotal point of our total presentation will be man himself, whole and entire, body and soul, heart and conscience, mind and will.

Therefore, this sacred Synod proclaims the highest destiny of man and champions the godlike seed which has been sown in him. It offers to mankind the honest assistance of the Church in fostering that brotherhood of all men which corresponds to this destiny of theirs. Inspired by no earthly ambition, the Church seeks but a solitary goal: to carry forward the work of Christ Himself under the lead of the befriending Spirit. And Christ entered this world to give witness to the truth, to rescue and not to sit in judgment, to serve and not to be served.[2]

INTRODUCTORY STATEMENT

THE SITUATION OF MEN IN THE MODERN WORLD

Hope and Anguish

4. To carry out such a task, the Church has always had the duty of scrutinizing the signs of the times and of interpreting them in the light of the gospel. Thus, in language intelligible to each generation, she can respond to the perennial questions which men ask about this present life and the life to come, and about the relationship of the one to the other. We must therefore recognize and understand the world in which we live, its expectations, its longings, and its often dramatic characteristics. Some of the main features of the modern world can be sketched as follows:

Today, the human race is passing through a new stage of its history. Profound and rapid changes are spreading by degrees around the whole world. Triggered by the intelligence and creative energies of man, these changes recoil upon him, upon his decisions and desires, both individual and collective, and upon his manner of thinking and acting with respect to things and to people. Hence we can already speak of a true social and cultural transformation, one which has repercussions on man's religious life as well.

As happens in any crisis of growth, this transformation has brought serious difficulties in its wake. Thus while man extends his power in every direction, he does not always succeed in subjecting it to his own welfare. Striving to penetrate farther into the deeper recesses of his own mind, he frequently appears more unsure of himself. Gradually and more precisely he lays bare the laws of society, only to be paralyzed by uncertainty about the direction to give it.

Never has the human race enjoyed such an abundance of wealth, resources, and economic power. Yet a huge proportion of the world's citizens is still tormented by hunger and poverty, while countless numbers suffer from total illiteracy. Never before today has man been so keenly aware of freedom, yet at the same time, new forms of social and psychological slavery make their appearance.

Although the world of today has a very vivid sense of its unity and of how one man depends on another in needful solidarity, it is most grievously torn into opposing camps by conflicting forces. For political, social, economic, racial, and ideological disputes still continue bitterly, and with them the peril of a war which would reduce everything to ashes. True, there is a growing exchange of ideas, but the very words by which key concepts are expressed take on quite different meanings in diverse ideological systems. Finally, man painstakingly searches for a better world, without working with equal zeal for the betterment of his own spirit.

Caught up in such numerous complications, very many of our contemporaries are kept from accurately identifying permanent values and adjusting them properly to fresh discoveries. As a result, buffeted between hope and anxiety and pressing one another with questions about the present course of events, they are burdened down with uneasiness. This same course of events leads men to look for answers. Indeed, it forces them to do so.

Profoundly Changed Conditions

5. Today's spiritual agitation and the changing conditions of life are part of a broader and deeper revolution. As a result of the latter, intellectual formation is ever increasingly based on the mathematical and natural sciences and on those dealing with man himself, while in the practical order the technology which stems from these sciences takes on mounting importance.

This scientific spirit exerts a new kind of impact on the cultural sphere and on modes of thought. Technology is now transforming the face of the earth, and is already trying to master outer space. To a certain extent, the human intellect is also broadening its dominion over time: over the past by means of historical knowledge; over the future by the art of projecting and by planning.

Advances in biology, psychology, and the social sciences

not only bring men hope of improved self-knowledge. In conjunction with technical methods, they are also helping men to exert direct influence on the life of social groups. At the same time, the human race is giving ever-increasing thought to forecasting and regulating its own population growth.

History itself speeds along on so rapid a course that an individual person can scarcely keep abreast of it. The destiny of the human community has become all of a piece, where once the various groups of men had a kind of private history of their own. Thus, the human race has passed from a rather static concept of reality to a more dynamic, evolutionary one. In consequence, there has arisen a new series of problems, a series as important as can be, calling for new efforts of analysis and synthesis.

Changes in the Social Order

6. By this very circumstance, the traditional local communities such as father-centered families, clans, tribes, villages, various groups and associations stemming from social contacts experience more thorough changes every day.

The industrial type of society is gradually being spread, leading some nations to economic affluence, and radically transforming ideas and social conditions established for centuries. Likewise, the practice and pursuit of city living has grown, either because of a multiplication of cities and their inhabitants, or by a transplantation of city life to rural settings.

New and more efficient media of social communication are contributing to the knowledge of events. By setting off chain reactions, they are giving the swiftest and widest possible circulation to styles of thought and feeling.

It is also noteworthy how many men are being induced to migrate on various counts, and are thereby changing their manner of life. Thus a man's ties with his fellows are constantly being multiplied. At the same time "socialization" brings further ties, without, however, always promoting appropriate personal development and truly personal relationships ("personalization").

This kind of evolution can be seen more clearly in those nations which already enjoy the conveniences of economic and technological progress, though it is also astir among peoples still striving for such progress and eager to secure for themselves the advantages of an industrialized and urbanized society. These peoples, especially those among them who are attached to older traditions, are simultaneously undergoing a movement toward more mature and personal exercise of liberty.

Psychological, Moral, and Religious Changes

7. A change in attitudes and in human structures frequently calls accepted values into question. This is especially true of young people, who have grown impatient on more than one occasion, and indeed become rebels in their distress. Aware of their own influence in the life of society, they want to assume a role in it sooner. As a result, parents and educators frequently experience greater difficulties day by day in discharging their tasks.

The institutions, laws, and modes of thinking and feeling as handed down from previous generations do not always seem to be well adapted to the contemporary state of affairs. Hence arises an upheaval in the manner and even the norms of behavior.

Finally, these new conditions have their impact on religion. On the one hand a more critical ability to distinguish religion from a magical view of the world and from the superstitions which still circulate purifies religion and exacts day by day a more personal and explicit adherence to faith. As a result many persons are achieving a more vivid sense of God.

On the other hand, growing numbers of people are abandoning religion in practice. Unlike former days, the denial of God or of religion, or the abandonment of them, are no longer unusual and individual occurrences. For today it is not rare for such decisions to be presented as requirements of scientific progress or of a certain new humanism. In numerous places these views are voiced not only in the teachings of philosophers, but on every side they influence literature, the arts, the interpretation of the humanities and of history, and civil laws themselves. As a consequence, many people are shaken.

Imbalances in the Modern World

8. Because they are coming so rapidly, and often in a disorderly fashion, all these changes beget contradictions and imbalances, or intensify them. Indeed the very fact that men are more conscious than ever of the inequalities in the world has the same effect.

Within the individual person there too often develops an imbalance between an intellect which is modern in practical matters, and a theoretical system of thought which can neither master the sum total of its ideas, nor arrange them adequately into a synthesis. Likewise, an imbalance arises between a concern for practicality and efficiency, and the demands of moral conscience; also, very often, between the conditions of collective existence and the requisites of personal thought, and even of contemplation. Specialization in any human activity can at length deprive a man of a comprehensive view of reality.

As for the family, discord results from demographic, economic, and social pressures, or from difficulties which arise between succeeding generations, or from new social relationships between men and women.

Significant differences crop up too between races and between various kinds of social orders; between wealthy nations and those which are less influential or are needy; finally, between international institutions born of the popular desire for peace, and the ambition to propagate one's own ideology, as well as collective greed existing in nations or other groups.

What results is mutual distrust, enmities, conflicts, and hardships. Of such is man at once the cause and the victim.

The Broader Desires of Mankind

9. Meanwhile, the conviction grows not only that humanity can and should increasingly consolidate its control over creation, but even more, that it devolves on humanity to establish a political, social, and economic order which will to an ever-better extent serve man and help individuals as well as groups to affirm and develop the dignity proper to them.

As a result very many persons are quite aggressively demanding those benefits of which with vivid awareness they judge themselves to be deprived either through injustice or unequal distribution. Nations on the road to progress, like those recently made independent, desire to participate in the goods of modern civilization, not only in the political field but also economically, and to play their part freely on the world scene. Still they continually fall behind while very often their dependence on wealthier nations deepens more rapidly, even in the economic sphere.

People hounded by hunger call upon those better off. Where they have not yet won it, women claim for themselves an equity with men before the law and in fact. Laborers and farmers seek not only to provide for the necessities of life but to develop the gifts of their personality by their labors, and indeed to take part in regulating economic, social, political, and cultural life. Now, for the first time in human history, all people are convinced that the benefits of culture ought to be and actually can be extended to everyone.

Still, beneath all these demands lies a deeper and more widespread longing. Persons and societies thirst for a full and free life worthy of man—one in which they can subject to their own welfare all that the modern world can offer them so abundantly. In addition, nations try harder every day to bring about a kind of universal community.

Since all these things are so, the modern world shows itself at once powerful and weak, capable of the noblest deeds or the foulest. Before it lies the path to freedom or to slavery, to progress or retreat, to brotherhood or hatred. Moreover, man is becoming aware that it is his responsibility to guide aright the forces which he has unleashed and which can enslave him or minister to him. That is why he is putting questions to himself.

Man's Deeper Questionings

10. The truth is that the imbalances under which the modern world labors are linked with that more basic imbalance rooted in the heart of man. For in man himself many elements wrestle with one another. Thus, on the one hand, as a creature he experiences his limitations in a multitude of

ways. On the other, he feels himself to be boundless in his desires and summoned to a higher life.

Pulled by manifold attractions, he is constantly forced to choose among them and to renounce some. Indeed, as a weak and sinful being, he often does what he would not, and fails to do what he would.[3] Hence he suffers from internal divisions, and from these flow so many and such great discords in society.

No doubt very many whose lives are infected with a practical materialism are blinded against any sharp insight into this kind of dramatic situation. Or else, weighed down by wretchedness, they are prevented from giving the matter any thought.

Thinking that they have found serenity in an interpretation of reality everywhere proposed these days, many look forward to a genuine and total emancipation of humanity wrought solely by human effort. They are convinced that the future rule of man over the earth will satisfy every desire of his heart.

Nor are there lacking men who despair of any meaning to life and praise the boldness of those who think that human existence is devoid of any inherent significance and who strive to confer a total meaning on it by their own ingenuity alone.

Nevertheless, in the face of the modern development of the world, an ever-increasing number of people are raising the most basic questions or recognizing them with a new sharpness: What is man? What is this sense of sorrow, of evil, of death, which continues to exist despite so much progress? What is the purpose of these victories, purchased at so high a cost? What can man offer to society, what can he expect from it? What follows this earthly life?

The Church believes that Christ, who died and was raised up for all,[4] can through His Spirit offer man the light and the strength to measure up to his supreme destiny. Nor has any other name under heaven been given to man by which it is fitting for him to be saved.[5] She likewise holds that in her most benign Lord and Master can be found the key, the focal point, and the goal of all human history.

The Church also maintains that beneath all changes there are many realities which do not change and which have their ultimate foundation in Christ, who is the same yesterday and today, yes and forever.[6] Hence in the light of Christ,[7] the image of the unseen God, the firstborn of every creature, the Council wishes to speak to all men in order to illuminate the mystery of man and to cooperate in finding the solution to the outstanding problems of our time.

PART I

THE CHURCH AND MAN'S CALLING

The Impulses of the Spirit Demand a Response

11. The People of God believes that it is led by the Spirit of the Lord, who fills the earth. Motivated by this faith, it labors to decipher authentic signs of God's presence and purpose in the happenings, needs, and desires in which this People has a part along with other men of our age. For faith throws a new light on everything, manifests God's design for man's total vocation, and thus directs the mind to solutions which are fully human.

This Council, first of all, wishes to assess in this light those values which are most highly prized today, and to relate them to their divine source. For insofar as they stem from endowments conferred by God on man, these values are exceedingly good. Yet they are often wrenched from their rightful function by the taint in man's heart, and hence stand in need of purification.

What does the Church think of man? What recommendations seem needful for the upbuilding of contemporary society? What is the ultimate significance of human activity throughout the world? People are waiting for an answer to these questions. From the answers it will be increasingly clear that the People of God and the human race in whose midst it lives render service to each other. Thus the mission of the

Church will show its religious, and by that very fact, it supremely human character.

CHAPTER I

THE DIGNITY OF THE HUMAN PERSON

Man as Made in God's Image

12. According to the almost unanimous opinion of believers and unbelievers alike, all things on earth should be related to man as their center and crown.

But what is man? About himself he has expressed, and continues to express, many divergent and even contradictory opinions. In these he often exalts himself as the absolute measure of all things or debases himself to the point of despair. The result is doubt and anxiety.

The Church understands these problems. Endowed with light from God, she can offer solutions to them so that man's true situation can be portrayed and his defects explained, while at the same time his dignity and destiny are justly acknowledged.

For sacred Scripture teaches that man was created "to the image of God," is capable of knowing and loving his Creator, and was appointed by Him as master of all earthly creatures[8] that he might subdue them and use them to God's glory.[9] "What is man that thou art mindful of him or the son of man that thou visitest him? Thou hast made him a little less than the angels, thou hast crowned him with glory and honor: thou hast set him over the works of thy hands, thou hast subjected all things under his feet" (Ps. 8:5–6).

But God did not create man as a solitary. For from the beginning "male and female he created them" (Gen. 1:27). Their companionship produces the primary form of interpersonal communion. For by his innermost nature man is a social being, and unless he relates himself to others he can neither live nor develop his potential.

Therefore, as we read elsewhere in holy Scripture, God saw "all the things that he had made, and they were very good" (Gen. 1:31).

Sin

13. Although he was made by God in a state of holiness, from the very dawn of history man abused his liberty, at the urging of personified Evil. Man set himself against God and sought to find fulfillment apart from God. Although he knew God, he did not glorify Him as God, but his senseless mind was darkened and he served the creature rather than the Creator.[10]

What divine revelation makes known to us agrees with experience. Examining his heart, man finds that he has inclinations toward evil too, and is engulfed by manifold ills which cannot come from his good Creator. Often refusing to acknowledge God as his beginning, man has disrupted also his proper relationship to his own ultimate goal. At the same time he became out of harmony with himself, with others, and with all created things.

Therefore man is split within himself. As a result, all of human life, whether individual or collective, shows itself to be a dramatic struggle between good and evil, between light and darkness. Indeed, man finds that by himself he is incapable of battling the assaults of evil successfully, so that everyone feels as though he is bound by chains.

But the Lord Himself came to free and strengthen man, renewing him inwardly and casting out that prince of this world (cf. Jn. 12:31) who held him in the bondage of sin.[11] For sin has diminished man, blocking his path to fulfillment.

The call to grandeur and the depths of misery are both a part of human experience. They find their ultimate and simultaneous explanation in the light of God's revelation.

The Make-up of Man

14. Though made of body and soul, man is one. Through his bodily composition he gathers to himself the elements of the material world. Thus they reach their crown through him, and through him raise their voice in free praise of the Creator.[12]

For this reason man is not allowed to despise his bodily life. Rather, he is obliged to regard his body as good and honorable since God created it and will raise it up on the last day. Nevertheless, wounded by sin, man experiences rebellious stirrings in his body. But the very dignity of man postulates that man glorify God in his body[13] and forbid it to serve the evil inclinations of his heart.

Now, man is not wrong when he regards himself as superior to bodily concerns, and as more than a speck of nature or a nameless constituent of the city of man. For by his interior qualities he outstrips the whole sum of mere things. He finds re-enforcement in this profound insight whenever he enters into his own heart. God, who probes the heart,[14] awaits him there. There he discerns his proper destiny beneath the eyes of God. Thus, when man recognizes in himself a spiritual and immortal soul, he is not being mocked by a deceptive fantasy springing from mere physical or social influences. On the contrary he is getting to the depths of the very truth of the matter.

The Dignity of the Mind; Truth; Wisdom

15. Man judges rightly that by his intellect he surpasses the material universe, for he shares in the light of the divine mind. By relentlessly employing his talents through the ages, he has indeed made progress in the practical sciences, technology, and the liberal arts. In our times he has won superlative victories, especially in his probing of the material world and in subjecting it to himself.

Still he has always searched for more penetrating truths, and finds them. For his intelligence is not confined to observable data alone. It can with genuine certitude attain to reality itself as knowable, though in consequence of sin that certitude is partly obscured and weakened.

The intellectual nature of the human person is perfected by wisdom and needs to be. For wisdom gently attracts the mind of man to a quest and a love for what is true and good. Steeped in wisdom, man passes through visible realities to those which are unseen.

Our era needs such wisdom more than bygone ages if the discoveries made by man are to be further humanized. For the future of the world stands in peril unless wiser men are forthcoming. It should also be pointed out that many nations, poorer in economic goods, are quite rich in wisdom and can offer noteworthy advantages to others.

It is, finally, through the gift of the Holy Spirit that man comes by faith to the contemplation and appreciation of the divine plan.[15]

The Dignity of the Moral Conscience

16. In the depths of his conscience, man detects a law which he does not impose upon himself, but which holds him to obedience. Always summoning him to love good and avoid evil, the voice of conscience can when necessary speak to his heart more specifically: do this, shun that. For man has in his heart a law written by God. To obey it is the very dignity of man; according to it he will be judged.[16]

Conscience is the most secret core and sanctuary of a man. There he is alone with God, whose voice echoes in his depths.[17] In a wonderful manner conscience reveals that law which is fulfilled by love of God and neighbor.[18] In fidelity to conscience, Christians are joined with the rest of men in the search for truth, and for the genuine solution to the numerous problems which arise in the life of individuals and from social relationships. Hence the more that a correct conscience holds sway, the more persons and groups turn aside from blind choice and strive to be guided by objective norms of morality.

Conscience frequently errs from invincible ignorance without losing its dignity. The same cannot be said of a man who cares but little for truth and goodness, or of a conscience which by degrees grows practically sightless as a result of habitual sin.

The Excellence of Liberty

17. Only in freedom can man direct himself toward goodness. Our contemporaries make much of this freedom and pursue it eagerly; and rightly so, to be sure. Often, however, they foster it perversely as a license for doing whatever pleases them, even if it is evil.

For its part, authentic freedom is an exceptional sign of the divine image within man. For God has willed that man be left "in the hand of his own counsel"[19] so that he can seek his Creator spontaneously, and come freely to utter and blissful perfection through loyalty to Him. Hence man's dignity demands that he act according to a knowing and free choice. Such a choice is personally motivated and prompted from within. It does not result from blind internal impulse nor from mere external pressure.

Man achieves such dignity when, emancipating himself from all captivity to passion, he pursues his goal in a spontaneous choice of what is good, and procures for himself, through effective and skillful action, apt means to that end. Since man's freedom has been damaged by sin, only by the help of God's grace can he bring such a relationship with God into full flower. Before the judgment seat of God each man must render an account of his own life, whether he has done good or evil.[20]

The Mystery of Death

18. It is in the face of death that the riddle of human existence becomes most acute. Not only is man tormented by pain and by the advancing deterioration of his body, but even more by a dread of perpetual extinction. He rightly follows the intuition of his heart when he abhors and repudiates the absolute ruin and total disappearance of his own person.

Man rebels against death because he bears in himself an eternal seed which cannot be reduced to sheer matter. All the endeavors of technology, though useful in the extreme, cannot calm his anxiety. For a prolongation of biological life is unable to satisfy that desire for a higher life which is inescapably lodged in his breast.

Although the mystery of death utterly beggars the imagination, the Church has been taught by divine revelation, and herself firmly teaches, that man has been created by God for a blissful purpose beyond the reach of earthly misery. In addition, that bodily death from which man would have been immune had he not sinned[21] will be vanquished, according to the Christian faith, when man who was ruined by his own doing is restored to wholeness by an almighty and merciful Savior.

For God has called man and still calls him so that with his entire being he might be joined to Him in an endless sharing of a divine life beyond all corruption. Christ won this victory when He rose to life, since by His death He freed man from death.[22] Hence to every thoughtful man a solidly established faith provides the answer to his anxiety about what the future holds for him. At the same time faith gives him the power to be united in Christ with his loved ones who have already been snatched away by death. Faith arouses the hope that they have found true life with God.

The Forms and Roots of Atheism

19. An outstanding cause of human dignity lies in man's call to communion with God. From the very circumstance of his origin, man is already invited to converse with God. For man would not exist were he not created by God's love and constantly preserved by it. And he cannot live fully according to truth unless he freely acknowledges that love and devotes himself to his Creator.

Still, many of our contemporaries have never recognized this intimate and vital link with God, or have explicitly rejected it. Thus atheism must be accounted among the most serious problems of this age, and is deserving of closer examination.

The word atheism is applied to phenomena which are quite distinct from one another. For while God is expressly denied by some, others believe that man can assert absolutely nothing about Him. Still others use such a method so to scrutinize the question of God as to make it seem devoid of meaning. Many, unduly transgressing the limits of the positive sciences, contend that everything can be explained by this kind of scientific reasoning alone, or, by contrast, they altogether disallow that there is any absolute truth.

Some laud man so extravagantly that their faith in God lapses into a kind of anemia, though they seem more inclined to affirm man than to deny God. Again some form for themselves such a fallacious idea of God that when they repudiate this figment they are by no means rejecting the God of the gospel. Some never get to the point of raising questions about

God, since they seem to experience no religious stirrings nor do they see why they should trouble themselves about religion.

Moreover, atheism results not rarely from a violent protest against the evil in this world, or from the absolute character with which certain human values are unduly invested, and which thereby already accords them the stature of God. Modern civilization itself often complicates the approach to God, not for any essential reason, but because it is excessively engrossed in earthly affairs.

Undeniably, those who willfully shut out God from their hearts and try to dodge religious questions are not following the dictates of their consciences. Hence they are not free of blame.

Yet believers themselves frequently bear some responsibility for this situation. For, taken as a whole, atheism is not a spontaneous development but stems from a variety of causes, including a critical reaction against religious beliefs, and in some places against the Christian religion in particular. Hence believers can have more than a little to do with the birth of atheism. To the extent that they neglect their own training in the faith, or teach erroneous doctrine, or are deficient in their religious, moral, or social life, they must be said to conceal rather than reveal the authentic face of God and religion.

Systematic Atheism

20. Modern atheism often takes on a systematic expression, which, in addition to other arguments against God, stretches the desire for human independence to such a point that it finds difficulties with any kind of dependence on God. Those who profess atheism of this sort maintain that it gives man freedom to be an end unto himself, the sole artisan and creator of his own history. They claim that this freedom cannot be reconciled with the affirmation of a Lord who is author and purpose of all things, or at least that this freedom makes such an affirmation altogether superfluous. The sense of power which modern technical progress generates in man can give color to such a doctrine.

Not to be overlooked among the forms of modern atheism

is that which anticipates the liberation of man especially through his economic and social emancipation. This form argues that by its nature religion thwarts such liberation by arousing man's hope for a deceptive future life, thereby diverting him from the constructing of the earthly city. Consequently, when the proponents of this doctrine gain governmental power they vigorously fight against religion. They promote atheism by using those means of pressure which public power has at its disposal. Such is especially the case in the work of educating the young.

The Church's Attitude Toward Atheism

21. In her loyal devotion to God and men, the Church has already repudiated[23] and cannot cease repudiating, sorrowfully but as firmly as possible, those poisonous doctrines and actions which contradict reason and the common experience of humanity, and dethrone man from his native excellence.

Still, she strives to detect in the atheistic mind the hidden causes for the denial of God. Conscious of how weighty are the questions which atheism raises, and motivated by love for all men, she believes these questions ought to be examined seriously and more profoundly.

The Church holds that the recognition of God is in no way hostile to man's dignity, since this dignity is rooted and perfected in God. For man was made an intelligent and free member of society by the God who created him. Ever more importantly, man is called as a son to commune with God and to share in His happiness. She further teaches that a hope related to the end of time does not diminish the importance of intervening duties, but rather undergirds the acquittal of them with fresh incentives. By contrast, when a divine substructure and the hope of life eternal are wanting, man's dignity is most grievously lacerated, as current events often attest. The riddles of life and death, of guilt and of grief go unsolved, with the frequent result that men succumb to despair.

Meanwhile, every man remains to himself an unsolved puzzle, however obscurely he may perceive it. For on certain occasions no one can entirely escape the kind of self-questioning mentioned earlier, especially when life's major events take place. To this questioning only God fully and most certainly provides an answer as He summons man to higher knowledge and humbler probing.

The remedy which must be applied to atheism, however, is to be sought in a proper presentation of the Church's teaching as well as in the integral life of the Church and her members. For it is the function of the Church, led by the Holy Spirit who renews and purifies her ceaselessly,[24] to make God the Father and His Incarnate Son present and in a sense visible.

This result is achieved chiefly by the witness of a living and mature faith, namely, one trained to see difficulties clearly and to master them. Very many martyrs have given luminous witness to this faith and continue to do so. This faith needs to prove its fruitfulness by penetrating the believer's entire life, including its worldly dimensions, and by activating him toward justice and love, especially regarding the needy. What does the most to reveal God's presence, however, is the brotherly charity of the faithful who are united in spirit as they work together for the faith of the gospel[25] and who prove themselves a sign of unity.

While rejecting atheism, root and branch, the Church sincerely professes that all men, believers and unbelievers alike, ought to work for the rightful betterment of this world in which all alike live. Such an ideal cannot be realized, however, apart from sincere and prudent dialogue. Hence the Church protests against the distinction which some state authorities unjustly make between believers and unbelievers, thereby ignoring fundamental rights of the human person. The Church calls for the active liberty of believers to build up in this world God's temple too. She courteously invites atheists to examine the gospel of Christ with an open mind.

Above all the Church knows that her message is in harmony with the most secret desires of the human heart when she champions the dignity of the human vocation, restoring hope to those who have already despaired of anything higher than their present lot. Far from diminishing man, her message brings to his development light, life, and freedom. Apart from this message nothing will avail to fill up the heart of man: "Thou hast made us for Thyself," O Lord, "and our hearts are restless till they rest in Thee."[26]

Christ as the New Man

22. The truth is that only in the mystery of the incarnate Word does the mystery of man take on light. For Adam, the first man, was a figure of Him who was to come,[27] namely, Christ the Lord. Christ, the final Adam, by the revelation of the mystery of the Father and His love, fully reveals man to man himself and makes his supreme calling clear. It is not surprising, then, that in Him all the aforementioned truths find their root and attain their crown.

He who is "the image of the invisible God" (Col. 1:15),[28] is Himself the perfect man. To the sons of Adam He restores the divine likeness which had been disfigured from the first sin onward. Since human nature as He assumed it was not annulled,[29] by that very fact it has been raised up to a divine dignity in our respect too. For by His incarnation the Son of God has united Himself in some fashion with every man. He worked with human hands, He thought with a human mind, acted by human choice,[30] and loved with a human heart. Born of the Virgin Mary, He has truly been made one of us, like us in all things except sin.[31]

As an innocent lamb He merited life for us by the free shedding of His own blood. In Him God reconciled us[32] to Himself and among ourselves. From bondage to the devil and sin, He delivered us, so that each of us can say with the Apostle: The Son of God "loved me and gave himself up for me" (Gal. 2:20). By suffering for us He not only provided us with an example for our imitation.[33] He blazed a trail, and if we follow it, life and death are made holy and take on a new meaning.

The Christian man, conformed to the likeness of that Son who is the firstborn of many brothers,[34] receives "the firstfruits of the Spirit" (Rom. 8:23) by which he becomes capable of discharging the new law of love.[35] Through this Spirit, who is "the pledge of our inheritance" (Eph. 1:14), the whole man is renewed from within, even to the achievement of "the redemption of the body" (Rom. 8:23): "If the

Spirit of him who raised Jesus from the dead dwells in you, then he who raised Jesus Christ from the dead will also bring to life your mortal bodies because of his Spirit who dwells in you" (Rom. 8:11).[36]

Pressing upon the Christian, to be sure, are the need and the duty to battle against evil through manifold tribulations and even to suffer death. But, linked with the paschal mystery and patterned on the dying Christ, he will hasten forward to resurrection in the strength which comes from hope.[37]

All this holds true not only for Christians, but for all men of good will in whose hearts grace works in an unseen way.[38] For, since Christ died for all men,[39] and since the ultimate vocation of man is in fact one, and divine, we ought to believe that the Holy Spirit in a manner known only to God offers to every man the possibility of being associated with this paschal mystery.

Such is the mystery of man, and it is a great one, as seen by believers in the light of Christian revelation. Through Christ and in Christ, the riddles of sorrow and death grow meaningful. Apart from His gospel, they overwhelm us. Christ has risen, destroying death by His death. He has lavished life upon us[40] so that, as sons in the Son, we can cry out in the Spirit: Abba, Father![41]

CHAPTER II

THE COMMUNITY OF MANKIND

The Council's Intention

23. One of the salient features of the modern world is the growing interdependence of men one on the other, a development very largely promoted by modern technical advances. Nevertheless, brotherly dialogue among men does not reach its perfection on the level of technical progress, but on the deeper level of interpersonal relationship. These demand a mutual respect for the full spiritual dignity of the person. Christian revelation contributes greatly to the promotion of

this communion between persons, and at the same time leads us to a deeper understanding of the laws of social life which the Creator has written into man's spiritual and moral nature.

Since rather recent documents of the Church's teaching authority have dealt at considerable length with Christian doctrine about human society,[42] this Council is merely going to call to mind some of the more basic truths, treating their foundations under the light of revelation. Then it will dwell more at length on certain of their implications having special significance for our day.

God's Plan Gives Man's Vocation a Communitarian Nature

24. God, who has fatherly concern for everyone, has willed that all men should constitute one family and treat one another in a spirit of brotherhood. For having been created in the image of God, who "from one man has created the whole human race and made them live all over the face of the earth" (Acts 17:26), all men are called to one and the same goal, namely, God Himself.

For this reason, love for God and neighbor is the first and greatest commandment. Sacred Scripture, however, teaches us that the love of God cannot be separated from love of neighbor: "If there is any other commandment, it is summed up in this saying, Thou shalt love thy neighbor as thyself. . . . Love therefore is the fulfillment of the Law" (Rom. 13:9–10; cf. 1 Jn. 4:20). To men growing daily more dependent on one another, and to a world becoming more unified every day, this truth proves to be of a paramount importance.

Indeed, the Lord Jesus, when He prayed to the Father, "that all may be one . . . as we are one" (Jn. 17:21–22) opened up vistas closed to human reason. For He implied a certain likeness between the union of the divine Persons, and in the union of God's sons in truth and charity. This likeness reveals that man, who is the only creature on earth which God willed for itself, cannot fully find himself except through a sincere gift of himself.[43]

The Interdependence of Person and Society

25. Man's social nature makes it evident that the progress of the human person and the advance of society itself hinge on each other. For the beginning, the subject and the goal of all social institutions is and must be the human person, which for its part and by its very nature stands completely in need of social life.[44] This social life is not something added on to man. Hence, through his dealings with others, through reciprocal duties, and through fraternal dialogue he develops all his gifts and is able to rise to his destiny.

Among those social ties which man needs for his development, some, like the family and political community, relate with greater immediacy to his innermost nature. Others originate rather from his free decision. In our era, for various reasons, reciprocal ties and mutual dependencies increase day by day and give rise to a variety of associations and organizations, both public and private. This development, which is called socialization, while certainly not without its dangers, brings with it many advantages with respect to consolidating and increasing the qualities of the human person, and safeguarding his rights.[45]

But if by this social life the human person is greatly aided in responding to his destiny, even in its religious dimensions, it cannot be denied that men are often diverted from doing good and spurred toward evil by the social circumstances in which they live and are immersed from their birth. To be sure, the disturbances which so frequently occur in the social order result in part from the natural tensions of economic, political, and social forms. But at a deeper level they flow from man's pride and selfishness, which contaminate even the social sphere. When the structure of affairs is flawed by the consequences of sin, man, already born with a bent toward evil, finds there new inducements to sin, which cannot be overcome without strenuous efforts and the assistance of grace.

Promoting the Common Good

26. Every day human interdependence grows more tightly drawn and spreads by degrees over the whole world. As a re-

sult the common good, that is, the sum of those conditions of social life which allow social groups and their individual members relatively thorough and ready access to their own fulfillment, today takes on an increasingly universal complexion and consequently involves rights and duties with respect to the whole human race. Every social group must take ao count of the needs and legitimate aspirations of other groups, and even of the general welfare of the entire human family.[46]

At the same time, however, there is a growing awareness of the exalted dignity proper to the human person, since he stands above all things, and his rights and duties are universal and inviolable. Therefore, there must be made available to all men everything necessary for leading a life truly human, such as food, clothing, and shelter; the right to choose a state of life freely and to found a family; the right to education, to employment, to a good reputation, to respect, to appropriate information, to activity in accord with the upright norm of one's own conscience, to protection of privacy and to rightful freedom in matters religious too.

Hence, the social order and its development must unceasingly work to the benefit of the human person if the disposition of affairs is to be subordinate to the personal realm and not contrariwise, as the Lord indicated when He said that the Sabbath was made for man, and not man for the Sabbath.[47]

This social order requires constant improvement. It must be founded on truth, built on justice, and animated by love; in freedom it should grow every day toward a more humane balance.[48] An improvement in attitudes and widespread changes in society will have to take place if these objectives are to be gained.

God's Spirit, who with a marvelous providence directs the unfolding of time and renews the face of the earth, is not absent from this development. The ferment of the gospel, too, has aroused and continues to arouse in man's heart the irresistible requirements of his dignity.

Reverence for the Human Person

27. Coming down to practical and particularly urgent consequences, the Council lays stress on reverence for man; everyone must consider his every neighbor without exception as

another self, taking into account first of all his life and the means necessary to living it with dignity,[49] so as not to imitate the rich man who had no concern for the poor man Lazarus.[50]

In our times a special obligation binds us to make ourselves the neighbor of absolutely every person, and of actively helping him when he comes across our path, whether he be an old person abandoned by all, a foreign laborer unjustly looked down upon, a refugee, a child born of an unlawful union and wrongly suffering for a sin he did not commit, or a hungry person who disturbs our conscience by recalling the voice of the Lord: "As long as you did it for one of these, the least of my brethren, you did it for me" (Mt. 25:40).

Furthermore, whatever is opposed to life itself, such as any type of murder, genocide, abortion, euthanasia, or willful self-destruction, whatever violates the integrity of the human person, such as mutilation, torments inflicted on body or mind, attempts to coerce the will itself; whatever insults human dignity, such as subhuman living conditions, arbitrary imprisonment, deportation, slavery, prostitution, the selling of women and children; as well as disgraceful working conditions, where men are treated as mere tools for profit, rather than as free and responsible persons; all these things and others of their like are infamies indeed. They poison human society, but they do more harm to those who practice them than those who suffer from the injury. Moreover, they are a supreme dishonor to the Creator.

Reverence and Love for Enemies

28. Respect and love ought to be extended also to those who think or act differently than we do in social, political, and religious matters, too. In fact, the more deeply we come to understand their ways of thinking through such courtesy and love, the more easily will we be able to enter into dialogue with them.

This love and good will, to be sure, must in no way render us indifferent to truth and goodness. Indeed love itself impels the disciples of Christ to speak the saving truth to all men. But it is necessary to distinguish between error, which always merits repudiation, and the person in error, who never loses the dignity of being a person, even when he is flawed by false or inadequate religious notions.[51] God alone is the judge and searcher of hearts; for that reason He forbids us to make judgments about the internal guilt of anyone.[52]

The teaching of Christ even requires that we forgive injuries,[53] and extends the law of love to include every enemy, according to the command of the New Law: "You have heard that it was said, 'Thou shalt love thy neighbor, and shalt hate thy enemy.' But I say to you, love your enemies, do good to those who hate you, and pray for those who persecute and calumniate you" (Mt. 5:43–44).

The Essential Equality of Men; and Social Justice

29. Since all men possess a rational soul and are created in God's likeness, since they have the same nature and origin, have been redeemed by Christ, and enjoy the same divine calling and destiny, the basic equality of all must receive increasingly greater recognition.

True, all men are not alike from the point of view of varying physical power and the diversity of intellectual and moral resources. Nevertheless, with respect to the fundamental rights of the person, every type of discrimination, whether social or cultural, whether based on sex, race, color, social condition, language, or religion, is to be overcome and eradicated as contrary to God's intent. For in truth it must still be regretted that fundamental personal rights are not yet being universally honored. Such is the case of a woman who is denied the right and freedom to choose a husband, to embrace a state of life, or to acquire an education or cultural benefits equal to those recognized for men.

Moreover, although rightful differences exist between men, the equal dignity of persons demands that a more humane and just condition of life be brought about. For excessive economic and social differences between the members of the one human family or population groups cause scandal, and militate against social justice, equity, the dignity of the human person, as well as social and international peace.

Human institutions, both private and public, must labor to minister to the dignity and purpose of man. At the same time let them put up a stubborn fight against any kind of slavery, whether social or political, and safeguard the basic rights of man under every political system. Indeed human institutions themselves must be accommodated by degrees to the highest of all realities, spiritual ones, even though meanwhile, a long enough time will be required before they arrive at the desired goal.

More Than an Individualistic Ethic Is Required

30. Profound and rapid changes make it particularly urgent that no one, ignoring the trend of events or drugged by laziness, content himself with a merely individualistic morality. It grows increasingly true that the obligations of justice and love are fulfilled only if each person, contributing to the common good, according to his own abilities and the needs of others, also promotes and assists the public and private institutions dedicated to bettering the conditions of human life.

Yet there are those who, while professing grand and rather noble sentiments, nevertheless in reality live always as if they cared nothing for the needs of society. Many in various places even make light of social laws and precepts, and do not hesitate to resort to various frauds and deceptions in avoiding just taxes or other debts due to society. Others think little of certain norms of social life, for example those designed for the protection of health, or laws establishing speed limits. They do not even avert to the fact that by such indifference they imperil their own life and that of others.

Let everyone consider it his sacred obligation to count social necessities among the primary duties of modern man, and to pay heed to them. For the more unified the world becomes, the more plainly do the offices of men extend beyond particular groups and spread by degrees to the whole world. But this challenge cannot be met unless individual men and their associations cultivate in themselves the moral and social virtues, and promote them in society. Thus, with the needed help of divine grace, men who are truly new and artisans of a new humanity can be forthcoming.

Responsibility and Participation

31. In order for individual men to discharge with greater exactness the obligations of their conscience toward themselves and the various groups to which they belong, they must be carefully educated to a higher degree of culture through the use of the immense resources available today to the human race. Above all the education of youth from every social background has to be undertaken, so that there can be produced not only men and women of refined talents, but those great-souled persons who are so desperately required by our times.

Now a man can scarcely arrive at the needed sense of responsibility unless his living conditions allow him to become conscious of his dignity, and to rise to his destiny by spending himself for God and for others. But human freedom is often crippled when a man falls into extreme poverty, just as it withers when he indulges in too many of life's comforts and imprisons himself in a kind of splendid isolation. Freedom acquires new strength, by contrast, when a man consents to the unavoidable requirements of social life, takes on the manifold demands of human community.

Hence, the will to play one's role in common endeavors should be everywhere encouraged. Praise is due to those national procedures which allow the largest possible number of citizens to participate in public affairs with genuine freedom. Account must be taken, to be sure, of the actual conditions of each people and the vigor required by public authority.

If every citizen is to feel inclined to take part in the activities of the various groups which make up the social body, these must offer advantages which will attract members and dispose them to serve others. We can justly consider that the future of humanity lies in the hands of those who are strong enough to provide coming generations with reasons for living and hoping.

The Incarnate Word and Human Solidarity

32. God did not create man for life in isolation, but for the formation of social unity. So also "it has pleased God to make men holy and save them not merely as individuals,

without any mutual bonds, but by making them into a single people, a people which acknowledges Him in truth and serves Him in holiness."[54] So from the beginning of salvation history He has chosen men not just as individuals but as members of a certain community. Revealing His mind to them, God called these chosen ones "His people" (Ex. 3:7-12), and, furthermore, made a covenant with them on Sinai.[55]

This communitarian character is developed and consummated in the work of Jesus Christ. For the very Word made flesh willed to share in the human fellowship. He was present at the wedding of Cana, visited the house of Zacchaeus, ate with publicans and sinners. He revealed the love of the Father and the sublime vocation of man in terms of the most common of social realities and by making use of the speech and the imagery of plain everyday life. Willingly obeying the laws of his country, He sanctified those human ties, especially family ones, from which social relationships arise. He chose to lead the life proper to an artisan of His time and place.

In His preaching He clearly taught the sons of God to treat one another as brothers. In His prayers He pleaded that all His disciples might be "one." Indeed, as the Redeemer of all, He offered Himself for all even to point of death. "Greater love than this no one has, that one lay down his life for his friends" (Jn. 15:13). He commanded His apostles to preach to all peoples the gospel message so that the human race might become the Family of God, in which the fullness of the Law would be love.

As the first-born of many brethren and through the gift of His Spirit, He founded after His death and resurrection a new brotherly community composed of all those who receive Him in faith and in love. This He did through His Body, which is the Church. There everyone, as members one of the other, would render mutual service according to the different gifts bestowed on each.

This solidarity must be constantly increased until that day on which it will be brought to perfection. Then, saved by grace, men will offer flawless glory to God as a family beloved of God and of Christ their Brother.

CHAPTER III

MAN'S ACTIVITY THROUGHOUT THE WORLD

The Problem Defined

33. Through his labors and his native endowments man has ceaselessly striven to better his life. Today, however, especially with the help of science and technology, he has extended his mastery over nearly the whole of nature and continues to do so. Thanks primarily to increased opportunities for many kinds of interchange among nations, the human family is gradually recognizing that it comprises a single world community and is making itself so. Hence many benefits once looked for, especially from heavenly powers, man has now enterprisingly procured for himself.

In the face of these immense efforts which already preoccupy the whole human race, men raise numerous questions among themselves. What is the meaning and value of this feverish activity? How should all these things be used? To the achievement of what goal are the strivings of individuals and societies heading?

The Church guards the heritage of God's Word and draws from it religious and moral principles, without always having at hand the solution to particular problems. She desires thereby to add the light of revealed truth to mankind's store of experience, so that the path which humanity has taken in recent times will not be a dark one.

The Value of Human Activity

34. Throughout the course of the centuries, men have labored to better the circumstances of their lives through a monumental amount of individual and collective effort. To believers, this point is settled: considered in itself, such human activity accords with God's will. For man, created to God's image, received a mandate to subject to himself the earth and all that it contains, and to govern the world with justice and holiness,[56] a mandate to relate himself and the

totality of things to Him who was to be acknowledged as the Lord and Creator of all. Thus, by the subjection of all things to man, the name of God would be wonderful in all the earth.[57]

This mandate concerns even the most ordinary everyday activities. For while providing the substance of life for themselves and their families, men and women are performing their activities in a way which appropriately benefits society. They can justly consider that by their labor they are unfolding the Creator's work, consulting the advantages of their brother men, and contributing by their personal industry to the realization in history of the divine plan.[58]

Thus, far from thinking that works produced by man's own talent and energy are in opposition to God's power, and that the rational creature exists as a kind of rival to the Creator, Christians are convinced that the triumphs of the human race are a sign of God's greatness and the flowering of His own mysterious design. For the greater man's power becomes, the farther his individual and community responsibility extends. Hence it is clear that men are not deterred by the Christian message from building up the world, or impelled to neglect the welfare of their fellows. They are, rather, more stringently bound to do these very things.[59]

The Regulation of Human Activity

35. Just as human activity proceeds from man, so it is ordered toward man. For when a man works he not only alters things and society, he develops himself as well. He learns much, he cultivates his resources, he goes outside of himself and beyond himself.

Rightly understood, this kind of growth is of greater value than any external riches which can be garnered. A man is more precious for what he is than for what he has.[60] Similarly, all that men do to obtain greater justice, wider brotherhood, and a more humane ordering of social relationships has greater worth than technical advances. For these advances can supply the material for human progress, but of themselves alone they can never actually bring it about.

Hence, the norm of human activity is this: that in accord

with the divine plan and will, it should harmonize with the genuine good of the human race, and allow men as individuals and as members of society to pursue their total vocation and fulfill it.

The Rightful Independence of Earthly Affairs

36. Now, many of our contemporaries seem to fear that a closer bond between human activity and religion will work against the independence of men, of societies, or of the sciences.

If by the autonomy of earthly affairs we mean that created things and societies themselves enjoy their own laws and values which must be gradually deciphered, put to use, and regulated by men, then it is entirely right to demand that autonomy. Such is not merely required by modern man, but harmonizes also with the will of the Creator. For by the very circumstance of their having been created, all things are endowed with their own stability, truth, goodness, proper laws, and order. Man must respect these as he isolates them by the appropriate methods of the individual sciences or arts.

Therefore, if methodical investigation within every branch of learning is carried out in a genuinely scientific manner and in accord with moral norms, it never truly conflicts with faith. For earthly matters and the concerns of faith derive from the same God.[61] Indeed, whoever labors to penetrate the secrets of reality with a humble and steady mind, is, even unawares, being led by the hand of God, who holds all things in existence, and gives them their identity.

Consequently, we cannot but deplore certain habits of mind, sometimes found too among Christians, which do not sufficiently attend to the rightful independence of science. The arguments and controversies which they spark lead many minds to conclude that faith and science are mutually opposed.[62]

But if the expression, the independence of temporal affairs, is taken to mean that created things do not depend on God, and that man can use them without any reference to their Creator, anyone who acknowledges God will see how false such a meaning is. For without the Creator the creature would disappear. For their part, however, all believers of whatever religion have always heard His revealing voice in the discourse of creatures. But when God is forgotten the creature itself grows unintelligible.

Human Activity as Infected by Sin

37. Sacred Scripture teaches the human family what the experience of the ages confirms: that while human progress is a great advantage to man, it brings with it a strong temptation. For when the order of values is jumbled, and bad is mixed with the good, individuals and groups pay heed solely to their own interests, and not to those of others. Thus it happens that the world ceases to be a place of true brotherhood. In our own day, the magnified power of humanity threatens to destroy the race itself.

For a monumental struggle against the powers of darkness pervades the whole history of man. The battle was joined from the very origins of the world and will continue until the last day, as the Lord has attested.[63] Caught in this conflict, man is obliged to wrestle constantly if he is to cling to what is good. Nor can he achieve his own integrity without valiant efforts and the help of God's grace.

That is why Christ's Church, trusting in the design of the Creator, acknowledges that human progress can serve man's true happiness. Yet she cannot help echoing the Apostle's warning: "Be not conformed to this world" (Rom. 12:2). By the world is here meant that spirit of vanity and malice which transforms into an instrument of sin those human energies intended for the service of God and man.

Hence if anyone wants to know how this unhappy situation can be overcome, Christians will tell him that all human activity, constantly imperiled by man's pride and deranged self-love, must be purified and perfected by the power of Christ's cross and resurrection. For, redeemed by Christ and made a new creature in the Holy Spirit, man is able to love the things themselves created by God, and ought to do so. He can receive them from God, and respect and reverence them as flowing constantly from the hand of God.

Grateful to his Benefactor for these creatures, using and enjoying them in detachment and liberty of spirit, man is led forward into a true possession of the world, as having nothing, yet possessing all things.[64] "All are yours, and you are Christ's, and Christ is God's" (1 Cor. 3:22–23).

Human Activity Finds Perfection in the Paschal Mystery

38. For God's Word, through whom all things were made, was Himself made flesh and dwelt on the earth of men.[65] Thus He entered the world's history as a perfect man, taking that history up into Himself and summarizing it.[66] He Himself revealed to us that "God is Love" (1 Jn. 4:8). At the same time He taught us that the new command of love was the basic law of human perfection and hence of the world's transformation.

To those, therefore, who believe in divine love, He gives assurance that the way of love lies open to all men and that the effort to establish a universal brotherhood is not a hopeless one. He cautions them at the same time that this love is not something to be reserved for important matters, but must be pursued chiefly in the ordinary circumstances of life.

Undergoing death itself for all of us sinners,[67] He taught us by example that we too must shoulder that cross which the world and the flesh inflict upon those who search after peace and justice. Appointed Lord by His resurrection and given plenary power in heaven and on earth,[68] Christ is now at work in the hearts of men through the energy of His Spirit. He arouses not only a desire for the age to come, but, by that very fact, He animates, purifies, and strengthens those noble longings too by which the human family strives to make its life more human and to render the whole earth submissive to this goal.

Now, the gifts of the Spirit are diverse. He calls some to give clear witness to the desire for a heavenly home and to keep that desire green among the human family. He summons others to dedicate themselves to the earthly service of men and to make ready the material of the celestial realm by this ministry of theirs. Yet He frees all of them so that by putting aside love of self and bringing all earthly resources into the service of human life they can devote themselves to that future when humanity itself will become an offering accepted by God.[69]

The Lord left behind a pledge of this hope and strength for life's journey in that sacrament of faith where natural elements refined by man are changed into His glorified Body and Blood, providing a meal of brotherly solidarity and a foretaste of the heavenly banquet.

A New Earth and a New Heaven

39. We do not know the time for the consummation of the earth and of humanity.[70] Nor do we know how all things will be transformed. As deformed by sin, the shape of this world will pass away.[71] But we are taught that God is preparing a new dwelling place and a new earth where justice will abide,[72] and whose blessedness will answer and surpass all the longings for peace which spring up in the human heart.[73]

Then, with death overcome, the sons of God will be raised up in Christ. What was sown in weakness and corruption will be clothed with incorruptibility.[74] While charity and its fruits endure,[75] all that creation[76] which God made on man's account will be unchained from the bondage of vanity.

Therefore, while we are warned that it profits a man nothing if he gain the whole world and lose himself,[77] the expectation of a new earth must not weaken but rather stimulate our concern for cultivating this one. For here grows the body of a new human family, a body which even now is able to give some kind of foreshadowing of the new age.

Earthly progress must be carefully distinguished from the growth of Christ's kingdom. Nevertheless, to the extent that the former can contribute to the better ordering of human society, it is of vital concern to the kingdom of God.[78]

For after we have obeyed the Lord, and in His Spirit nurtured on earth the values of human dignity, brotherhood and freedom, and indeed all the good fruits of our nature and enterprise, we will find them again, but freed of stain, burnished and transfigured. This will be so when Christ hands over to the Father a kingdom eternal and universal: "a kingdom of truth and life, of holiness and grace, of justice, love and peace."[79] On this earth that kingdom is already present in mystery. When the Lord returns, it will be brought into full flower.

CHAPTER IV

THE ROLE OF THE CHURCH IN THE MODERN WORLD

The Church and the World as Mutually Related

40. Everything we have said about the dignity of the human person, and about the human community and the profound meaning of human activity, lays the foundation for the relationship between the Church and the world, and provides the basis for dialogue between them.[80] In this chapter, presupposing everything which has already been said by this Council concerning the mystery of the Church, we must now consider this same Church inasmuch as she exists in the world, living and acting with it.

Coming forth from the eternal Father's love,[81] founded in time by Christ the Redeemer, and made one in the Holy Spirit,[82] the Church has a saving and an eschatological purpose which can be fully attained only in the future world. But she is already present in this world, and is composed of men, that is, of members of the earthly city who have a call to form the family of God's children during the present history of the human race, and to keep increasing it until the Lord returns.

United on behalf of heavenly values and enriched by them, this family has been "constituted and organized in the world as a society"[83] by Christ, and is equipped with "those means which befit it as a visible and social unity."[84] Thus the Church, at once a visible assembly and a spiritual community,[85] goes forward together with humanity and experiences the same earthly lot which the world does. She serves as a leaven and as a kind of soul for human society[86] as it is to be renewed in Christ and transformed into God's family.

That the earthly and the heavenly city penetrate each

other is a fact accessible to faith alone. It remains a mystery of human history, which sin will keep in great disarray until the splendor of God's sons is fully revealed. Pursuing the saving purpose which is proper to her, the Church not only communicates divine life to men, but in some way casts the reflected light of that life over the entire earth.

This she does most of all by her healing and elevating impact on the dignity of the person, by the way in which she strengthens the seams of human society and imbues the everyday activity of men with a deeper meaning and importance. Thus, through her individual members and her whole community, the Church believes she can contribute greatly toward making the family of man and its history more human.

In addition, the Catholic Church gladly holds in high esteem the things which other Christian Churches or ecclesial communities have done or are doing cooperatively by way of achieving the same goal. At the same time, she is firmly convinced that she can be abundantly and variously helped by the world in the matter of preparing the ground for the gospel. This help she gains from the talents and industry of individuals and from human society as a whole. The Council now sets forth certain general principles for the proper fostering of this mutual exchange and assistance in concerns which are in some way common to the Church and the world.

The Help Which the Church Strives to Bring to Individuals

41. Modern man is on the road to a more thorough development of his own personality, and to a growing discovery and vindication of his own rights. Since it has been entrusted to the Church to reveal the mystery of God, who is the ultimate goal of man, she opens up to man at the same time the meaning of his own existence, that is, the innermost truth about himself. The Church truly knows that only God, whom she serves, meets the deepest longings of the human heart, which is never fully satisfied by what this world has to offer.

She also knows that man is constantly worked upon by God's Spirit, and hence can never be altogether indifferent to the problems of religion. The experience of past ages proves this, as do numerous indications in our own times. For man will always yearn to know, at least in an obscure way, what is the meaning of his life, of his activity, of his death. The very presence of the Church recalls these problems to his mind.

But only God, who created man to His own image and ransomed him from sin, provides a fully adequate answer to these questions. This He does through what He has revealed in Christ His Son, who became man. Whoever follows after Christ, the perfect man, becomes himself more of a man.

Thanks to this belief, the Church can anchor the dignity of human nature against all tides of opinion, for example, those which undervalue the human body or idolize it. By no human law can the personal dignity and liberty of man be so aptly safeguarded as by the gospel of Christ which has been entrusted to the Church.

For this gospel announces and proclaims the freedom of the sons of God, and repudiates all the bondage which ultimately results from sin.[87] The gospel has a sacred reverence for the dignity of conscience and its freedom of choice, constantly advises that all human talents be employed in God's service and men's, and, finally, commends all to the charity of all.[88]

All this corresponds with the basic law of the Christian dispensation. For though the same God is Savior and Creator, Lord of human history as well as of salvation history, in the divine arrangement itself the rightful autonomy of the creature, and particularly of man, is not withdrawn. Rather it is re-established in its own dignity and strengthened in it.

Therefore, by virtue of the gospel committed to her, the Church proclaims the rights of man. She acknowledges and greatly esteems the dynamic movements of today by which these rights are everywhere fostered. Yet these movements must be penetrated by the spirit of the gospel and protected against any kind of false autonomy. For we are tempted to think that our personal rights are fully ensured only when we are exempt from every requirement of divine law. But this way lies not the maintenance of the dignity of the human person, but its annihilation.

The Help Which the Church Strives to Give to Society

42. The union of the human family is greatly fortified and fulfilled by the unity, founded on Christ,[89] of the family of God's sons.

Christ, to be sure, gave His Church no proper mission in the political, economic, or social order. The purpose which He set before her is a religious one.[90] But out of this religious mission itself come a function, a light, and an energy which can serve to structure and consolidate the human community according to the divine law. As a matter of fact, when circumstances of time and place create the need, she can and indeed should initiate activities on behalf of all men. This is particularly true of activities designed for the needy, such as the works of mercy and similar undertakings.

The Church further recognizes that worthy elements are found in today's social movements, especially an evolution toward unity, a process of wholesome socialization and of association in civic and economic realms. For the promotion of unity belongs to the innermost nature of the Church, since she is, "by her relationship with Christ, both a sacramental sign and an instrument of intimate union with God, and of the unity of all mankind."[91]

Thus she shows the world that an authentic union, social and external, results from a union of minds and hearts, namely, from that faith and charity by which her own unity is unbreakably rooted in the Holy Spirit. For the force which the Church can inject into the modern society of man consists in that faith and charity put into vital practice, not in any external dominion exercised by merely human means.

Moreover, in virtue of her mission and nature, she is bound to no particular form of human culture, nor to any political, economic, or social system. Hence the Church by her very universality can be a very close bond between diverse human communities and nations, provided these trust her and truly acknowledge her right to true freedom in fulfilling her mission. For this reason, the Church admonishes her own sons, but also humanity as a whole, to overcome all strife between nations and races in this family spirit of God's children, and in the same way, to give internal strength to human associations which are just.

This Council, therefore, looks with great respect upon all the true, good, and just elements found in the very wide variety of institutions which the human race has established for itself and constantly continues to establish. The Council affirms, moreover, that the Church is willing to assist and promote all these institutions to the extent that such a service depends on her and can be associated with her mission. She has no fiercer desire than that, in pursuit of the welfare of all, she may be able to develop herself freely under any kind of government which grants recognition to the basic rights of person and family and to the demands of the common good.

The Help Which the Church Strives to Give to Human Activity Through Christians

43. This Council exhorts Christians, as citizens of two cities, to strive to discharge their earthly duties conscientiously and in response to the gospel spirit. They are mistaken who, knowing that we have here no abiding city but seek one which is to come,[92] think that they may therefore shirk their earthly responsibilities. For they are forgetting that by the faith itself they are more than ever obliged to measure up to these duties, each according to his proper vocation.[93]

Nor, on the contrary, are they any less wide of the mark who think that religion consists in acts of worship alone and in the discharge of certain moral obligations, and who imagine they can plunge themselves into earthly affairs in such a way as to imply that these are altogether divorced from the religious life. This spirit between the faith which many profess and their daily lives deserves to be counted among the more serious errors of our age. Long since, the prophets of the Old Testament fought vehemently against this scandal[94] and even more so did Jesus Christ Himself in the New Testament threaten it with grave punishments.[95]

Therefore, let there be no false opposition between professional and social activities on the one part, and religious life on the other. The Christian who neglects his temporal duties neglects his duties toward his neighbor and even God, and jeopardizes his eternal salvation. Christians should rather rejoice that they can follow the example of Christ, who worked as an artisan. In the exercise of all their earthly activities, they can thereby gather their humane, domestic, professional, social, and technical enterprises into one vital synthesis with religious values, under whose supreme direction all things are harmonized unto God's glory.

Secular duties and activities belong properly although not exclusively to laymen. Therefore acting as citizens of the world, whether individually or socially, they will observe the laws proper to each discipline, and labor to equip themselves with a genuine expertise in their various fields. They will gladly work with men seeking the same goals. Acknowledging the demands of faith and endowed with its force, they will unhesitatingly devise new enterprises, where they are appropriate, and put them into action.

Laymen should also know that it is generally the function of their well-formed Christian conscience to see that the divine law is inscribed in the life of the earthly city. From priests they may look for spiritual light and nourishment. Let the layman not imagine that his pastors are always such experts, that to every problem which arises, however complicated, they can readily give him a concrete solution or even that such is their mission. Rather, enlightened by Christian wisdom and giving close attention to the teaching authority of the Church,[96] let the layman take on his own distinctive role.

Often enough the Christian view of things will itself suggest some specific solution in certain circumstances. Yet it happens rather frequently, and legitimately so, that with equal sincerity some of the faithful will disagree with others on a given matter. Even against the intentions of their proponents, however, solutions proposed on one side or another may be easily confused by many people with the gospel message. Hence it is necessary for people to remember that no one is allowed in the aforementioned situations to appropriate the Church's authority for his opinion. They should always try to enlighten one another through honest discussion, preserving mutual charity and caring above all for the common good.

Since they have an active role to play in the whole life of the Church, laymen are not only bound to penetrate the world with a Christian spirit. They are also called to be witnesses to Christ in all things in the midst of human society.

Bishops, to whom is assigned the task of ruling the Church of God, should, together with their priests, so preach the message of Christ that all the earthly activities of the faithful will be bathed in the light of the gospel. All pastors should remember too that by their daily conduct and concern[97] they are revealing the face of the Church to the world. Men will judge the power and truth of the Christian message thereby. By their lives and speech, in union with religious and their faithful, may pastors demonstrate that even now the Church, by her presence alone and by all the gifts which she possesses, is an unspent fountain of those virtues which the modern world most needs.

By unremitting study they should fit themselves to do their part in establishing dialogue with the world and with men of all shades of opinion. Above all let them take to heart the words which this Council has spoken: "Because the human race today is joining more and more in civic, economic, and social unity, it is that much more necessary that priests, united in concern and effort under the leadership of the bishops and the Supreme Pontiff, wipe out every ground of division, so that the whole human race may be brought into the unity of the family of God."[98]

Although by the power of the Holy Spirit the Church has remained the faithful spouse of her Lord and has never ceased to be the sign of salvation on earth, still she is very well aware that among her members,[99] both clerical and lay, some have been unfaithful to the Spirit of God during the course of many centuries. In the present age, too, it does not escape the Church how great a distance lies between the message she offers and the human failings of those to whom the gospel is entrusted.

Whatever be the judgment of history on these defects, we

ought to be conscious of them, and struggle against them energetically, lest they inflict harm on the spread of the gospel. The Church also realizes that in working out her relationship with the world she always has great need of the ripening which comes with the experience of the centuries. Led by the Holy Spirit, Mother Church unceasingly exhorts her sons "to purify and renew themselves so that the sign of Christ can shine more brightly on the face of the Church."[100]

The Help Which the Church Receives from the Modern World

44. Just as it is in the world's interest to acknowledge the Church as a historical reality, and to recognize her good influence, so the Church herself knows how richly she has profited by the history and development of humanity.

Thanks to the experience of past ages, the progress of the sciences, and the treasures hidden in the various forms of human culture, the nature of man himself is more clearly revealed and new roads to truth are opened. These benefits profit the Church, too, for from the beginning of her history, she has learned to express the message of Christ with the help of the ideas and terminology of various peoples, and has tried to clarify it with the wisdom of philosophers, too.

Her purpose has been to adapt the gospel to the grasp of all as well as to the needs of the learned, insofar as such was appropriate. Indeed, this accommodated preaching of the revealed Word ought to remain the law of all evangelization. For thus each nation develops the ability to express Christ's message in its own way. At the same time, a living exchange is fostered between the Church and the diverse cultures of people.[101]

To promote such an exchange, the Church requires special help, particularly in our day, when things are changing very rapidly and the ways of thinking are exceedingly various. She must rely on those who live in the world, are versed in different institutions and specialties, and grasp their innermost significance in the eyes of both believers and unbelievers. With the help of the Holy Spirit, it is the task of the entire People of God, especially pastors and theologians, to hear, distinguish, and interpret the many voices of our age, and to judge them in the light of the divine Word. In this way, revealed truth can always be more deeply penetrated, better understood, and set forth to greater advantage.

Since the Church has a visible and social structure as a sign of her unity in Christ, she can and ought to be enriched by the development of human social life. The reason is not that the constitution given her by Christ is defective, but so that she may understand it more penetratingly, express it better, and adjust it more successfully to our times.

She gratefully understands that in her community life no less than in her individual sons, she receives a variety of helps from men of every rank and condition. For whoever promotes the human community at the family level, culturally, in its economic, social, and political dimensions, both nationally and internationally, such a one, according to God's design, is contributing greatly to the Church community as well, to the extent that it depends on things outside itself. Indeed, the Church admits that she has greatly profited and still profits from the antagonism of those who oppose or persecute her.[102]

Christ, the Alpha and the Omega

45. While helping the world and receiving many benefits from it, the Church has a single intention: that God's kingdom may come, and that the salvation of the whole human race may come to pass. For every benefit which the People of God during its earthly pilgrimage can offer to the human family stems from the fact that the Church is "the universal sacrament of salvation,"[103] simultaneously manifesting and exercising the mystery of God's love for man.

For God's Word, by whom all things were made, was Himself made flesh so that as perfect man He might save all men and sum up all things in Himself. The Lord is the goal of human history, the focal point of the longings of history and of civilization, the center of the human race, the joy of every heart, and the answer to all its yearnings.[104] He it is whom the Father raised from the dead, lifted on high, and stationed at His right hand, making Him Judge of the living and the dead. Enlivened and united in His Spirit, we journey toward the consummation of human history, one which fully accords with the counsel of God's love: "To re-establish all things in Christ, both those in the heavens and those on the earth" (Eph. 1:10).

The Lord Himself speaks: "Behold, I come quickly! And my reward is with me, to render to each one according to his works. I am the Alpha and the Omega, the first and the last, the beginning and the end" (Apoc. 22:12–13).

PART II

SOME PROBLEMS OF SPECIAL URGENCY

Preface

46. This Council has set forth the dignity of the human person and the work which men have been destined to undertake throughout the world both as individuals and as members of society. There are a number of particularly urgent needs characterizing the present age, needs which go to the roots of the human race. To a consideration of these in the light of the gospel and of human experience, the Council would now direct the attention of all.

Of the many subjects arousing universal concern today, it may be helpful to concentrate on these: marriage and the family, human culture, life in its economic, social, and political dimensions, the bonds between the family of nations, and peace. On each of these may there shine the radiant ideals proclaimed by Christ. By these ideals may Christians be led, and all mankind enlightened, as they search for answers to questions of such complexity.

CHAPTER I

FOSTERING THE NOBILITY OF MARRIAGE AND THE FAMILY

Marriage and Family in the Modern World

47. The well-being of the individual person and of human and Christian society is intimately linked with the healthy

condition of that community produced by marriage and family. Hence Christians and all men who behold this community in high esteem sincerely rejoice in the various ways by which men today find help in fostering this community of love and perfecting its life, and by which spouses and parents are assisted in their lofty calling. Those who rejoice in such aids look for additional benefits from them and labor to bring them about.

Yet the excellence of this institution is not everywhere reflected with equal brilliance. For polygamy, the plague of divorce, so-called free love, and other disfigurements have an obscuring effect. In addition, married love is too often profaned by excessive self-love, the worship of pleasure, and illicit practices against human generation. Moreover, serious disturbances are caused in families by modern economic conditions, by influences at once social and psychological, and by the demands of civil society. Finally, in certain parts of the world problems resulting from population growth are generating concern.

All these situations have produced anxious consciences. Yet, the power and strength of the institution of marriage and family can also be seen in the fact that time and again, despite the difficulties produced, the profound changes in modern society reveal the true character of this institution in one way or another.

Therefore, by presenting certain key points of Church doctrine in a clearer light, this Council wishes to offer guidance and support to those Christians and other men who are trying to keep sacred and to foster the natural dignity of the married state and its superlative value.

The Sanctity of Marriage and the Family

48. The intimate partnership of married life and love has been established by the Creator and qualified by His laws. It is rooted in the conjugal covenant of irrevocable personal consent. Hence, by that human act whereby spouses mutually bestow and accept each other, a relationship arises which by divine will and in the eyes of society too is a lasting one. For the good of the spouses and their offspring as well as of

society, the existence of this sacred bond no longer depends on human decisions alone.

For God Himself is the author of matrimony, endowed as it is with various benefits and purposes.[105] All of these have a very decisive bearing on the continuation of the human race, on the personal development and eternal destiny of the individual members of a family, and on the dignity, stability, peace, and prosperity of the family itself and of human society as a whole. By their very nature, the institution of matrimony itself and conjugal love are ordained for the procreation and education of children, and find in them their ultimate crown.

Thus a man and a woman, who by the marriage convenant of conjugal love "are no longer two, but one flesh" (Mt. 19:6), render mutual help and service to each other through an intimate union of their persons and of their actions. Through this union they experience the meaning of their oneness and attain to it with growing perfection day by day. As a mutual gift of two persons, this intimate union, as well as the good of the children, imposes total fidelity on the spouses and argues for an unbreakable oneness between them.[106]

Christ the Lord abundantly blessed this many-faceted love, welling up as it does from the foundation of divine love and structured as it is on the model of His union with the Church. For as God of old made Himself present[107] to His people through a covenant of love and fidelity, so now the Savior of men and the Spouse[108] of the Church comes into the lives of married Christians through the sacrament of matrimony. He abides with them thereafter so that, just as He loved the Church and handed Himself over on her behalf,[109] the spouses may love each other with perpetual fidelity through mutual self-bestowal.

Authentic married love is caught up into divine love and is governed and enriched by Christ's redeeming power and the saving activity of the Church. Thus this love can lead the spouses to God with powerful effect and can aid and strengthen them in the sublime office of being a father or a mother.[110]

For this reason, Christian spouses have a special sacrament

by which they are fortified and receive a kind of consecration in the duties and dignity of their state.[111] By virtue of this sacrament, as spouses fulfill their conjugal and family obligations, they are penetrated with the spirit of Christ. This spirit suffuses their whole lives with faith, hope, and charity. Thus they increasingly advance their own perfection, as well as their mutual sanctification, and hence contribute jointly to the glory of God.

As a result, with their parents leading the way by example and family prayer, children and indeed everyone gathered around the family hearth will find a readier path to human maturity, salvation, and holiness. Graced with the dignity and office of fatherhood and motherhood, parents will energetically acquit themselves of a duty which devolves primarily on them, namely education, and especially religious education.

As living members of the family, children contribute in their own way to making their parents holy. For they will respond to the kindness of their parents with sentiments of gratitude, with love and trust. They will stand by them as children should when hardships overtake their parents and old age brings its loneliness. Widowhood, accepted bravely as a continuation of the marriage vocation, will be esteemed by all.[112] Families will share their spiritual riches generously with other families too. Thus the Christian family, which springs from marriage as a reflection of the loving covenant uniting Christ with the Church,[113] and as a participation in that covenant, will manifest to all men the Savior's living presence in the world, and the genuine nature of the Church. This the family will do by the mutual love of the spouses, by their generous fruitfulness, their solidarity and faithfulness, and by the loving way in which all members of the family work together.

Conjugal Love

49. The biblical Word of God several times urges the betrothed and the married to nourish and develop their wedlock by pure conjugal love and undivided affection.[114] Many men of our own age also highly regard true love between husband and wife as it manifests itself in a variety of ways

depending on the worthy customs of various peoples and times.

This love is an eminently human one since it is directed from one person to another through an affection of the will. It involves the good of the whole person. Therefore it can enrich the expressions of body and mind with a unique dignity, ennobling these expressions as special ingredients and signs of the friendship distinctive of marriage. This love the Lord has judged worthy of special gifts, healing, perfecting, and exalting gifts of grace and of charity.

Such love, merging the human with the divine, leads the spouses to a free and mutual gift of themselves, a gift proving itself by gentle affection and by deed. Such love pervades the whole of their lives.[115] Indeed, by its generous activity it grows better and grows greater. Therefore it far excels mere erotic inclination, which, selfishly pursued, soon enough fades wretchedly away.

This love is uniquely expressed and perfected through the marital act. The actions within marriage by which the couple are united intimately and chastely are noble and worthy ones. Expressed in a manner which is truly human, these actions signify and promote that mutual self-giving by which spouses enrich each other with a joyful and a thankful will.

Sealed by mutual faithfulness and hallowed above all by Christ's sacrament, this love remains steadfastly true in body and in mind, in bright days or dark. It will never be profaned by adultery or divorce. Firmly established by the Lord, the unity of marriage will radiate from the equal personal dignity of wife and husband, a dignity acknowledged by mutual and total love.

The steady fulfillment of the duties of this Christian vocation demands notable virtue. For this reason, strengthened by grace for holiness of life, the couple will painstakingly cultivate and pray for constancy of love, largeheartedness, and the spirit of sacrifice.

Authentic conjugal love will be more highly prized, and wholesome public opinion created regarding it, if Christian couples give outstanding witness to faithfulness and harmony in the same love, and to their concern for educating their children; also, if they do their part in bringing about the needed cultural, psychological, and social renewal on behalf of marriage and the family.

Especially in the heart of their own families, young people should be aptly and seasonably instructed about the dignity, duty, and expression of married love. Trained thus in the cultivation of chastity, they will be able at a suitable age to enter a marriage of their own after an honorable courtship.

The Fruitfulness of Marriage

50. Marriage and conjugal love are by their nature ordained toward the begetting and educating of children. Children are really the supreme gift of marriage and contribute very substantially to the welfare of their parents. The God Himself who said, "It is not good for man to be alone" (Gen. 2:18) and "who made man from the beginning male and female" (Mt. 19:4), wished to share with man a certain special participation in His own creative work. Thus He blessed male and female, saying: "Increase and multiply" (Gen. 1:28).

Hence, while not making the other purposes of matrimony of less account, the true practice of conjugal love, and the whole meaning of the family life which results from it, have this aim: that the couple be ready with stout hearts to cooperate with the love of the Creator and the Savior, who through them will enlarge and enrich His own family day by day.

Parents should regard as their proper mission the task of transmitting human life and educating those to whom it has been transmitted. They should realize that they are thereby cooperators with the love of God the Creator, and are, so to speak, the interpreters of that love. Thus they will fulfill their task with human and Christian responsibility. With docile reverence toward God, they will come to the right decision by common counsel and effort.

They will thoughtfully take into account both their own welfare and that of their children, those already born and those which may be foreseen. For this accounting they will reckon with both the material and the spiritual conditions of the times as well as of their state in life. Finally, they will consult the interests of the family group, of temporal society, and of the Church herself.

The parents themselves should ultimately make this judgment, in the sight of God. But in their manner of acting, spouses should be aware that they cannot proceed arbitrarily. They must always be governed according to a conscience dutifully conformed to the divine law itself, and should be submissive toward the Church's teaching office, which authentically interprets that law in the light of the gospel. That divine law reveals and protects the integral meaning of conjugal love, and impels it toward a truly human fulfillment.

Thus, trusting in divine Providence and refining the spirit of sacrifice,[116] married Christians glorify the Creator and strive toward fulfillment in Christ when, with a generous human and Christian sense of responsibility, they acquit themselves of the duty to procreate. Among the couples who fulfill their God-given task in this way, those merit special mention who with wise and common deliberation, and with a gallant heart, undertake to bring up suitably even a relatively large family.[117]

Marriage to be sure is not instituted solely for procreation. Rather, its very nature as an unbreakable compact between persons, and the welfare of the children, both demand that the mutual love of the spouses, too, be embodied in a rightly ordered manner, that it grow and ripen. Therefore, marriage persists as a whole manner and communion of life, and maintains its value and indissolubility, even when offspring are lacking—despite, rather often, the very intense desire of the couple.

Harmonizing Conjugal Love with Respect for Human Life

51. This Council realizes that certain modern conditions often keeps couples from arranging their married lives harmoniously, and that they find themselves in circumstances where at least temporarily the size of their families should not be increased. As a result, the faithful exercise of love and the full intimacy of their lives are hard to maintain. But where

the intimacy of married life is broken off, it is not rare for its faithfulness to be imperiled and its quality of fruitfulness ruined. For then the upbringing of the children and the courage to accept new ones are both endangered.

To these problems there are those who presume to offer dishonorable solutions. Indeed, they do not recoil from the taking of life. But the Church issues the reminder that a true contradiction cannot exist between the divine laws pertaining to the transmission of life and those pertaining to the fostering of authentic conjugal love.

For God, the Lord of life, has conferred on men the surpassing ministry of safeguarding life—a ministry which must be fulfilled in a manner which is worthy of man. Therefore from the moment of its conception life must be guarded with the greatest care, while abortion and infanticide are unspeakable crimes. The sexual characteristics of man and the human faculty of reproduction wonderfully exceed the dispositions of lower forms of life. Hence the acts themselves which are proper to conjugal love and which are exercised in accord with genuine human dignity must be honored with great reverence.

Therefore when there is question of harmonizing conjugal love with the responsible transmission of life, the moral aspect of any procedure does not depend solely on sincere intentions or on an evaluation of motives. It must be determined by objective standards. These, based on the nature of the human person and his acts, preserve the full sense of mutual self-giving and human procreation in the context of true love. Such a goal cannot be achieved unless the virtue of conjugal chastity is sincerely practiced. Relying on these principles, sons of the Church may not undertake methods of regulating procreation which are found blameworthy by the teaching authority of the Church in its unfolding of the divine law.[118]

Everyone should be persuaded that human life and the task of transmitting it are not realities bound up with this world alone. Hence they cannot be measured or perceived only in terms of it, but always have a bearing on the eternal destiny of men.

All Must Promote the Good Estate of Marriage and the Family

52. The family is a kind of school of deeper humanity. But if it is to achieve the full flowering of its life and mission, it needs the kindly communion of minds and the joint deliberation of spouses, as well as the painstaking cooperation of parents in the education of their children. The active presence of the father is highly beneficial to their formation. The children, especially the younger among them, need the care of their mother at home. This domestic role of hers must be safely preserved, though the legitimate social progress of women should not be underrated on that account.

Children should be so educated that as adults they can, with a mature sense of responsibility, follow their vocation, including a religious one, and choose their state of life. If they marry, they can thereby establish their family in favorable moral, social, and economic conditions. Parents or guardians should by prudent advice provide guidance to their young with respect to founding a family, and the young ought to listen gladly. At the same time no pressure, direct or indirect, should be put on the young to make them enter marriage or choose a specific partner.

Thus the family is the foundation of society. In it the various generations come together and help one another to grow wiser and to harmonize personal rights with the other requirements of social life. All those, therefore, who exercise influence over communities and social groups should work efficiently for the welfare of marriage and the family.

Public authority should regard it as a sacred duty to recognize, protect, and promote their authentic nature, to shield public morality, and to favor the prosperity of domestic life. The right of parents to beget and educate their children in the bosom of the family must be safeguarded. Children, too who unhappily lack the blessing of a family should be protected by prudent legislation and various undertakings, and provided with the help they need.

Redeeming the present time,[119] and distinguishing eternal realities from their changing expressions, Christians should actively promote the values of marriage and the family, both by the example of their own lives and by cooperation with other men of good will. Thus when difficulties arise, Christians will provide, on behalf of family life, those necessities and helps which are suitably modern. To this end, the Christian instincts of the faithful, the upright moral conscience of men, and the wisdom and experience of persons versed in the sacred sciences will have much to contribute.

Those, too, who are skilled in other sciences, notably the medical, biological, social, and psychological, can considerably advance the welfare of marriage and the family, along with peace of conscience, if by pooling their efforts they labor to explain more thoroughly the various conditions favoring a proper regulation of births.

It devolves on priests duly trained about family matters to nurture the vocation of spouses by a variety of pastoral means, by preaching God's Word, by liturgical worship, and by other spiritual aids to conjugal and family life; to sustain them sympathetically and patiently in difficulties, and to make them courageous through love. Thus families which are truly noble will be formed.

Various organizations, especially family associations, should try by their programs of instruction and action to strengthen young people and spouses themselves, particularly those recently wed, and to train them for family, social, and apostolic life.

Finally, let the spouses themselves, made to the image of the living God and enjoying the authentic dignity of persons, be joined to one another[120] in equal affection, harmony of mind, and the work of mutual sanctification. Thus they will follow Christ who is the principle of life.[121] Thus, too, by the joys and sacrifices of their vocation and through their faithful love, married people will become witnesses of the mystery of that love which the Lord revealed to the world by His dying and His rising up to life again.[122]

CHAPTER II

THE PROPER DEVELOPMENT OF CULTURE

Introduction

53. It is a fact bearing on the very person of man that he can come to an authentic and full humanity only through culture, that is, through the cultivation of natural goods and values. Wherever human life is involved, therefore, nature and culture are quite intimately connected.

The word "culture" in its general sense indicates all those factors by which man refines and unfolds his manifold spiritual and bodily qualities. It means his effort to bring the world itself under his control by his knowledge and his labor. It includes the fact that by improving customs and institutions he renders social life more human both within the family and in the civic community. Finally, it is a feature of culture that throughout the course of time man expresses, communicates, and conserves in his works great spiritual experiences and desires, so that these may be of advantage to the progress of many, even of the whole human family.

Hence it follows that human culture necessarily has a historical and social aspect and that the word "culture" often takes on a sociological and ethnological sense. It is in this sense that we speak of a plurality of cultures.

Various conditions of community living, as well as various patterns for organizing the goods of life, arise from diverse ways of using things, of laboring, of expressing oneself, of practicing religion, of forming customs, of establishing laws and juridical institutions, of advancing the arts and sciences, and of promoting beauty. Thus the customs handed down to it form for each human community its proper patrimony. Thus, too, is fashioned the specific historical environment which enfolds the men of every nation and age and from which they draw the values which permit them to promote human and civic culture.

SECTION 1: THE CIRCUMSTANCES OF CULTURE IN THE WORLD TODAY

New Forms of Living

54. The living conditions of modern man have been so profoundly changed in their social and cultural dimensions, that we can speak of a new age in human history.[123] Fresh avenues are open, therefore, for the refinement and the wider diffusion of culture. These avenues have been paved by the enormous growth of natural, human, and social sciences, by progress in technology, and by advances in the development and organization of the means by which men communicate with one another.

Hence the culture of today possesses particular characteristics. For example, the so-called exact sciences sharpen critical judgment to a very fine edge. Recent psychological research explains human activity more profoundly. Historical studies make a signal contribution to bringing men to see things in their changeable and evolutionary aspects. Customs and usages are becoming increasingly uniform. Industrialization, urbanization, and other causes of community living create new forms of culture (mass-culture), from which arise new ways of thinking, acting, and making use of leisure. The growth of communication between the various nations and social groups opens more widely to all the treasures of different cultures.

Man the Author of Culture

55. In every group or nation, there is an ever-increasing number of men and women who are conscious that they themselves are the artisans and the authors of the culture of their community. Throughout the world there is a similar growth in the combined sense of independence and responsibility. Such a development is of paramount importance for the spiritual and moral maturity of the human race. This truth grows clearer if we consider how the world is becoming unified and how we have the duty to build a better world

based upon truth and justice. Thus we are witnesses of the birth of a new humanism, one in which man is defined first of all by his responsibility toward his brothers and toward history.

Problems and Duties

56. In these conditions, it is no wonder that, feeling his responsibility for the progress of culture, man nourishes higher hopes but also looks anxiously upon many contradictions which he will have to resolve:

What must be done to prevent the increased exchanges between cultures, which ought to lead to a true and fruitful dialogue between groups and nations, from disturbing the life of communities, destroying ancestral wisdom, or jeopardizing the uniqueness of each people?

How can the vitality and growth of a new culture be fostered without the loss of living fidelity to the heritage of tradition? This question is especially urgent when a culture resulting from the enormous scientific and technological progress must be harmonized with an education nourished by classical studies as adapted to various traditions.

As special branches of knowledge continue to shoot out so rapidly, how can the necessary synthesis of them be worked out, and how can men preserve the ability to contemplate and to wonder, from which wisdom comes?

What can be done to make all men on earth share in cultural values, when the culture of the more sophisticated grows ever more refined and complex?

Finally, how is the independence which culture claims for itself to be recognized as legitimate without the promotion of a humanism which is merely earth-bound, and even contrary to religion itself?

In the thick of these tensions, human culture must evolve today in such a way that it can develop the whole human person harmoniously and at the same time assist men in those duties which all men, especially Christians, are called to fulfill in the fraternal unity of the one human family.

SECTION 2: SOME PRINCIPLES OF PROPER CULTURAL DEVELOPMENT

Faith and Culture

57. Christians, on pilgrimage toward the heavenly city, should seek and savor the things which are above.[124] This duty in no way decreases, but rather increases, the weight of their obligation to work with all men in constructing a more human world. In fact, the mystery of the Christian faith furnishes them with excellent incentives and helps toward discharging this duty more energetically and especially toward uncovering the full meaning of this activity, a meaning which gives human culture its eminent place in the integral vocation of man.

For when, by the work of his hands or with the aid of technology, man develops the earth so that it can bear fruit and become a dwelling worthy of the whole human family, and when he consciously takes part in the life of social groups, he carries out the design of God. Manifested at the beginning of time, the divine plan is that man should subdue[125] the earth, bring creation to perfection, and develop himself. When a man so acts he simultaneously obeys the great Christian commandment that he place himself at the service of his brother men.

Furthermore, when a man applies himself to the various disciplines of philosophy, of history, and of mathematical and natural science, and when he cultivates the arts, he can do very much to elevate the human family to a more sublime understanding of truth, goodness, and beauty, and to the formation of judgments which embody universal values. Thus mankind can be more clearly enlightened by that marvelous Wisdom which was with God from all eternity, arranging all things with Him, playing upon the earth, delighting in the sons of men.[126]

In this way, the human spirit grows increasingly free of its bondage to creatures and can be more easily drawn to the worship and contemplation of the Creator. Moreover, under the impulse of grace, man is disposed to acknowledge the Word of God. Before He became flesh in order to save all things and to sum them up in Himself, "He was in the world" already as "the true light that enlightens every man" (Jn. 1:9–10).[127]

No doubt today's progress in science and technology can foster a certain exclusive emphasis on observable data, and an agnosticism about everything else. For the methods of investigation which these sciences use can be wrongly considered as the supreme rule for discovering the whole truth. By virtue of their methods, however, these sciences cannot penetrate to the intimate meaning of things. Yet the danger exists that man, confiding too much in modern discoveries, may even think that he is sufficient unto himself and no longer seek any higher realities.

These unfortunate results, however, do not necessarily follow from the culture of today, nor should they lead us into the temptation of not acknowledging its positive values. For among its values are these: scientific study and strict fidelity toward truth in scientific research, the necessity of working together with others in technical groups, a sense of international solidarity, an ever clearer awareness of the responsibility of experts to aid men and even to protect them, the desire to make the conditions of life more favorable for all, especially for those who are deprived of the opportunity to exercise responsibility or who are culturally poor.

All of these values can provide some preparation for the acceptance of the message of the gospel—a preparation which can be animated with divine love by Him who came to save the world.

The Many Links Between the Gospel and Culture

58. There are many links between the message of salvation and human culture. For God, revealing Himself to His people to the extent of a full manifestation of Himself in His Incarnate Son, has spoken according to the culture proper to different ages.

Living in various circumstances during the course of time, the Church, too, has used in her preaching the discoveries of different cultures to spread and explain the message of Christ to all nations, to probe it and more deeply understand it and to give it better expression in liturgical celebrations and in the life of the diversified community of the faithful.

But at the same time, the Church, sent to all peoples of every time and place, is not bound exclusively and indissolubly to any race or nation, nor to any particular way of life or any customary pattern of living, ancient or recent. Faithful to her own tradition and at the same time conscious of her universal mission, she can enter into communion with various cultural modes, to her own enrichment and theirs too.

The good news of Christ constantly renews the life and culture of fallen man. It combats and removes the errors and evils resulting from sinful allurements which are a perpetual threat. It never ceases to purify and elevate the morality of peoples. By riches coming from above, it makes fruitful, as it were from within, the spiritual qualities and gifts of every people and of every age. It strengthens, perfects, and restores[128] them in Christ. Thus by the very fulfillment of her own mission[129] the Church stimulates and advances human and civic culture. By her action, even in its liturgical form, she leads men toward interior liberty.

Harmony Between the Forms of Culture

59. For the aforementioned reasons, the Church recalls to the mind of all that culture must be made to bear on the integral perfection of the human person, and on the good of the community and the whole of society. Therefore the human spirit must be cultivated in such a way that there results a growth in its ability to wonder, to understand, to contemplate, to make personal judgments, and to develop a religious, moral, and social sense.

Because it flows immediately from man's spiritual and social nature, culture has constant need of a just freedom if it is to develop. It also needs the legitimate possibility of exercising its independence according to its own principles. Rightly, therefore, it demands respect and enjoys a certain inviolability, at least as long as the rights of the individual and of the community, whether particular or universal, are preserved within the context of the common good.

This sacred Synod, therefore, recalling the teaching of the

first Vatican Council, declares that there are "two orders of knowledge" which are distinct, namely, faith and reason. It declares that the Church does not indeed forbid that "when the human arts and sciences are practiced they use their own principles and their proper method, each in its own domain." Hence, "acknowledging this just liberty," this sacred Synod affirms the legitimate autonomy of human culture and especially of the sciences.[130]

All these considerations demand too, that, within the limits of morality and the general welfare, a man be free to search for the truth, voice his mind, and publicize it; that he be free to practice any art he chooses; and finally that he have appropriate access to information about public affairs.[131]

It is not the function of public authority to determine what the proper nature of forms of human culture should be. It should rather foster the conditions and the means which are capable of promoting cultural life among all citizens and even within the minorities of a nation.[132] Hence in this matter men must insist above all else that culture be not diverted from its own purpose made to serve political or economic interests.

SECTION 3: SOME ESPECIALLY URGENT DUTIES OF CHRISTIANS WITH REGARD TO CULTURE

Recognizing and Implementing the Right to Culture

60. The possibility now exists of liberating most men from the misery of ignorance. Hence it is a duty most befitting our times that men, especially Christians, should work strenuously on behalf of certain decisions which must be made in the economic and political fields, both nationally and internationally. By these decisions universal recognition and implementation should be given to the right of all men to a human and civic culture favorable to personal dignity and free from any discrimination on the grounds of race, sex, nationality, religious or social conditions.

Therefore it is necessary to provide every man with a sufficient abundance of cultural benefits, especially those which constitute so-called basic culture. Otherwise, because of illiteracy and a lack of responsible activity, very many will be prevented from collaborating in a truly human manner for the sake of the common good.

Efforts must be made to see that men who are capable of higher studies can pursue them. In this way, as far as possible, they can be prepared to undertake in society those duties, offices, and services which are in harmony with their natural aptitude and with the competence they will have acquired.[133] Thus all the individuals and the social groups comprising a given people will be able to attain the full development of their culture, a development in accord with their qualities and traditions.

Energetic efforts must also be expended to make everyone conscious of his right to culture and of the duty he has to develop himself culturally and to assist others. For existing conditions of life and of work sometimes thwart the cultural strivings of men and destroy in them the desire for self-improvement. This is especially true of country people and laborers. They need to be provided with working conditions which will not block their human development but rather favor it.

Women are now employed in almost every area of life. It is appropriate that they should be able to assume their full proper role in accordance with their own nature. Everyone should acknowledge and favor the proper and necessary participation of women in cultural life.

Cultural Education

61. Today it is more difficult than ever for a synthesis to be formed of the various branches of knowledge and the arts. For while the mass and the diversity of cultural factors are increasing, there is a decline in the individual man's ability to grasp and unify these elements. Thus the ideal of "the universal man" is disappearing more and more. Nevertheless, it remains each man's duty to preserve a view of the whole human person, a view in which the values of intellect, will, conscience, and fraternity are pre-eminent. These values are all rooted in God the Creator and have been wonderfully restored and elevated in Christ.

The family is, as it were, the primary mother and nurse of this attitude. There, in an atmosphere of love, children can more easily learn the true structure of reality. There, too, tested forms of human culture impress themselves upon the mind of the developing adolescent in a kind of automatic way.

Opportunities for the same kind of education can also be found in modern society, thanks especially to the increased circulation of books and to the new means of cultural and social communication. All such opportunities can foster a universal culture.

The widespread reduction in working hours, for instance, brings increasing advantages to numerous people. May these leisure hours be properly used for relaxation of spirit and the strengthening of mental and bodily health. Such benefits are available through spontaneous study and activity and through travel, which refines human qualities and enriches men with mutual understanding. These benefits are obtainable too from physical exercise and sports events, which can help to preserve emotional balance, even at the community level, and to establish fraternal relations among men of all conditions, nations, and races.

Hence let Christians work together to animate the cultural expressions and group activities characteristic of our times with a human and a Christian spirit.

All these benefits, however, cannot educate men to a full self-development unless at the same time deep thought is given to what culture and science mean in terms of the human person.

Harmony Between Culture and Christian Formation

62. Although the Church has contributed much to the development of culture, experience shows that, because of circumstances, it is sometimes difficult to harmonize culture with Christian teaching.

These difficulties do not necessarily harm the life of faith. Indeed they can stimulate the mind to a more accurate and penetrating grasp of the faith. For recent studies and findings of science, history, and philosophy raise new questions which influence life and demand new theological investigations.

Furthermore, while adhering to the methods and requirements proper to theology, theologians are invited to seek continually for more suitable ways of communicating doctrine to the men of their times. For the deposit of faith or revealed truths are one thing; the manner in which they are formulated without violence to their meaning and significance is another.[134]

In pastoral care, appropriate use must be made not only of theological principles, but also of the findings of the secular sciences, especially of psychology and sociology. Thus the faithful can be brought to live the faith in a more thorough and mature way.

Literature and the arts are also, in their own way, of great importance to the life of the Church. For they strive to probe the unique nature of man, his problems, and his experiences as he struggles to know and perfect both himself and the world. They are preoccupied with revealing man's place in history and in the world, with illustrating his miseries and joys, his needs and strengths, and with foreshadowing a better life for him. Thus they are able to elevate human life as it is expressed in manifold forms, depending on time and place.

Efforts must therefore be made so that those who practice these arts can feel that the Church gives recognition to them in their activities, and so that, enjoying an orderly freedom, they can establish smoother relations with the Christian community. Let the Church also acknowledge new forms of art which are adapted to our age and are in keeping with the characteristics of various nations and regions. Adjusted in their mode of expression and conformed to liturgical requirements, they may be introduced into the sanctuary when they raise the mind to God.[135]

In this way the knowledge of God can be better revealed. Also, the preaching of the gospel can become clearer to man's mind and show its relevance to the conditions of human life.

May the faithful, therefore, live in very close union with the men of their time. Let them strive to understand perfectly their way of thinking and feeling, as expressed in their culture. Let them blend modern science and its theories and the understanding of the most recent discoveries with Christian morality and doctrine. Thus their religious practice and morality can keep pace with their scientific knowledge and with an ever-advancing technology. Thus too they will be able to test and interpret all things in a truly Christian spirit.

Through a sharing of resources and points of view, let those who teach in seminaries, colleges, and universities try to collaborate with men well versed in the other sciences. Theological inquiry should seek a profound understanding of revealed truth without neglecting close contact with its own times. As a result, it will be able to help those men skilled in various fields of knowledge to gain a better understanding of the faith.

This common effort will very greatly aid in the formation of priests. It will enable them to present to our contemporaries the doctrine of the Church concerning God, man, and the world in a manner better suited to them, with the result that they will receive it more willingly.[136] Furthermore, it is to be hoped that many laymen will receive an appropriate formation in the sacred sciences, and that some will develop and deepen these studies by their own labors. In order that such persons may fulfill their proper function, let it be recognized that all the faithful, clerical and lay, possess a lawful freedom of inquiry and of thought, and the freedom to express their minds humbly and courageously about those matters in which they enjoy competence.[137]

CHAPTER III

SOCIO-ECONOMIC LIFE

Some Aspects of Economic Life

63. In the socio-economic realm, too, the dignity and total vocation of the human person must be honored and advanced along with the welfare of society as a whole. For man is the source, the center, and the purpose of all socio-economic life.

As in other areas of social life, modern economy is marked by man's increasing domination over nature, by closer and more intense relationships between citizens, groups, and countries and by their mutual dependence, and by more frequent intervention on the part of government. At the same time progress in the methods of production and in the exchange of goods and services has made the economy an apt instrument for meeting the intensified needs of the human family more successfully.

Reasons for anxiety, however, are not lacking. Many people, especially in economically advanced areas, seem to be hypnotized, as it were, by economics, so that almost their entire personal and social life is permeated with a certain economic outlook. These people can be found both in nations which favor a collective economy as well as in others.

Again, we are at a moment in history when the development of economic life could diminish social inequalities if that development were guided and coordinated in a reasonable and human way. Yet all too often it serves only to intensify the inequalities. In some places it even results in a decline in the social status of the weak and in contempt for the poor.

While an enormous mass of people still lack the absolute necessities of life, some, even in less advanced countries, live sumptuously or squander wealth. Luxury and misery rub shoulders. While the few enjoy very great freedom of choice, the many are deprived of almost all possibility of acting on their own initiative and responsibility, and often subsist in living and working conditions unworthy of human beings.

A similar lack of economic and social balance is to be noted between agriculture, industry, and the services, and also between different parts of one and the same country. The contrast between the economically more advanced countries and other countries is becoming more serious day by day, and the very peace of the world can be jeopardized in consequence.

Our contemporaries are coming to feel these inequalities with an ever sharper awareness. For they are thoroughly convinced that the wider technical and economic potential which the modern world enjoys can and should correct this unhappy state of affairs. Hence, numerous reforms are needed at the socio-economic level, along with universal changes in ideas and attitudes.

Now in this area the Church maintains certain principles

of justice and equity as they apply to individuals, societies, and international relations. In the course of the centuries and with the light of the gospel she has worked out these principles as right reason demanded. In modern times especially, the Church has enlarged upon them. This sacred Council wishes to re-enforce these principles according to the circumstances of the times and to set forth certain guidelines, primarily with regard to the requirements of economic development.[138]

SECTION 1: ECONOMIC DEVELOPMENT

In the Service of Man

64. Today, more than ever before, progress in the production of agricultural and industrial goods and in the rendering of services is rightly aimed at making provision for the growth of a people and at meeting the rising expectations of the human race. Therefore, technical progress must be fostered, along with a spirit of initiative, an eagerness to create and expand enterprises, the adaptation of methods of production—in a word, all the elements making for such development.

The fundamental purpose of this productivity must not be the mere multiplication of products. It must not be profit or domination. Rather, it must be the service of man, and indeed of the whole man, viewed in terms of his material needs and the demands of his intellectual, moral, spiritual, and religious life. And when we say man, we mean every man whatsoever and every group of men, of whatever race and from whatever part of the world. Consequently, economic activity is to be carried out according to its own methods and laws but within the limits of morality,[139] so that God's plan for mankind can be realized.[140]

Under Man's Control

65. Economic development must be kept under the control of mankind. It must not be left to the sole judgment of a few men or groups possessing excessive economic power, or of the political community alone, or of certain especially power-

ful nations. It is proper, on the contrary, that at every level the largest possible number of people have an active share in directing that development. When it is a question of international developments, all nations should so participate. It is also necessary for the spontaneous activities of individuals and of independent groups to be coordinated with the efforts of public authorities. These activities and these efforts should be aptly and harmoniously interwoven.

Growth must not be allowed merely to follow a kind of automatic course resulting from the economic activity of individuals. Nor must it be entrusted solely to the authority of government. Hence, theories which obstruct the necessary reforms in the name of a false liberty must be branded as erroneous. The same is true of those theories which subordinate the basic rights of individual persons and groups to the collective organization of production.[141]

Citizens, for their part, should remember that they have the right and the duty, which must be recognized by civil authority, to contribute according to their ability to the true progress of their own community. Especially in underdeveloped areas, where all resources must be put to urgent use, those men gravely endanger the public good who allow their resources to remain unproductive or who deprive their community of the material and spiritual aid it needs. The personal right of migration, however, is not to be impugned.

Removing Huge Differences

66. If the demands of justice and equity are to be staisfied, vigorous efforts must be made, without violence to the rights of persons or to the natural characteristics of each country, to remove as quickly as possible the immense economic inequalities which now exist. In many cases, these are worsening and are connected with individual and group discrimination.

In many areas, too, farmers experience special difficulties in raising products or in selling them. In such cases, country people must be helped to increase and to market what they produce, to make the necessary advances and changes, and to obtain a fair return. Otherwise, as too often happens, they will remain in the condition of lower-class citizens. Let farmers, especially young ones, skillfully apply themselves to perfecting their professional competence. Without it, no agricultural progress can take place.[142]

Justice and equity likewise require that the mobility which is necessary in a developing economy be regulated in such a way as to keep the life of individuals and their families from becoming insecure and precarious. Hence, when workers come from another country or district and contribute by their labor to the economic advancement of a nation or region, all discrimination with respect to wages and working conditions must be carefully avoided.

The local people, moreover, especially public authorities, should all treat them not as mere tools of production but as persons, and must help them to arrange for their families to live with them and to provide themselves with decent living quarters. The native should also see that these workers are introduced into the social life of the country or region which receives them. Employment opportunities, however, should be created in their own areas as far as possible.

In those economic affairs which are today subject to change, as in the new forms of industrial society in which automation, for example, is advancing, care must be taken that sufficient and suitable work can be obtained, along with appropriate technical and professional formation. The livelihood and the human dignity of those especially who are in particularly difficult circumstances because of illness or old age should be safeguarded.

SECTION 2: CERTAIN PRINCIPLES GOVERNING SOCIO-ECONOMIC LIFE AS A WHOLE

Labor and Leisure

67. Human labor which is expended in the production and exchange of goods or in the performance of economic services is superior to the other elements of economic life. For the latter have only the nature of tools.

Whether it is engaged in independently or paid for by someone else, this labor comes immediately from the person. In a sense, the person stamps the things of nature with his seal and subdues them to his will. It is ordinarily by his labor that a man supports himself and his family, is joined to his fellow men and serves them, and is enabled to exercise genuine charity and be a partner in the work of bringing God's creation to perfection. Indeed, we hold that by offering his labor to God a man becomes associated with the redemptive work itself of Jesus Christ, who conferred an eminent dignity on labor when at Nazareth He worked with His own hands.

From all these considerations there arise every man's duty to labor faithfully and also his right to work. It is the duty of society, moreover, according to the circumstances prevailing in it, and in keeping with its proper role, to help its citizens find opportunities for adequate employment. Finally, payment for labor must be such as to furnish a man with the means to cultivate his own material, social, cultural, and spiritual life worthily, and that of his dependents. What this payment should be will vary according to each man's assignment and productivity, the conditions of his place of employment, and the common good.[143]

Since economic activity is generally exercised through the combined labors of human beings, any way of organizing and directing that activity which would be detrimental to any worker would be wrong and inhuman. It too often happens, however, even in our day, that in one way or another workers are made slaves of their work. This situation can by no means be justified by so-called economic laws. The entire process of productive work, therefore, must be adapted to the needs of the person and to the requirements of his life, above all his domestic life. Such is especially the case with respect to mothers of families, but due consideration to every person's sex and age.

The opportunity should also be afforded to workers to develop their own abilities and personalities through the work they perform. Though they should apply their time and energy to their employment with a due sense of responsibility, all workers should also enjoy sufficient rest and leisure to cultivate their family, cultural, social, and religious life. They should also have the opportunity to develop on their own the resources and potentialities to which, perhaps, their professional work gives but little scope.

Economic Participation and Conflict

68. In economic enterprises it is persons who work together, that is, free and independent human beings created to the image of God. Therefore the active participation of everyone in the running of an enterprise should be promoted.[144] This participation should be exercised in appropriately determined ways. It should take into account each person's function, whether it be one of ownership, hiring, management, or labor. It should provide for the necessary unity of operations.

However, decisions concerning economic and social conditions, on which the future of the workers and their children depends, are rather often made not within the enterprise itself but by institutions on a higher level. Hence the workers themselves should have a share also in controlling these institutions, either in person or through freely elected delegates.

Among the basic rights of the human person must be counted the right of freely founding labor unions. These unions should be truly able to represent the workers and to contribute to the proper arrangement of economic life. Another such right is that of taking part freely in the activity of these unions without risk of reprisal. Through this sort of orderly participation, joined with an ongoing formation in economic and social matters, all will grow day by day in the awareness of their own function and responsibility. Thus they will be brought to feel that according to their own proper capacities and aptitudes they are associates in the whole task of economic and social development and in the attainment of the universal common good.

When, however, socio-economic disputes arise, efforts must be made to come to a peaceful settlement. Recourse must always be had above all to sincere discussion between the parties. Even in present-day circumstances, however, the strike can still be a necessary, though ultimate, means for the defense of the workers' own rights and the fulfillment of their just demands. As soon as possible, however, ways should be sought to resume negotiations and the discussion of reconciliation.

The Common Purpose of Created Things

69. God intended the earth and all that it contains for the use of every human being and people. Thus, as all men follow justice and unite in charity, created good should abound for them on a reasonable basis.[145] Whatever the forms of ownership may be, as adapted to the legitimate institutions of people according to diverse and changeable circumstances, attention must always be paid to the universal purpose for which created goods are meant. In using them, therefore, a man should regard his lawful possessions not merely as his own but also as common property in the sense that they should accrue to the benefit of not only himself but of others.[146]

For the rest, the right to have a share of earthly goods sufficient for oneself and one's family belongs to everyone. The Fathers and Doctors of the Church held this view, teaching that men are obliged to come to the relief to the poor, and to do so not merely out of their superfluous goods.[147] If a person is in extreme necessity, he has the right to take from the riches of others what he himself needs.[148] Since there are so many people in this world afflicted with hunger, this sacred Council urges all, both individuals and governments, to remember the saying of the Fathers: "Feed the man dying of hunger, because if you have not fed him you have killed him."[149] According to their ability, let all individuals and governments undertake a genuine sharing of their goods. Let them use these goods especially to provide individuals and nations with the means for helping and developing themselves.

In economically less advanced societies, it is not rare for the communal purpose of earthly goods to be partially satisfied through the customs and traditions proper to a community. By such means the absolute essentials are furnished to each member. If, however, customs cannot answer the new needs of this age, an effort must be made to avoid regarding them as altogether unchangeable. At the same time, rash action should not be taken against worthy customs which, provided that they are suitably adapted to present-day circumstances, do not cease to be very useful.

Similarly, in highly developed nations a body of social institutions dealing with insurance and security can, for its part, make the common purpose of earthly goods effective. Family and social services, especially those which provide for culture and education, should be further promoted. Still, care must be taken lest, as a result of all these provisions, the citizenry fall into a kind of sluggishness toward society, and reject the burdens of office and of public service.

Distribution and Money

70. The distribution of goods should be directed toward providing employment and sufficient income for the people of today and of the future. Whether individuals, groups, or public authorities make the decisions concerning this distribution and the planning of the economy, they are bound to keep these objectives in mind. They must realize their serious obligation of seeing to it that provision is made for the necessities of a decent life on the part of individuals and of the whole community. They must also look out for the future and establish a proper balance between the needs of present-day consumption, both individual and collective, and the necessity of distributing goods on behalf of the coming generation. They should also bear constantly in mind the urgent needs of underdeveloped countries and regions. In financial transactions they should beware of hurting the welfare of their own country or of other countries. Care should also be taken lest the economically weak countries unjustly suffer loss from a change in the value of money.

Ownership and Property

71. Ownership and other forms of private control over material goods contribute to the expression of personality. Moreover, they furnish men with an occasion for exercising their role in society and in the economy. Hence it is very important to facilitate the access of both individuals and communities to some control over material goods.

Private ownership or some other kind of dominion over material goods provides everyone with a wholly necessary area of independence, and should be regarded as an extension of human freedom. Finally, since it adds incentives for carrying on one's function and duty, it constitutes a kind of prerequisite for civil liberties.[150]

The forms of such dominion or ownership are varied today and are becoming increasingly diversified. They all remain a source of security not to be underestimated, even in the face of the public funds, rights, and services provided by society. This is true not only of material goods but also of intangible goods, such as professional skills.

The right of private control, however, is not opposed to the right inherent in various forms of public ownership. Still, goods can be transferred to the public domain only by the competent authority, according to the demands and within the limits of the common good, and with fair compensation. It is a further right of public authority to guard against any misuse of private property which injures the common good.[151]

By its very nature, private property has a social quality deriving from the law of the communal purpose of earthly goods.[152] If this social quality is overlooked, property often becomes an occasion of greed and of serious disturbances. Thus, to those who attack the concept of private property, a pretext is given for calling the right itself into question.

In many underdeveloped areas there are large or even gigantic rural estates which are only moderately cultivated or lie completely idle for the sake of profit. At the same time the majority of the people are either without land or have only very small holdings, and there is evident and urgent need to increase land productivity.

It is not rare for those who are hired to work for the landowners, or who till a portion of the land as tenants, to receive a wage or income unworthy of human beings, to lack decent housing, and to be exploited by middlemen. Deprived of all security, they live under such personal servitude that almost every opportunity for acting on their own initiative and responsibility is denied to them, and all advancement in human culture and all sharing in social and political life are ruled out.

Depending on circumstances, therefore, reforms must be instituted if income is to grow, working conditions improve, job security increase, and an incentive to working on one's own initiative be provided. Indeed, insufficiently cultivated estates should be distributed to those who can make these lands fruitful. In this case, the necessary ways and means, especially educational aids and the right facilities for cooperative organization, must be supplied. Still, whenever the common good requires expropriation, compensation must be reckoned in equity after all the circumstances have been weighed.

Economics and Christ's Kingdom

72. Christians who take an active part in modern socio-economic development and defend justice and charity should be convinced that they can make a great contribution to the prosperity of mankind and the peace of the world. Whether they do so as individuals or in association, let their example be a shining one. After acquiring whatever skills and experience are absolutely necessary, they should in faithfulness to Christ and His gospel observe the right order of values in their earthly activities. Thus their whole lives, both individual and social, will be permeated with the spirit of the beatitudes, notably with the spirit of poverty.

Whoever in obedience to Christ seeks first the kingdom of God will as a consequence receive a stronger and purer love for helping all his brothers and for perfecting the work of justice under the inspiration of charity.[153]

CHAPTER IV

THE LIFE OF THE POLITICAL COMMUNITY

Modern Politics

73. Our times have witnessed profound changes too in the institutions of peoples and in the ways that peoples are joined together. These changes are resulting from the cultural, economic, and social evolution of these same peoples. The changes are having a great impact on the life of the political community, especially with regard to universal rights and duties both in the exercise of civil liberty and in the at-

tainment of the common good, and with regard to the regulation of the relations of citizens among themselves, and with public authority.

From a keener awareness of human dignity there arises in many parts of the world a desire to establish a political-juridical order in which personal rights can gain better protection. These include the rights of free assembly, of common action, of expressing personal opinions, and of professing a religion both privately and publicly. For the protection of personal rights is a necessary condition for the active participation of citizens, whether as individuals or collectively, in the life and government of the state.

Among numerous people, cultural, economic, and social progress has been accompanied by the desire to assume a larger role in organizing the life of the political community. In many consciences there is a growing intent that the rights of national minorities be honored while at the same time these minorities honor their duties toward the political community. In addition men are learning more every day to respect the opinions and religious beliefs of others. At the same time a broader spirit of cooperation is taking hold. Thus all citizens, and not just a privileged few, are actually able to enjoy personal rights.

Men are voicing disapproval of any kind of government which blocks civil or religious liberty, multiplies the victims of ambition and political crimes, and wrenches the exercise of authority from pursuing the common good to serving the advantage of a certain faction or of the rulers themselves. There are some such governments holding power in the world.

No better way exists for attaining a truly human political life than by fostering an inner sense of justice, benevolence, and service for the common good, and by strengthening basic beliefs about the true nature of the political community, and about the proper exercise and limits of public authority.

Nature and Goal of Politics

74. Individuals, families, and various groups which compose the civic community are aware of their own insufficiency in the matter of establishing a fully human condition of life.

They see the need for that wider community in which each would daily contribute his energies toward the ever better attainment of the common good.[154] It is for this reason that they set up the political community in its manifold expressions.

Hence the political community exists for that common good in which the community finds it full justification and meaning, and from which it derives its pristine and proper right. Now, the common good embraces the sum of those conditions of social life by which individuals, families, and groups can achieve their own fulfillment in a relatively thorough and ready way.[155]

Many different people go to make up the political community, and these can lawfully incline toward diverse ways of doing things. Now, if the political community is not to be torn to pieces as each man follows his own viewpoint, authority is needed. This authority must dispose the energies of the whole citizenry toward the common good, not mechanically or despotically, but primarily as a moral force which depends on freedom and the conscientious discharge of the burdens of any office which has been undertaken.

It is therefore obvious that the political community and public authority are based on human nature and hence belong to an order of things divinely foreordained. At the same time the choice of government and the method of selecting leaders is left to the free will of citizens.[156]

It also follows that political authority, whether in the community as such or in institutions representing the state, must always be exercised within the limits of morality and on behalf of the dynamically conceived common good, according to a juridical order enjoying legal status. When such is the case citizens are conscience-bound to obey.[157] This fact clearly reveals the responsibility, dignity, and importance of those who govern.

Where public authority oversteps its competence and oppresses the people, these people should nevertheless obey to the extent that the objective common good demands. Still it is lawful for them to defend their own rights and those of their fellow citizens against any abuse of this authority, provided that in so doing they observe the limits imposed by natural law and the gospel.

The practical ways in which the political community structures itself and regulates public authority can vary according to the particular character of a people and its historical development. But these methods should always serve to mold men who are civilized, peace-loving, and well disposed toward all—to the advantage of the whole human family.

Political Participation

75. It is in full accord with human nature that juridical-political structures should, with ever better success and without any discrimination, afford all their citizens the chance to participate freely and actively in establishing the constitutional bases of a political community, governing the state, determining the scope and purpose of various institutions, and choosing leaders.[158] Hence let all citizens be mindful of their simultaneous right and duty to vote freely in the interest of advancing the common good. The Church regards as worthy of praise and consideration the work of those who, as a service to others, dedicate themselves to the welfare of the state and undertake the burdens of this task.

If conscientious cooperation between citizens is to achieve its happy effect in the normal course of public affairs, a positive system of law is required. In it should be established a division of governmental roles and institutions and, at the same time, an effective and independent system for the protection of rights. Let the rights of all persons, families, and associations, along with the exercise of those rights, be recognized, honored, and fostered.[159] The same holds for those duties which bind all citizens. Among the latter should be remembered that of furnishing the commonwealth with the material and spiritual services required for the common good.

Authorities must beware of hindering family, social, or cultural groups, as well as intermediate bodies and institutions. They must not deprive them of their own lawful and effective activity, but should rather strive to promote them willingly and in an orderly fashion. For their part, citizens both as individuals and in association should be on guard against granting government too much authority and inappropriately seeking from it excessive conveniences and advantages, with a consequent weakening of the sense of responsibility on the part of individuals, families, and social groups.

Because of the increased complexity of modern circumstances, government is more often required to intervene in social and economic affairs, by way of bringing about conditions more likely to help citizens and groups freely attain to complete human fulfillment with greater effect. The proper relationship between socialization[160] on the one hand and personal independence and development on the other can be variously interpreted according to the locales in question and the degree of progress achieved by a given people.

When the exercise of rights is temporarily curtailed on behalf of the common good, it should be restored as quickly as possible after the emergency passes. In any case it harms humanity when government takes on totalitarian or dictatorial forms injurious to the rights of persons or social groups.

Citizens should develop a generous and loyal devotion to their country, but without any narrowing of mind. In other words, they must always look simultaneously to the welfare of the whole human family, which is tied together by the manifold bonds linking races, peoples, and nations.

Let all Christians appreciate their special and personal vocation in the political community. This vocation requires that they give conspicuous example of devotion to the sense of duty and of service to the advancement of the common good. Thus they can also show in practice how authority is to be harmonized with freedom, personal initiative with consideration for the bonds uniting the whole social body, and necessary unity with beneficial diversity.

Christians should recognize that various legitimate though conflicting views can be held concerning the regulation of temporal affairs. They should respect their fellow citizens when they promote such views honorably even by group action. Political parties should foster whatever they judge necessary for the common good. But they should never prefer their own advantage over this same common good.

Civic and political education is today supremely necessary

for the people, especially young people. Such education should be painstakingly provided, so that all citizens can make their contribution to the political community. Let those who are suited for it, or can become so, prepare themselves for the difficult but most honorable art of politics.[161] Let them work to exercise this art without thought of personal convenience and without benefit of bribery. Prudently and honorably let them fight against injustice and oppression, the arbitrary rule of one man or one party, and lack of tolerance. Let them devote themselves to the welfare of all sincerely and fairly, indeed with charity and political courage.

Politics and the Church

76. It is highly important, especially in pluralistic societies, that a proper view exist of the relation between the political community and the Church. Thus the faithful will be able to make a clear distinction between what a Christian conscience leads them to do in their own name as citizens, whether as individuals or in association, and what they do in the name of the Church and in union with her shepherds.

The role and competence of the Church being what it is, she must in no way be confused with the political community, nor bound to any political system. For she is at once a sign and a safeguard of the transcendence of the human person.

In their proper spheres, the political community and the Church are mutually independent and self-governing. Yet, by a different title, each serves the personal and social vocation of the same human beings. This service can be more effectively rendered for the good of all, if each works better for wholesome mutual cooperation, depending on the circumstances of time and place. For man is not restricted to the temporal sphere. While living in history he fully maintains his eternal vocation.

The Church, founded on the Redeemer's love, contributes to the wider application of justice and charity within and between nations. By preaching the truth of the gospel and shedding light on all areas of human activity through her teaching and the example of the faithful, she shows respect for the political freedom and responsibility of citizens and fosters these values.

The apostles, their successors, and those who assist these successors have been sent to announce to men Christ, the Savior of the world. Hence in the exercise of their apostolate they must depend on the power of God, who very often reveals the might of the gospel through the weakness of its witnesses. For those who dedicate themselves to the ministry of God's Word should use means and helps proper to the gospel. In many respects these differ from the supports of the earthly city.

There are, indeed, close links between earthly affairs and those aspects of man's condition which transcend this world. The Church herself employs the things of time to the degree that her own proper mission demands. Still she does not lodge her hope in privileges conferred by civil authority. Indeed, she stands ready to renounce the exercise of certain legitimately acquired rights if it becomes clear that their use raises doubt about the sincerity of her witness or that new conditions of life demand some other arrangement.

But it is always and everywhere legitimate for her to preach the faith with true freedom, to teach her social doctrine, and to discharge her duty among men without hindrance. She also has the right to pass moral judgments, even on matters touching the political order, whenever basic personal rights or the salvation of souls make such judgments necessary. In so doing, she may use only those helps which accord with the gospel and with the general welfare as it changes according to time and circumstance.

Holding faithfully to the gospel and exercising her mission in the world, the Church consolidates peace among men, to God's glory.[162] For it is her task to uncover, cherish, and ennoble[163] all that is true, good, and beautiful in the human community.

CHAPTER V

THE FOSTERING OF PEACE AND THE
PROMOTION OF A COMMUNITY OF NATIONS

Introduction

77. In our generation, when men continue to be afflicted by acute hardships and anxieties arising from ongoing wars or the threat of them, the whole human family has reached an hour of supreme crisis in its advance toward maturity. Moving gradually together and everywhere more conscious already of its oneness, this family cannot accomplish its task of constructing for all men everywhere a world more genuinely human unless each person devotes himself with renewed determination to the reality of peace. Thus it happens that the gospel message, which is in harmony with the loftier strivings and aspirations of the human race, takes on a new luster in our days as it declares that the artisans of peace are blessed, "for they shall be called children of God" (Mt. 5:9).

Consequently, as it points out the authentic and most noble meaning of peace and condemns the frightfulness of war, this Council fervently desires to summon Christians to cooperate with all men in making secure among themselves a peace based on justice and love, and in setting up agencies of peace. This Christians should do with the help of Christ, the Author of peace.

The Nature of Peace

78. Peace is not merely the absence of war. Nor can it be reduced solely to the maintenance of a balance of power between enemies. Nor is it brought about by dictatorship. Instead, it is rightly and appropriately called "an enterprise of justice" (Is. 32:7). Peace results from that harmony built into human society by its divine Founder, and actualized by men as they thirst after ever greater justice.

The common good of men is in its basic sense determined by the eternal law. Still the concrete demands of this common good are constantly changing as time goes on. Hence peace is never attained once and for all, but must be built up ceaselessly. Moreover, since the human will is unsteady and wounded by sin, the achievement of peace requires that everyone constantly master his passions and that lawful authority keep vigilant.

But such is not enough. This peace cannot be obtained on earth unless personal values are safeguarded and men freely and trustingly share with one another the riches of their inner spirits and their talents. A firm determination to respect other men and peoples and their dignity, as well as the studied practice of brotherhood, are absolutely necessary for the establishment of peace. Hence peace is likewise the fruit of love, which goes beyond what justice can provide.

That earthly peace which arises from love of neighbor symbolizes and results from the peace of Christ, who comes forth from God the Father. For by His cross the incarnate Son, the Prince of Peace, reconciled all men with God. By thus restoring the unity of all men in one people and one body, He slew hatred in His own flesh.[164] After being lifted on high by His resurrection, He poured the Spirit of love into the hearts of men.

For this reason, all Christians are urgently summoned "to practice the truth in love" (Eph. 4:15) and to join with all true peacemakers in pleading for peace and bringing it about.

Motivated by this same spirit, we cannot fail to praise those who renounce the use of violence in the vindication of their rights and who resort to methods of defense which are otherwise available to weaker parties too, provided that this can be done without injury to the rights and duties of others or of the community itself.

Insofar as men are sinful, the threat of war hangs over them, and hang over them it will until the return of Christ. But to the extent that men vanquish sin by a union of love, they will vanquish violence as well, and make these words come true: "They shall beat their swords into plowshares and their spears into pruning hooks; one nation shall not raise the sword against another, nor shall they train for war again" (Is. 2:4).

SECTION 1: THE AVOIDANCE OF WAR

Curbing the Savagery of War

79. In spite of the fact that recent wars have wrought physical and moral havoc on our world, conflicts still produce their devastating effect day by day somewhere in the world. Indeed, now that every kind of weapon produced by modern science is used in war, the fierce character of warfare threatens to lead the combatants to a savagery far surpassing that of the past. Furthermore, the complexity of the modern world and the intricacy of international relations allow guerrilla warfare to be drawn out by new methods of deceit and subversion. In many cases the use of terrorism is regarded as a new way to wage war.

Contemplating this melancholy state of humanity, the Council wishes to recall first of all the permanent binding force of universal natural law and its all-embracing principles. Man's conscience itself gives ever more emphatic voice to these principles. Therefore, actions which deliberately conflict with these same principles, as well as orders commanding such actions, are criminal. Blind obedience cannot excuse those who yield to them. Among such must first be counted those actions designed for the methodical extermination of an entire people, nation, or ethnic minority. These actions must be vehemently condemned as horrendous crimes. The courage of those who openly and fearlessly resist men who issue such commands merits supreme commendation.

On the subject of war, quite a large number of nations have subscribed to various international agreements aimed at making military activity and its consequences less inhuman. Such are conventions concerning the handling of wounded or captured soldiers, and various similar agreements. Agreements of this sort must be honored. Indeed they should be improved upon so that they can better and more workably lead to restraining the frightfulness of war.

All men, especially government officials and experts in these matters, are bound to do everything they can to effect these improvements. Moreover, it seems right that laws make humane provisions for the case of those who for reasons of conscience refuse to bear arms, provided however, that they accept some other form of service to the human community.

Certainly, war has not been rooted out of human affairs. As long as the danger of war remains and there is no competent and sufficiently powerful authority at the international level, governments cannot be denied the right to legitimate defense once every means of peaceful settlement has been exhausted. Therefore, government authorities and others who share public responsibility have the duty to protect the welfare of the people entrusted to their care and to conduct such grave matters soberly.

But it is one thing to undertake military action for the just defense of the people, and something else again to seek the subjugation of other nations. Nor does the possession of war potential make every military or political use of it lawful. Neither does the mere fact that war has unhappily begun mean that all is fair between the warring parties.

Those who are pledged to the service of their country as members of its armed forces should regard themselves as agents of security and freedom on behalf of their people. As long as they fulfill this role properly, they are making a genuine contribution to the establishment of peace.

Total War

80. The horror and perversity of war are immensely magnified by the multiplication of scientific weapons. For acts of war involving these weapons can inflict massive and indiscriminate destruction far exceeding the bounds of legitimate defense. Indeed, if the kind of instruments which can now be found in the armories of the great nations were to be employed to their fullest, an almost total and altogether reciprocal slaughter of each side by the other would follow, not to mention the widespread devastation which would take place in the world and the deadly aftereffects which would be spawned by the use of such weapons.

All these considerations compel us to undertake an evaluation of war with an entirely new attitude.[165] The men of our time must realize that they will have to give a somber reckoning for their deeds of war. For the course of the future will depend largely on the decisions they make today.

With these truths in mind, this most holy Synod makes its own the condemnations of total war already pronounced by recent Popes,[166] and issues the following declaration:

Any act of war aimed indiscriminately at the destruction of entire cities or of extensive areas along with their population is a crime against God and man himself. It merits unequivocal and unhesitating condemnation.

The unique hazard of modern warfare consists in this: it provides those who possess modern scientific weapons with a kind of occasion for perpetrating just such abominations. Moreover, through a certain inexorable chain of events, it can urge men on to the most atrocious decisions. That such in fact may never happen in the future, the bishops of the whole world, in unity assembled, beg all men, especially government officials and military leaders, to give unremitting thought to the awesome responsibility which is theirs before God and the entire human race.

The Arms Race

81. Scientific weapons, to be sure, are not amassed solely for use in war. The defensive strength of any nation is considered to be dependent upon its capacity for immediate retaliation against an adversary. Hence this accumulation of arms, which increases each year, also serves, in a way heretofore unknown, as a deterrent to possible enemy attack. Many regard this state of affairs as the most effective way by which peace of a sort can be maintained between nations at the present time.

Whatever be the case with this method of deterrence, men should be convinced that the arms race in which so many countries are engaged is not a safe way to preserve a steady peace. Nor is the so-called balance resulting from this race a sure and authentic peace. Rather than being eliminated thereby, the causes of war threaten to grow gradually stronger.

While extravagant sums are being spent for the furnishing of ever new weapons, an adequate remedy cannot be provided for the multiple miseries afflicting the whole modern world. Disagreements between nations are not really and radically healed. On the contrary other parts of the world are infected with them. New approaches initiated by reformed attitudes must be adopted to remove this trap and to restore genuine peace by emancipating the world from its crushing anxiety.

Therefore, it must be said again: the arms race is an utterly treacherous trap for humanity, and one which injures the poor to an intolerable degree. It is much to be feared that if this race persists, it will eventually spawn all the lethal ruin whose path it is now making ready.

Warned by the calamities which the human race has made possible, let us make use of the interlude granted us from above and in which we rejoice. In greater awareness of our own responsibility let us find means for resolving our disputes in a manner more worthy of man. Divine Providence urgently demands of us that we free ourselves from the age-old slavery of war. But if we refuse to make this effort, we do not know where the evil road we have ventured upon will lead us.

The Total Banning of War, and International Action for Avoiding War

82. It is our clear duty, then, to strain every muscle as we work for the time when all war can be completely outlawed by international consent. This goal undoubtedly requires the establishment of some universal public authority acknowledged as such by all, and endowed with effective power to safeguard, on the behalf of all, security, regard for justice, and respect for rights.

But before this hoped-for authority can be set up, the highest existing international centers must devote themselves vigorously to the pursuit of better means for obtaining common security. Peace must be born of mutual trust between nations rather than imposed on them through fear of one another's weapons. Hence everyone must labor to put an end at last to the arms race, and to make a true beginning of disarmament, not indeed a unilateral disarmament, but one proceeding at an equal pace according to agreement, and backed up by authentic and workable safeguards.[167]

In the meantime, efforts which have already been made

and are still under way to eliminate the danger of war are not to be underrated. On the contrary, support should be given to the good will of the very many leaders who work hard to do away with war, which they abominate. Though burdened by the enormous preoccupations of their high office, these men are nonetheless motivated by the very grave peacemaking task to which they are bound, even if they cannot ignore the complexity of matters as they stand.

We should fervently ask God to give these men the strength to go forward perseveringly and to follow through courageously on this work of building peace with vigor. It is a work of supreme love for mankind. Today it most certainly demands that these leaders extend their thoughts and their spirit beyond the confines of their own nation, that they put aside national selfishness and ambition to dominate other nations, and that they nourish a profound reverence for the whole of humanity, which is already making its way so laboriously toward greater unity.

The problems of peace and of disarmament have already been the subject of extensive, strenuous, and relentless examination. Together with international meetings dealing with these problems, such studies should be regarded as the first steps toward solving these serious questions. They should be promoted with even greater urgency in the hope that they will yield practical results in the future.

Nevertheless, men should take heed not to entrust themselves only to the efforts of others, while remaining careless about their own attitudes. For government officials, who must simultaneously guarantee the good of their own people and promote the universal good, depend on public opinion and feeling to the greatest possible extent. It does them no good to work at building peace so long as feelings of hostility, contempt, and distrust, as well as racial hatred and unbending ideologies, continue to divide men and place them in opposing camps.

Hence arises a surpassing need for renewed education of attitudes and for new inspiration in the area of public opinion. Those who are dedicated to the work of education, particularly of the young, or who mold public opinion, should regard as their most weighty task the effort to instruct all in fresh sentiments of peace. Indeed, every one of us should have a change of heart as we regard the entire world and those tasks which we can perform in unison for the betterment of our race.

But we should not let false hope deceive us. For enmities and hatred must be put away and firm, honest agreements concerning world peace reached in the future. Otherwise, for all its marvelous knowledge, humanity, which is already in the middle of a grave crisis, will perhaps be brought to that mournful hour in which it will experience no peace other than the dreadful peace of death.

But, while we say this, the Church of Christ takes her stand in the midst of the anxiety of this age, and does not cease to hope with the utmost confidence. She intends to propose to our age over and over again, in season and out of season, this apostolic message: "Behold, now is the acceptable time" for a change of heart; "behold, now is the day of salvation!"[168]

SECTION 2: BUILDING UP THE INTERNATIONAL COMMUNITY

The Causes and Cures of Discord

83. If peace is to be established, the primary requisite is to eradicate the causes of dissension between men. Wars thrive on these, especially on injustice. Many of these causes stem from excessive economic inequalities and from excessive slowness in applying the needed remedies. Other causes spring from a quest for power and from contempt for personal rights. If we are looking for deeper explanations, we can find them in human jealousy, distrust, pride, and other egotistic passions.

Man cannot tolerate so many breakdowns in right order. What results is that the world is ceaselessly infected with arguments between men and acts of violence, even when war is not raging. Moreover, these same evils are found in relationships between nations. Hence, if such evils are to be overcome or prevented, and violence kept from becoming unbridled, it is altogether necessary that international institutions cooperate to a better and surer extent and that they be coordinated. Also, unwearying efforts must be made to create agencies for the promotion of peace.

The Community of Nations and International Organizations

84. Today the bonds of mutual dependence become increasingly close between all citizens and all the peoples of the world. The universal common good needs to be intelligently pursued and more effectively achieved. Hence it is now necessary for the family of nations to create for themselves an order which corresponds to modern obligations, particularly with reference to those numerous regions still laboring under intolerable need.

For the attainment of these goals, agencies of the international community should do their part to provide for the various necessities of men. In the field of social life this means food, health, education, and employment. In certain situations which can obtain anywhere, it means the general need to promote the growth of developing nations, to attend to the hardships of refugees scattered throughout the world, or to assist migrants and their families.

The international agencies, both universal and regional, which already exist assuredly deserve well of the human race. These stand forth as the first attempts to lay international foundations under the whole human community for the solving of the critical problems of our age, the promotion of global progress, and the prevention of any kind of war. The Church rejoices at the spirit of true fraternity flourishing between Christians and non-Christians in all these areas. This spirit strives to see that ever more intense efforts are made for the relief of the world's enormous miseries.

International Cooperation at the Economic Level

85. The modern interconnection between men also demands the establishment of greater international cooperation in the economic field. For although nearly all peoples have gained their independence, it is still far from true that they are free from excessive inequalities and from every form of undue dependence, or that they have put behind them danger of serious internal difficulties.

The development of any nation depends on human and financial assistance. Through education and professional formation, the citizens of each nation should be prepared to shoulder the various offices of economic and social life. Such preparation needs the help of foreign experts. When they render assistance these experts should do so not in a lordly fashion, but as helpers and co-workers.

The developing nations will be unable to procure the necessary material assistance unless the practices of the modern business world undergo a profound change. Additional help should be offered by advanced nations, in the form of either grants or investments. These offers should be made generously and without avarice. They should be accepted honorably.

If an economic order is to be created which is genuine and universal, there must be an abolition of excessive desire for profit, nationalistic pretensions, the lust for political domination, militaristic thinking, and intrigues designed to spread and impose ideologies.

Proposals are made in favor of numerous economic and social systems. It is to be hoped that experts in such affairs will find common bases for a healthy world trade. This hope will be more readily realized if individuals put aside their personal prejudices and show that they are prepared to undertake sincere discussions.

Some Useful Norms

86. The following norms would seem to be appropriate for this cooperation:

a) Developing nations should strongly desire to seek the complete human fulfillment of their citizens as the explicit and fixed goal of progress. Let them be mindful that progress begins and develops primarily from the efforts and endowments of the people themselves. Hence, instead of depending solely on outside help, they should rely chiefly on the full unfolding of their own resources and the cultivation of their own qualities and tradition. Those who have greater influence on others should be outstanding in this respect.

b) As for the advanced nations, they have a very heavy obligation to help the developing peoples in the discharge of the aforementioned responsibilities. If this world-wide collaboration is to be established, certain psychological and material adjustments will be needed among the advanced nations and should be brought about.

Thus these nations should carefully consider the welfare of weaker and poorer nations when negotiating with them. For such nations need for their own livelihood the income derived from the sale of domestic products.

c) The international community should see to the coordination and stimulation of economic growth. These objectives must be pursued in such a way, however, that the resources organized for this purpose can be shared as effectively and justly as possible. This same community should regulate economic relations throughout the world so that they can unfold in a way which is fair. In so doing, however, the community should honor the principle of subsidiarity.

Let adequate organizations be established for fostering and harmonizing international trade, especially with respect to the less advanced countries, and for repairing the deficiencies caused by an excessive disproportion in the power possessed by various nations. Such regulatory activity, combined with technical, cultural, and financial help, ought to afford the needed assistance to nations striving for progress, enabling them to achieve economic growth expeditiously.

d) In many instances there exists a pressing need to reform economic and social structures. But nations must beware of technical solutions immaturely proposed, especially those which offer men material advantages while militating against his spiritual nature and development. For, "Not by bread alone does man live, but by every word that comes forth from the mouth of God" (Mt. 4:4). Each branch of the human family possesses in itself and in its worthier traditions some part of the spiritual treasure entrusted by God to humanity, even though many do not know the source of this treasure.

International Cooperation in the Matter of Population

87. International cooperation becomes supremely necessary

with respect to those peoples who, in addition to many other problems, are today often enough burdened in a special way with the difficulties stemming from a rapid population growth. There is an urgent need for all nations, especially the richer ones, to cooperate fully and intensely in an exploration as to how there can be prepared and distributed to the human community whatever is required for the livelihood and proper training of men. Some peoples, indeed, would greatly better their conditions of life if they could be duly trained to abandon ancient methods of farming in favor of modern techniques. With necessary prudence they should adapt these techniques to their own situations. In addition they need to establish a better social order and regulate the distribution of land with greater fairness.

Within the limits of their own competence, government officials have rights and duties with regard to the population problems of their own nation, for instance, in the matter of social legislation as it affects families, of migration to cities, of information relative to the condition and needs of the nation. Since the minds of men are so powerfully disturbed about this problem, the Council also desires that, especially in universities, Catholic experts in all these aspects should skillfully pursue their studies and projects and give them an ever wider scope.

Many people assert that it is absolutely necessary for population growth to be radically reduced everywhere or at least in certain nations. They say this must be done by every possible means and by every kind of government intervention. Hence this Council exhorts all to beware against solutions contradicting the moral law, solutions which have been promoted publicly or privately, and sometimes actually imposed.

For in view of the inalienable human right to marry and beget children, the question of how many children should be born belongs to the honest judgment of parents. The question can in no way be committed to the decision of government. Now since the judgment of the parents supposes a rightly formed conscience, it is highly important that everyone be given the opportunity to practice upright and truly human responsibility. This responsibility respects the divine law and takes account of circumstances and the times. It requires that educational and social conditions in various places be changed for the better, and especially that religious instruction or at least full moral training be provided.

Human beings should also be judiciously informed of scientific advances in the exploration of methods by which spouses can be helped in arranging the number of their children. The reliability of these methods should be adequately proven and their harmony with the moral order should be clear.

The Duty of Christians to Provide Support

88. Christians should collaborate willingly and whole-heartedly in establishing an international order involving genuine respect for all freedoms and amicable brotherhood between all men. This objective is all the more pressing since the greater part of the world is still suffering from so much poverty that it is as if Christ Himself were crying out in these poor to beg the charity of the disciples.

Some nations with a majority of citizens who are counted as Christians have an abundance of this world's goods, while others are deprived of the necessities of life and are tormented with hunger, disease, and every kind of misery. This situation must not be allowed to continue, to the scandal of humanity. For the spirit of poverty and of charity are the glory and authentication of the Church of Christ.

Christians, especially young people, are to be praised and supported, therefore, when they volunteer their services to help other men and nations. Indeed, it is the duty of the whole People of God, following the word and example of the bishops, to do their utmost to alleviate the sufferings of the modern age. As was the ancient custom in the Church, they should meet this obligation out of the substance of their goods, and not only out of what is superfluous.

Without being inflexible and completely uniform, the collection and distribution of aid should be conducted in an orderly fashion in dioceses, nations, and throughout the entire world. (Wherever it seems appropriate, this activity of Catholics should be carried on in unison with other Christian brothers.) For the spirit of charity does not forbid but rather requires that charitable activity be exercised in a provident and orderly manner. Therefore, it is essential for those who intend to dedicate themselves to the service of the developing nations to be properly trained in suitable institutions.

Effective Presence of the Church on the International Scene

89. In pursuit of her divine mission, the Church preaches the gospel to all men and dispenses the treasures of grace. Thus, by imparting knowledge of the divine and natural law, she everywhere contributes to strengthening peace and to placing brotherly relations between individuals and peoples on solid ground. Therefore, to encourage and stimulate cooperation among men, the Church must be thoroughly present in the midst of the community of nations. She must achieve such a presence both through her public institutions and through the full and sincere collaboration of all Christians, a collaboration motivated solely by the desire to be of service to all.

This goal will come about more effectively if the faithful themselves, conscious of their responsibility as men and as Christians, strive to stir up in their own area of influence a willingness to cooperate readily with the international community. In both religious and civic education, special care must be given to the proper formation of youth in this respect.

The Role of Christians in International Institutions

90. An outstanding form of international activity on the part of Christians undoubtedly consists in the cooperative effort which, as individuals and in groups, they make to institutes established for the encouragement of cooperation among nations. The same is true of their efforts to establish such agencies. There are also various international Catholic associations which can serve in many ways to construct a peaceful and fraternal community of nations. These deserve to be strengthened by an increase in the number of well-qualified associates and in the needed resources. Let them be fortified too by a suitable coordination of their energies. For

today effective action as well as the need for dialogue demand joint projects.

Moreover, such associations contribute much to the development of a universal outlook—something certainly appropriate for Catholics. They also help to form an awareness of genuine universal solidarity and responsibility.

Finally, this Council desires that by way of fulfilling their role properly in the international community, Catholics should seek to cooperate actively and in a positive manner both with their separated brothers, who together with them profess the gospel of love, and with all men thirsting for true peace.

In view of the immense hardships which still afflict the majority of men today, the Council regards it as most opportune that some agency of the universal Church be set up for the world-wide promotion of justice for the poor and of Christ's kind of love for them. The role of such an organization will be to stimulate the Catholic community to foster progress in needy regions, and social justice on the international scene.

CONCLUSION

The Role of Individual Believers and Dioceses

91. Drawn from the treasures of Church teaching, the proposals of this sacred Synod look to the assistance of every man of our time, whether he believes in God, or does not explicitly recognize Him. Their purpose is to help men gain a sharper insight into their full destiny, so that they can fashion the world more to man's surpassing dignity, search for a brotherhood which is universal and more deeply rooted, and meet the urgencies of our age with a gallant and unified effort born of love.

Undeniably this conciliar program is but a general one in several of its parts—and deliberately so, given the immense variety of situations and forms of human culture in the world. Indeed, while it presents teaching already accepted in the Church, the program will have to be further pursued and amplified, since it often deals with matters in a constant state of development. Still, we have relied on the Word of God and the spirit of the gospel. Hence we entertain the hope that many of our proposals will be able to bring substantial benefit to everyone, especially after they have been adapted to individual nations and mentalities by the faithful, under the guidance of their pastors.

Dialogue Between All Men

92. By virtue of her mission to shed on the whole world the radiance of the gospel message, and to unify under one Spirit all men of whatever nation, race, or culture, the Church stands forth as a sign of that brotherliness which allows honest dialogue and invigorates it.

Such a mission requires in the first place that we foster within the Church herself mutual esteem, reverence, and harmony, through the full recognition of lawful diversity. Thus all those who compose the one People of God, both pastors and the general faithful, can engage in dialogue with ever-abounding fruitfulness. For the bonds which unite the faithful are mightier than anything which divides them. Hence, let there be unity in what is necessary, freedom in what is unsettled, and charity in any case.

Our hearts embrace also those brothers and communities not yet living with us in full communion. To them we are linked nonetheless by our profession of the Father and the Son and the Holy Spirit, and by the bond of charity. We are mindful that the unity of Christians is today awaited and desired by many, too, who do not believe in Christ. For the further it advances toward truth and love under the powerful impulse of the Holy Spirit, the more this unity will be a harbinger of unity and peace for the world at large.

Therefore, by common effort and in ways which are today increasingly appropriate for seeking this splendid goal effectively, let us take pains to pattern ourselves after the gospel more exactly every day, and thus work as brothers in rendering service to the human family. For in Christ Jesus this family is called into the family of the sons of God.

We also turn our thoughts to all who acknowledge God, and who preserve in their traditions precious elements of religion and humanity. We want frank conversation to compel us all to receive the inspirations of the Spirit faithfully and to measure up to them energetically.

For our part, the desire for such dialogue, which can lead to truth through love alone, excludes no one, though an appropriate measure of prudence must undoubtedly be exercised. We include those who cultivate beautiful qualities of the human spirit, but do not yet acknowledge the Source of these qualities.

We include those who oppress the Church and harass her in manifold ways. Since God the Father is the origin and purpose of all men, we are all called to be brothers. Therefore, if we have been summoned to the same destiny, which is both human and divine, we can and we should work together without violence and deceit in order to build up the world in genuine peace.

Building Up the World and Fulfilling Its Purpose

93. Mindful of the Lord's saying: "By this will all men know that you are my disciples, if you have love for one another" (Jn. 13:35), Christians cannot yearn for anything more ardently than to serve the men of the modern world ever more generously and effectively. Therefore, holding faithfully to the gospel and benefiting from its resources, and united with every man who loves and practices justice, Christians have shouldered a gigantic task demanding fulfillment in this world. Concerning this task they must give a reckoning to Him who will judge every man on the last day.

Not everyone who cries, "Lord, Lord," will enter into the kingdom of heaven, but those who do the Father's will and take a strong grip on the work at hand. Now, the Father wills that in all men we recognize Christ our brother and love Him effectively in word and in deed. By thus giving witness to the truth, we will share with others the mystery of the heavenly Father's love. As a consequence, men throughout the world will be aroused to a lively hope—the gift of the Holy Spirit—that they will finally be caught up in peace and utter happiness in that fatherland radiant with the splendor of the Lord.

"Now, to him who is able to accomplish all things in a

measure far beyond what we ask or conceive, in keeping with
the power that is at work in us—to him be glory in the
Church and in Christ Jesus down through all the ages of
time without end. Amen" (Eph. 3:20–21).

Each and every one of the things set forth in this Pastoral
Constitution has won the consent of the Fathers of this most
sacred Council. We too, by the apostolic authority conferred
on us by Christ, join with the Venerable Fathers in approving, decreeing, and establishing these things in the Holy
Spirit, and we direct that what has thus been enacted in
synod be published to God's glory.

Rome, at St. Peter's, December 7, 1965

I, Paul, Bishop of the Catholic Church

NOTES

1. The pastoral constitution De Ecclesia in Mundo Huius Tem-
poris is made up of two parts; yet it constitutes an organic unity.

By way of explanation: the constitution is called "pastoral" because, while resting on doctrinal principles, it seeks to express the
relation of the Church to the world and modern mankind. The result is that, on the one hand, a pastoral slant is present in the first
part, and, on the other hand, a doctrinal slant is present in the second part.

In the first part, the Church develops her teaching on man, on
the world which is the enveloping context of man's existence, and
on man's relations to his fellow men. In part two, the Church gives
closer consideration to various aspects of modern life and human society; special consideration is given to those questions and problems
which, in this general area, seem to have a greater urgency in our
day. As a result, in part two the subject matter which is viewed in
the light of doctrinal principles is made up of diverse elements.
Some elements have a permanent value; others, only a transitory
one.

Consequently, the Constitution must be interpreted according to
the general norms of theological interpretation. Interpreters must
bear in mind—especially in part two—the changeable circumstances
which the subject matter, by its very nature, involves.

2. Cf. Jn. 18:37; Mt. 10:28; Mk. 10:45.

3. Cf. Rom. 7:14ff.

4. Cf. 2 Cor. 5:15.

5. Cf. Acts 4:12.

6. Cf. Heb. 13:8.

7. Cf. Col. 1:15.

8. Cf. Gen. 1:26; Wis. 2:23.

9. Cf. Eccl. (Sir.) 17:3–10.

10. Cf. Rom. 1:21–25.

11. Cf. Jn. 8:34.

12. Cf. Dan. 3:57–90.

13. Cf. 1 Cor. 6:13–20.

14. Cf. 1 Kg. 16:7; Jer. 17:10.

15. Cf. Eccl. (Sir.) 17:7–8.

16. Cf. Rom. 2:15–16.

17. Cf. Pius XII, radio address on the correct formation of a Christian conscience in the young, Mar. 23, 1952: AAS (1952), p. 271.

18. Cf. Mt. 22:37–40; Gal. 5:14.

19. Cf. Eccl. (Sir.) 15:14.

20. Cf. 2 Cor. 5:10.

21. Cf. Wis. 1:13; 2:23–24; Rom. 5:21; 6:23; Jas. 1:15.

22. Cf. 1 Cor. 15:56–57.

23. Cf. Pius XI, encyclical letter *Divini Redemptoris*, March 19, 1937: AAS 29 (1937), pp. 65–106; Pius XII, encyclical letter *Ad Apostolorum Principis*, June 29, 1958: AAS 50 (1958), pp. 601–614; John XXIII, encyclical letter *Mater et Magistra*, May 15, 1961: AAS 35 (1961), pp. 451–453; Paul VI, encyclical letter *Ecclesiam Suam*, Aug. 6, 1964: AAS 56 (1964), pp. 651–653.

24. Cf. Second Vatican Council, dogmatic constitution *Lumen Gentium*, Chap. I, Art. 8: AAS 57 (1965), p. 12.

25. Cf. Phil. 1:27.

26. St. Augustine, *Confessions* I, 1: PL 32, 661.

27. Cf. Rom. 5:14. Cf. Tertullian, *De carnis resurrectione* 6: "The shape that the slime of the earth was given was intended with a view to Christ, the future man.": p. 2, 282; CSEL 47, p. 33, l. 12–13.

28. Cf. 2 Cor. 4:4.

29. Cf. Second Council of Constantinople, can. 7: "The divine Word was not changed into a human nature, nor was a human nature absorbed by the Word." Denz. 219 (428). Cf. also Third Council of Constantinople: "For just as His most holy and immaculate human nature, though deified, was not destroyed (Theotheisa ouk anerethe), but rather remained in its proper state and mode of being": Denz. 291 (556). Cf. Council of Chalcedon: "to be acknowledged in two natures, without confusion, change, division, or separation." Denz. 148 (302).

30. Cf. Third Council of Constantinople: "and so His human will, though deified, is not destroyed": Denz. 291 (556).

31. Cf. Heb. 4:15.

32. Cf. 2 Cor. 5:18–19; Col. 1:20–22.

33. Cf. 1 Pet. 2:21; Mt. 16:24; Lk. 14:27.

34. Cf. Rom. 8:29; Col. 3:10–14.

35. Cf. Rom. 8:1–11.

36. Cf. 2 Cor. 4:14.

37. Cf. Phil. 3:19; Rom. 8:17.

38. Cf. Second Vatican Council, dogmatic constitution *Lumen Gentium*, Chap. II, Art. 16: AAS 57 (1965), p. 20.

39. Cf. Rom. 8:32.

40. Cf. the Byzantine Easter Liturgy.

41. Cf. Rom. 8:15 and Gal. 4:6; cf. also Jn. 1:22 and Jn. 3:1–2.

42. Cf. John XXIII, encyclical letter *Mater et Magistra*, May 15, 1961: AAS 53 (1961), pp. 401–464, and encyclical letter *Pacem in Terris*, Apr. 11, 1963: AAS 55 (1963), pp. 257–304; Paul VI, encyclical letter *Ecclesiam Suam*, Aug. 6, 1964: AAS 54 (1964), pp. 609–659.

43. Cf. Lk. 17:33.

44. Cf. St. Thomas, 1 *Ethica Lect.* 1.

45. Cf. John XXIII, encyclical letter *Mater et Magistra*: AAS 53 (1961), p. 418. Cf. also Pius XI, encyclical letter *Quadragesimo Anno*: AAS 23 (1931), pp. 222ff.

46. Cf. John XXIII, encyclical letter *Mater et Magistra*: AAS 53 (1961).

47. Cf. Mk. 2:27.

48. Cf. John XXIII, encyclical letter *Pacem in Terris*: AAS 55 (1963), p. 266.

49. Cf. Jas. 2:15–16.

50. Cf. Lk. 16:18–31.

51. Cf. John XXIII, encyclical letter *Pacem in Terris*: AAS 55 (1963), pp. 299 and 300.

52. Cf. Lk. 6:37–38; Mt. 7:1–2; Rom. 2:1–11; 14:10; 14:10–12.

53. Cf. Mt. 5:43–47.

54. Cf. dogmatic constitution *Lumen Gentium*, Chap. II, Art. 9: AAS 57 (1965), pp. 12–13.

55. Cf. Ex. 24:1–8.

56. Cf. Gen. 1:26–27; 9:3; Wis. 9:3.

57. Cf. Ps. 8:7 and 10.

58. Cf. John XXIII, encyclical letter *Pacem in Terris*: AAS 55 (1963), p. 297.

59. Cf. *Message to All Mankind* sent by the Fathers at the beginning of the Second Vatican Council, Oct. 20, 1962: AAS 54 (1962), p. 823.

60. Cf. Paul VI, address to the diplomatic corps, Jan. 7, 1965: AAS 57 (1965), p. 232.

61. Cf. First Vatican Council, *Dogmatic Constitution on the Catholic Faith*, Chap. III: Denz. 1785–1786 (3004–3005).

62. Cf. Msgr. Pio Paschini, *Vita e opere di Galileo Galilei*, 2 volumes, Vatican Press (1964).

63. Cf. Mt. 24:13; 13:24–30 and 36–43.

64. Cf. 2 Cor. 6:10.

65. Cf. Jn. 1:3 and 14.

66. Cf. Eph. 1:10.

67. Cf. Jn. 3:16; Rom. 5:8.

68. Cf. Acts 2:36; Mt. 28:18.

69. Cf. Rom. 15:16.

70. Cf. Acts 1:7.

71. Cf. 1 Cor. 7:31; St. Irenaeus, *Adversus haereses*, V, 36, PG, VIII, 1221.

72. Cf. 2 Cor. 5:2; 2 Pet. 3:13.

73. Cf. 1 Cor. 2:9; Apoc. 21:4–5.

74. Cf. 1 Cor. 15:42 and 53.

75. Cf. 1 Cor. 13:8; 3:14.

76. Cf. Rom. 8:19–21.

77. Cf. Lk. 9:25.

78. Cf. Pius XI, encyclical letter *Quadragesimo Anno*: AAS 23 (1931), p. 207.

79. Preface of the Feast of Christ the King.

80. Cf. Paul VI, encyclical letter *Ecclesiam Suam*, III, AAS 56 (1964), pp. 637–659.

81. Cf. Tit. 3:4: "love of mankind."

82. Cf. Eph. 1:3; 5:6, 13–14, 23.

83. Second Vatican Council, dogmatic constitution *Lumen Gentium*, Chap. I, Art. 8: AAS 57 (1965), p. 12.

84. *Ibid.*, Chap. II, Art. 9: AAS 57 (1965), p. 14; cf. Art. 8: AAS loc. cit., p. 11.

85. *Ibid.*, Chap. I, Art. 8: AAS 57 (1965), p. 11.

86. Cf. *ibid.*, Chap. IV, Art. 38: AAS 57 (1965), p. 43 with note 120.

87. Cf. Rom. 8:14–17.

88. Cf. Mt. 22:39.

89. Dogmatic constitution *Lumen Gentium*, Chap. II, Art. 9: AAS 57 (1956), pp. 12–14.

90. Cf. Pius XII, Address to the International Union of Institutes of Archeology, History and History of Art, Mar. 9, 1956: AAS 48 (1965), p. 212: "Its divine Founder, Jesus Christ, has not given it any mandate or fixed any end of the cultural order. The goal which Christ assigns to it is strictly religious. . . . The Church must lead men to God, in order that they may be given over to him without reserve. . . . The Church can never lose sight of the strictly religious, supernatural goal. The meaning of all its activities, down to the last canon of its code, can only cooperate directly or indirectly in this goal."

91. Dogmatic constitution *Lumen Gentium*, Chap. I, Art. 1: AAS 57 (1965), p. 5.

92. Cf. Heb. 13:14.

93. Cf. 2 Th. 3:6–13; Eph. 4:28.

94. Cf. Is. 58:1–12.

95. Cf. Mt. 23:3–23; Mk. 7:10–13.

96. Cf. John XXIII, encyclical letter *Mater et Magistra*, IV: AAS 53 (1961), pp. 456–457; cf. I: AAS loc. cit., pp. 407, 410–411.

97. Cf. dogmatic constitution *Lumen Gentium*, Chap. III, Art. 28: AAS 57 (1965), p. 35.

98. *Ibid.*, Art. 28: AAS loc. cit., pp. 35–36.

99. Cf. St. Ambrose, *De virginitate*, Chap. VIII, Art. 48: ML 16, 278.

100. Cf. dogmatic constitution *Lumen Gentium*, Chap. II, Art. 15: AAS 57 (1965), p. 20.

101. Cf. dogmatic constitution *Lumen Gentium*, Chap. II, Art. 13: AAS 57 (1965), p. 17.

102. Cf. Justin, *Dialogus cum Tryphone*, Chap. 100; MG 6, 729 (ed. Otto), 1897, pp. 391–393: ". . . but the greater the number of persecutions which are inflicted upon us, so much the greater the number of other men who become devout believers through the name of Jesus." Cf. Tertullian *Apologeticus*, Chap. L, 13: "Every time you mow us down like grass, we increase in number: the blood of Christians is a seed!" Cf. dogmatic constitution *Lumen Gentium*, Chap. II, Art. 9: AAS 57 (1965), p. 14.

103. Cf. dogmatic constitution *Lumen Gentium*, Chap. II, Art. 15: AAS 57 (1965), p. 20.

104. Cf. Paul VI, address given on Feb. 3, 1965.

105. Cf. St. Augustine, *De bono coniugii*: PL 40, 375–76 and 394; St. Thomas, *Summa Theol.*, Suppl. Quaest. 49, Art. 3 ad 1; *Decretum pro Armenis*: Denz.-Schoen. 1327; Pius XI, encyclical letter *Casti Connubii*: AAS 22 (1930), pp. 547–548; Denz.-Schoen. 3703–3714.

106. Cf. Pius XI, encyclical letter *Casti Connubii*: AAS 22 (1930), pp. 546–547; Denz.-Schoen. 3706.

107. Cf. Os. 2; Jer. 3, 6–13; Ezek. 16 and 23; Is. 54.

108. Cf. Mt. 9:15; Mk. 2:19–20; Lk. 5:34–35; Jn. 3:29; cf. also 2 Cor. 11:2; Eph. 5:27; Apoc. 19:7–8; 21:2 and 9.

109. Cf. Eph. 5:25.

110. Cf. Second Vatican Council, dogmatic constitution *Lumen Gentium*: AAS 57 (1965), pp. 15–16; 40–41; 47.

111. Pius XI, encyclical letter *Casti Connubii*: AAS 22 (1930), p. 583.

112. Cf. 1 Tim. 5:3.

113. Cf. Eph. 5:32.

114. Cf. Gen. 2:22–24; Pr. 5:15–20; 31:10–31; Tob. 8:4–8; Cant. 1:2–3; 1:16; 4:16; 5:1; 7:8–14; 1 Cor. 7:3–6; Eph. 5:25–33.

115. Cf. Pius XI, encyclical letter *Casti Connubii*: AAS 22 (1930), p. 547 and 548; Denz.-Schoen. 3707.

116. Cf. 1 Cor. 7:5.

117. Cf. Pius XII, Address *Tra le viste*, Jan. 20, 1958: AAS 50 (1958), p. 91.

118. Cf. Pius XI, encyclical letter *Casti Connubii*: AAS 22 (1930), Denz.-Schoen., 3716–3718; Pius XII, *Allocutio Conventui Unionis Italicae inter Obstetrices*, Oct. 29, 1951: AAS 43 (1951), pp. 835–854; Paul VI, address to a group of cardinals, June 23, 1964: AAS 56 (1964), pp. 581–589. Certain questions which need further and more careful investigation have been handed over, at the command of the supreme Pontiff, to a commission for the study of population, family, and births, in order that, after it fulfills its function, the Supreme Pontiff may pass judgment. With the doctrine of the magisterium in this state, this holy Synod does not intend to propose immediately concrete solutions. (In the Latin text this is footnote 14 of Chap. I, in Part 2 of the document. —Ed.)

119. Cf. Eph. 5:16; Col. 4:5.

120. Cf. *Sacramentarium Gregorianum*: PL 78, 262.

121. Cf. Rom. 5:15 and 18; 6:5–11; Gal. 2:20.

122. Cf. Eph. 5:25–27.

123. Cf. introductory statement of this Constitution, Art. 4ff.

124. Cf. Col. 3:1–2.

125. Cf. Gen. 1:28.

126. Cf. Pr. 8:30–31.

127. Cf. St. Irenaeus, *Adversus haereses*: III, 11, 8 (ed. Sagnard, p. 200; cf. *ibid.*, 16, 6: pp. 290–292; 21, 10–22: pp. 370–372; 22, 3: p. 378; etc.).

128. Cf. Eph. 1:10.

129. Cf. the words of Pius XI to Father M. D. Roland-Gosselin: "It is necessary never to lose sight of the fact that the objective of the Church is to evangelize, not to civilize. If it civilizes, it is for the sake of evangelization" (Semaines sociales de France, Versailles, 1936, pp. 461–462).

130. First Vatican Council, *Constitution on the Catholic Faith*: Denz. 1795, 1799 (3015, 3019). Cf. Pius XI, encyclical letter *Quadragesimo Anno*: AAS 23 (1931), p. 190.

131. Cf. John XXIII, encyclical letter *Pacem in Terris*: AAS 55 (1963), p. 260.

132. Cf. John XXIII, encyclical letter: *Pacem in Terris*: AAS 55 (1963), p. 283; Pius XII, radio address, Dec. 24, 1941: AAS 34 (1942), pp. 16–17.

133. John XXIII, encyclical letter *Pacem in Terris*: AAS 55 (1963), p. 260.

134. Cf. John XXIII, speech delivered on Oct. 11, 1962, at the beginning of the Council: AAS 54 (1962), p. 792.

135. Cf. *Constitution on the Sacred Liturgy*, Art. 123, AAS 56

(1964), p. 131; Paul VI, discourse to the artists of Rome: AAS 56 (1964), pp. 439–442.

136. Cf. Second Vatican Council, Decree on Priestly Formation and Declaration on Christian Education.

137. Cf. dogmatic constitution Lumen Gentium, Chap. IV, Art. 37: AAS 57 (1965), pp. 42–43.

138. Cf. Pius XII, address on Mar. 23, 1952: AAS 44 (1952), p. 273; John XXIII, allocution to the Catholic Association of Italian Workers, May 1, 1959: AAS 51 (1959), p. 358.

139. Cf. Pius XI, encyclical letter Quadragesimo Anno: AAS 23 (1931), pp. 190ff; Pius XII, address of Mar. 23, 1952: AAS 44 (1952), pp. 276ff; John XXIII encyclical letter Mater et Magistra: AAS 53 (1961), p. 450; Vatican Council II, Decree Inter Mirifica (On the Instruments of Social Communication), Chapter I, Art. 6: AAS 56 (1964), p. 147.

140. Cf. Mt. 16:26; Lk. 16:1–31; Col. 3:17.

141. Cf. Leo XIII, encyclical letter Libertas, in Acta Leonis XIII; t. VIII, pp. 220ff; Pius XI, encyclical letter Quadragesimo Anno: AAS 23 (1931), pp. 191ff; Pius XI, encyclical letter Divini Redemptoris: AAS 39 (1937), pp. 65ff; Pius XII, Christmas message, 1941: AAS 34 (1942), pp. 10ff; John XXIII, encyclical letter Mater et Magistra: AAS 53 (1961), pp. 401–464.

142. In reference to agricultural problems cf. especially John XXIII, encyclical letter Mater et Magistra: AAS 53 (1961), pp. 341ff.

143. Cf. Leo XIII, encyclical letter Rerum Novarum: AAS 23 (1890–91), p. 649, p. 662; Pius XI, encyclical letter Quadragesimo Anno: AAS 23 (1931), pp. 200–201; Pius XI, encyclical letter Divini Redemptoria: AAS 29 (1937), p. 92; Pius XII, radio address on Christmas Eve, 1942: AAS 35 (1943), p. 20; Pius XII, allocution of June 13, 1943, AAS 35, p.172; Pius XII, radio address to the workers of Spain, Mar. 11, 1951: AAS 43 (1951), p. 215; John XXIII, encyclical letter Mater et Magistra: AAS 53 (1961), p. 419.

144. Cf. John XXIII, encyclical letter Mater et Magistra: AAS 53 (1961), pp. 408, 424, 427; however, the word "curatione" has been taken from the Latin text of the encyclical letter Quadragesimo Anno: AAS 23 (1931), p. 199. Under the aspect of the evolution of the question cf. also: Pius XII, allocution of June 3, 1950; AAS 42 (1950), pp. 485–488; Paul VI, allocution of June 8, 1964: AAS 56 (1964), pp. 574–579.

145. Cf. Pius XII, encyclical Sertum Laetitiae: AAS 31 (1939), p. 642; John XXIII, consistorial allocution: AAS 52 (1960), pp. 5–11; John XXIII, encyclical letter Mater et Magistra: AAS 53 (1961), p. 411.

146. Cf. St. Thomas, Summa Theol.: II–II q. 32, a. 5 ad 2; ibid q. 66, a. 2; cf. explanation in Leo XIII, encyclical letter Rerum Novarum: AAS 23 (1890–91), p. 651; cf. also Pius XII allocution of June 1, 1941: AAS 33 (1941), p. 199; Pius XII, Christmas radio address 1954: AAS 47 (1955), p. 27.

147. Cf. St. Basil, Hom. in illud Lucae "Destruam horrea mea," Art. 2 (PG 31, 263); Lactantius, Divinarum institutionum, lib. V. On Justice (PL 6, 565 B): St. Augustine, In Ioann. Ev. Tr. 50, Art, 6 (PL 35, 1760); St. Augustine, Enarratio in Ps. CXLVII, 12 (PL 37, 192); St. Gregory the Great, Homiliae in Ev., hom. 20 (PL 76, 1165); St. Gregory the Great, Regulae Pastoralis liber, pars III, c. 21 (PL 77, 87); St. Bonaventure, in III Sent. d. 33, dub 1 (ed. Quaracchi III, 728); St. Bonaventure, In IV Sent. d. 15, p. II a. 2. q. 1 (ed. cit. IV, 371b); q. de superfluo (ms. Assisi, Bibl. Comun. 186, ff. 112a–113a); St. Albert the Great, in III Sent., d. 33, a. 3, sol. 1 (ed. Borgnet XXVIII, 611); Id In IV Sent. d. 15, a. 16 (ed. cit. XXIX, 494–497). As for the determination of what is superfluous in our day and age, cf. John XXIII, radio-television message of Sept. 11, 1962: AAS 54 (1962), p. 682: "The obligation of every man, the urgent obligation of the Christian man, is to reckon what is superfluous by the measure of the needs of others, and to see to it that the administration and the distribution of created goods serve the common good."

148. In that case, the old principle holds true: "In extreme necessity all goods are common, that is, all goods are to be shared." On the other hand, for the order, extension, and manner by which the principle is applied in the proposed text, besides the modern authors cf. St. Thomas, Summa Theol. II–II, q. 66, a. 7. Obviously, for the correct application of the principle, all the conditions that are morally required must be met.

149. Cf. Gratian, Decretum, C.21, dist. LXXXVI (ed. Friedberg I, 302). This axiom is also found already in PL 54, 591 A (cf. in Antonianum 27 [1952], 349–366).

150. Cf. Leo XIII, encyclical letter Rerum Novarum: AAS 23 (1890–91), pp. 643–646; Pius XI, encyclical letter Quadragesimo Anno: AAS 23 (1931), p. 191; Pius XII, radio message of June 1, 1941: AAS 33 (1941), p. 199; Pius XII, radio message on Christmas Eve, 1942: AAS 35 (1943), p. 17; Pius XII, radio message of Sept. 1, 1944: AAS 36 (1944), p. 253; John XXIII, encyclical letter Mater et Magistra: AAS 53 (1961), pp. 428–429.

151. Cf. Pius XI, encyclical letter Quadragesimo Anno: AAS 23 (1931), p. 214; John XXIII, encyclical letter Mater et Magistra: AAS 53 (1961), p. 429.

152. Cf. Pius XII, radio message of Pentecost 1941: AAS 44 (1941), p. 199; John XXIII, encyclical letter Mater et Magistra: AAS 53 (1961), p. 430.

153. For the right use of goods according to the doctrine of the New Testament, cf. Lk. 3:11; 10:30ff; 11:41; 1 Pet. 5:3; Mk. 8:36; 12:39–41; Jas. 5:1–6; 1 Tim. 6:8; Eph. 4:28; 2 Cor. 8:13; 1 Jn. 3:17ff.

154. Cf. John XXIII, encyclical letter Mater et Magistra: AAS 53 (1961), p. 417.

155. Cf. John XXIII, ibid.

156. Cf. Rom. 13:1–5.

157. Cf. Rom. 13:5.

158. Cf. Pius XII, radio message, Dec. 24, 1942: AAS 35 (1943), pp. 9–24; Dec. 24, 1944: AAS 37 (1945), pp. 11–17; John XXIII, encyclical letter *Pacem in Terris*: AAS 55 (1963), pp. 263, 271, 277, and 278.

159. Cf. Pius XII, radio message of June 7, 1941: AAS 33 (1941), p. 200; John XXIII, encyclical letter *Pacem in Terris*: l.c., p. 273 and 274.

160. Cf. John XXIII, encyclical letter *Mater et Magistra*: AAS 53 (1961), p. 416.

161. Pius XI, allocution *Ai dirigenti della Federazione Universitaria Cattolica*: Discorsi di Pio XI (ed. Bertetto), Turin, vol. 1 (1960), p. 743.

162. Cf. Lk. 2:14.

163. Cf. Second Vatican Council, dogmatic constitution *Lumen Gentium*, Art. 13: AAS 57 (1965), p. 17.

164. Cf. Eph. 2:16; Col. 1:20–22.

165. Cf. John XXIII, encyclical letter *Pacem in Terris*, Apr. 11, 1963: AAS 55 (1963), p. 291: "Therefore in this age of ours which prides itself on its atomic power, it is irrational to believe that war is still an apt means of vindicating violated rights."

166. Cf. Pius XII, allocution of Sept. 30, 1954: AAS 46 (1954), p. 589; radio message of Dec. 24, 1954: AAS 47 (1955), pp. 15ff; John XXIII, encyclical letter *Pacem in Terris*: AAS 55 (1963), pp. 286–291; Paul VI, allocution to the United Nations, Oct. 4, 1965.

167. Cf. John XXIII, encyclical letter *Pacem in Terris* where reduction of arms is mentioned: AAS 55 (1963), p. 287.

168. Cf. 2 Cor. 2:6.

DECLARATION ON RELIGIOUS FREEDOM
(DIGNITATIS HUMANAE)

The topic of religious freedom has been a subject of deep concern to North American Catholics. In the nineteenth century, the papacy had made clear its opposition to Church-state separation and freedom of conscience; yet American Catholics had long affirmed their unswerving loyalty to their Constitution, which incorporated these arrangements and principles into the nation's fundamental law. Rome tolerated the American experiment, but warned from time to time against an American tendency to take its arrangements as normative for the universal Church. American Catholics, sincerely loyal to both Church and nation, consistently were open to the charge of opportunism—accepting the First Amendment because they were powerless to change it. At mid-twentieth century, the American Jesuit John Courtney Murray began writing on the issue, providing a theoretical understanding of both Church and nation which could place Catholic loyalty within the framework of a development doctrine. Silenced for a decade, his voice emerged as a highly influential one at the Council, as did the voices of several European theologians who approached the issue in different ways. The result was one of the Council's most startling documents, the Declaration on Religious Freedom, which endorsed the separation of Church and state and gave particular emphasis to the "right and indeed duty of every man to follow his conscience." Initially understood as providing a basis for the reconciliation of the Church with the pluralist, liberal societies of the West, the principles of the document could and did become important instruments for further change. As long-time conservative opponents of religious liberty had recognized, affirmation of it in principle not only would endanger the integrity of the Church as a social and cultural institution but would also undermine the foundations of its own internal unity and discipline. Nevertheless, the document manifested the fulfillment of Pope John's emphasis on human rights; it removed major barriers to Catholic participation in ecumenical and worldly activity and secured the role of human rights in the Church and in so-called Catholic countries. It manifested that fundamental commitment to the human person as the center of social life which was already bringing major changes in social teaching.

Traditionally, conscience had been viewed as the extension or application of the general principles of natural law to a particular action. As a result, conscience was seen as an act of the person, not as a part of the person. Conscience had usually been defined as a judgment of reason, based on knowledge coming from an awareness of the basic principles of natural law and training in moral development, on the conformity or nonconformity of a particular act with the objective standards of natural law. This judgment is then binding on the individual because it tells the individual what the law is at this particular time and in this particular situation. Conscience, therefore, is the ultimate subjective norm of morality in that it is to apply the objective norms of natural law to this particular act. But to say this, from the point of view of the tradition, was not to say that conscience could not err or that conscience was the total source of morality. One always had to evaluate conscientious decisions in the light of both Catholic dogma and the general norms of the natural law, especially as these were interpreted by the teaching magisterium of the Church.

The Council document accepts this general view of conscience but puts it in a framework that is broader than that of natural law. The Council says that conscience is the most secret core and sanctuary of a person. Conscience reveals that law which is fulfilled by the love of God and neighbor and therefore unites the Christian in the search for truth with the whole human community. The document also talks about the formation of conscience. This is to be done primarily within the community. There must be both a hearing and a testing of the message of Jesus. Within the Church community, this will be done by a sincere effort to understand and apply the teaching of the magisterium of the Church. But it must also include, as the Council itself suggests, a reflection of what tradition has called the *sensus fidelium*, the sense of what the community actually believes. Also, in articulating one's own conscientious decision, a dialectic will be set up between revelation, the manifestation of God's will through Scripture and tradition, and natural law, the objective created order of the universe. By attempting to test and reconcile one's conscientious decisions with both of these sources of morality and by one's fidelity to the community belief, one can be more sure that decisions arrived at in conscience are close to the ethical demands of the community.

The Council's definition of religious liberty is so important that it deserves to be quoted in full.

> . . . the human person has a right to religious freedom. This freedom means that all men are to be immune from coercion on the part of individuals or of social groups and of any human power, in such wise that in matters religious no one is to be forced to act in a manner contrary to his own beliefs. Nor is anyone to be restrained from acting in accordance with his own beliefs, whether privately or publicly, whether alone or in association with others, within due limits.

The strong implication of this definition is that truth must be sought in a manner proper to the human person and his or her dignity. This means that all inquiries must be free. Also it means that humans are to assist one another as honestly as possible in the quest for truth. As such this definition is a strong condemnation of all forms of propaganda and ideologies which hinder individuals from attaining the truth. The search for truth would also include such phenomena as teaching, communication, and dialogue. It is only in the dialectic that arises out of full involvement within the community that truth can be achieved.

A second strong implication of the definition is that persons both perceive and acknowledge imperatives of divine law through decisions which are arrived at conscientiously. This is again a very strong reaffirmation of the tradition, namely that when persons make conscientious decisions that are arrived at as honestly as possible, they must follow these decisions so that they may come to God. Consequently the Council emphasizes that individuals must not be forced to act against their conscience. Neither are people to be restrained from acting in accordance with their consciences, especially in matters religious. This point is of particular importance to American Catholics, for the American legal tradition, in terms of the First Amendment to the Constitution, has emphasized a strong distinction between religious beliefs and religious actions. This constitutional tradition affirms that while anyone may believe anything he or she chooses to believe, individuals are not so free in acting out their religious beliefs. There may be vested state interests that are of concern and that may force regulation of one's acting out a particular religious belief. While this American tradition has found application mainly in laws prohibiting polygamy on the part of Mormons, and prohibiting Jehovah's Witnesses from refusing blood transfusions, the distinction gained notoriety during the Vietnam war. Here it was used to prohibit Catholic selective conscientious objectors from refusing service on the basis of religious reasons. While the Roman Catholic ethical tradition has always affirmed the right of an individual to object selectively to a particular war on the grounds that was unjust, the Supreme Court and the Selective Service refused to allow such an option for American Catholics. According to the Declaration on Religious Freedom, this was a clear violation of their religious rights, because they were being forced to act against their consciences. Some recent court decisions have suggested that a softening of the distinction between belief and action may be forthcoming. However, as it stands, the legal tradition's emphasis on the absolute dichotomy between religious belief and religious action may prove to be a severe test of the seriousness with which American Catholics put into practice their belief in the Council's definition of religious freedom.

On the other hand, the Council does recognize that this right to religious freedom is exercised in human societies; hence its exercise must be subject to certain regulatory norms. These are spelled out in paragraph 7 of the document, but they merit summarization here. First, the moral principles of personal and social responsibility are to be observed. Second, individuals and groups must have respect for the rights of others and for their own duties toward others and for the welfare of all. Third, individuals must deal with others in justice and civility. Finally, government regulatory action, which is justified, must be controlled by judicial norms which are in conformity with the objective moral order. Although the Council suggests several guidelines by which this fourth principle may be put into practice, nonetheless this will be the area at which the issue will be joined most critically. In many ways religious claims can be extremely threatening to the society, and therefore the society will resist these claims as strongly as possible in the name of vested state interests, national security, or some other significant rubric. Nonetheless it is at this point that individuals must strongly proclaim the Council's teaching that no one is to be restrained from acting out his or her religious beliefs.

This document represents most clearly the victory of the language of rights over the language of duties in Roman Catholic social theology. While the document recognizes that individuals do have duties toward society and affirms the objective obligations that come from the natural law, nonetheless the total emphasis is on the religious claim in conscience of the individual over and against the demands and duties imposed upon the individual by society. Even though this right is somewhat modified by its articulation within a social context, nonetheless the intent is clear: Individuals cannot be forced to act against their conscience or be restrained from acting in accordance with their conscience. This validates a strong moral claim of the individual against the power of the state and so sets the individual clearly apart from the community and the state. For this reason, the document on religious freedom may be the most radical of all the Council documents and therefore the most dangerous, because it does imply that at certain points social duties cannot be used as a way of coercing an individual to abrogate his or her individual right of religious freedom. Because of this the document is also the strongest of all the Council documents.

It affirms that an individual is of ultimate importance and that when an individual in conscientious decisions in relation to both God and the community chooses a course of action, this individual cannot be restrained from so acting. By this affirmation the document greatly enhances the value and dignity of each individual and the conscientious decisions this individual makes. In so doing, the Council comes closest to the heart of the American tradition which values the individual in the contributions that he or she can make to the society. But it also accepts the American political tradition, derived from contract theory, which recognizes that the individual typically stands in an adversary relation to society and makes claims over and against society. And just as the repercussions of this contract theory of individual rights have continued to provide the basis for creativity and revolution within the American tradition, so it has also done for the Church since Vatican II. The effects of this document have severely shaken the foundations of Roman Catholicism since Vatican II; it remains to be seen what further implications and consequences this doctrine will have for the future of Catholicism.

DIGNITATIS HUMANAE

DECLARATION ON RELIGIOUS FREEDOM

ON THE RIGHT OF THE PERSON AND OF COMMUNITIES
TO SOCIAL AND CIVIL FREEDOM IN MATTERS RELIGIOUS

PAUL BISHOP, SERVANT OF THE SERVANTS OF GOD,
TOGETHER WITH THE FATHER OF
THE SACRED COUNCIL,
FOR EVERLASTING MEMORY

1. A sense of the dignity of the human person has been impressing itself more and more deeply on the consciousness of contemporary man.[1] And the demand is increasingly made that men should act on their own judgment, enjoying and making use of a responsible freedom, not driven by coercion but motivated by a sense of duty. The demand is also made that constitutional limits should be set to the powers of government, in order that there may be no encroachment on the rightful freedom of the person and of associations.

This demand for freedom in human society chiefly regards the quest for the values proper to the human spirit. It regards, in the first place, the free exercise of religion in society.

This Vatican Synod takes careful note of these desires in the minds of men. It proposes to declare them to be greatly in accord with truth and justice. To this end, it searches into the sacred tradition and doctrine of the Church—the treasury out of which the Church continually brings forth new things that are in harmony with the things that are old.

First, this sacred Synod professes its belief that God himself has made known to mankind the way in which men are to serve Him, and thus be saved in Christ and come to blessedness. We believe that this one true religion subsists in the Catholic and apostolic Church, to which the Lord Jesus committed the duty of spreading it abroad among all men. Thus He spoke to the apostles: "Go, therefore, and make disciples of all nations, baptizing them in the name of the Father, and of the Son, and of the Holy Spirit, teaching them to observe all that I have commanded you" (Mt. 28:19-20). On their part, all men are bound to seek the truth, especially in what concerns God and His Church, and to embrace the truth they come to know, and to hold fast to it.

This sacred Synod likewise professes its belief that it is upon the human conscience that these obligations fall and exert their binding force. The truth cannot impose itself except by virtue of its own truth, as it makes its entrace into the mind at once quietly and with power. Religious freedom, in turn, which men demand as necessary to fulfill their duty to worship God, has to do with immunity from coercion in civil society. Therefore, it leaves untouched traditional Catholic doctrine on the moral duty of men and societies toward the true religion and toward the one Church of Christ.

Over and above all this, in taking up the matter of religious freedom this sacred Synod intends to develop the doctrine of recent Popes on the inviolable rights of the human person and on the constitutional order of society.

CHAPTER I

GENERAL PRINCIPLE OF RELIGIOUS FREEDOM

2. This Vatican Synod declares that the human person has a right to religious freedom. This freedom means that all men are to be immune from coercion on the part of individuals or of social groups and of any human power, in such wise that in matters religious no one is to be forced to act in a manner contrary to his own beliefs. Nor is anyone to be restrained from acting in accordance with his own beliefs, whether privately or publicly, whether alone or in association with others, within due limits.

The Synod further declares that the right to religious freedom has its foundation in the very dignity of the human person, as this dignity is known through the revealed Word of

God and by reason itself.[2] This right of the human person to religious freedom is to be recognized in the constitutional law whereby society is governed. Thus it is to become a civil right.

It is in accordance with their dignity as persons—that is, beings endowed with reason and free will and therefore privileged to bear personal responsibility—that all men should be at once impelled by nature and also bound by a moral obligation to seek the truth, especially religious truth. They are also bound to adhere to the truth, once it is known, and to order their whole lives in accord with the demands of truth.

However, men cannot discharge these obligations in a manner in keeping with their own nature unless they enjoy immunity from external coercion as well as psychological freedom. Therefore, the right to religious freedom has its foundation, not in the subjective disposition of the person, but in his very nature. In consequence, the right to this immunity continues to exist even in those who do not live up to their obligation of seeking the truth and adhering to it. Nor is the exercise of this right to be impeded, provided that the just requirements of public order are observed.

3. Further light is shed on the subject if one considers that the highest norm of human life is the divine law—eternal, objective, and universal—whereby God orders, directs, and governs the entire universe and all the ways of the human community, by a plan conceived in wisdom and love. Man has been made by God to participate in this law, with the result that, under the gentle disposition of divine Providence, he can come to perceive ever increasingly the unchanging truth. Hence every man has the duty, and therefore the right, to seek the truth in matters religious, in order that he may with prudence form for himself right and true judgments of conscience, with the use of all suitable means.

Truth, however, is to be sought after in a manner proper to the dignity of the human person and his social nature. The inquiry is to be free, carried on with the aid of teaching or instruction, communication, and dialogue. In the course of these, men explain to one another the truth they have discovered, or think they have discovered, in order thus to assist one another in the quest for truth. Moreover, as the truth is

discovered, it is by a personal assent that men are to adhere
to it.

On his part, man perceives and acknowledges the imperatives of the divine law through the mediation of conscience.
In all his activity a man is bound to follow his conscience
faithfully, in order that he may come to God, for whom he
was created. It follows that he is not to be forced to act in a
manner contrary to his conscience. Nor, on the other hand, is
he to be restrained from acting in accordance with his conscience, especially in matters religious.

For, of its very nature, the exercise of religion consists before all else in those internal, voluntary, and free acts
whereby man sets the course of his life directly toward God.
No merely human power can either command or prohibit
acts of this kind.[3]

However, the social nature of man itself requires that he
should give external expression to his internal acts of religion;
that he should participate with others in matters religious;
that he should profess his religion in community. Injury,
therefore, is done to the human person and to the very order
established by God for human life, if the free exercise of
religion is denied in society when the just requirements of
public order do not so require.

There is a further consideration. The religious acts whereby
men, in private and in public and out of a sense of personal
conviction, direct their lives to God transcend by their very
nature the order of terrestrial and temporal affairs. Government, therefore, ought indeed to take account of the religious
life of the people and show it favor, since the function of
government is to make provision for the common welfare.
However, it would clearly transgress the limits set to its
power were it to presume to direct or inhibit acts that are
religious.

4. The freedom of immunity from coercion in matters
religious which is the endowment of persons as individuals is
also to be recognized as their right when they act in community. Religious bodies are a requirement of the social nature
both of man and of religion itself.

Provided the just requirements of public order are observed, religious bodies rightfully claim freedom in order that

they may govern themselves according to their own norms, honor the Supreme Being in public worship, assist their members in the practice of the religious life, strengthen them by instruction, and promote institutions in which they may join together for the purpose of ordering their own lives in accordance with their religious principles.

Religious bodies also have the right not to be hindered, either by legal measures or by administrative action on the part of government, in the selection, training, appointment, and transferral of their own ministers, in communicating with religious authorities and communities abroad, in erecting buildings for religious purposes, and in the acquisition and use of suitable funds or properties.

Religious bodies also have the right not to be hindered in their public teaching and witness to their faith, whether by the spoken or by the written word. However, in spreading religious faith and in introducing religious practices, everyone ought at all times to refrain from any manner of action which might seem to carry a hint of coercion or of a kind of persuasion that would be dishonorable or unworthy, especially when dealing with poor or uneducated people. Such a manner of action would have to be considered an abuse of one's own right and a violation of the right of others.

In addition, it comes within the meaning of religious freedom that religious bodies should not be prohibited from freely undertaking to show the special value of their doctrine in what concerns the organization of society and the inspiration of the whole of human activity. Finally, the social nature of man and the very nature of religion afford the foundation of the right of men freely to hold meetings and to establish educational, cultural, charitable, and social organizations, under the impulse of their own religious sense.

5. Since the family is a society in its own original right, it has the right freely to live its own domestic religious life under the guidance of parents. Parents, moreover, have the right to determine, in accordance with their own religious beliefs, the kind of religious education that their children are to receive.

Government, in consequence, must acknowledge the right of parents to make a genuinely free choice of schools and of

other means of education. The use of this freedom of choice
is not to be made a reason for imposing unjust burdens on
parents, whether directly or indirectly. Besides, the rights of
parents are violated if their children are forced to attend lessons or instruction which are not in agreement with their
religious beliefs. The same is true if a single system of education, from which all religious formation is excluded, is imposed upon all.

6. The common welfare of society consists in the entirety
of those conditions of social life under which men enjoy the
possibility of achieving their own perfection in a certain
fullness of measure and also with some relative ease. Hence
this welfare consists chiefly in the protection of the rights,[4]
and in the performance of the duties, of the human person.
Therefore, the care of the right to religious freedom devolves
upon the people as a whole, upon social groups, upon government, and upon the Church and other religious communities, in virtue of the duty of all toward the common welfare,
and in the manner proper to each.

The protection and promotion of the inviolable rights of
man ranks among the essential duties of government.[5] Therefore, government is to assume the safeguard of the religious
freedom of all its citizens, in an effective manner, by just
laws and by other appropriate means. Government is also to
help create conditions favorable to the fostering of religious
life, in order that the people may be truly enabled to exercise
their religious rights and to fulfill their religious duties, and
also in order that society itself may profit by the moral qualities of justice and peace which have their origin in men's
faithfulness to God and to His holy will.[6]

If, in view of peculiar circumstances obtaining among certain peoples, special legal recognition is given in the constitutional order of society to one religious body, it is at the
same time imperative that the right of all citizens and
religious bodies to religious freedom should be recognized
and made effective in practice.

Finally, government is to see to it that the equality of citizens before the law, which is itself an element of the common welfare, is never violated for religious reasons whether

openly or covertly. Nor is there to be discrimination among citizens.

It follows that a wrong is done when government imposes upon its people, by force or fear or other means, the profession or repudiation of any religion, or when it hinders men from joining or leaving a religious body. All the more is it a violation of the will of God and of the sacred rights of the person and the family of nations, when force is brought to bear in any way in order to destroy or repress religion, either in the whole of mankind or in a particular country or in a specific community.

7. The right to religious freedom is exercised in human society; hence its exercise is subject to certain regulatory norms. In the use of all freedoms, the moral principle of personal and social responsibility is to be observed. In the exercise of their rights, individual men and social groups are bound by the moral law to have respect both for the rights of others and for their own duties toward others and for the common welfare of all. Men are to deal with their fellows in justice and civility.

Furthermore, society has the right to defend itself against possible abuses committed on pretext of freedom of religion. It is the special duty of government to provide this protection. However, government is not to act in arbitrary fashion or in an unfair spirit of partisanship. Its action is to be controlled by juridical norms which are in conformity with the objective moral order.

These norms arise out of the need for effective safeguard of the rights of all citizens and for peaceful settlement of conflicts of rights. They flow from the need for an adequate care of genuine public peace, which comes about when men live together in good order and in true justice. They come, finally, out of the need for a proper guardianship of public morality. These matters constitute the basic component of the common welfare: they are what is meant by public order.

For the rest, the usages of society are to be the usages of freedom in their full range. These require that the freedom of man be respected as far as possible, and curtailed only when and in so far as necessary.

8. Many pressures are brought to bear upon men of our day, to the point where the danger arises lest they lose the possibility of acting on their own judgment. On the other hand, not a few can be found who seem inclined to use the name of freedom as the pretext for refusing to submit to authority and for making light of the duty of obedience.

Therefore, this Vatican Synod urges everyone, especially those who are charged with the task of educating others, to do their utmost to form men who will respect the moral order and be obedient to lawful authority. Let them form men too who will be lovers of true freedom—men, in other words, who will come to decisions on their own judgment and in the light of truth, govern their activities with a sense of responsibility, and strive after what is true and right, willing always to join with others in cooperative effort.

Religious freedom, therefore, ought to have this further purpose and aim, namely that men may come to act with greater responsibility in fulfilling their duties in community life.

CHAPTER II

RELIGIOUS FREEDOM IN THE LIGHT OF REVELATION

9. The declaration of this Vatican Synod on the right of man to religious freedom has its foundation in the dignity of the person. The requirements of this dignity have come to be more adequately known to human reason through centuries of experience. What is more, this doctrine of freedom has roots in divine revelation, and for this reason Christians are bound to respect it all the more conscientiously.

Revelation does not indeed affirm in so many words the right of man to immunity from external coercion in matters religious. It does, however, disclose the dignity of the human person in its full dimensions. It gives evidence of the respect which Christ showed toward the freedom with which man is to fulfill his duty of belief in the Word of God. It gives us lessons too in the spirit which disciples of such a Master ought to make their own and to follow in every situation.

Thus, further light is cast on the general principles upon which the doctrine of this Declaration on Religious Freedom is based. In particular, religious freedom in society is entirely consonant with the freedom of the act of Christian faith.

10. It is one of the major tenets of Catholic doctrine that man's response to God in faith must be free. Therefore no one is to be forced to embrace the Christian faith[7] against his own will. This doctrine is contained in the Word of God and it was constantly proclaimed by the Fathers of the Church.[8] The act of faith is of its very nature a free act. Man, redeemed by Christ the Savior and through Christ Jesus called to be God's adopted son,[9] cannot give his adherence to God revealing Himself unless the Father draw him[10] to offer to God the reasonable and free submission of faith.

It is therefore completely in accord with the nature of faith that in matters religious every manner of coercion on the part of men should be excluded. In consequence, the principle of religious freedom makes no small contribution to the creation of an environment in which men can without hindrance be invited to Christian faith, and embrace it of their own free will, and profess it effectively in their whole manner of life.

11. God calls men to serve Him in spirit and in truth. Hence they are bound in conscience but they stand under no compulsion. God has regard for the dignity of the human person whom He Himself created; man is to be guided by his own judgment and he is to enjoy freedom.

This truth appears at its height in Christ Jesus, in whom God perfectly manifested Himself and His ways with men. Christ is our Master and our Lord.[11] He is also meek and humble of heart.[12] And in attracting and inviting His disciples He acted patiently.[13] He wrought miracles to shed light on His teaching and to establish its truth. But His intention was to rouse faith in His hearers and to confirm them in faith, not to exert coercion upon them.[14]

He did indeed denounce the unbelief of some who listened to Him; but He left vengeance to God in expectation of the day of judgment.[15] When He sent His apostles into the world, He said to them: "He who believes and is baptized shall be saved, but he who does not believe shall be condemned" (Mk. 16:16); but He Himself, noting that cockle had been sown amid the wheat, gave orders that both should be allowed to grow until the harvest time, which will come at the end of the world.[16]

He refused to be a political Messiah, ruling by force[17]; He preferred to call Himself the Son of Man, who came "to serve and to give his life as a ransom for many" (Mk. 10:45). He showed Himself the perfect Servant of God[18]; "a bruised reed he will not break, and a smoking wick he will not quench" (Mt. 12:20).

He acknowledged the power of government and its rights when He commanded that tribute be given to Caesar. But He gave clear warning that the higher rights of God are to be kept inviolate: "Render, therefore, to Caesar the things that are Caesar's, and to God the things that are God's" (Mt. 22:21).

In the end, when He completed on the cross the work of redemption whereby He achieved salvation and true freedom for men, He also brought His revelation to completion. He bore witness to the truth,[19] but He refused to impose the truth by force on those who spoke against it. Not by force of blows does his rule assert its claims.[20] Rather, it is established by witnessing to the truth and by hearing the truth, and it extends its dominion by the love whereby Christ, lifted up on the cross, draws all men to Himself.[21]

Taught by the word and example of Christ, the apostles followed the same way. From the very origins of the Church the disciples of Christ strove to convert men to faith in Christ as the Lord—not, however, by the use of coercion or by devices unworthy of the gospel, but by the power, above all, of the Word of God.[22] Steadfastly they proclaimed to all the plan of God our Savior, "who wishes all men to be saved and to come to the knowledge of the truth" (1 Tim. 2:4). At the same time, however, they showed respect for weaker souls even though these persons were in error. Thus they made it plain that "every one of us will render an account of himself to God" (Rom. 14:12),[23] and for this reason is bound to obey his conscience.

Like Christ Himself, the apostles were unceasingly bent upon bearing witness to the truth of God. They showed special courage in speaking "the word of God with boldness"

(Acts 4:31)[24] before the people and their rulers. With a firm faith they held that the gospel is indeed the power of God unto salvation for all who believe.[25] Therefore they rejected all "carnal weapons."[26] They followed the example of the gentleness and respectfulness of Christ. And they preached the Word of God in the full confidence that there was resident in this Word itself a divine power able to destroy all the forces arrayed against God[27] and to bring men to faith in Christ and to His service.[28] As the Master, so too the apostles recognized legitimate civil authority. "For there exists no authority except from God," the Apostle teaches, and therefore commands: "Let everyone be subject to the higher authorities . . . : he who resists the authority resists the ordinance of God" (Rom. 13:1–2).[29]

At the same time, however, they did not hesitate to speak out against governing powers which set themselves in opposition to the holy will of God: "We must obey God rather than men" (Acts 5:29).[30] This is the way along which countless martyrs and other believers have walked through all ages and over all the earth.

12. The Church therefore is being faithful to the truth of the gospel, and is following the way of Christ and the apostles when she recognizes, and gives support to, the principle of religious freedom as befitting the dignity of man and as being in accord with divine revelation. Throughout the ages, the Church has kept safe and handed on the doctrine received from the Master and from the apostles. In the life of the People of God as it has made its pilgrim way through the vicissitudes of human history, there have at times appeared ways of acting which were less in accord with the spirit of the gospel and even opposed to it. Nevertheless, the doctrine of the Church that no one is to be coerced into faith has always stood firm.

Thus the leaven of the gospel has long been about its quiet work in the minds of men. To it is due in great measure the fact that in the course of time men have come more widely to recognize their dignity as persons, and the conviction has grown stronger that in religious matters the person in society is to be kept free from all manner of human coercion.

13. Among the things which concern the good of the

Church and indeed the welfare of society here on earth—things therefore which are always and everywhere to be kept secure and defended against all injury—this certainly is pre-eminent, namely, that the Church should enjoy that full measure of freedom which her care for the salvation of men requires.[31] This freedom is sacred, because the only-begotten Son endowed with it the Church which He purchased with His blood. It is so much the property of the Church that to act against it is to act against the will of God. The freedom of the Church is the fundamental principle in what concerns the relations between the Church and governments and the whole civil order.

In human society and in the face of government, the Church claims freedom for herself in her character as a spiritual authority, established by Christ the Lord. Upon this authority there rests, by divine mandate, the duty of going out into the whole world and preaching the gospel to every creature.[32] The Church also claims freedom for herself in her character as a society of men who have the right to live in society in accordance with the precepts of Christian faith.[33]

In turn, where the principle of religious freedom is not only proclaimed in words or simply incorporated in law but also given sincere and practical application, there the Church succeeds in achieving a stable situation of right as well as of fact and the independence which is necessary for the fulfillment of her divine mission. This independence is precisely what the authorities of the Church claim in society.[34]

At the same time, the Christian faithful, in common with all other men, possess the civil right not to be hindered in leading their lives in accordance with their conscience. Therefore, a harmony exists between the freedom of the Church and the religious freedom which is to be recognized as the right of all men and communities and sanctioned by constitutional law.

14. In order to be faithful to the divine command, "Make disciples of all nations" (Mt. 28:19), the Catholic Church must work with all urgency and concern "that the Word of God may run and be glorified" (2 Th. 3:1). Hence the

Church earnestly begs of her children that, first of all, "supplications, prayers, intercessions, and thanksgivings be made for all men. . . . For this is good and agreeable in the sight of God our Savior, who wishes all men to be saved and to come to the knowledge of the truth" (1 Tim. 2:1–4).

In the formation of their consciences, the Christian faithful ought carefully to attend to the sacred and certain doctrine of the Church.[35] The Church is, by the will of Christ, the teacher of the truth. It is her duty to give utterance to, and authoritatively to teach, that Truth which is Christ Himself, and also to declare and confirm by her authority those principles of the moral order which have their origin in human nature itself. Furthermore, let Christians walk in wisdom in the face of those outside, "in the Holy Spirit, in unaffected love, in the word of truth" (2 Cor. 6:6–7). Let them be about their task of spreading the light of life with all confidence[36] and apostolic courage, even to the shedding of their blood.

The disciple is bound by a grave obligation toward Christ his Master ever more adequately to understand the truth received from Him, faithfully to proclaim it, and vigorously to defend it, never—be it understood—having recourse to means that are incompatible with the spirit of the gospel. At the same time, the charity of Christ urges him to act lovingly, prudently and patiently in his dealings with those who are in error or in ignorance with regard to the faith.[37] All is to be taken into account—the Christian duty to Christ, the life-giving Word which must be proclaimed, the rights of the human person, and the measure of grace granted by God through Christ to men, who are invited freely to accept and profess the faith.

15. The fact is that men of the present day want to be able freely to profess their religion in private and in public. Religious freedom has already been declared to be a civil right in most constitutions, and it is solemnly recognized in international documents.[38] The further fact is that forms of government still exist under which, even though freedom of religious worship receives constitutional recognition, the powers of government are engaged in the effort to deter citi-

zens from the profession of religion and to make life difficult and dangerous for religious communities.

This sacred Synod greets with joy the first of these two facts, as among the signs of the times. With sorrow, however, it denounces the other fact, as only to be deplored. The Synod exhorts Catholics, and it directs a plea to all men, most carefully to consider how greatly necessary religious freedom is, especially in the present condition of the human family.

All nations are coming into even closer unity. Men of different cultures and religions are being brought together in closer relationships. There is a growing consciousness of the personal responsibility that weighs upon every man. All this is evident.

Consequently, in order that relationships of peace and harmony may be established and maintained within the whole of mankind, it is necessary that religious freedom be everywhere provided with an effective constitutional guarantee, and that respect be shown for the high duty and right of man freely to lead his religious life in society.

May the God and Father of all grant that the human family, through careful observance of the principle of religious freedom in society, may be brought by the grace of Christ and the power of the Holy Spirit to the sublime and unending "freedom of the glory of the sons of God" (Rom. 8:21).

Each and every one of the things set forth in this Declaration has won the consent of the Fathers of this most sacred Council. We too, by the apostolic authority conferred on us by Christ, join with the Venerable Fathers in approving, decreeing, and establishing these things in the Holy Spirit, and we direct that what has thus been enacted in synod be published to God's glory.

Rome, at St. Peter's, December 7, 1965

I, Paul, Bishop of the Catholic Church

NOTES

1. Cf. John XXIII, encyclical *Pacem in Terris*, Apr. 11, 1963: AAS 55 (1963), p. 279; *ibid.*, p. 265; Pius XII, radio message, Dec. 24, 1944: AAS 37 (1945), p. 14.

2. Cf. John XXIII, encyclical *Pacem in Terris*, Apr. 11, 1963: AAS 55 (1963), pp. 260–261; Pius XII, radio message, Dec. 24, 1942: AAS 35 (1943), p. 19; Pius XI, encyclical *Mit Brennender Sorge*, Mar. 14, 1937: AAS 29 (1937), p. 160; Leo XIII, encyclical *Libertas Praestantissimum*, June 20, 1888: Acts of Leo XIII 8 (1888), pp. 237–238.

3. Cf. John XXIII, encyclical *Pacem in Terris*, Apr. 11, 1963: AAS 55 (1963), p. 270; Paul VI, radio message, Dec. 22, 1964: AAS 57 (1963), pp. 181–182.

4. Cf. John XXIII encyclical *Mater et Magistra*, May 15, 1961: AAS 53 (1961), p. 417; *idem*, encyclical *Pacem in Terris*, Apr. 11, 1963: AAS 55 (1963), p. 273.

5. Cf. John XXIII, encyclical *Pacem in Terris*, Apr. 11, 1963: AAS 55 (1963), pp. 273–274; Pius XII, radio message, June 1, 1941: AAS 33 (1941), p. 200.

6. Cf. Leo XIII, encyclical *Immortale Dei*, Nov. 1, 1885: AAS 18 (1885), p. 161.

7. Cf. CIC, c. 1351; Pius XII, allocution to prelate auditors and other officials and administrators of the tribune of the Holy Roman Rota, Oct. 6, 1946: AAS 38 (1946), p. 394; *idem*, encyclical *Mystici Corporis*, June 29, 1943: AAS 35 (1943), p. 243.

8. Cf. Lactantius, *Divinarum Institutionum*, Book V, 19: CSEL 19, pp. 463–464, 465: PL 6, 614 and 616 (ch. 20); St. Ambrose, *Epistola ad Valentianum Imp.*, Letter 21: PL 16, 1005; St. Augustine, *Contra Litteras Petiliani*, Book II, ch. 83: CSEL 52, p. 112: PL 43, 315; cf. C. 23, q. 5, c. 33 (ed. Friedburg, col. 939); *idem*, Letter 23: PL 33, 98; *idem*, Letter 34: PL 33, 132; *idem*, Letter 35: PL 33, 135; St. Gregory the Great, *Epistola ad Virgilium et Theodorum Episcopos Massiliae Galliarum*, Register of Letters I, 45: MGH Ep. 1, p. 72; PL 77, 510–511 (Book I, ep. 47); *idem*, *Epistola ad Johannem Episcopum Constantinopolitanum*, Register of Letters III, 52: MGH Letter 1, p. 210: PL 77, 649 (Book III, Letter 53); cf. D. 45, c. 1 (ed. Friedberg, col. 160); Council of Toledo IV, c. 57: Mansi 10, 633; cf. D. 45, c. 5 (ed. Friedberg, col. 161–162); Clement III: X., V. 6, 9: ed. Friedberg, col. 774; Innocent III, *Epistola ad Arelatensem Archiepiscopum*, X., III, 42, 3: ed. Friedberg, col. 646.

9. Cf. Eph. 1:5.

10. Cf. Jn. 6:44.

11. Cf. Jn. 13:13.

12. Cf. Mt. 11:29.

13. Cf. Mt. 11:28–30; Jn. 6:67–68.

14. Cf. Mt. 9:28–29; Mk. 9:23–24; 6:5–6; Paul VI, encyclical *Ecclesiam Suam*, Aug. 6, 1964: AAS 56 (1964), pp. 642–643.

15. Cf. Mt. 11:20–24; Rom. 12:19–20; 2 Th. 1:8.

16. Cf. Mt. 13:30 and 40–42.

17. Cf. Mt. 4:8–10; Jn. 6:15.

18. Cf. Is. 42:1–4.

19. Cf. Jn. 18:37.

20. Cf. Mt. 26:51–53; Jn. 18:36.

21. Cf. Jn. 12:32.

22. Cf. 1 Cor. 2:3–5; 1 Th. 2:3–5.

23. Cf. Rom. 14:1–23; 1 Cor. 8:9–13; 10:23–33.

24. Cf. Eph. 6:19–20.

25. Rom. 1:16.

26. Cf. 2 Cor. 10:4; 1 Th. 5:8–9.

27. Cf. Eph. 6:11–17.

28. Cf. 2 Cor. 10:3–5.

29. Cf. 1 Pet. 2:13–17.

30. Cf. Acts 4:19–20.

31. Cf. Leo XIII, letter *Officio Sanctissimo*, Dec. 22, 1887: AAS 20 (1887), p. 269; *idem*, letter *Ex Litteris*, Apr. 7, 1887: AAS 19 (1886), p. 465.

32. Cf. Mk. 16:15; Mt. 28:18–20; Pius XII, encyclical *Summi Pontificatus*, Oct. 20, 1939: AAS 31 (1939), pp. 445–446.

33. Cf. Pius XI, letter *Firmissimam Constantiam*, Mar. 28, 1937: AAS 29 (1937), p. 196.

34. Cf. Pius XII, allocution *Ci Riesce*, Dec. 6, 1953: AAS 45 (1953), p. 802.

35. Cf. Pius XII, radio message, Mar. 23, 1952: AAS 44 (1952), pp. 270–278.

36. Cf. Acts 4:29.

37. Cf. John XXIII, encyclical *Pacem in Terris*, Apr. 11, 1963: AAS 55 (1963), pp. 299–300.

38. Cf. John XXIII, encyclical *Pacem in Terris*, Apr. 11, 1963: AAS 55 (1963), pp. 295–296.

ON THE DEVELOPMENT OF PEOPLES
(POPULORUM PROGRESSIO)

The choice of the successor to Pope John XXIII was almost a foregone conclusion. Archbishop Giovanni Cardinal Montini of Milan had been widely mentioned as a likely candidate five years earlier. During John's reign he enjoyed many marks of papal favor and played an important role in the first session of the Council. On the fifth ballot, June 21, 1963, he was selected and chose the name Paul VI. Ascending the throne of Peter in the midst of the most profound wave of change to sweep the Church since the Reformation, Paul VI was to need all the skills of conciliation and compromise acquired in a long career of papal service to keep the universal Church both united and on the road to renewal and reform. Fully committed to the success of the Council, he was equally determined to maintain the power and dignity of the papal office, a set of loyalties which would cause him much anguish in the years ahead.

Paul's reign has reflected the tensions present at his ascension. He has often seemed to be on both sides of questions, articulating a progressive view of the role of the papacy in the Church, while strongly defending the prerogatives of his office: traveling the world to dramatize the Church's commitment to ecumenical dialogue and world peace, while continuing many practices of papal centralization, diplomacy, and finance which seemed to some to contradict these fine gestures. Most important for many American Catholics, he appointed a broadly representative commission to advise him on the birth-control question—then went against its advice by affirming the Church's established position, an action which sent shock waves through the Church in the United States and particularly called into question the moral and juridical authority of the Church's teaching office.

In *Populorum Progressio*, Pope Paul placed the social question in its worldwide context. Development, the attainment of full self-development on the part of the poor of the world, was now "the new name for peace." Even more than his predecessors, Pope Paul offered an economic interpretation of the sources of war and argued even more strenuously for economic justice as the surest road to peace. "Left to itself," he argued, the international economic system "works rather to widen the differences in the world's levels of life, not to diminish them; rich peoples enjoy rapid growth whereas the poor develop slowly." He deplored the predominance of profits and the continued belief in free trade, which operated mainly to the benefit of the rich and the powerful. As a matter of justice "the superfluous wealth of rich countries should be placed at the service of poor nations."

On the surface, at least, *Populorum Progressio* seems the most radical of the papal pronouncements on social issues. The Pope rejects quite unequivocally many of the basic precepts of capitalism, including unrestricted private property, the profit motive, and reliance on free trade in the world economy. There is a note of urgency missing from earlier statements, a sense that in the absence of clear and decisive action the arms race and the disparity between the rich and the poor nations of the world will accelerate and the world will be faced with disaster. He emphasized most strongly the right in justice of the poorer nations to the aid of the wealthier and, while overall the call is for the wealthy to fulfill their moral duty, there is at least a suggestion that, in the extreme situation, the poor retain the right to a violent solution of their problems. Already hedged by many modifications, that statement was to be even more modified in later speeches. Yet the principles of human rights, social development, and popular participation so strong in Pope John's encyclicals were continued with even greater force by Pope Paul, and they were and remain principles of almost revolutionary power.

A major thematic area of concern is Paul's vision of development. For him, development is not to be limited to mere economic growth. "It has to promote the good of every man and of the whole man." This development takes place on an individual level and is oriented to what Pope Paul calls a transcendent humanism, human maturity open to further maturity. Also development takes place on the social level because each individual is a part of the whole. True development does not come from increased possessions or technical advances but from a new humanism, allowing individuals to renew themselves by embracing the higher values of "love and friendship, of prayer and contemplation." True and integral human development consists of the following qualities: the acquisition of knowledge, culture, and the necessities of life; the desire for cooperation and peace, with a corresponding recognition of human dignity; the recognition of supreme values and the destiny of the person and the acceptance of faith which opens individuals to union with God. This concept of development is personalistic in its content and thrust. It focuses on individual and social values and describes the social institutions in which humans live as the context in which development occurs and as a context which is to be examined and changed in light of continued development.

Speaking on property, Pope Paul states that private property "does not constitute for anyone an absolute and unconditioned right." Thus no one is justified in keeping for one's exclusive use what is not needed when others lack the basic human necessities. Speaking to the situation of "landed estates" which can sometimes impede general prosperity, Paul VI teaches that "the common good sometimes demands their expropriation." Also people with excessive incomes should not transfer them abroad to derive purely individual benefits, because this can bring harm to their country. In trying to achieve balance between private rights and social necessities, public authority is to serve as the mediator and to provide a solution—with the active participation of both individuals and the community.

In terms of aid, each nation has the obligation to produce "more and better quality goods to give all its inhabitants a truly human standard of living." Also the developed nations should put part of their own production and talents at the disposal of nations who lack these resources. This wealth should be distributed through coordinated planning so that the results can be fully effective. To this end, Pope Paul reissued his plea for the establishment of a world fund made up of money formerly budgeted for arms but now used to relieve world poverty. This could temper the temptation to practice neocolonialism which can occur through politically oriented trade and aid relations. It would also allow lower interest rates on loans. Such a fund would allow the receiving countries political freedom and the integrity of their own social institutions.

Trade is a new dimension of social teaching included in *Populorum Progressio*. Paul VI points to the fact that manufactured goods always have a ready market and an increasing value. Raw materials, however, are often subject to great fluctuation in value and in quantity and quality. As a result, countries with underdeveloped industries tend to remain poor. Because of this inequality the principle of free trade is no longer able to govern international trade relations: "prices which are 'freely' set in the market can produce unfair results." Thus an economy based solely on the law of free competition is no longer valid because it tends to create an economic dictatorship. Freedom of trade, therefore, must be subject to the demands of social justice.

In addition to giving a general description of the content of a concept of development, the encyclical also gives guidelines to help bring the definition to reality. Public authority has the responsibility to define objectives, and the means to achieve these and to initiate their implementation. However private institutions and other groups are to be involved in this work also. These programs are to be directed to the service of individuals and are to show as much "concern for social progress as for economic growth." Economic and technological growth and development for their own sake have no meaning; they derive their meaning and purpose from humans, whom they serve. The main areas of concentration are aid to developing nations, the establishment of equitable trade relations, and the creation of social systems which will ensure justice to all. Finally, the goal of development is peace, a more perfect form of justice among individuals built up day after day in the pursuit of an order intended by God. Development means people working for their own improvement and regional agreements among developing nations for mutual support. Consequently, programs of internationl cooperation are "the milestones on the road to development that leads to peace."

The reaction to *Populorum Progressio* demonstrated the many problems and dilemmas inherent in the increasingly specific criticism contained in Catholic social teaching. On the one hand, conservatives regarded the document as a kind of pseudo radicalism—"warmed-over Marxism," the *Wall Street Journal* said. The Pope's words could easily be turned on the Church itself: If, indeed, "the superfluous wealth of the rich countries should be placed at the service of poor nations," what, then, of the superfluous wealth of the Church? In the absence of public and forthright financial disclosure by the Church in Rome and elsewhere, rumors of Church wealth flourished, evidence of considerable wealth was available, and the charge of hypocrisy was easily made. Furthermore, the moderate liberal leadership of the West could ask, what is "superfluous wealth," and how exactly is it to be placed in the service of poor nations? While many might agree with the Pope's description of the problem, and might even share the sense of urgency, they might also feel helpless to find a solution which did not involve either dependence upon the benevolence of the wealthy or resort to violence in revolutionary struggles. As with so many other dimensions of postconciliar Catholicism, new windows had been opened, new demands had been made, but the exact direction which the Church and the world should follow was unclear. The result was that papal pronouncements could seem irrelevant to the real issues at stake. When note was taken of the continued opposition to Socialism and Communism, and the practical opposition to revolution, many felt that irrelevance had in fact become irresponsibility. In the years that followed, as local Churches attempted to develop their own theological reflection on "the signs of the times" new voices would emerge to call the Church into the midst of contemporary life. Poised in delicate balance between the Church's comfortable, established role in the developed world and its moral commitment to freedom, justice, and peace, Pope Paul VI attempted to provide leadership for the present with a sense of continuity with the past. It was a most difficult task.

The retention of so many of the forms of the past, particularly the forms of diplomatic relations, suggested an approach to social questions characteristic of a state or of an ideologically oriented movement. Yet, the emerging social theology suggested that while the Church made its own set of moral and ethical criteria on the basis of which it could condemn certain situations as contradictions of Christian teaching, and while these same standards could allow it to offer criticism of methods of solving social problems, actual, concrete policies and programs designed to promote world peace or social justice required judgment of the political and economic order in which the Church had no special expertise. The tendency of the heavily democratic language of development and participation suggested that such programs and policies must come from the people themselves, utilizing the best social science expertise available to them. Rather than telling the world how to solve its problems, the Church was taking on the role of a moral critic and prophet, seeking a full commitment to basic human values in its own life, and encouraging its people to become active, helpful, and committed participants in all its movements and struggles for human liberation. Accordingly, while continuing to speak a message of hope to the people of the world, the Church gradually directed more and more of its attention to itself, urging its local Churches and their people to make the principles of justice and peace their own, to embody those principles in the day-to-day life of their Christian communities, and to join actively, as individuals and as groups with other people to alleviate suffering and to build a just and peaceful world.

POPULORUM PROGRESSIO

ENCYCLICAL LETTER OF HIS HOLINESS,
PAUL VI, POPE, TO THE BISHOPS, PRIESTS,
RELIGIOUS, THE FAITHFUL, AND
TO ALL MEN OF GOOD WILL

1. The development of peoples has the Church's close attention, particularly the development of those peoples who are striving to escape from hunger, misery, endemic diseases and ignorance; of those who are looking for a wider share in the benefits of civilization and a more active improvement of their human qualities; of those who are aiming purposefully at their complete fulfillment. Following on the Second Vatican Ecumenical Council a renewed consciousness of the demands of the Gospel makes it her duty to put herself at the service of all, to help them grasp their serious problem in all its dimensions, and to convince them that solidarity in action at this turning point in human history is a matter of urgency.

2. Our predecessors in their great encyclicals, Leo XIII in *Rerum Novarum*,[1] Pius XI in *Quadragesimo Anno*[2] and John XXIII in *Mater et Magistra*[3] and *Pacem in Terris*[4]— not to mention the messages of Pius XII[5] to the world—did not fail in the duty of their office of shedding the light of the Gospel on the social questions of their times.

3. Today the principal fact that we must all recognise is that the social question has become world-wide. John XXIII stated this in unambiguous terms[6] and the Council echoed him in its Pastoral Constitution on *The Church in the Modern World*.[7] This teaching is important and its application urgent. Today the peoples in hunger are making a dramatic appeal to the peoples blessed with abundance. The Church shudders at this cry of anguish and calls each one to give a loving response of charity to this brother's cry for help.

4. Before We became Pope, two journeys, to Latin America in 1960 and to Africa in 1962, brought Us into direct contact with the acute problems pressing on continents full of life and hope. Then on becoming Father of all We made further journeys, to the Holy Land and India, and were able to see and virtually touch the very serious difficulties besetting peoples of long-standing civilisations who are at grips with the problem of development. While the Second Vatican Ecumenical Council was being held in Rome, providential circumstances permitted Us to address in person the General Assembly of the United Nations, and We pleaded the cause of poor peoples before this distinguished body.

5. Then quite recently, in Our desire to carry out the wishes of the Council and give specific expression to the Holy See's contribution to this great cause of peoples in development, We considered it Our duty to set up a Pontifical Commission in the Church's central administration, charged with "bringing to the whole of God's People the full knowledge of the part expected of them at the present time, so as to further the progress of poorer peoples, to encourage social justice among nations, to offer to less developed nations the means whereby they can further their own progress":[8] its name, which is also its programme, is *Justice and Peace*. We think that this can and should bring together men of good will with our Catholic sons and our Christian brothers. So it is to all that We address this solemn appeal for concrete action towards man's complete development and the development of all mankind.

PART I

FOR MAN'S COMPLETE DEVELOPMENT

1. THE DATA OF THE PROBLEM

6. Freedom from misery; the greater assurance of finding subsistence, health and fixed employment; an increased share of responsibility without oppression of any kind and in security from situations that do violence to their dignity as men;

better education—in brief, to seek to do more, know more and have more in order to be more: that is what men aspire to now when a greater number of them are condemned to live in conditions that make this lawful desire illusory. Besides, peoples who have recently gained national independence experience the need to add to this political freedom a fitting autonomous growth, social as well as economic, in order to assure their citizens of a full human enhancement and to take their rightful place with other nations.

7. Though insufficient for the immensity and urgency of the task, the means inherited from the past are not lacking. It must certainly be recognised that colonising powers have often furthered their own interests, power or glory, and that their departure has sometimes left a precarious economy, bound up for instance with the production of one kind of crop whose market prices are subject to sudden and considerable variation. Yet while recognising the damage done by a certain type of colonialism and its consequences, one must at the same time acknowledge the qualities and achievement of colonisers who brought their science and technical knowledge and left beneficial results of their presence in so many underprivileged regions. The structures established by them persist, however incomplete they may be; they diminished ignorance and sickness, brought the benefits of communications and improved living conditions.

8. Yet once this is admitted, it remains only too true that the resultant situation is manifestly inadequate for facing the hard reality of modern economics. Left to itself it works rather to widen the differences in the world's levels of life, not to diminish them: rich peoples enjoy rapid growth whereas the poor develop slowly. The imbalance is on the increase: some produce a surplus of foodstuffs, others cruelly lack them and see their exports made uncertain.

9. At the same time social conflicts have taken on world dimensions. The acute disquiet which has taken hold of the poor classes in countries that are becoming industrialised, is now embracing those whose economy is almost exclusively agrarian: farming people, too, are becoming aware of their "undeserved hardship."[9] There is also the scandal of glaring inequalities not merely in the enjoyment of possessions but

even more in the exercise of power. While a small restricted group enjoys a refined civilisation in certain regions, the remainder of the population, poor and scattered, is "deprived of nearly all possibility of personal initiative and of responsibility, and often times even its living and working conditions are unworthy of the human person."[10]

10. Furthermore, the conflict between traditional civilisations and the new elements of industrial civilisation break down structures which do not adapt themselves to new conditions. Their framework, sometimes rigid, was the indispensable prop to personal and family life; older people remain attached to it, the young escape from it, as from a useless barrier, to turn eagerly to new forms of life in society. The conflict of the generations is made more serious by a tragic dilemma: whether to retain ancestral institutions and convictions and renounce progress, or to admit techniques and civilisations from outside and reject along with the traditions of the past all their human richness. In effect, the moral, spiritual and religious supports of the past too often give way without securing in return any guarantee of a place in the new world.

11. In this confusion the temptation becomes stronger to risk being swept away towards types of messianism which give promises but create illusions. The resulting dangers are patent: violent popular reactions, agitation towards insurrection, and a drifting towards totalitarian ideologies. Such are the data of the problem. Its seriousness is evident to all.

2. THE CHURCH AND DEVELOPMENT

12. True to the teaching and example of her divine Founder, Who cited the preaching of the Gospel to the poor as a sign of His mission,[11] the Church has never failed to foster the human progress of the nations to which she brings faith in Christ. Her missionaries have built, not only churches, but also hostels and hospitals, schools and universities. Teaching the local populations the means of deriving the best advantages from their natural resources, missionaries have often protected them from the greed of foreigners. Without doubt their work, inasmuch as it was human, was

not perfect, and sometimes the announcement of the authentic Gospel message was infiltrated by many ways of thinking and acting which were characteristic of their home country. But the missionaries were also able to develop and foster local institutions. In many a region they were among the pioneers in material progress as well as in cultural advancement. Let it suffice to recall the example of Father Charles de Foucauld, whose charity earned him the title "Universal Brother," and who edited an invaluable dictionary of the Touareg language. We ought to pay tribute to these pioneers who have been too often forgotten, but who were urged on by the love of Christ, just as we honour their imitators and successors who today still continue to put themselves at the generous and unselfish service of those to whom they announce the Gospel.

13. However, local and individual undertakings are no longer enough. The present situation of the world demands concerted action based on a clear vision of all economic, social, cultural, and spiritual aspects. Experienced in human affairs, the Church, without attempting to interfere in any way in the politics of States, "seeks but a solitary goal: to carry forward the work of Christ Himself under the lead of the befriending Spirit. And Christ entered this world to give witness to the truth, to rescue and not to sit in judgment, to serve and not to be served."[12] Founded to establish on earth the Kingdom of Heaven and not to conquer any earthly power, the Church clearly states that the two realms are distinct, just as the two powers, ecclesiastical and civil, are supreme, each in its own domain.[13] But, since the Church lives in history, she ought to "scrutinize the signs of the times and interpret them in the light of the Gospel."[14] Sharing the noblest aspirations of men and suffering when she sees them not satisfied, she wishes to help them attain their full flowering, and that is why she offers men what she possesses as her characteristic attribute: a global vision of man and of the human race.

Christian Vision of Development

14. Development cannot be limited to mere economic growth. In order to be authentic, it must be complete: in-

tegral, that is, it has to promote the good of every man and of the whole man. As an eminent specialist has very rightly and emphatically declared: "We do not believe in separating the economic from the human, nor development from the civilisations in which it exists. What we hold important is man, each man and each group of men, and we even include the whole of humanity."[15]

15. In the design of God, every man is called upon to develop and fulfill himself, for every life is a vocation. At birth, everyone is granted, in germ, a set of aptitudes and qualities for him to bring to fruition. Their coming to maturity, which will be the result of education received from the environment and personal efforts, will allow each man to direct himself toward the destiny intended for him by his Creator. Endowed with intelligence and freedom, he is responsible for his fulfilment as he is for his salvation. He is aided, or sometimes impeded, by those who educate him and those with whom he lives, but each one remains, whatever be these influences affecting him, the principal agent of his own success or failure. By the unaided effort of his own intelligence and his will, each man can grow in humanity, can enhance his personal worth, can become more a person.

16. However, this self-fulfilment is not something optional. Just as the whole of creation is ordained to its Creator, so spiritual beings should of their own accord orientate their lives to God, the first truth and the supreme good. Thus it is that human fulfilment constitutes, as it were, a summary of our duties. But there is much more: this harmonious enrichment of nature by personal and responsible effort is ordered to a further perfection. By reason of his union with Christ, the source of life, man attains to new fulfilment of himself, to a transcendent humanism which gives him his greatest possible perfection: this is the highest goal of personal development.

17. But each man is a member of society. He is part of the whole of mankind. It is not just certain individuals, but all men who are called to this fullness of development. Civilisations are born, develop and die. But humanity is advancing along the path of history like the waves of a rising tide encroaching gradually on the shore. We have inherited from

past generations, and we have benefitted from the work of our contemporaries: for this reason we have obligations towards all, and we cannot refuse to interest ourselves in those who will come after us to enlarge the human family. The reality of human solidarity, which is a benefit for us, also imposes a duty.

18. This personal and communal development would be threatened if the true scale of values were undermined. The desire for necessities is legitimate, and work undertaken to obtain them is a duty: If any man will not work, neither let him eat.[16] But the acquiring of temporal goods can lead to greed, to the insatiable desire for more, and can make increased power a tempting objective. Individuals, families and nations can be overcome by avarice, be they poor or rich, and all can fall victim to a stifling materialism.

19. Increased possession is not the ultimate goal of nations nor of individuals. All growth is ambivalent. It is essential if man is to develop as a man, but in a way it imprisons man if he considers it the supreme good, and it restricts his vision. Then we see hearts harden and minds close, and men no longer gather together in friendship but out of self-interest, which soon leads to oppositions and disunity. The exclusive pursuit of possessions thus becomes an obstacle to individual fulfilment and to man's true greatness. Both for nations and for individual men, avarice is the most evident form of moral underdevelopment.

20. If further development calls for the work of more and more technicians, even more necessary is the deep thought and reflection of wise men in search of a new humanism which will enable modern man to find himself anew by embracing the higher values of love and friendship, of prayer and contemplation.[17] This is what will permit the fullness of authentic development, a development which is for each and all the transition from less human conditions to those which are more human.

21. Less human conditions: the lack of material necessities for those who are without the minimum essential for life, the moral deficiencies of those who are mutilated by selfishness. Less human conditions: oppressive social structures, whether due to the abuses of ownership or to the abuses of power, to

the exploitation of workers or to unjust transactions. Conditions that are more human: the passage from misery towards the possession of necessities, victory over social scourges, the growth of knowledge, the acquisition of culture. Additional conditions that are more human: increased esteem for the dignity of others, the turning toward the spirit of poverty,[18] cooperation for the common good, the will and desire for peace. Conditions that are still more human: the acknowledgement by man of supreme values, and of God their source and their finality. Conditions that, finally and above all, are more human: faith, a gift of God accepted by the good will of man, and unity in the charity of Christ, Who calls us all to share as sons in the life of the living God, the Father of all men.

3. ACTION TO BE UNDERTAKEN

The Universal Purpose of Created Things

22. "Fill the earth and subdue it":[19] the Bible, from the first page on, teaches us that the whole of creation is for man, that it is his responsibility to develop it by intelligent effort and by means of his labour to perfect it, so to speak, for his use. If the world is made to furnish each individual with the means of livelihood and the instruments for his growth and progress, each man has therefore the right to find in the world what is necessary for himself. The recent Council reminded us of this: "God intended the earth and all that it contains for the use of every human being and people. Thus, as all men follow justice and unite in charity, created goods should abound for them on a reasonable basis."[20] All other rights whatsoever, including those of property and of free commerce, are to be subordinated to this principle. They should not hinder but on the contrary favour its application. It is a grave and urgent social duty to redirect them to their primary finality.

23. "If someone who has the riches of this world sees his brother in need and closes his heart to him, how does the love of God abide in him?"[21] It is well known how strong were the words used by the Fathers of the Church to

describe the proper attitude of persons who possess anything towards persons in need. To quote Saint Ambrose: "You are not making a gift of your possessions to the poor person. You are handing over to him what is his. For what has been given in common for the use of all, you have arrogated to yourself. The world is given to all, and not only to the rich."[22] That is, private property does not constitute for anyone an absolute and unconditioned right. No one is justified in keeping for his exclusive use what he does not need, when others lack necessities. In a word "according to the traditional doctrine as found in the Fathers of the Church and the great theologians, the right to property must never be exercised to the detriment of the common good." If there should arise a conflict "between acquired private rights and primary community exigencies," it is the responsibility of public authorities "to look for a solution, with the active participation of individuals and social groups."[23]

24. If certain landed estates impede the general prosperity because they are extensive, unused or poorly used, or because they bring hardship to peoples or are detrimental to the interests of the country, the common good sometimes demands their expropriation. While giving a clear statement on this,[24] the Council recalled no less clearly that the available revenue is not to be used in accordance with mere whim, and that no place must be given to selfish speculation. Consequently it is unacceptable that citizens with abundant incomes from the resources and activity of their country should transfer a considerable part of this income abroad purely for their own advantage, without care for the manifest wrong they inflict on their country by doing this.[25]

Industrialisation

25. The introduction of industry is a necessity for economic growth and human progress; it is also a sign of development and contributes to it. By persistent work and use of his intelligence man gradually wrests nature's secrets from her and finds a better application for her riches. As his self-mastery increases, he develops a taste for research and discovery, an ability to take a calculated risk, boldness in enterprises, generosity in what he does and a sense of responsibility.

26. But it is unfortunate that on these new conditions of society a system has been constructed which considers profit as the key motive for economic progress, competition as the supreme law of economics, and private ownership of the means of production as an absolute right that has no limits and carries no corresponding social obligation. This unchecked liberalism leads to dictatorship rightly denounced by Pius XI as producing "the international imperialism of money."[26] One cannot condemn such abuses too strongly by solemnly recalling once again that the economy is at the service of man.[27] But if it is true that a type of capitalism has been the source of excessive suffering, injustices and fratricidal conflicts whose effects still persist, it would also be wrong to attribute to industrialisation itself evils that belong to the woeful system which accompanied it. On the contrary one must recognise in all justice the irreplaceable contribution made by the organisation of labour and of industry to what development has accomplished.

27. Similarly with work: while it can sometimes be given exaggerated significance, it is for all something willed and blessed by God. Man created to His image "must cooperate with his Creator in the perfecting of creation and communicate to the earth the spiritual imprint he himself has received."[28] God, Who has endowed man with intelligence, imagination and sensitivity, has also given him the means of completing His work in a certain way: whether he be artist or craftsman, engaged in management, industry or agriculture, everyone who works is a creator. Bent over a material that resists his efforts, a man by his work gives his imprint to it, acquiring, as he does so, perseverance, skill and a spirit of invention. Further, when work is done in common, when hope, hardship, ambition and joy are shared, it brings together and firmly unites the wills, minds and hearts of men: in its accomplishment, men find themselves to be brothers.[29]

28. Work of course can have contrary effects, for it promises money, pleasure and power, invites some to selfishness, others to revolt; it also develops professional awareness, sense of duty and charity to one's neighbour. When it is more scientific and better organised, there is a risk of its dehumanising those who perform it, by making them its servants,

for work is human only if it remains intelligent and free. John XXIII gave a reminder of the urgency of giving everyone who works his proper dignity by making him a true sharer in the work he does with others: "every effort should be made that the enterprise become a community of persons in the dealings, activities and standing of all its members."[30] Man's labour means much more still for the Christian: the mission of sharing in the creation of the supernatural world[31] which remains incomplete until we all come to build up together that perfect Man of whom St. Paul speaks "who realises the fulness of Christ."[32]

Urgency of the Task to Be Done

29. We must make haste: too many are suffering, and the distance is growing that separates the progress of some and the stagnation, not to say the regression, of others. Yet the work required should advance smoothly if there is not to be the risk of losing indispensable equilibrium. A hasty agrarian reform can fail. Industrialisation if introduced suddenly can displace structures still necessary, and produce hardships in society which would be a setback in terms of human values.

30. There are certainly situations whose injustice cries to heaven. When whole populations destitute of necessities live in a state of dependence barring them from all initiative and responsibility, and all opportunity to advance culturally and share in social and political life, recourse to violence, as a means to right these wrongs to human dignity, is a grave temptation.

31. We know, however, that a revolutionary uprising—save where there is manifest, long-standing tyranny which would do great damage to fundamental personal rights and dangerous harm to the common good of the country—produces new injustices, throws more elements out of balance and brings on new disasters. A real evil should not be fought against at the cost of greater misery.

32. We want to be clearly understood: the present situation must be faced with courage and the injustices linked with it must be fought against and overcome. Development demands bold transformations, innovations that go deep. Urgent reforms should be undertaken without delay. It is for

each one to take his share in them with generosity, particularly those whose education, position and opportunities afford them wide scope for action. May they show an example, and give of their own possessions as several of Our brothers in the episcopacy have done.[33] In so doing they will live up to men's expectations and be faithful to the Spirit of God, since it is "the ferment of the Gospel which has aroused and continues to arouse in man's heart the irresistible requirements of his dignity."[34]

Programmes and Planning

33. Individual initiative alone and the mere free play of competition could never assure successful development. One must avoid the risk of increasing still more the wealth of the rich and the dominion of the strong, whilst leaving the poor in their misery and adding to the servitude of the oppressed. Hence programmes are necessary in order "to encourage, stimulate, coordinate, supplement and integrate"[35] the activity of individuals and of intermediary bodies. It pertains to the public authorities to choose, even to lay down the objectives to be pursued, the ends to be achieved, and the means for attaining these, and it is for them to stimulate all the forces engaged in this common activity. But let them take care to associate private initiative and intermediary bodies with this work. They will thus avoid the danger of complete collectivisation or of arbitrary planning, which, by denying liberty, would prevent the exercise of the fundamental rights of the human person.

34. This is true since every programme, made to increase production, has, in the last analysis, no other *raison d'être* than the service of man. Such programmes should reduce inequalities, fight discriminations, free man from various types of servitude and enable him to be the instrument of his spiritual growth. To speak of development, is in effect to show as much concern for social progress as for economic growth. It is not sufficient to increase overall wealth for it to be distributed equitably. It is not sufficient to promote technology to render the world a more human place in which to live. The mistakes of their predecessors should warn those on the road to development of the dangers to be avoided in this field. To-

morrow's technocracy can beget evils no less redoubtable than those due to the liberalism of yesterday. Economics and technology have no meaning except from man whom they should serve. And man is only truly man in as far as, master of his own acts and judge of their worth, he is author of his own advancement, in keeping with the nature which was given to him by his Creator and whose possibilities and exigencies he himself freely assumes.

35. It can even be affirmed that economic growth depends in the very first place upon social progress: thus basic education is the primary object of any plan of development. Indeed hunger for education is no less debasing than hunger for food: an illiterate is a person with an undernourished mind. To be able to read and write, to acquire a professional formation, means to recover confidence in oneself and to discover that one can progress along with the others. As We said in Our message to the UNESCO Congress held in 1965 at Teheran, for man literacy is "a fundamental factor of social integration, as well as of personal enrichment, and for society it is a privileged instrument of economic progress and of development."[36] We also rejoice at the good work accomplished in this field by private initiative, by the public authorities and by international organisations: these are the primary agents of development, because they render man capable of acting for himself.

36. But man finds his true identity only in his social milieu, where the family plays a fundamental role. The family's influence may have been excessive, at some periods of history and in some places when it was exercised to the detriment of the fundamental rights of the individual. The long-standing social frameworks, often too rigid and badly organised, existing in developing countries, are, nevertheless, still necessary for a time, yet progressively relaxing their excessive hold on the population. But the natural family, monogamous and stable, such as the divine plan conceived it[37] and as Christianity sanctified it, must remain the place where "the various generations come together and help one another to grow wiser and to harmonise personal rights with the other requirements of social life."[38]

37. It is true that too frequently an accelerated demo-

graphic increase adds its own difficulties to the problems of development: the size of the population increases more rapidly than available resources, and things are found to have reached apparently an impasse. From that moment the temptation is great to check the demographic increase by means of radical measures. It is certain that public authorities can intervene, within the limit of their competence, by favouring the availability of appropriate information and by adopting suitable measures, provided that these be in conformity with the moral law and that they respect the rightful freedom of married couples. Where the inalienable right to marriage and procreation is lacking, human dignity has ceased to exist. Finally, it is for the parents to decide, with full knowledge of the matter, on the number of their children, taking into account their responsibilities towards God, themselves, the children they have already brought into the world, and the community to which they belong. In all this they must follow the demands of their own conscience enlightened by God's law authentically interpreted, and sustained by confidence in Him.[39]

38. In the task of development, man, who finds his life's primary environment in the family, is often aided by professional organisations. If it is their objective to promote the interests of their members, their responsibility is also great with regard to the educative task which at the same time they can and ought to accomplish. By means of the information they provide and the formation they propose, they can do much to give to all a sense of the common good and of the consequent obligations that fall upon each person.

39. All social action involves a doctrine. The Christian cannot admit that which is based upon a materialistic and atheistic philosophy, which respects neither the religious orientation of life to its final end, nor human freedom and dignity. But, provided that these values are safeguarded, a pluralism of professional organisations and trade unions is admissible, and from certain points of view useful, if thereby liberty is protected and emulation stimulated. And We most willingly pay homage to all those who labour in them to give unselfish service to their brothers.

40. In addition to professional organisations, there are also

institutions which are at work. Their role is no less important for the success of development. "The future of the world stands in peril," the Council gravely affirms, "unless wiser men are forthcoming." And it adds: "many nations, poorer in economic goods, are quite rich in wisdom and able to offer noteworthy advantages to others."[40] Rich or poor, each country possesses a civilisation handed down by their ancestors: institutions called for by life in this world, and higher manifestations of the life of the spirit, manifestations of an artistic, intellectual and religious character. When the latter possess true human values, it would be grave error to sacrifice them to the former. A people that would act in this way would thereby lose the best of its patrimony; in order to live, it would be sacrificing its reasons for living. Christ's teaching also applies to people: "What does it profit a man to gain the whole world if he suffers the loss of his soul."[41]

41. Less well-off peoples can never be sufficiently on their guard against this temptation which comes to them from wealthy nations. For these nations all too often set an example of success in a highly technical and culturally developed civilisation; they also provide the model for a way of acting that is principally aimed at the conquest of material prosperity. Not that material prosperity of itself precludes the activity of the human spirit. On the contrary, the human spirit, "increasingly free of its bondage to creatures, can be more easily drawn to the worship and contemplation of the Creator."[42] However, "modern civilization itself often complicates the approach to God, not for any essential reason, but because it is excessively engrossed in earthly affairs."[43] Developing nations must know how to discriminate among those things that are held out to them; they must be able to assess critically, and eliminate those deceptive goods which would only bring about a lowering of the human ideal, and to accept those values that are sound and beneficial, in order to develop them alongside their own, in accordance with their own genius.

42. What must be aimed at is complete humanism.[44] And what is that if not the fully rounded development of the whole man and of all men? A humanism closed in on itself, and not open to the values of the spirit and to God Who is

their source, could achieve apparent success. True, man can organise the world apart from God, but "without God man can organise it in the end only to man's detriment. An isolated humanism is an inhuman humanism."[45] There is no true humanism but that which is open to the Absolute and is conscious of a vocation which gives human life its true meaning. Far from being the ultimate measure of all things, man can only realise himself by reaching beyond himself. As Pascal has said so well: "Man infinitely surpasses man."[46]

PART II

The Development of the Human Race in the Spirit of Solidarity

43. There can be no progress towards the complete development of man without the simultaneous development of all humanity in the spirit of solidarity. As We said at Bombay: "Man must meet man, nation meet nation, as brothers and sisters, as children of God. In this mutual understanding and friendship, in this sacred communion, we must also begin to work together to build the common future of the human race."[47] We also suggested a search for concrete and practical ways of organisation and cooperation, so that all available resources be pooled and thus a true communion among all nations be achieved.

44. This duty is the concern especially of better-off nations. Their obligations stem from a brotherhood that is at once human and supernatural, and take on a threefold aspect: the duty of human solidarity—the aid that the rich nations must give to developing countries; the duty of social justice—the rectification of inequitable trade relations between powerful nations and weak nations; the duty of universal charity—the effort to bring about a world that is more human towards all men, where all will be able to give and receive, without one group making progress at the expense of the other. The question is urgent, for on it depends the future of the civilisation of the world.

1. AID FOR THE WEAK

45. "If a brother or a sister be naked," says Saint James, "if they lack their daily nourishment, and one of you says to them: 'Go in peace, be warmed and be filled,' without giving them what is necessary for the body, what good does it do?"[48] Today no one can be ignorant any longer of the fact that in whole continents countless men and women are ravished by hunger, countless numbers of children are undernourished, so that many of them die in infancy, while the physical growth and mental development of many others are retarded and as a result whole regions are condemned to the most depressing despondency.

46. Anguished appeals have already been sounded in the past: that of John XXIII was warmly received.[49] We Ourselves repeated it in Our Christmas Message of 1963,[50] and again in 1966 on behalf of India.[51] The campaign against hunger being carried on by the Food and Agriculture Organisation (FAO) and encouraged by the Holy See has been generously supported. Our *Caritas Internationalis* is at work everywhere, and many Catholics, at the urging of Our Brothers in the episcopacy, contribute generously of their means and spend themselves without counting the cost in assisting those who are in want, continually widening the circle of those they look upon as neighbors.

47. But neither all this nor the private and public funds that have been invested, nor the gifts and loans that have been made, can suffice. It is not just a matter of eliminating hunger, nor even of reducing poverty. The struggle against destitution, though urgent and necessary, is not enough. It is a question, rather, of building a world where every man, no matter what his race, religion or nationality, can live a fully human life, freed from servitude imposed on him by other men or by natural forces over which he has not sufficient control; a world where freedom is not an empty word and where the poor man Lazarus can sit down at the same table with the rich man.[52] This demands great generosity, much sacrifice and unceasing effort on the part of the rich man. Let

each one examine his conscience, a conscience that conveys a new message for our times. Is he prepared to support out of his own pocket works and undertakings organised in favour of the most destitute? Is he ready to pay higher taxes so that the public authorities can intensify their efforts in favour of development? Is he ready to pay a higher price for imported goods so that the producer may be more justly rewarded? Or to leave this country, if necessary and if he is young, in order to assist in this development of the young nations?

48. The same duty of solidarity that rests on individuals exists also for nations: "Advanced nations have a very heavy obligation to help the developing peoples."[53] It is necessary to put this teaching of the Council into effect. Although it is normal that a nation should be the first to benefit from the gifts that Providence has bestowed on it as the fruit of the labours of its people, still no country can claim on that account to keep its wealth for itself alone. Every nation must produce more and better quality goods to give to all its inhabitants a truly human standard of living, and also to contribute to the common development of the human race. Given the increasing needs of the under-developed countries, it should be considered quite normal for an advanced country to devote a part of its production to meet their needs, and to train teachers, engineers, technicians and scholars prepared to put their knowledge and their skill at the disposal of less fortunate peoples.

49. We must repeat once more that the superfluous wealth of rich countries should be placed at the service of poor nations. The rule which up to now held good for the benefit of those nearest to us, must today be applied to all the needy of this world. Besides, the rich will be the first to benefit as a result. Otherwise their continued greed will certainly call down upon them the judgement of God and the wrath of the poor, with consequences no one can foretell. If today's flourishing civilisations remain selfishly wrapped up in themselves, they could easily place their highest values in jeopardy, sacrificing their will to be great to the desire to possess more. To them we could apply also the parable of the rich man whose fields yielded an abundant harvest and who

did not know where to store his harvest: "God said to him: 'Fool, this night do they demand your soul of you.' "[54]

50. In order to be fully effective, these efforts ought not remain scattered or isolated, much less be in competition for reasons of power or prestige: the present situation calls for concerted planning. A planned programme is of course better and more effective than occasional aid left to individual good-will. It presupposes, as We said above, careful study, the selection of ends and the choice of means, as well as a reorganisation of efforts to meet the needs of the present and the demands of the foreseeable future. More important, a concerted plan has advantages that go beyond the field of economic growth and social progress; for in addition it gives significance and value to the work undertaken. While shaping the world it sets a higher value on man.

51. But it is necessary to go still further. At Bombay We called for the establishment of a great *World Fund*, to be made up of part of the money spent on arms, to relieve the most destitute of this world.[55] What is true of the immediate struggle against want, holds good also when there is a question of development. Only world-wide collaboration, of which a common fund would be both means and symbol, will succeed in overcoming vain rivalries and in establishing a fruitful and peaceful exchange between peoples.

52. There is certainly no need to do away with bilateral and multilateral agreements: they allow ties of dependence and feelings of betterness, left over from the era of colonialism, to yield place to the happier relationship of friendship, based on a footing of constitutional and political equality. However, if they were to be fitted into the framework of world-wide collaboration, they would be beyond all suspicion, and as a result there would be less distrust on the part of the receiving nations. These would have less cause for fearing that, under the cloak of financial aid or technical assistance, there lurk certain manifestations of what has come to be called neo-colonialism, in the form of political pressures and economic suzerainty aimed at maintaining or acquiring complete dominance.

53. Besides, who does not see that such a fund would

make it easier to take measures to prevent certain wasteful expenditures, the result of fear or pride? When so many people are hungry, when so many families suffer from destitution, when so many remain steeped in ignorance, when so many schools, hospitals and homes worthy of the name remain to be built, all public or private squandering of wealth, all expenditure prompted by motives of national or personal ostentation, every exhausting armaments race, becomes an intolerable scandal. We are conscious of Our duty to denounce it. Would that those in authority listened to Our words before it is too late!

54. This means that it is absolutely necessary to create among all peoples that dialogue for whose establishment We expressed Our hope in Our first Encyclical *Ecclesiam Suam.*[56] This dialogue between those who contribute wealth and those who benefit from it, will provide the possibility of making an assessment of the contribution necessary, not only drawn up in terms of the generosity and the available wealth of the donor nations, but also conditioned by the real needs of the receiving countries and the use to which the financial assistance can be put. Developing countries will thus no longer risk being overwhelmed by debts whose repayment swallows up the greater part of their gains. Rates of interest and time for repayment of the loan could be so arranged as not to be too great a burden on either party, taking into account free gifts, interest-free or low-interest loans, and the time needed for liquidating the debts. Guarantees could be given to those who provide the capital that it will be put to use according to an agreed plan and with a reasonable measure of efficiency, since there is no question of encouraging parasites or the indolent. And the receiving countries could demand that there be no interference in their political life or subversion of their social structures. As sovereign states they have the right to conduct their own affairs, to decide on their policies and to move freely towards the kind of society they choose. What must be brought about, therefore, is a system of cooperation freely undertaken, an effective and mutual sharing, carried out with equal dignity on either side, for the construction of a more human world.

55. The task might seem impossible in those regions where

Most 3rd world dealing with impossible debt problems 1st world terribly overextended in 3rd world. Lends 3rd world money the cares of day-to-day survival fill the entire existence of families incapable of planning the kind of work which would open the way to a future that is less desperate. These, however, are the men and women who must be helped, who must be persuaded to work for their own betterment and endeavour to acquire gradually the means to that end. This common task will not succeed without concerted, constant and courageous efforts. But let everyone be convinced of this: the very life of poor nations, civil peace in developing countries, and world peace itself are at stake.

2. EQUITY IN TRADE RELATIONS

56. The efforts which are being made to assist developing nations on a financial and technical basis, though considerable, would be illusory if their benefits were to be partially nullified as a consequence of the trade relations existing between rich and poor countries. The confidence of these latter would be severely shaken if they had the impression that what was being given them with one hand was being taken away with the other.

57. Of course, highly industrialised nations export for the most part manufactured goods, while countries with less developed economics have only food, fibres and other raw materials to sell. As a result of technical progress the value of manufactured goods is rapidly increasing and they can always find an adequate market. On the other hand, raw materials produced by under-developed countries are subject to wide and sudden fluctuations in price, a state of affairs far removed from the progressively increasing value of industrial products. As a result, nations whose industrialisation is limited are faced with serious difficulties when they have to rely on their exports to balance their economy and to carry out their plans for development. The poor nations remain ever poor while the rich ones become still richer.

58. In other words, the rule of free trade, taken by itself, is no longer able to govern international relations. Its advantages are certainly evident when the parties involved are not affected by any excessive inequalities of economic power: it is an incentive to progress and a reward for effort. That is why

industrially developed countries see in it a law of justice. But
the situation is no longer the same when economic conditions differ too widely from country to country: prices which
are "freely" set in the market can produce unfair results. One
must recognise that it is the fundamental principle of
liberalism, as the rule for commercial exchange, which is
questioned here.

59. The teaching of Leo XIII in *Rerum Novarum* is always valid: if the positions of the contracting parties are too
unequal, the consent of the parties does not suffice to guarantee the justice of their contract, and the rule of free
agreement remains subservient to the demands of the natural
law.[57] What was true of the just wage for the individual is
also true of international contracts: an economy of exchange
can no longer be based solely on the law of free competition,
a law which, in its turn, too often creates an economic dictatorship. Freedom of trade is fair only if it is subject to the
demands of social justice.

60. Moreover, this has been understood by the developed
nations themselves, which are striving, by means of appropriate measures, to re-establish within their own economies
a balance, which competition, if left to itself, tends to compromise. Thus it happens that these nations often support
their agriculture at the price of sacrifices imposed on economically more favoured sectors. Similarly, to maintain the commercial relations which are developing among themselves, especially within a common market, the financial, fiscal, and
social policy of these nations tries to restore comparable opportunities to competing industries which are not equally
prospering.

61. In this area one cannot employ two systems of weights
and measures. What holds for a national economy or among
developed countries is valid also in commercial relations between rich nations and poor nations. Without abolishing the
competitive market, it should be kept within the limits which
make it just and moral, and therefore human. In trade between developed and under-developed economies, conditions
are too disparate and the degrees of genuine freedom available too unequal. In order that international trade be human

and moral, social justice requires that it restore to the participants a certain equality of opportunity. This equality is a long-term objective, but to reach it, we must begin now to create true equality in discussions and negotiations. Here again international agreements on a rather wide scale would be helpful: they would establish general norms for regulating certain prices, for guaranteeing certain types of production, for supporting certain new industries. Who is there who does not see that such a common effort aimed at increased justice in business relations between peoples would bestow on developing nations positive assistance, the effects of which would be not only immediate but lasting?

62. Among still other obstacles which are opposed to the formation of a world which is more just and which is better organised toward a universal solidarity, We wish to speak of nationalism and racism. It is only natural that communities which have recently reached their political independence should be jealous of a national unity which is still fragile, and that they should strive to protect it. Likewise, it is to be expected that nations endowed with an ancient culture should be proud of the patrimony which their history has bequeathed to them. But these legitimate feelings should be ennobled by that universal charity which embraces the entire human family. Nationalism isolates people from their true good. It would be especially harmful where the weakness of national economies demands rather the pooling of efforts, of knowledge and of funds, in order to implement programmes of development and to increase commercial and cultural exchange.

63. Racism is not the exclusive lot of young nations, where sometimes it hides beneath the rivalries of clans and political parties, with heavy losses for justice and at the risk of civil war. During the colonial period it often flared up between the colonists and the indigenous population, and stood in the way of mutually profitable understanding, often giving rise to bitterness in the wake of genuine injustices. It is still an obstacle to collaboration among disadvantaged nations and a cause of division and hatred within countries whenever individuals and families see the inviolable rights of the human

person held in scorn, as they themselves are unjustly subjected to a regime of discrimination because of their race or their colour.

64. We are deeply distressed by such a situation which is laden with threats for the future. We are, nonetheless, hopeful: a more deeply felt need for collaboration, a heightened sense of unity will finally triumph over misunderstandings and selfishness. We hope that the countries whose development is less advanced will be able to take advantage of their proximity in order to organise among themselves, on a broadened territorial basis, areas for concerted development: to draw up programmes in common, to coordinate investments, to distribute the means of production, and to organise trade. We hope also that multilateral and international bodies, by means of the reorganisation which is required, will discover the ways that will allow peoples which are still underdeveloped to break through the barriers which seem to enclose them and to discover for themselves, in full fidelity to their own proper genius, the means for their social and human progress.

65. Such is the goal we must attain. World unity, ever more effective, should allow all peoples to become the artisans of their destiny. The past has too often been characterized by relationships of violence between nations; may the day dawn when international relations will be marked with the stamp of mutual respect and friendship, of interdependence in collaboration, the betterment of all seen as the responsibility of each individual. The younger or weaker nations ask to assume their active part in the construction of a better world, one which shows deeper respect for the rights and the vocation of the individual. This is a legitimate appeal; everyone should hear it and respond to it.

3. UNIVERSAL CHARITY

66. The world is sick. Its illness consists less in the unproductive monopolisation of resources by a small number of men than in the lack of brotherhood among individuals and peoples.

67. We cannot insist too much on the duty of welcoming

others—a duty springing from human solidarity and Christian charity—which is incumbent both on the families and the cultural organisations of the host countries. Centres of welcome and hostels must be multiplied, especially for youth. This must be done first to protect them from loneliness, the feeling of abandonment and distress, which undermine all moral resistance. This is also necessary to protect them from the unhealthy situation in which they find themselves, forced as they are to compare the extreme poverty of their homeland with the luxury and waste which often surround them. It should be done also to protect them against the subversive teachings and temptations to aggression which assail them, as they recall so much "unmerited misery."[58] Finally, and above all, this hospitality should aim to provide them, in the warm atmosphere of a brotherly welcome, with the example of wholesome living, an esteem for genuine and effective Christian charity, an esteem for spiritual values.

68. It is painful to think of the numerous young people who come to more advanced countries to receive the science, the competence, and the culture which will make them more qualified to serve their homeland, and who certainly acquire there a formation of high quality, but who often lose the esteem for the spiritual values which often were to be found, as a precious patrimony, in the civilisations where they had grown up.

69. The same welcome is due to emigrant workers, who live in conditions which are often inhuman, and who economise on what they earn in order to send a little relief to their family living in misery in their native land.

70. Our second recommendation is for those whose business calls them to countries recently opened to industrialisation: industrialists, merchants, leaders or representatives of larger enterprises. It happens that they are not lacking in social sensitivity in their own country; why then do they return to the unhuman principles of individualism when they operate in less-developed countries? Their advantaged situation should on the contrary move them to become the initiators of social progress and of human advancement in the area where their business calls them. Their very sense of organisation should suggest to them the means for making

intelligent use of the labour of the indigenous population, of forming qualified workers, of training engineers and staffs, of giving scope to their initiative, of introducing them progressively into higher positions, thus preparing them to share, in the near future, in the responsibilities of management. At least let justice always rule the relations between superiors and their subordinates. Let standard contracts with reciprocal obligations govern these relationships. Finally, let no one, whatever his status, be subjected unjustly to the arbitrariness of others.

71. We are happy that experts are being sent in larger and larger numbers on development missions by institutions, whether international or bilateral, or by private organisations: "they ought not conduct themselves in a lordly fashion, but as helpers and co-workers."[59] A people quickly perceives whether those who come to help them do so with or without affection, whether they come merely to apply their techniques or to recognise in man his full value.

Their message is in danger of being rejected if it is not presented in the context of brotherly love.

72. Hence, necessary technical competence must be accompanied by authentic signs of disinterested love. Freed of all nationalistic pride and of every appearance of racism, experts should learn how to work in close collaboration with all. They realise that their competence does not confer on them a superiority in every field. The civilisation which formed them contains, without doubt, elements of universal humanism, but it is not the only civilisation nor does it enjoy a monopoly of valuable elements. Moreover it cannot be imported without undergoing adaptations. The men on these missions will be intent on discovering, along with its history, the component elements of the cultural riches of the country receiving them. Mutual understanding will be established which will enrich both cultures.

73. Between civilisations, as between persons, sincere dialogue indeed creates brotherhood. The work of development will draw nations together in the attainment of goals pursued with a common effort if all, from governments and their representatives to the last expert, are inspired by brotherly love and moved by the sincere desire to build a civilisation

founded on world solidarity. A dialogue based on man, and not on commodities or technical skills, will then begin. It will be fruitful if it brings to the peoples who benefit from it the means of self-betterment and spiritual growth, if the technicians act as educators, and if the instruction imparted is characterised by so lofty a spiritual and moral tone that it guarantees not merely economic, but human development. When aid programmes have been terminated, the relationships thus established will endure. Who does not see of what importance they will be for the peace of the world?

74. Many young people have already responded with warmth and enthusiasm to the appeal of Pius XII for lay missionaries.[60] Many also are those who have spontaneously put themselves at the disposition of official or private organisations which are collaborating with developing nations. We are pleased to learn that in certain nations "military service" can be partially accomplished by doing "social service," a "service pure and simple." We bless these undertakings and the good will which inspires them. May all those who wish to belong to Christ hear His appeal: "I was hungry and you gave me to eat, thirsty and you gave me to drink, a stranger and you took me in, naked and you clothed me, sick and you visited me, a prisoner and you came to see me."[61] No one can remain indifferent to the lot of his brothers who are still buried in wretchedness, and victims of insecurity, slaves of ignorance. Like the heart of Christ, the heart of the Christian must sympathise with this misery: "I have pity on this multitude."[62]

75. The prayer of all ought to rise with fervour to the Almighty. Having become aware of such great misfortunes, the human race will apply itself with intelligence and steadfastness to abolish them. This prayer should be matched by the resolute commitment of each individual—according to the measure of his strength and possibilities—to the struggle against under-development. May individuals, social groups, and nations join hands in brotherly fashion, the strong aiding the weak to grow, exerting all their competence, enthusiasm and disinterested love. More than any other, the individual who is animated by true charity labours skillfully to discover the causes of misery, to find the means to combat it, to over-

come it resolutely. A creator of peace, he "will follow his
path, lighting the lamps of joy and playing their brilliance
and loveliness on the hearts of men across the surface of the
globe, leading them to recognise, across all frontiers, the faces
of their brothers, the faces of their friends."[63]

4. DEVELOPMENT IS THE NEW NAME FOR PEACE

76. Excessive economic, social and cultural inequalities
among peoples arouse tensions and conflicts, and are a danger
to peace. As We said to the Fathers of the Council when
We returned from Our journey of peace to the United Nations: "The condition of the peoples in process of development ought to be the object of our consideration; or better:
our charity for the poor in the world—and there are multitudes of them—must become more considerate, more active,
more generous."[64] To wage war on misery and to struggle
against injustice is to promote, along with improved conditions, the human and spiritual progress of all men, and therefore the common good of humanity. Peace cannot be limited
to a mere absence of war, the result of an ever precarious balance of forces. No, peace is something that is built up day
after day, in the pursuit of an order intended by God, which
implies a more perfect form of justice among men.[65]

77. The peoples themselves have the prime responsibility
to work for their own development. But they will not bring
this about in isolation. Regional agreements among weak nations for mutual support, understandings of wider scope entered into for their help, more far-reaching agreements to establish programmes for closer cooperation among groups of
nations—these are the milestones on the road to development that leads to peace.

78. This international collaboration on a world-wide scale
requires institutions that will prepare, coordinate and direct
it, until finally there is established an order of justice which
is universally recognised. With all Our heart, We encourage
these organisations which have undertaken this collaboration
for the development of the peoples of the world, and Our
wish is that they grow in prestige and authority. "Your vocation," as We said to the representatives of the United Na-

tions in New York, "is to bring not some people but all peoples to treat each other as brothers. . . . Who does not see the necessity of thus establishing progressively a world authority, capable of acting effectively in the juridical and political sectors?"[66]

79. Some would consider such hopes utopian. It may be that these persons are not realistic enough, and that they have not perceived the dynamism of a world which desires to live more fraternally—a world which, in spite of its ignorance, its mistakes and even its sins, its relapses into barbarism and its wanderings far from the road of salvation, is, even unawares, taking slow but sure steps towards its Creator. This road towards a greater humanity requires effort and sacrifice; but suffering itself, accepted for the love of our brethren, favours the progress of the entire human family. Christians know that union with the sacrifice of our Saviour contributes to the building up of the Body of Christ in its plentitude: the assembled people of God.[67]

80. We are all united in this progress toward God. We have desired to remind all men how crucial is the present moment, how urgent the work to be done. The hour for action has now sounded. At stake are the survival of so many innocent children and, for so many families overcome by misery, the access to conditions fit for human beings; at stake are the peace of the world and the future of civilisation. It is time for all men and all peoples to face up to their responsibilities.

A Final Appeal

81. First, We appeal to all Our sons. In countries undergoing development no less than in others, the laymen should take up as their own proper task the renewal of the temporal order. If the role of the Hierarchy is to teach and to interpret authentically the norms of morality to be followed in this matter, it belongs to the laymen, without waiting passively for orders and directives, to take the initiative freely and to infuse a Christian spirit into the mentality, customs, laws and structures of the community in which they live.[68] Changes are necessary, basic reforms are indispensable: the laymen should strive resolutely to permeate them with the

spirit of the Gospel. We ask Our Catholic sons who belong to the more favoured nations, to bring their talents and give their active participation to organisations, be they of an official or private nature, civil or religious, which are working to overcome the difficulties of the developing nations. They will certainly desire to be in the first ranks of those who collaborate to establish as fact and reality an international morality based on justice and equity.

82. We are sure that all Christians, our brethren, will wish to expand their common cooperative effort in order to help mankind vanquish selfishness, pride and rivalries, to overcome ambitions and injustices, to open up to all the road to a more human life, where each man will be loved and helped as his brother, as his neighbour. And, still deeply impressed by the memory of Our unforgettable encounter in Bombay with our non-Christian brethren, We invite them anew to work with all their heart and their intelligence towards this goal, that all the children of men may lead a life worthy of the children of God.

83. Finally, We turn to all men of good will who believe that the way to peace lies in the area of development. Delegates to international organisations, government officials, gentlemen of the press, educators: all of you, each in your own way, are the builders of a new world. We entreat Almighty God to enlighten your minds and strengthen your determination to alert public opinion and to involve the peoples of the world. Educators, it is your task to awaken in persons, from their earliest years, a love for the peoples who live in misery. Gentlemen of the press, it is up to you to place before our eyes the story of the efforts exerted to promote mutual assistance among peoples, as well as the spectacle of the miseries which men tend to forget in order to quiet their consciences. Thus at least the wealthy will know that the poor stand outside their doors waiting to receive some left-overs from their banquets.

84. Government officials, it is your concern to mobilise your peoples to form a more effective world solidarity, and above all to make them accept the necessary taxes on their luxuries and their wasteful expenditures, in order to bring about development and to save the peace. Delegates to inter-

national organisations, it depends on you to see that the dangerous and futile rivalry of powers should give place to collaboration which is friendly, peaceful and free of vested interests, in order to achieve a responsible development of mankind, in which all men will have an opportunity to find their fulfilment.

85. If it is true that the world is in trouble because of the lack of thinking, then We call upon men of reflection and of learning, Catholics, Christians, those who hold God in honour, who thirst for an absolute, for justice and for truth: We call upon all men of good will. Following Christ, We make bold to ask you earnestly: "seek and you shall find,"[69] open the paths which lead to mutual assistance among peoples, to a deepening of human knowledge, to an enlargement of heart, to a more brotherly way of living within a truly universal human society.

86. All of you who have heard the appeal of suffering peoples, all of you who are working to answer their cries, you are the apostles of a development which is good and genuine, which is not wealth that is self-centered and sought for its own sake, but rather an economy which is put at the service of man, the bread which is daily distributed to all, as a source of brotherhood and a sign of Providence.

87. With a full heart We bless you, and We appeal to all men of good will to join you in a spirit of brotherhood. For, if the new name for peace is development, who would not wish to labour for it with all his powers? Yes, We ask you, all of you, to heed Our cry of anguish, in the name of the Lord.

From the Vatican, on the Feast of Easter, the twenty-sixth day of March in the year one thousand nine hundred and sixty-seven.

PAUL PP. VI

NOTES

1. Cf. *Acta Leonis XIII*, t. XI (1892), pp. 97–148.
2. Cf. A.A.S. 23 (1931), pp. 177–228.
3. Cf. A.A.S. 53 (1961), pp. 401–64.

4. Cf. A.A.S. 55 (1963), pp. 257–304.

5. Cf. in particular the Radio Message of June 1, 1941, for the 50th anniversary of *Rerum Novarum*, in AAS 33 (1941), pp. 195–205; Christmas Radio Message of 1942, in AAS 35 (1943), pp. 9–24; Address to a group of workers on the anniversary of *Rerum Novarum*, May 14, 1953, in AAS 45 (1953), pp. 402–8.

6. Cf. Encyclical *Mater et Magistra*, May 15, 1961: AAS 53 (1961), p. 440.

7. *Gaudium et Spes*, §§ 63–72: AAS 58 (1966), pp. 1084–94.

8. Motu Proprio *Catholicam Christi Ecclesiam*, Jan. 6, 1967, AAS 59 (1967), p. 27.

9. Encyclical *Rerum Novarum*, May 15, 1891: *Acta Leonis XIII*, t. XI (1892), p. 98.

10. *Gaudium et Spes*, § 63, ¶ 5.

11. Cf. Lk. 7:22.

12. *Gaudium et Spes*, § 63, ¶ 5.

13. Cf. Encyclical *Immortale Dei*, Nov. 1, 1885: *Acta Leonis XIII* t. V (1885), p. 127.

14. *Gaudium et Spes* § 4, ¶ 1.

15. L.-J. Lebret, O.P., *Dynamique concrète du développement*, Paris: Economie et Humanisme, Les Editions Ouvrières, 1961, p. 28.

16. 2 Thes 3:10.

17. Cf., for example, J. Maritain, *Les conditions spirituelles du progrès et de la paix*, in *Rencontre des cultures à l'UNESCO sous le signe du Concile œcuménique Vatican II*, Paris: Mame, 1966, p. 66.

18. Cf. Mt 5:3.

19. Gen. 1:28.

20. *Gaudium et Spes*, § 69, ¶ 1.

21. 1 Jn 3:17.

22. *De Nabuthe*, c. 12, n. 53, (P.L. 14, 747). Cf. J.-R. Palanque, *Saint Ambroise et l'empire romain*, Paris: de Boccard, 1933, pp. 336f.

23. Letter to the 52nd Session of the French Social Weeks (Brest, 1965), in *L'homme et la révolution urbaine*, Lyons Chronique sociale, 1965, pp. 8 and 9. Cf. *L'Osservatore Romano*, July 10, 1965, *Documentation catholique*, t. 62, Paris, 1965, col. 1365.

24. *Gaudium et Spes*, § 71, ¶ 8.

25. Cf. *Ibid.*, § 65, ¶ 3.

26. Encyclical *Quadragesimo Anno*, May 15, 1931, AAS 23 (1931), p. 212.

27. Cf., for example, Colin Clark, *The Conditions of Economic Progress*, 3rd ed., London: Macmillan and Co., and New York: St. Martin's Press, 1960, pp. 3–6.

28. Letter to the 51st Session of the French Social Weeks (Lyons, 1964), in *Le travail et les travailleurs dans la societé con-*

temporaine, Lyons, Chronique sociale, 1965, p. 6. Cf. *L'Osservatore Romano*, July 10, 1964; *Documentation catholique*, t. 61, Paris, 1964, col. 931.

29. Cf., for example, M.-D. Chenu, O.P., *Pour une théologie du travail*, Paris: Editions du Seuil, 1955, Eng. tr.: *The Theology of Work: An Exploration*, Dublin: Gill and Son, 1963.

30. *Mater et Magistra*, AAS 53 (1961), p. 423.

31. Cf., for example, O. von Nell-Breuning, S.J., *Wirtschaft und Gesell-schaft*, t. 1: *Grundfragen*, Freiburg: Herder, 1956, pp. 183–84.

32. Eph 4:13.

33. Cf., for example, Bishop Manue Larrain Errázuriz of Talca, Chile, President of CELAM, *Lettre pastorale sur le developpement et la paix*, Paris: Pax Christi, 1965.

34. *Gaudium et Spes*, § 26, ⫿ 5.

35. *Mater et Magistra*, AAS 53 (1961), p. 414.

36. *L'Osservatore Romano*, Sept. 11, 1965; *Documentation catholique*, t. 62, Paris, 1965, col. 1674–75.

37. Mt 19:16.

38. *Gaudium et Spes*, § 52, ⫿ 3.

39. Cf. *Ibid.*, §§ 50–51 and note 14; and § 87, ⫿⫿ 4, 5.

40. *Ibid.*, § 15, ⫿ 4.

41. Mt 16:26.

42. *Gaudium et Spes*, § 57, ⫿ 4.

43. *Ibid.*, § 19.

44. Cf., for example, J. Maritain, *L'humanisme intégral*, Paris: Aubier, 1936. Eng. tr.: *True Humanism*, London: Geoffrey Bles; and New York: Charles Scribner's Sons, 1938.

45. H. de Lubac, S.J., *Le drame de l'humanisme athée*, Paris: Spes, 1945, p. 10. Eng. tr. *The Drama of Atheistic Humanism*, London: Sheed and Ward, 1949, p. VII.

46. *Pensées*, ed. Brunschvicg, n. 434. Cf. M. Zundel, *L'homme passe l'homme*, Le Caire, Editions du lien, 1944.

47. Address to the Representatives of non-Christian Religions, Dec. 3, 1964, AAS 57 (1965), p. 132.

48. Jas 2: 15–16.

49. Cf. *Mater et Magistra*, AAS 53 (1961), pp. 440f.

50. Cf. AAS 56 (1964), pp. 57–58.

51. Cf. *Encicliche e Discorsi di Paolo VI*, vol. IX, Roma, ed. Paoline, 1966, pp. 132–36, *Documentation catholique*, t. 43, Paris, 1966, col. 403–6.

52. Cf. Lk 16:19–31.

53. *Gaudium et Spes*, § 86, ⫿ 3.

54. Lk 12:20.

55. Message to the world, entrusted to Journalists on Dec. 4, 1964. Cf. AAS 57 (1965), p. 135.

56. CF. AAS 56 (1964), pp. 639f.

57. Cf. *Acta Leonis XIII*, t. XI (1892), p. 131.

58. Cf. *Ibid.*, p. 98.

59. *Gaudium et Spes*, § 85, ¶ 2.

60. Cf. Encyclical *Fidei Donum*, Apr. 21, 1957, AAS 49 (1957), p. 246.

61. Mt 25:35–36.

62. Mk 8:2.

63. Address of John XXIII upon Reception of the Balzan Prize for Peace, May 10, 1963, AAS 55 (1963), p. 455.

64. A.A.S. 57 (1965), p. 896.

65. Cf. Encyclical *Pacem in Terris*, Apr. 11, 1963, AAS 55 (1963), p. 301.

66. AAS 57 (1965), p. 880.

67. Cf. Eph 4:12; *Lumen Gentium*, n. 13.

68. Cf. *Apostolicam Actuositatem*, nn. 7, 13 and 24.

69. Lk 11:9.

A CALL TO ACTION:
LETTER ON THE EIGHTIETH
ANNIVERSARY OF *RERUM NOVARUM*
(OCTOGESIMA ADVENIENS)

Pope Paul's second major message on social issues took the
form of an open letter to Cardinal Roy of Quebec, chairman
of the Pontifical Commission on Justice and Peace. Timed to
coincide with the eightieth anniversary of *Rerum Novarum*
and the tenth anniversary of *Mater et Magistra*, the letter
was published as "A Call to Action." It was addressed
directly to Catholics and urged them to begin more seriously
to incorporate the new sense of Christian responsibility in
the world into all phases of their lives. It emphasized that action for justice was a personal responsibility of every Christian, that this responsibility rested also on Christian organizations and institutions, and that it involved both the effort
to bear witness to the principles of justice in personal and
community life and acting to give those principles life in the
society around them. The direction set by "A Call to Action," then, seemed fully appropriate to the situation in
which the Church found itself. Action was imperative, the
principles of action relatively clear, and the forms and styles
of action remained open to the reflection and decision of the
local Churches around the world. The imperatives set by
Pope John for the Church to become related authentically
and responsibly in all phases of its life to the contemporary
struggle of humanity for justice and peace now had the
renewed sanction of the papal office.

Even though this social message had papal approbation,

nonetheless Pope Paul emphasized that it was up to Christian communities to analyze the situation which was proper to their own country in the light of the gospel and to draw principles of reflection, norms of judgment, and directives for action from both the gospel and the Church's message. Rather than prescribe a specific program of action binding on all, the message recognized that situations in different countries were not the same and therefore no universal program could be presented. Therefore options and commitments had to be discussed in order to bring about a specific social, political, and economic change needed in a particular situation. This emphasis on self-determination, while not totally new, finds renewed support in this message and gives encouragement to those Catholics who have been involved in the social process and have been attempting to derive a Christian orientation toward the various problems in which they and their society find themselves.

A new problem that the Pope addresses in this letter is that of urbanization and industrialization. The almost exponential growth of these two phenomena has raised a host of new social problems: unemployment, mobility, unionization, and technological development. In the light of these problems the Pope asks whether humanity, "having rationally endeavored to control nature, is . . . not now becoming the slave of the objects which [it] makes?" This question arises because of the ways in which urbanization has impacted the ways of life of individuals: in the family, the neighborhood, and the Christian community. The Pope sees individuals as facing a new loneliness, a result of the anonymity, poverty, indifference, waste, and overconsumption that are often found in cities. The Pope strongly suggests that these developments lend themselves easily to new forms of exploitation and domination. To combat this, the Pope suggests a renovation of the neighborhood and the communities in which people live in urban environments. This will be means by which individuals can escape from the isolation created by the urban environment and can find and help build new communities. The Pope sees this as a way of putting into practice many of the demands of Christian justice so that individuals can exercise their legitimate rights and also respond in a genuine sense of obligation to those who are in need. As a symbol of hope, the Pope focuses on the image of the new Jerusalem, the Holy City, as a place where God also may be encountered.

Another issue, connected with the problems of urbanization and the development of technology is the environment. Because of the increasing domination of humans over nature and also the ways in which individuals and social organizations have used the environment, problems that were unthought of twenty years ago are now becoming not only evident but extremely critical and raise severe questions about the future capability of the earth to support the human race. As a result the Pope perceives that the environment may no longer be under the control of individuals; this may create a future situation which may be intolerable for human existence. He therefore calls for a new sense of responsibility on the part of individuals to examine the consequences of our actions, which are creating the destiny that will be shared by all inhabitants of the planet earth. We need to ask if we should do all that we can. Such a radical question will strike at the heart of many of our current values and needs; but if we are to survive in a meaningful way, this hard question must be faced, and Christians must assume their social responsibility in re-examining the traditional concept of stewardship of the earth.

Moving on to the question of political action and involvement on the part of Christians who are attempting to live out their social responsibility, the Pope raises the issue of the ideologies which lie behind political programs. The letter argues that every social ideology is ambiguous and that the Christian faith must be recognized to transcend and occasionally oppose some ideologies in that it recognizes a relationship to God and to the realities of responsibility and freedom. If one accepts an ideology as sufficient in itself, then one makes a new idol of this, with all of the possible concomitant dangers that go with this, such as coerciveness and totalitarianism. An ideology which suggests the liberation of individuals may end by making them slaves. Thus, while encouraging Christians to participate in social action and political programs, the Pope warns that we must not make these ends in themselves, lest we be seduced by a new and more treacherous form of slavery. The Christian must always keep in mind significant values such as liberty, responsibility, and openness to the spiritual as a way of guarding the intrinsic development of each individual.

The Pope specifically attacks the ideology of Marxism with its atheistic materialism, its dialectic of violence, its absorption of individual freedom into the collectivity, its denial of human transcendence, and its substitution of license for freedom. While recognizing that Marxism has various levels—the class struggle, the collective exercise of political and economic power under the direction of a single party, a socialist ideology based on historical materialism, and a scientific method of social and political analysis—he argues that it will be illusory and dangerous to accept the elements of Marxist analysis without recognizing their relationships with ideology, the class struggle, and the kinds of totalitarian and violent societies to which this process leads. Because of this perception of the inherent violence that Marxism has within itself, the Pope rejects it as a means by which Christians may analyze their society and plan programs of social reform.

In spite of the suspicions of a variety of ideologies, the letter recognizes that the problems of our day are urgent and that therefore Christians are called to action and participation in the social and political processes of the countries in which we live. In doing this Christians will serve a twofold function: first, helping individuals discover the truth, and second, putting this into practice by the active living of the gospel. The Pope very strongly points out that it is not enough to recall the principles of actions, to point out injustice, and to utter pious words of denunciation; such words lack meaning unless they are accompanied by responsible political and social action. Thus the Pope places the responsibility for social reform squarely on the shoulders of each Christian. Such responsibility must also lead the Christian to join in organizations or parties which would help promote social reform. Such involvement cannot be left to others; it is the responsibility of Christians both as Christians and as members of society to be involved in actualizing the values of justice and peace which are the basis of true community and true international harmony.

This new call to action, even though suspicious of many current political movements and ideologies, nonetheless recognizes that Christians must become involved in the process of social reform as part of their mission as Christians. Even though it may be difficult to read the signs of the times and even though specific programs may not bring the fulfillment of one's hopes, nonetheless Christians cannot be excused from putting into practice the demands of the gospel for a more harmonious human community. The letter recognizes that many of the problems that we face are new and may be extremely difficult to resolve; however, the difficulty of the task does not absolve the Christian from his or her duty to fulfill as best as possible the demands of the gospel. In fact, the urgency of the situation lends new support to the obligations that Christians have to contribute their best energies to social renewal.

OCTOGESIMA ADVENIENS

A CALL TO ACTION

APOSTOLIC LETTER OF HIS HOLINESS
POPE PAUL VI
TO CARDINAL MAURICE ROY,
PRESIDENT OF THE COUNCIL OF THE LAITY
AND OF THE PONTIFICAL COMMISSION
JUSTICE AND PEACE,
ON THE OCCASION
OF THE EIGHTIETH ANNIVERSARY OF
THE ENCYCLICAL RERUM NOVARUM

Venerable Brother,

1. The eightieth anniversary of the publication of the encyclical *Rerum Novarum*, the message of which continues to inspire action for social justice, prompts us to take up again and to extend the teaching of our predecessors, in response to the new needs of a changing world. The Church, in fact, travels forward with humanity and shares its lot in the setting of history. At the same time that she announces to men the Good News of God's love and of salvation in Christ, she clarifies their activity in the light of the Gospel and in this way helps them to correspond to God's plan of love and to realize the fullness of their aspirations.

Universal Appeal for More Justice

2. It is with confidence that we see the Spirit of the Lord pursuing his work in the hearts of men and in every place gathering together Christian communities conscious of their responsibilities in society. On all the continents, among all races, nations and cultures, and under all conditions the Lord continues to raise up authentic apostles of the Gospel.

We have had the opportunity to meet these people, to admire them and to give them our encouragement in the course of our recent journeys. We have gone into the crowds and have heard their appeals, cries of distress and at the same time cries of hope. Under these circumstances we have seen in a new perspective the grave problems of our time. These problems of course are particular to each part of the world, but at the same time they are common to all mankind, which is questioning itself about its future and about the tendency and the meaning of the changes taking place. Flagrant inequalities exist in the economic, cultural and political development of the nations: while some regions are heavily industrialized, others are still at the agricultural stage; while some countries enjoy prosperity, others are struggling against starvation; while some peoples have a high standard of culture, others are still engaged in eliminating illiteracy. From all sides there rises a yearning for more justice and a desire for a better guaranteed peace in mutual respect among individuals and peoples.

Diversity of Situations

3. There is of course a wide diversity among the situations in which Christians—willingly or unwillingly—find themselves according to regions, socio-political systems and cultures. In some places they are reduced to silence, regarded with suspicion and as it were kept on the fringe of society, enclosed without freedom in a totalitarian system. In other places they are a weak minority whose voice makes itself heard with difficulty. In some other nations, where the Church sees her place recognized, sometimes officially so, she too finds herself subjected to the repercussions of the crisis which is unsettling society; some of her members are tempted by radical and violent solutions from which they believe that they can expect a happier outcome. While some people, unaware of present injustices, strive to prolong the existing situation, others allow themselves to be beguiled by revolutionary ideologies which promise them, not without delusion, a definitively better world.

4. In the face of such widely varying situations it is difficult for us to utter a unified message and to put forward a solution which has universal validity. Such is not our ambi-

tion, nor is it our mission. It is up to the Christian communities to analyze with objectivity the situation which is proper to their own country, to shed on it the light of the Gospel's unalterable words and to draw principles of reflection, norms of judgment and directives for action from the social teaching of the Church. This social teaching has been worked out in the course of history and notably, in this industrial era, since the historic date of the message of Pope Leo XIII on "the condition of the workers," and it is an honor and joy for us to celebrate today the anniversary of that message. It is up to these Christian communities, with the help of the Holy Spirit, in communion with the bishops who hold responsibility and in dialogue with other Christian berthren and all men of goodwill, to discern the options and commitments which are called for in order to bring about the social, political and economic changes seen in many cases to be urgently needed. In this search for the changes which should be promoted, Christians must first of all renew their confidence in the forcefulness and special character of the demands made by the Gospel. The Gospel is not out-of-date because it was proclaimed, written and lived in a different socio-cultural context. Its inspiration, enriched by the living experience of Christian tradition over the centuries, remains ever new for converting men and for advancing the life of society. It is not however to be utilized for the profit of particular temporal options, to the neglect of its universal and eternal message.[1]

Specific Message of the Church

5. Amid the disturbances and uncertainties of the present hour, the Church has a specific message to proclaim and a support to give to men in their efforts to take in hand and give direction to their future. Since the period in which the encyclical *Rerum Novarum* denounced in a forceful and imperative manner the scandal of the condition of the workers in the nascent industrial society, historical evolution has led to an awareness of other dimensions and other applications of social justice. The encyclicals *Quadragesimo Anno*[2] and *Mater et Magistra*[3] already noted this fact. The recent Council for its part took care to point them out, in particular in the Pastoral Constitution *Gaudium et Spes*. We ourself have

already continued these lines of thought in our encyclical *Populorum Progressio.* "Today," we said, "the principal fact that we must all recognize is that the social question has become worldwide."[4] "A renewed consciousness of the demands of the Gospel makes it the Church's duty to put herself at the service of all, to help them grasp their serious problem in all its dimensions, and to convince them that solidarity in action at this turning point in human history is a matter of urgency."[5]

6. It will moreover be for the forthcoming Synod of Bishops itself to study more closely and to examine in greater detail the Church's mission in the face of grave issues raised today by the question of justice in the world. But the anniversary of *Rerum Novarum,* venerable brother, gives us the opportunity today to confide our preoccupations and thoughts in the face of this problem to you as President of the Pontifical Commission Justice and Peace and of the Council of Laity. In this way it is also our wish to offer these bodies of the Holy See our encouragement in their ecclesial activity in the service of men.

Extent of Present-day Changes

7. In so doing, our purpose—without however forgetting the permanent problems already dealt with by our predecessors—is to draw attention to a number of questions. These are questions which because of their urgency, extent and complexity must in the years to come take first place among the preoccupations of Christians, so that with other men the latter may dedicate themselves to solving the new difficulties which put the very future of man in jeopardy. It is necessary to situate the problems created by the modern economy in the wider context of a new civilization. These problems include human conditions of production, fairness in the exchange of goods and in the division of wealth, the significance of the increased needs of consumption and the sharing of responsibility. In the present changes, which are so profound and so rapid, each day man discovers himself anew, and he questions himself about the meaning of his own being and of his collective survival. Reluctant to gather the lessons of a past that he considers over and done with and too differ-

ent from the present, man nevertheless needs to have light shed upon his future—a future which he perceives to be as uncertain as it is changing—by permanent eternal truths. These are truths which are certainly greater than man but, if he so wills, he can himself find their traces.[6]

NEW SOCIAL PROBLEMS

Urbanization

8. A major phenomenon draws our attention, as much in the industrialized countries as in those which are developing: urbanization.

After long centuries, agrarian civilization is weakening. Is sufficient attention being devoted to the arrangement and improvement of the life of the country people, whose inferior and at times miserable economic situation provokes the flight to the unhappy crowded conditions of the city outskirts, where neither employment nor housing awaits them?

This unceasing flight from the land, industrial growth, continual demographic expansion and the attraction of urban centers bring about concentrations of population, the extent of which is difficult to imagine, for people are already speaking in terms of a "megalopolis" grouping together tens of millions of persons. Of course there exist medium-sized towns, the dimension of which ensures a better balance in the population. While being able to offer employment to those that progress in agriculture makes available, they permit an adjustment of the human environment which better avoids the proletarianism and crowding of the great built-up areas.

9. The inordinate growth of these centers accompanies industrial expansion, without being identified with it. Based on technological research and the transformation of nature, industrialization constantly goes forward, giving proof of incessant creativity. While certain enterprises develop and are concentrated, others die or change their location. Thus new social problems are created: professional or regional unemployment, redeployment and mobility of persons, permanent

adaptation of workers and disparity of conditions in the different branches of industry. Unlimited competition utilizing the modern means of publicity incessantly launches new products and tries to attract the consumer, while earlier industrial installations which are still capable of functioning become useless. While very large areas of the population are unable to satisfy their primary needs, superfluous needs are ingeniously created. It can thus rightly be asked if, in spite of all his conquests, man is not turning back against himself the results of his activity. Having rationally endeavored to control nature,[7] is he not now becoming the slave of the objects which he makes?

Christians in the City

10. Is not the rise of an urban civilization which accompanies the advance of industrial civilization a true challenge to the wisdom of man, to his capacity for organization and to his farseeing imagination? Within industrial society urbanization upsets both the ways of life and the habitual structures of existence: the family, the neighborhood, and the very framework of the Christian community. Man is experiencing a new loneliness; it is not in the face of a hostile nature which it has taken him centuries to subdue, but in an anonymous crowd which surrounds him and in which he feels himself a stranger. Urbanization, undoubtedly an irreversible stage in the development of human societies, confronts man with difficult problems. How is he to master its growth, regulate its organization, and successfully accomplish its animation for the good of all?

In this disordered growth, new proletariats are born. They install themselves in the heart of the cities sometimes abandoned by the rich; they dwell on the outskirts—which become a belt of misery besieging in a still-silent protest with luxury which blatantly cries out from centers of consumption and waste. Instead of favoring fraternal encounter and mutual aid, the city fosters discrimination and also indifference. It lends itself to new forms of exploitation and of domination whereby some people in speculating on the needs of others derive inadmissible profits. Behind the façades, much misery is hidden, unsuspected even by the closest neighbors; other forms of misery spread where human dignity founders: delinquency, criminality, abuse of drugs and eroticism.

11. It is in fact the weakest who are the victims of dehumanizing living conditions, degrading for conscience and harmful for the family institution. The promiscuity of working people's housing makes a minimum of intimacy impossible; young couples waiting in vain for a decent dwelling at a price they can afford are demoralized and their union can thereby even be endangered; youth escape from a home which is too confined and seek in the street compensations and companionships which cannot be supervised. It is the grave duty of those responsible to strive to control this process and to give it direction.

There is an urgent need to remake at the level of the street, of the neighborhood or of the great agglomerative dwellings the social fabric whereby man may be able to develop the needs of his personality. Centers of special interest and of culture must be created or developed at the community and parish levels with different forms of associations, recreational centers, and spiritual and community gatherings where the individual can escape from isolation and form anew fraternal relationships.

12. To build up the city, the place where men and their expanded communities exist, to create new modes of neighborliness and relationships, to perceive an original application of social justice and to undertake responsibility for this collective future, which is foreseen as difficult, is a task in which Christians must share. To those who are heaped up in an urban promiscuity which becomes intolerable it is necessary to bring a message of hope. This can be done by brotherhood which is lived and by concrete justice. Let Christians, conscious of this new responsibility, not lose heart in view of the vast and faceless society; let them recall Jonah who traversed Niniveh, the great city, to proclaim therein the good news of God's mercy and was upheld in his weakness by the sole strength of the word of Almighty God. In the Bible, the city is in fact often the place of sin and pride—the pride of man who feels secure enough to be able to build his life without God and even to affirm that he is powerful against

God. But there is also the example of Jerusalem, the Holy City, the place where God is encountered, the promise of the city which comes from on high.[8]

Youth

13. Urban life and industrial change bring strongly to light questions which until now were poorly grasped. What place, for example, in this world being brought to birth, should be given to youth? Everywhere dialogue is proving to be difficult between youth, with its aspirations, renewal and also insecurity for the future, and the adult generations. It is obvious to all that here we have a source of serious conflicts, division and opting out, even within the family, and a questioning of modes of authority, education for freedom and the handing on of values and beliefs, which strikes at the deep roots of society.

The Role of Women

Similarly, in many countries a charter for women which would put an end to an actual discrimination and would establish relationships of equality in rights and of respect for their dignity is the object of study and at times of lively demands. We do not have in mind that false equality which would deny the distinctions laid down by the Creator himself and which would be in contradiction with woman's proper role, which is of such capital importance, at the heart of the family as well as within society. Developments in legislation should on the contrary be directed to protecting her proper vocation and at the same time recognizing her independence as a person, and her equal rights to participate in cultural, economic, social and political life.

Workers

14. As the Church solemnly reaffirmed in the recent Council, "the beginning, the subject and the goal of all social institutions is and must be the human person."[9] Every man has the right to work, to a chance to develop his qualities and his personality in the exercise of his profession, to equitable remuneration which will enable him and his family "to lead a

worthy life on the material, social, cultural and spiritual level,"[10] and to assistance in case of need arising from sickness or age.

Although for the defense of these rights democratic societies accept today the principle of labor union rights, they are not always open to their exercise. The important role of union organizations must be admitted: their object is the representation of the various categories of workers, their lawful collaboration in the economic advance of society, and the development of the sense of their responsibility for the realization of the common good. Their activity, however, is not without its difficulties. Here and there the temptation can arise of profiting from a position of force to impose, particularly by strikes—the right to which as a final means of defense remains certainly recognized—conditions which are too burdensome for the overall economy and for the social body, or to desire to obtain in this way demands of a directly political nature. When it is a question of public services, required for the life of an entire nation, it is necessary to be able to assess the limit beyond which the harm caused to society becomes inadmissible.

Victims of Changes

15. In short, progress has already been made in introducing, in the area of human relationships, greater justice and greater sharing of responsibilities. But in this immense field much remains to be done. Further reflection, research and experimentation must be actively pursued, unless one is to be late in meeting the legitimate aspirations of the workers—aspirations which are being increasingly asserted according as their education, their consciousness of their dignity and the strength of their organizations increase.

Egoism and domination are permanent temptations for men. Likewise an ever finer discernment is needed, in order to strike at the roots of newly arising situations of injustice and to establish progressively a justice which will be less and less imperfect. In industrial change, which demands speedy and constant adaptation, those who will find themselves injured will be more numerous and at a greater disadvantage from the point of view of making their voices heard. The

Church directs her attention to these new "poor"—the handicapped and the maladjusted, the old, different groups of those on the fringe of society, and so on—in order to recognize them, help them, defend their place and dignity in a society hardened by competition and the attraction of success.

Discrimination

16. Among the victims of situations of injustice—unfortunately no new phenomenon—must be placed those who are discriminated against, in law or in fact, on account of their race, origin, color, culture, sex or religion.

Racial discrimination possesses at the moment a character of very great relevance by reason of the tension which it stirs up both within certain countries and on the international level. Men rightly consider unjustifiable and reject as inadmissible the tendency to maintain or introduce legislation or behavior systematically inspired by racialist prejudice. The members of mankind share the same basic rights and duties, as well as the same supernatural destiny. Within a country which belongs to each one, all should be equal before the law, find equal admittance to economic, cultural, civic and social life, and benefit from a fair sharing of the nation's riches.

Right to Emigrate

17. We are thinking also of the precarious situation of a great number of emigrant workers whose condition as foreigners makes it all the more difficult for them to make any sort of social vindication, in spite of their real participation in the economic effort of the country that receives them. It is urgently necessary for people to go beyond a narrowly nationalist attitude in their regard and to give them a charter which will assure them a right to emigrate, favor their integration, facilitate their professional advancement and give them access to decent housing where, if such is the case, their families can join them.[11]

Linked to this category are the people who, to find work, or to escape a disaster or a hostile climate, leave their regions and find themselves without roots among other people.

It is everyone's duty, but especially that of Christians,[12] to work with energy for the establishment of universal brother-hood, the indispensable basis for authentic justice and the condition for enduring peace: "We cannot in truthfulness call upon that God who is the Father of all if we refuse to act in a brotherly way toward certain men, created to God's image. A man's relationship with God the Father and his relationship with his brother men are so linked together that Scripture says: 'He who does not love does not know God' (1 Jn 4:8)."[13]

Creating Employment

18. With demographic growth, which is particularly pronounced in the young nations, the number of those failing to find work and driven to misery or parasitism will grow in the coming years unless the conscience of man rouses itself and gives rise to a general movement of solidarity through an effective policy of investment and or organization of production and trade, as well as of education. We know the attention given to these problems within international organizations, and it is our lively wish that their members will not delay bringing their actions into line with their declarations.

It is disquieting in this regard to note a kind of fatalism which is gaining a hold even on people in positions of responsibility. This feeling sometimes leads to Malthusian solutions inculcated by active propaganda for contraception and abortion. In this critical situation, it must on the contrary be affirmed that the family, without which no society can stand, has a right to the assistance which will assure it of the conditions for a healthy development. "It is certain," we said in our encyclical *Populorum Progressio*, "that public authorities can intervene, within the limit of their competence, by favoring the availability of appropriate information and by adopting suitable measures, provided that these be in conformity with the moral law and that they respect the rightful freedom of married couples. Where the inalienable right to marriage and procreation is lacking, human dignity has ceased to exist."[14]

19. In no other age has the appeal to the imagination of society been so explicit. To this should be devoted enterprises of invention and capital as important as those invested for ar-

maments or technological achievements. If man lets himself rush ahead without foreseeing in good time the emergence of new social problems, they will become too grave for a peaceful solution to be hope for.

Media of Social Communication

20. Among the major changes of our times, we do not wish to forget to emphasize the growing role being assumed by the media of social communication and their influence on the transformation of mentalities, of knowledge, of organizations and of society itself. Certainly they have many positive aspects. Thanks to them news from the entire world reaches us practically in an instant, establishing contacts which supersede distances and creating elements of unity among all men. A greater spread of education and culture is becoming possible. Nevertheless, by their very action the media of social communication are reaching the point of representing as it were a new power. One cannot but ask about those who really hold this power, the aims that they pursue and the means they use, and finally, about the effect of their activity on the exercise of individual liberty, both in the political and ideological spheres and in social, economic and cultural life. The men who hold this power have a grave moral responsibility with respect to the truth of the information that they spread, the needs and the reactions that they generate, and the values which they put forward. In the case of television, moreover, what is coming into being is an original mode of knowledge and a new civilization: that of the image.

Naturally, the public authorities cannot ignore the growing power and influence of the media of social communication and the advantages and risks which their use involves for the civic community and for its development and real perfecting.

Consequently they are called upon to perform their own positive function for the common good by encouraging every constructive expression, by supporting individual citizens and groups in defending the fundamental values of the person and of human society, and also by taking suitable steps to prevent the spread of what would harm the common heritage of values on which orderly civil progress is based.[15]

The Environment

21. While the horizon of man is thus being modified according to the images that are chosen for him, another transformation is making itself felt, one which is the dramatic and unexpected consequence of human activity. Man is suddenly becoming aware that by an ill-considered exploitation of nature he risks destroying it and becoming in his turn the victim of this degradation. Not only is the material environment becoming a permanent menace—pollution and refuse, new illnesses and absolute destructive capacity—but the human framework is no longer under man's control, thus creating an environment for tomorrow which may well be intolerable. This is a wide-ranging social problem which concerns the entire human family.

The Christian must turn to these new perceptions in order to take on responsibility, together with the rest of men, for a destiny which from now on is shared by all.

FUNDAMENTAL ASPIRATIONS AND CURRENTS OF IDEAS

22. While scientific and technological progress continues to overturn man's surroundings, his patterns of knowledge, work, consumption and relationships, two aspirations persistently make themselves felt in these new contexts, and they grow stronger to the extent that he becomes better informed and better educated: the aspiration to equality and the aspiration to participation, two forms of man's dignity and freedom.

Advantages and Limitations of Juridical Recognition

23. Through this statement of the rights of man and the seeking for international agreements for the application of these rights, progress has been made towards inscribing these two aspirations in deeds and structures.[16] Nevertheless various forms of discrimination continually reappear—ethnic, cultural, religious, political and so on. In fact, human rights are still too often disregarded, if not scoffed at, or else they re-

ceive only formal recognition. In many cases legislation does not keep up with real situations. Legislation is necessary, but it is not sufficient for setting up true relationships of justice and equality. In teaching us charity, the Gospel instructs us in the preferential respect due to the poor and the special situation they have in society: the more fortunate should renounce some of their rights so as to place their goods more generously at the service of others. If, beyond legal rules, there is really no deeper feeling of respect for and service to others, then even equality before the law can serve as an alibi for flagrant discrimination, continued exploitation and actual contempt. Without a renewed education in solidarity, an overemphasis on equality can give rise to an individualism in which each one claims his own rights without wishing to be answerable for the common good.

In this field, everyone sees the highly important contribution of the Christian spirit, which moreover answers man's yearning to be loved. "Love for man, the prime value of the earthly order," ensures the conditions for peace, both social peace and international peace, by affirming our universal brotherhood.[17]

The Political Society

24. The two aspirations, to equality and to participation, seek to promote a democratic type of society. Various models are proposed, some are tried out, none of them gives complete satisfaction, and the search goes on between ideological and pragmatic tendencies. The Christian has the duty to take part in this search and in the organization and life of political society. As a social being, man builds his destiny within a series of particular groupings which demand, as their completion and as a necessary condition for their development, a vaster society, one of a universal character, the political society. All particular activity must be placed within that wider society, and thereby it takes on the dimension of the common good.[18]

This indicates the importance of education for life in society, in which there are called to mind, not only information on each one's rights, but also their necessary correlative: the recognition of the duties of each one in regard to others. The sense and practice of duty are themselves conditioned by self-mastery and by the acceptance of responsibility and of the limits placed upon the freedom of the individual or of the group.

25. Political activity—need one remark that we are dealing primarily with an activity, not an ideology?—should be the projection of a plan of society which is consistent in its concrete means and in its inspiration, and which springs from a complete conception of man's vocation and of its differing social expressions. It is not for the State or even for political parties, which would be closed unto themselves, to try to impose an ideology by means that would lead to a dictatorship over minds, the worst kind of all. It is for cultural and religious groupings, in the freedom of acceptance which they presume, to develop in the social body, disinterestedly and in their own ways, those ultimate convictions on the nature, origin and end of man and society.

In this field, it is well to keep in mind the principle proclaimed at the Second Vatican Council: "The truth cannot impose itself except by virtue of its own truth, and it makes its entrance into the mind at once quietly and with power."[19]

Ideologies and Human Liberty

26. Therefore the Christian who wishes to live his faith in a political activity which he thinks of as service cannot without contradicting himself adhere to ideological systems which radically or substantially go against his faith and his concept of man. He cannot adhere to the Marxist ideology, to its atheistic materialism, to its dialectic of violence and to the way it absorbs individual freedom in the collectivity, at the same time denying all transcendence to man and his personal and collective history; nor can he adhere to the liberal ideology which believes it exalts individual freedom by withdrawing it from every limitation, by stimulating it through exclusive seeking of interest and power, and by considering social solidarities as more or less automatic consequences of individual initiatives, not as an aim and a major criterion of the value of the social organization.

27. Is there need to stress the possible ambiguity of every

social ideology? Sometimes it leads political or social activity to be simply the application of an abstract, purely theoretical idea; at other times it is thought which becomes a mere instrument at the service of activity as a simple means of a strategy. In both cases is it not man that risks finding himself alienated? The Christian faith is above and is sometimes opposed to the ideologies, in that it recognizes God, who is transcendent and the Creator, and who, through all the levels of creation, calls on man as endowed with responsibility and freedom.

28. There would also be the danger of giving adherence to an ideology which does not rest on a true and organic doctrine, to take refuge in it as a final and sufficient explanation of everything, and thus to build a new idol, accepting, at times without being aware of doing so, its totalitarian and coercive character. And people imagine they find in it a justification for their activity, even violent activity, and an adequate response to a generous desire to serve. The desire remains but it allows itself to be consumed by an ideology which, even if it suggests certain paths to man's liberation, ends up by making him a slave.

29. It has been possible today to speak of a retreat of ideologies. In this respect the present time may be favorable for an openness to the concrete transcendence of Christianity. It may also be a more accentuated sliding towards a new positivism: universalized technology as the dominant form of activity, as the overwhelming pattern of existence, even as a language, without the question of its meaning being really asked.

Historical Movements

30. But outside of this positivism which reduces man to a single dimension even if it be an important one today and by so doing mutilates him, the Christian encounters in his activity concrete historical movements sprung from ideologies and in part distinct from them. Our venerated predecessor Pope John XXIII in *Pacem in Terris* already showed that it is possible to make a distinction: "Neither can false philosophical teachings regarding the nature, origin and destiny of the universe and of man be identified with historical movements

that have economic, social, cultural or political ends, not
even when these movements have originated from those
teachings and have drawn and still draw inspiration therefrom. Because the teachings, once they are drawn up and
defined, remain always the same, while the movements, being
concerned with historical situations in constant evolution,
cannot but be influenced by these latter and cannot avoid,
therefore, being subject to changes, even of a profound nature. Besides, who can deny that those movements, insofar as
they conform to the dictates of right reason and are interpreters of the lawful aspirations of the human person, contain elements that are positive and deserving of approval?"[20]

Attraction of Socialist Currents

31. Some Christians are today attracted by socialist currents and their various developments. They try to recognize
therein a certain number of aspirations which they carry
within themselves in the name of their faith. They feel that
they are part of that historical current and wish to play a part
within it. Now this historical current takes on, under the
same name, different forms according to different continents
and cultures, even if it drew its inspiration, and still does in
many cases, from ideologies incompatible with faith. Careful
judgment is called for. Too often Christians attracted by socialism tend to idealize it in terms which, apart from anything else, are very general: a will for justice, solidarity and
equality. They refuse to recognize the limitations of the historical socialist movements, which remain conditioned by the
ideologies from which they originated. Distinctions must be
made to guide concrete choices between the various levels of
expression of socialism: a generous aspiration and a seeking
for a more just society, historical movements with a political
organization and aim, and an ideology which claims to give a
complete and self-sufficient picture of man. Nevertheless,
these distinctions must not lead one to consider such levels as
completely separate and independent. The concrete link
which, according to circumstances, exists between them must
be clearly marked out. This insight will enable Christians to
see the degree of commitment possible along these lines,

while safeguarding the values, especially those of liberty, responsibility and openness to the spiritual, which guarantee the integral development of man.

Historical Evolution of Marxism

32. Other Christians even ask whether an historical development of Marxism might not authorize certain concrete rapprochements. They note in fact a certain splintering of Marxism, which until now showed itself to be a unitary ideology which explained in atheistic terms the whole of man and the world since it did not go outside their development process. Apart from the ideological confrontation officially separating the various champions of Marxism-Leninism in their individual interpretations of the thought of its founders, and apart from the open opposition between the political systems which make use of its name today, some people lay down distinctions between Marxism's various levels of expression.

33. For some, Marxism remains essentially the active practice of class struggle. Experiencing the ever present and continually renewed force of the relationships of domination and exploitation among men, they reduce Marxism to no more than a struggle—at times with no other purpose—to be pursued and even stirred up in permanent fashion. For others, it is first and foremost the collective exercise of political and economic power under the direction of a single party, which would be the whole expression and guarantee of the welfare of all, and would deprive individuals and other groups of any possibility of initiative and choice. At a third level, Marxism, whether in power or not, is viewed as a socialist ideology based on historical materialism and the denial of everything transcendent. At other times, finally, it presents itself in a more attenuated form, one also more attractive to the modern mind: as a scientific activity, as a rigorous method of examining social and political reality, and as the rational link, tested by history, between theoretical knowledge and the practice of revolutionary tranformation. Although this type of analysis gives a privileged position to certain aspects of reality to the detriment of the rest, and interprets them in the light of its ideology, it nevertheless

furnishes some people not only with a working tool but also a certitude preliminary to action: the claim to decipher in a scientific manner the mainsprings of the evolution of society.

34. While, through the concrete existing form of Marxism, one can distinguish these various aspects and the questions they pose for the reflection and activity of Christians, it would be illusory and dangerous to reach a point of forgetting the intimate link which radically binds them together, to accept the elements of Marxist analysis without recognizing their relationships with ideology, and to enter into the practice of class struggle and its Marxist interpretation, while failing to note the kind of totalitarian and violent society to which this process leads.

The Liberal Ideology

35. On another side, we are witnessing a renewal of the liberal ideology. This current asserts itself both in the name of economic efficiency, and for the defense of the individual against the increasingly overwhelming hold of organizations, and as a reaction against the totalitarian tendencies of political powers. Certainly, personal initiative must be maintained and developed. But do not Christians who take this path tend to idealize liberalism in their turn, making it a proclamation in favor of freedom? They would like a new model, more adapted to present-day conditions, while easily forgetting that at the very root of philosophical liberalism is an erroneous affirmation of the autonomy of the individual in his activity, his motivation and the exercise of his liberty. Hence, the liberal ideology likewise calls for careful discernment on their part.

Christian Discernment

36. In this renewed encounter of the various ideologies, the Christian will draw from the sources of his faith and the Church's teaching the necessary principles and suitable criteria to avoid permitting himself to be first attracted by and then imprisoned within a system whose limitations and totalitarianism may well become evident to him too late, if he does not perceive them in their roots. Going beyond every system, without however failing to commit himself concretely

to serving his brothers, he will assert, in the very midst of his options, the specific character of the Christian contribution for a positive transformation of society.[21]

Rebirth of Utopias *Important in lib. th.*
It is the kingdom - the vision

that inspire us.

37. Today, moreover, the weaknesses of the ideologies are better perceived through the concrete systems in which they are trying to affirm themselves. Bureaucratic socialism, technocratic capitalism and authoritarian democracy are showing how difficult it is to solve the great human problem of living together in justice and equality. How in fact could they escape the materialism, egoism or constraint which inevitably go with them? This is the source of a protest which is springing up more or less everywhere, as a sign of a deep-seated sickness, while at the same time we are witnessing the rebirth of what it is agreed to call "utopias." These claim to resolve the political problem of modern societies better than the ideologies. It would be dangerous to disregard this. The appeal to a utopia is often a convenient excuse for those who wish to escape from concrete tasks in order to take refuge in an imaginary world. To live in a hypothetical future is a facile alibi for rejecting immediate responsibilities. But it must clearly be recognized that this kind of criticism of existing society often provokes the forward-looking imagination both to perceive in the present the disregarded possibility hidden within it, and to direct itself towards a fresh future; it thus sustains social dynamism by the confidence that it gives to the inventive powers of the human mind and heart; and, if it refuses no overture, it can also meet the Christian appeal. The Spirit of the Lord, who animates man renewed in Christ, continually breaks down the horizons within which his understanding likes to find security and the limits to which his activity would willingly restrict itself; there dwells within him a power which urges him to go beyond every system and every ideology. At the heart of the world there dwells the mystery of man discovering himself to be God's son in the course of a historical and psychological process in which constraint and freedom as well as the weight of sin and the breath of the Spirit alternate and struggle for the upper hand.

The dynamism of Christian faith here triumphs over the narrow calculations of egoism. Animated by the power of the Spirit of Jesus Christ, the Saviour of mankind, and upheld by hope, the Christian involves himself in the building up of the human city, one that is to be peaceful, just and fraternal and acceptable as an offering to God.[22] In fact, "the expectation of a new earth must not weaken but rather stimulate our concern for cultivating this one. For here grows the body of a new human family, a body which even now is able to give some kind of foreshadowing of the new age."[23]

The Questioning of the Human Sciences

38. In this world dominated by scientific and technological change, which threatens to drag it towards a new positivism, another more fundamental doubt is raised. Having subdued nature by using his reason, man now finds that he himself is as it were imprisoned within his own rationality; he in turn becomes the object of science. The "human sciences" are today enjoying a significant flowering. On the one hand they are subjecting to critical and radical examination the hitherto accepted knowledge about man, on the grounds that this knowledge seems either too empirical or too theoretical. On the other hand, methodological necessity and ideological presuppositions too often lead the human sciences to isolate, in the various situations, certain aspects of man, and yet to give these an explanation which claims to be complete or at least an interpretation which is meant to be all-embracing from a purely quantitative or phenomenological point of view. This scientific reduction betrays a dangerous presumption. To give a privileged position in this way to such an aspect of analysis is to mutilate man and, under the pretext of a scientific procedure, to make it impossible to understand man in his totality.

39. One must be no less attentive to the action which the human sciences can instigate, giving rise to the elaboration of models of society to be subsequently imposed on men as scientifically tested types of behavior. Man can then become the object of manipulations directing his desires and needs and modifying his behavior and even his system of values.

There is no doubt that there exists here a grave danger for the societies of tomorrow and for man himself. For even if all agree to build a new society at the service of men, it is still essential to know what sort of man is in question.

40. Suspicion of the human sciences affects the Christian more than others, but it does not find him disarmed. For, as we ourself wrote in *Populorum Progressio*, it is here that there is found the specific contribution of the Church to civilizations: "Sharing the noblest aspirations of men and suffering when she sees them not satisfied, she wishes to help them attain their full flowering, and that is why she offers men what she possesses as her characteristic attribute: a global vision of man and of the human race."[24] Should the Church in its turn contest the proceedings of the human sciences, and condemn their pretensions? As in the case of the natural sciences, the Church has confidence in this research also and urges Christians to play an active part in it.[25] Prompted by the same scientific demands and the desire to know man better, but at the same time enlightened by their faith, Christians who devote themselves to the human sciences will begin a dialogue between the Church and this new field of discovery, a dialogue which promises to be fruitful. Of course, each individual scientific discipline will be able, in its own particular sphere, to grasp only a partial—yet true—aspect of man; the complete picture and the full meaning will escape it. But within these limits the human sciences give promise of a positive function that the Church willingly recognizes. They can even widen the horizons of human liberty to a greater extent than the conditioning circumstances perceived enable one to foresee. They could thus assist Christian social morality, which no doubt will see its field restricted when it comes to suggesting certain models of society, while its function of making a critical judgment and taking an overall view will be strengthened by its showing the relative character of the behavior and values presented by such and such a society as definitive and inherent in the very nature of man. These sciences are a condition at once indispensable and inadequate for a better discovery of what is human. They are a language which becomes more and more complex, yet one that

deepens rather than solves the mystery of the heart of man;
nor does it provide the complete and definitive answer to the
desire which springs from his innermost being.

Ambiguous Nature of Progress

41. This better knowledge of man makes it possible to pass
a better critical judgment upon and to elucidate a fundamental notion that remains at the basis of modern societies
as their motive, their measure and their goal: namely, progress. Since the nineteenth century, western societies and, as a
result, many others have put their hopes in ceaselessly
renewed and indefinite progress. They saw this progress as
man's effort to free himself in face of the demands of nature
and of social constraints; progress was the condition for and
the yardstick of human freedom. Progress, spread by the
modern media of information and by the demand for wider
knowledge and greater consumption, has become an omni-
present ideology. Yet a doubt arises today regarding both its
value and its result. What is the meaning of this never-end-
ing, breathless pursuit of a progress that always eludes one
just when one believes one has conquered it sufficiently in
order to enjoy it in peace? If it is not attained, it leaves one
dissatisfied. Without doubt, there has been just condemnation of the limits and even the misdeeds of a merely quantitative economic growth; there is a desire to attain objectives
of a qualitative order also. The quality and the truth of
human relations, the degree of participation and of responsibility, are no less significant and important for the future of
society than the quantity and variety of the goods produced
and consumed.

Overcoming the temptation to wish to measure everything
in terms of efficiency and of trade, and in terms of the interplay of forces and interests, man today wishes to replace
these quantitative criteria with the intensity of communication, the spread of knowledge and culture, mutual
service and a combining of efforts for a common task. Is not
genuine progress to be found in the development of moral
consciousness, which will lead man to exercise a wider solidarity and to open himself freely to others and to God? For a
Christian, progress necessarily comes up against the escha-

tological mystery of death. The death of Christ and his resurrection and the outpouring of the Spirit of the Lord help man to place his freedom, in creativity and gratitude, within the context of the truth of all progress and the only hope which does not deceive.[26]

CHRISTIANS FACE TO FACE WITH THESE NEW PROBLEMS

Dynamism of the Church's Social Teaching

42. In the face of so many new questions the Church makes an effort to reflect in order to give an answer, in its own sphere, to men's expectations. If today the problems seem original in their breadth and their urgency, is man without the means of solving them? It is with all its dynamism that the social teaching of the Church accompanies men in their search. If it does not intervene to authenticate a given structure or to propose a ready-made model, it does not thereby limit itself to recalling general principles. It develops through reflection applied to the changing situations of this world, under the driving force of the Gospel as the source of renewal when its message is accepted in its totality and with all its demands. It also develops with the sensitivity proper to the Church which is characterized by a disinterested will to serve and by attention to the poorest.

Finally, it draws upon its rich experience of many centuries which enables it, while continuing its permanent preoccupations, to undertake the daring and creative innovations which the present state of the world requires.

For Greater Justice

43. There is a need to establish a greater justice in the sharing of goods, both within national communities and on the international level. In international exchanges there is a need to go beyond relationships based on force, in order to arrive at agreements reached with the good of all in mind. Relationships based on force have never in fact established justice in a true and lasting manner, even if at certain times the alteration of positions can often make it possible to find

easier conditions for dialogue. The use of force moreover leads to the setting in motion of opposing forces, and from this springs a climate of struggle which opens the way to situations of extreme violence and to abuses.[27]

But, as we have often stated, the most important duty in the realm of justice is to allow each country to promote its own development, within the framework of a cooperation free from any spirit of domination, whether economic or political. The complexity of the problems raised is certainly great, in the present intertwining of mutual dependences. Thus it is necessary to have the courage to undertake a revision of the relationships between nations, whether it is a question of the international division of production, the structure of exchanges, the control of profits, the monetary system—without forgetting the actions of human solidarity— to question the models of growth of the rich nations and change people's outlooks, so that they may realize the prior call of international duty, and to renew international organizations so that they may increase in effectiveness.

44. Under the driving force of new systems of production, national frontiers are breaking down, and we can see new economic powers emerging, the multinational enterprises, which by the concentration and flexibility of their means can conduct autonomous strategies which are largely independent of the national political powers and therefore not subject to control from the point of view of the common good. By extending their activities, these private organizations can lead to a new and abusive form of economic domination on the social, cultural and even political level. The excessive concentration of means and powers that Pope Pius XI already condemned on the fortieth anniversary of *Rerum Novarum* is taking on a new and very real image.

Change of Attitudes and Structures

45. Today men yearn to free themselves from need and dependence. But this liberation starts with the interior freedom that men must find again with regard to their goods and their powers; they will never reach it except through a transcendent love for man, and, in consequence, through a genuine readiness to serve. Otherwise, as one can see only too

clearly, the most revolutionary ideologies lead only to a change of masters; once installed in power in their turn, these new masters surround themselves with privileges, limit freedoms and allow other forms of injustice to become established.

Thus many people are reaching the point of questioning the very model of society. The ambition of many nations, in the competition that sets them in opposition and which carries them along, is to attain technological, economic and military power. This ambition then stands in the way of setting up structures in which the rhythm of progress would be regulated with a view to greater justice, instead of accentuating inequalities and living in a climate of distrust and struggle which would unceasingly compromise peace.

Christian Meaning of Political Activity

46. Is it not here that there appears a radical limitation to economics? Economic activity is necessary and, if it is at the service of man, it can be "a source of brotherhood and a sign of Providence."[28] It is the occasion of concrete exchanges between man, of rights recognized, of services rendered and of dignity affirmed in work. Though it is often a field of confrontation and domination, it can give rise to dialogue and foster cooperation. Yet it runs the risk of taking up too much strength and freedom.[29] This is why the need is felt to pass from economics to politics. It is true that in the term "politics" many confusions are possible and must be clarified, but each man feels that in the social and economic field, both national and international, the ultimate decision rests with political power.

Political power, which is the natural and necessary link for ensuring the cohesion of the social body, must have as its aim the achievement of the common good. While respecting the legitimate liberties of individuals, families and subsidiary groups, it acts in such a way as to create, effectively and for the well-being of all, the conditions required for attaining man's true and complete good, including his spiritual end. It acts within the limits of its competence, which can vary from people to people and from country to country. It always intervenes with care for justice and with devotion to the common good, for which it holds final responsibility. It does not, for all that, deprive individuals and intermediary bodies of the field of activity and responsibility which are proper to them and which lead them to collaborate in the attainment of this common good. In fact, "the true aim of all social activity should be to help individual members of the social body, but never to destroy or absorb them."[30] According to the vocation proper to it, the political power must know how to stand aside from particular interests in order to view its responsibility with regard to the good of all men, even going beyond national limits. To take politics seriously at its different levels—local, regional, national and worldwide—is to affirm the duty of man, of every man, to recognize the concrete reality and the value of the freedom of choice that is offered to him to seek to bring about both the good of the city and of the nation and of mankind. Politics are a demanding manner—but not the only one—of living the Christian commitment to the service of others. Without of course solving every problem, it endeavors to apply solutions to the relationships men have with one another. The domain of politics is wide and comprehensive, but it is not exclusive. An attitude of encroachment which would tend to set up politics as an absolute value would bring serious danger. While recognizing the autonomy of the reality of politics, Christians who are invited to take up political activity should try to make their choices consistent with the Gospel and, in the framework of a legitimate plurality, to give both personal and collective witness to the seriousness of their faith by effective and disinterested service of men.

Sharing in Responsibility

47. The passing to the political dimension also expressed a demand made by the man of today: a greater sharing in responsibility and in decision-making. This legitimate aspiration becomes more evident as the cultural level rises, as the sense of freedom develops and as man becomes more aware of how, in a world facing an uncertain future, the choices of today already condition the life of tomorrow. In *Mater et Magistra*[31] Pope John XXIII stressed how much the admittance to responsibility is a basic demand of man's nature, a

concrete exercise of his freedom and a path to his development, and he showed how, in economic life and particularly in enterprise, this sharing in responsibilities should be ensured.[32] Today the field is wider, and extends to the social and political sphere in which a reasonable sharing in responsibility and in decisions must be established and strengthened. Admittedly, it is true that the choices proposed for a decision are more and more complex; the considerations that must be borne in mind are numerous, and the foreseeing of the consequences involves risk, even if new sciences strive to enlighten freedom at these important moments. However, although limits are sometimes called for, these obstacles must not slow down the giving of wider participation in working out decisions, making choices and putting them into practice. In order to counterbalance increasing technocracy, modern forms of democracy must be devised, not only making it possible for each man to become informed and to express himself, but also by involving him in a shared responsibility.

Thus human groups will gradually begin to share and to live as communities. Thus freedom, which too often asserts itself as a claim for autonomy by opposing the freedom of others, will develop in its deepest human reality: to involve itself and to spend itself in building up active and lived solidarity. But, for the Christian, it is by losing himself in God who sets him free that man finds true freedom, renewed in the death and resurrection of the Lord.

CALL TO ACTION

Need to Become Involved in Action

48. In the social sphere, the Church has always wished to assume a double function: first to enlighten minds in order to assist them to discover the truth and to find the right path to follow amid the different teachings that call for their attention; and secondly to take part in action and to spread, with a real care for service and effectiveness, the energies of the Gospel. Is it not in order to be faithful to this desire that the Church has sent on an apostolic mission among the workers priests who, by sharing fully the condition of the

worker, are at that level the witnesses to the Church's solicitude and seeking?

It is to all Christians that we address a fresh and insistent call to action. In our encyclical on the Development of Peoples we urged that all should set themselves to the task: "Laymen should take up as their own proper task the renewal of the temporal order. If the role of the hierarchy is to teach and to interpret authentically the norms of morality to be followed in this matter, it belongs to the laity, without waiting passively for orders and directives, to take the initiative freely and to infuse a Christian spirit into the mentality, customs, laws and structures of the community in which they live."[33] Let each one examine himself, to see what he has done up to now, and what he ought to do. It is not enough to recall principles, state intentions, point to crying injustices and utter prophetic denunciations; these words will lack real weight unless they are accompanied for each individual by a livelier awareness of personal responsibility and by effective action. It is too easy to throw back on others responsibility for injustices, if at the same time one does not realize how each one shares in it personally, and how personal conversion is needed first. This basic humility will rid action of all inflexibility and sectarianism; it will also avoid discouragement in the face of a task which seems limitless in size. The Christian's hope comes primarily from the fact that he knows that the Lord is working with us in the world, continuing in his Body which is the Church—and, through the Church, in the whole of mankind—the Redemption which was accomplished on the Cross and which burst forth in victory on the morning of the Resurrection.[34] This hope springs also from the fact that the Christian knows that other men are at work, to undertake actions of justice and peace working for the same ends. For beneath an outward appearance of indifference, in the heart of every man there is a will to live in brotherhood and a thirst for justice and peace, which is to be expanded.

49. Thus, amid the diversity of situations, functions and organizations, each one must determine, in his conscience, the actions which he is called to share in. Surrounded by various currents into which, beside legitimate aspirations, there

insinuate themselves more ambiguous tendencies, the Christian must make a wise and vigilant choice and avoid involving himself in collaboration without conditions and contrary to the principles of a true humanism, even in the name of a genuinely felt solidarity. If in fact he wishes to play a specific part as a Christian in accordance with his faith—a part that unbelievers themselves expect of him—he must take care in the midst of his active commitment to clarify his motives and to rise above the objectives aimed at, by taking a more all-embracing view which will avoid the danger of selfish particularism and oppressive totalitarianism.

Pluralism of Options

50. In concrete situations, and taking account of solidarity in each person's life, one must recognize a legitimate variety of possible options. The same Christian faith can lead to different commitments.[35] The Church invites all Christians to take up a double task of inspiring and of innovating, in order to make structures evolve, so as to adapt them to the real needs of today. From Christians who at first sight seem to be in opposition, as a result of starting from differing options, she asks an effort at mutual understanding of the other's positions and motives; a loyal examination of one's behavior and its correctness will suggest to each one an attitude of more profound charity which, while recognizing the differences, believes nonetheless in the possibility of convergence and unity. "The bonds which unite the faithful are mightier than anything which divides them."[36]

It is true that many people, in the midst of modern structures and conditioning circumstances, are determined by their habits of thought and their functions, even apart from the safeguarding of material interests. Others feel so deeply the solidarity of classes and cultures that they reach the point of sharing without reserve all the judgments and options of their surroundings.[37] Each one will take great care to examine himself and to bring about that true freedom according to Christ which makes one receptive to the universal in the very midst of the most particular conditions.

51. It is in this regard too that Christian organizations, under their different forms, have a responsibility for collec-

tive action. Without putting themselves in the place of the institutions of civil society, they have to express, in their own way and rising above their particular nature, the concrete demands of the Christian faith for a just, and consequently necessary, transformation of society.[38]

Today more than ever the Word of God will be unable to be proclaimed and heard unless it is accompanied by the witness of the power of the Holy Spirit, working within the action of Christians in the service of their brothers, at the points in which their existence and their future are at stake.

52. In expressing these reflections to you, venerable brother, we are of course aware that we have not dealt with all the social problems that today face the man of faith and men of goodwill. Our recent declarations—to which has been added your message of a short time ago on the occasion of the launching of the Second Development Decade—particularly concerning the duties of the community of nations in the serious question of the integral and concerted development of man, are still fresh in people's minds. We address these present reflections to you with the aim of offering to the Council of the Laity and the Pontifical Commission Justice and Peace some fresh contributions, as well as an encouragement, for the pursuit of their task of "awakening the People of God to a full understanding of its role at the present time" and of "promoting the apostolate on the international level."[39]

It is with these sentiments, venerable brother, that we impart to you our Apostolic Blessing.

From the Vatican, May 14, 1971.

PAULUS P.P. VI

NOTES

1. *Gaudium et Spes*, § 10: AAS 58 (1966), p. 1033.
2. AAS 23 (1931), p. 209ff.
3. AAS 53 (1961), p. 429.
4. § 3, *AAS* 59 (1967), p. 258.
5. *Ibidem*, § 1: p. 257.

6. Cf. 2 Cor. 4:17.

7. *Populorum Progressio*, § 25: AAS 59 (1967), pp. 269–270.

8. Cf. Rev. 3:12; 21:2.

9. *Gaudium et Spes*, § 25: AAS 58 (1966), p. 1045.

10. *Ibidem*, § 67: p. 1089.

11. *Populorum Progressio*, § 69: AAS 59 (1967), pp. 290–291.

12. Cf. Mt. 25:35.

13. *Nostra Aetate*, § 5: AAS 58 (1966), p. 743.

14. § 37, AAS 59 (1967), p. 276.

15. *Inter Mirifica*, § 12: AAS 56 (1964), p. 149.

16. Cf. *Pacem in Terris*: AAS 55 (1963), p. 261ff.

17. Cf. Message for the World Day of Peace, 1971: AAS 63 (1971), pp. 5–9.

18. Cf. *Gaudium et Spes*, § 74: AAS 58 (1966), pp. 1095–1096.

19. *Dignitatis Humanae*, § 1: AAS 58 (1966), p. 930.

20. AAS 55 (1963), p. 300.

21. Cf. *Gaudium et Spes*, § 11: AAS 58 (1966), p. 1033.

22. Cf. Rom. 15:16.

23. *Gaudium et Spes*, § 39: AAS 58 (1966), p. 1057.

24. § 13: *Populorum Progressio*, AAS 59 (1967), p. 264.

25. Cf. *Gaudium et Spes*, § 36: AAS 58 (1966), p. 1054.

26. Cf. Rom. 5:5.

27. *Populorum Progressio*, §§ 56ff: AAS 59 (1967), pp. 285ff.

28. *Ibidem*, § 86: p. 299.

29. *Gaudium et Spes*, § 63: AAS 58 (1966), p. 1085.

30. *Quadragesimo Anno*: AAS 23 (1931), p. 203; cf. *Mater et Magistra*: AAS 53 (1961), pp. 414, 428; *Gaudium et Spes*, §§ 74–76: AAS 58 (1966), pp. 1095–1100.

31. AAS 53 (1961), pp. 420–422.

32. *Gaudium et Spes*, §§ 68, 75: AAS 58 (1966), pp. 1089–1090, 1097.

33. § 81: AAS 59 (1967), pp. 296–297.

34. Cf. Mt 28:30; Phil. 2:3–11.

35. *Gaudium et Spes*, § 43: AAS 58 (1966), p. 1061.

36. *Ibidem*, § 92: p. 1113.

37. Cf. 1 Thess 5:21.

38. *Lumen Gentium*, § 31: AAS 57 (1965), pp. 37–38; *Apostolicam Actuositatem* § 5: AAS 58 (1966), p. 842.

39. *Catholicam Christi Ecclesiam*, AAS 59 (1967), pp. 27 and 26.

JUSTICE IN THE WORLD

The Second Vatican Council had defined the pastoral office of bishops with emphasis on the notion of collegiality: the bishops, under the leadership of the Pope, sharing directly in the power of governing the Church. Pope Paul, to implement institutional expression of this principle, announced that after the Council regular synods of bishops would be chosen to meet in Rome to advise and consult with him. The 1971 Synod dealt with two major questions: the priesthood, and justice in the world. Much of the media coverage of this event centered on the explosive question of clerical celibacy. Although many priests had asked their episcopal representatives to work for modification of this traditional Catholic practice, open and prolonged debate of this topic was not allowed. The document on the ministerial priesthood thus had an unfinished quality and left many priests with a sense of frustration.

On the question of justice in the world, in contrast, there was considerable open debate. During the Synod it became clear that such questions were now to feel the powerful influence of a new element: an increasingly self-confident and articulate native leadership from the Churches of Asia, Africa, and Latin America. Also the Synod document "Justice in the World" had a quality of concreteness and realism which distinguished it from previous papal pronouncements, while at the same time it took several of the emerging principles of papal thought and gave them new force. The result was a strong, positive document sanctioned by papal and episcopal approval which was available to give powerful support to those in all nations working to bring the Church into a more active, vigilant, and pastoral relationship to the problems of world justice and peace.

Taking note of the Council's emphasis on "scrutinizing the signs of the times," the bishops began by stating that there exist "serious injustices which are building around the world of men a network of domination, oppression, and abuses which stifle freedom and which keep the greater part of humanity from sharing in the building up and enjoyment of a more just and a more fraternal world." This emphasis on structures of injustice directs attention away from a moralistic approach to justice and instead leads to a vision of structural change which incorporates principles of justice into human relationships. Pope Paul's appeal to the rich nations to share their wealth is now supplemented by the demand for basic structural change. And in this effort the bishops suggest that the Church must stand with the poor and the oppressed if it is to be faithful to its gospel mandate.

Various statements in the Synod document climax tendencies present since *Mater et Magistra*. The most quoted statement in the document comes at the conclusion of the introduction: "Action on behalf of justice and participation in the transformation of the world fully appear to us as a constitutive dimension of the preaching of the Gospel, or, in other words, of the Church's mission for the redemption of the human race and its liberation from every oppressive situation." This powerful statement draws the Church away from any sense that "the Church does not belong in politics" or that "social action" should only follow more "religious" efforts of the administration of the sacraments and spiritual development. It suggests instead that concern for justice must be a dimension of all phases of Christian life and that personal, communal, and collective action on behalf of justice is a critical, elementary responsibility of the Church. Given the urgency of the situation described in *Populorum Progressio* and elaborated here, this demand becomes even more forceful and immediate.

Chapter I of the document begins with the paradox of our civilization: the powerful, dynamic social and technological forces which can bring about a unified world society, and the

increasing strength of the forces of division and antagonism.
Increased nationalism, racial and class divisions, the arms
race, and the concentration of wealth and power in the hands
of a few have all contributed to potentially destroying the
seeds of unity and harmony that are present in the world.

The Synod proposes a determined will for development as
the means to counteract the injustice present in our world.
This right to development is seen as "a dynamic interpenetration of all those fundamental human rights upon which
the aspirations of individuals and nations are based." Part of
the clearing of the way for the actualization of such a right is
changing social structures which interfere with movements of
reform. This is an important point because the Synod is not
looking at individual conversion and charity as a means of social reform; it clearly recognizes that only if substantive structural changes are made can development occur which will satisfy the aspirations of the underdeveloped nations. Such a
right demands a much larger degree of self-determination on
the part of the developing nations, which must be coupled
with economic growth and participation. This responsible nationalism will allow the new nations to equalize relationships
with the developed nations and will also allow these nations
to acquire an identity of their own which can be used as the
basis for the development of a generation which wants to
build its own future.

The remainder of this chapter is devoted to a specific and
prophetic critique of social policies which have created victims of injustice. The Synod condemns, in terms that are
specific and strong, a variety of forms of injustice ranging
from the plight of migrants and refugees to that of those
suffering from religious and political persecution. Rarely have
ecclesiastical documents spoken in such condemnatory language of conditions of injustice in the world. The severity of
its critique should awaken us all to the obligation that we
have to work for the structural changes necessary to remedy
these forms of injustice.

Chapter II of the document grounds this critique of society in an incarnational theology which recognizes that
"Christ united in an indivisible way the relationship of man
to God and the relationship of man to other men." Since the

relation of individuals to their neighbors is intimately bound up with their relationship to God, our response to God is to be shown in love and service of our neighbors. The Synod also points out that love of neighbor and justice cannot be separated, for love implies a recognition of the dignity and rights of one's neighbor. Thus, "justice attains its inner fullness only in love." Consequently the Synod affirms that the mission of preaching the gospel dictates that we must dedicate ourselves to the liberation of humans in this world.

Since the preaching of the gospel message carries a demand for justice in the world, the Church has the right and duty to proclaim the principles of justice on social, national, and international levels and to denounce injustice wherever it is found. The bishops recognize, of course, that it is not proper for the Church to offer specific solutions or programs to solve a variety of problems of the world; the mission of the Church involves defending and promoting the dignity and rights of the human person. Christians, then, are to act as a leaven in the world and to accept their responsibilities in the world. Thus, while recognizing that the political mission of the Church is an indirect one, the Synod nonetheless affirms the responsibility of the Church and its members to speak out, strongly when necessary, against the injustice that is present.

In Chapter III, which discusses the practice of justice, the bishops propose an examination of the modes of acting and life style found within the Church, because those who venture to speak to others about justice must first be just. Consequently the document discusses, again in strong terms, elements of justice that must be present within the Church itself. This means, first of all, that rights must be preserved in the Church. No one is to be deprived of rights because he or she is associated with the Church. Nor should those who serve the Church be deprived of livelihood or customary forms of social security. Also the laity must be able to exercise more important functions, especially with regard to Church property and its administration. The Synod also recognizes that the rights of women within the Church must be extended and that they must receive a greater voice within it. The document speaks strongly of the necessity of the Church, the hierarchy, and its members leading a style of life that is proper to the followers of the poor Christ. Thus it is necessary that positions of privilege must be continually submitted to the test of evangelical witness which the Church is required to give. If the Church and its members are associated with the rich and the powerful who oppress the poor, it will never be a credible voice in seeking to achieve social justice.

The practice of justice also requires the Church to participate in education. These educational efforts must help individuals to live their lives in accordance with the evangelical principles of personal and social morality, and must help individuals to perceive that they are part of a human family which is destined to live in love and justice. Such education necessarily focuses on respect for the person and the dignity of each individual. This is the foundation upon which all other moral education must be based. The Synod notes that the recent papal teachings can be used as a way of providing general principles which can be applied to specific situations as a way of attempting to bring justice to the world. The liturgy, which is the heart and life of the Church, is a way of affirming both community and the mission of the Church. For, in hearing the Word of God and celebrating the reality of Christ among us, we are encouraged to take this life with us and to actualize it in the acts of justice that we bring to those we meet.

The document also recognizes that it will be necessary to operate on an international level to bring about a significant reform of the structures which are presently responsible for depriving others of both their human dignity and their personal rights. The Synod sets forth a series of eight propositions which provide general guidelines for the continued promulgation of the right to development. Of special importance is the role of the United Nations both with respect to its emphasis on the inalienable rights and dignity of the human being and also on the programs which can help bring about a greater equality within the structures of international relations. The other major theme in these general principles is that of the role of development as a means of aiding the underdeveloped nations through contributions to their economy, fairer prices for raw materials, and the opening of new markets to them. Within this theme, self-determination is seen as the major way by which development should occur.

Although there is a degree of pessimism in this document and although it speaks in strong prophetic terms about the depth of the injustice which lies within our world and threatens to destroy it, the Synod concludes its message on a note of hope. This is based on the Christian vision that creation is groaning in an act of giving birth as it waits for the glory of God to be revealed in it. The Synod bishops are encouraged by the efforts of individuals to lessen injustice, to lead lives of nonviolence, and to share in love and justice the goods of the earth with others. However, as has already been noted, the release of the love of God into the world is the responsibility both of the Church and of its individual members. For if we do not follow the example of Christ in actualizing the love of God through love of neighbor, then the message of hope that the Council offers will become mere rhetoric, because it is proclaimed with the lips but is neither believed nor lived in the lives of individual Christians.

JUSTICE IN THE WORLD

SYNOD OF BISHOPS
1971

INTRODUCTION

Gathered from the whole world, in communion with all who believe in Christ and with the entire human family, and opening our hearts to the Spirit who is making the whole of creation new, we have questioned ourselves about the mission of the People of God to further justice in the world.

Scrutinizing the "signs of the times" and seeking to detect the meaning of emerging history, while at the same time sharing the aspirations and questionings of all those who want to build a more human world, we have listened to the Word of God that we might be converted to the fulfilling of the divine plan for the salvation of the world.

Even though it is not for us to elaborate a very profound analysis of the situation of the world, we have nevertheless been able to perceive the serious injustices which are building around the world of men a network of domination, oppression and abuses which stifle freedom and which keep the greater part of humanity from sharing in the building up and enjoyment of a more just and more fraternal world.

At the same time we have noted the inmost stirring moving the world in its depths. There are facts constituting a contribution to the furthering of justice. In associations of men and among peoples themselves there is arising a new awareness which shakes them out of any fatalistic resignation and which spurs them on to liberate themselves and to be responsible for their own destiny. Movements among men are seen which express hope in a better world and a will to change whatever has become intolerable.

Listening to the cry of those who suffer violence and are oppressed by unjust systems and structures, and hearing the appeal of a world that by its perversity contradicts the plan of its Creator, we have shared our awareness of the Church's vocation to be present in the heart of the world by proclaiming the Good News to the poor, freedom to the oppressed, and joy to the afflicted. The hopes and forces which are moving the world in its very foundations are not foreign to the dynamism of the Gospel, which through the power of the Holy Spirit frees men from personal sin and from its consequences in social life.

The uncertainty of history and the painful convergences in the ascending path of the human community direct us to sacred history; there God has revealed himself to us, and made known to us, as it is brought progressively to realization, his plan of liberation and salvation which is once and for all fulfilled in the Paschal Mystery of Christ. Action on behalf of justice and participation in the transformation of the world fully appear to us as a constitutive dimension of the preaching of the Gospel, or, in other words, of the Church's mission for the redemption of the human race and its liberation from every oppressive situation.

CHAPTER I

JUSTICE AND WORLD SOCIETY

Crisis of Universal Solidarity

The world in which the Church lives and acts is held captive by a tremendous paradox. Never before have the forces working for bringing about a unified world society appeared so powerful and dynamic; they are rooted in the awareness of the full basic equality as well as of the human dignity of all. Since men are members of the same human family, they are indissolubly linked with one another in the one destiny of the whole world, in the responsibility for which they all share.

The new technological possibilities are based upon the unity of science, on the global and simultaneous character of communications, and on the birth of an absolutely interdependent economic world. Moreover, men are beginning to grasp a new and more radical dimension of unity; for they perceive that their resources, as well as the precious treasures of air and water—without which there cannot be life—and the small delicate biosphere of the whole complex of all life on earth, are not infinite, but on the contrary must be saved and preserved as a unique patrimony belonging to all mankind.

The paradox lies in the fact that within this perspective of unity the forces of division and antagonism seem today to be increasing in strength. Ancient divisions between nations and empires, between races and classes, today possess new technological instruments of destruction. The arms race is a threat to man's highest good, which is life; it makes poor peoples and individuals yet more miserable, while making richer those already powerful; it creates a continuous danger of conflagration, and in the case of nuclear arms, it threatens to destroy all life from the face of the earth. At the same time new divisions are being born to separate man from his neighbor. Unless combatted and overcome by social and political action, the influence of the new industrial and technological order favours the concentration of wealth, power and decision-making in the hands of a small public or private controlling group. Economic injustice and lack of social participation keep a man from attaining his basic human and civil rights.

In the last twenty-five years a hope has spread through the human race that economic growth would bring about such a quantity of goods that it would be possible to feed the hungry at least with the crumbs falling from the table, but this has proved a vain hope in underdeveloped areas and in pockets of poverty in wealthier areas, because of the rapid growth of population and of the labour force, because of rural stagnation and the lack of agrarian reform, and because of the massive migratory flow to the cities, where the industries, even though endowed with huge sums of money, nevertheless provide so few jobs that not infrequently one worker in four is left unemployed. These stifling oppressions constantly give rise to great numbers of "marginal" persons, ill-fed, inhumanly housed, illiterate and deprived of political power as well as of the suitable means of acquiring responsibility and moral dignity.

Furthermore, such is the demand for resources and energy by the richer nations, whether capitalist or socialist, and such are the effects of dumping by them in the atmosphere and the sea that irreparable damage would be done to the essential elements of life on earth, such as air and water, if their high rates of consumption and pollution, which are constantly on the increase, were extended to the whole of mankind.

The strong drive towards global unity, the unequal distribution which places decisions concerning three quarters of income, investment and trade in the hands of one third of the human race, namely the more highly developed part, the insufficiency of a merely economic progress, and the new recognition of the material limits of the biosphere—all this makes us aware of the fact that in today's world new modes of understanding human dignity are arising.

The Right to Development

In the face of international systems of domination, the bringing about of justice depends more and more on the determined will for development.

In the developing nations and in the so-called socialist world, that determined will asserts itself especially in a struggle for forms of claiming one's rights and self-expression, a struggle caused by the evolution of the economic system itself.

This aspiring to justice asserts itself in advancing beyond the threshold at which begins a consciousness of enhancement of personal worth (cf. *Populorum Progressio* § 15; A.A.S. 59, 1967, p. 265) with regard both to the whole man and the whole of mankind. This is expressed in an awareness of the right to development. The right to development must be seen as a dynamic interpenetration of all those fundamental human rights upon which the aspirations of individuals and nations are based.

This desire, however, will not satisfy the expectations of our time if it ignores the objective obstacles which social structures place in the way of conversion of hearts, or even of the realization of the ideal of charity. It demands on the contrary that the general condition of being marginal in society be overcome, so that an end will be put to the systematic barriers and vicious circles which oppose the collective advance towards enjoyment of adequate remuneration of the factors of production, and which strengthen the situation of discrimination with regard to access to opportunities and collective services from which a great part of the people are now excluded. If the developing nations and regions do not attain liberation through development, there is a real danger that the conditions of life created especially by colonial domination may evolve into a new form of colonialism in which the developing nations will be the victims of the interplay of international economic forces. That right to development is above all a right to hope according to the concrete measure of contemporary humanity. To respond to such a hope, the concept of evolution must be purified of those myths and false convictions which have up to now gone with a thought-pattern subject to a kind of deterministic and automatic notion of progress.

By taking their future into their own hands through a determined will for progress, the developing peoples—even if they do not achieve the final goal—will authentically manifest their own personalization. And in order that they may cope with the unequal relationships within the present world complex, a certain responsible nationalism gives them the impetus needed to acquire an identity of their own. From this basic self-determination can come attempts at putting together new political groupings allowing full development to these peoples; there can also come measures necessary for overcoming the inertia which could render fruitless such an effort—as in some cases population pressure; there can also come new sacrifices which the growth of planning demands of a generation which wants to build its own future.

On the other hand, it is impossible to conceive true progress without recognizing the necessity—within the political system chosen—of a development composed both of economic growth and participation; and the necessity too of an increase in wealth implying as well social progress by the entire community as it overcomes regional imbalance and islands of prosperity. Participation constitutes a right which is to be applied both in the economic and in the social and political field.

While we again affirm the right of people to keep their own identity, we see ever more clearly that the fight against a modernization destructive of the proper characteristics of nations remains quite ineffective as long as it appeals only to sacred historical customs and venerable ways of life. If modernization is accepted with the intention that it serve the good of the nation, men will be able to create a culture which will constitute a true heritage of their own in the manner of a true social memory, one which is active and formative of authentic creative personality in the assembly of nations.

Voiceless Injustices

We see in the world a set of injustices which constitute the nucleus of today's problems and whose solution requires the undertaking of tasks and functions in every sector of society, and even on the level of the global society towards which we are speeding in this last quarter of the twentieth century. Therefore we must be prepared to take on new functions and new duties in every sector of world society, if justice is really to be put into practice. Our action is to be directed above all at those men and nations which because of various forms of oppression and because of the present character of our society are silent, indeed voiceless, victims of injustice.

Take, for example, the case of migrants. They are often forced to leave their own country to find work, but frequently find the doors closed in their faces because of discriminatory attitudes, or, if they can enter, they are often obliged to lead an insecure life or are treated in an inhuman manner. The same is true of groups that are less well off on the social ladder such as workers and especially farm workers who play a very great part in the process of development.

To be especially lamented is the condition of so many millions of refugees, and of every group of people suffering persecution—sometimes in institutionalized form—for racial or ethnic origin or on tribal grounds. This persecution on tribal grounds can at times take on the characteristics of genocide.

In many areas justice is seriously injured with regard to people who are suffering persecution for their faith, or who are in many ways being ceaselessly subjected by political parties and public authorities to an action of oppressive atheization, or who are deprived of religious liberty either by being kept from honouring God in public worship, or by being prevented from publicly teaching and spreading their faith, or by being prohibited from conducting their temporal affairs according to the principles of their religion.

Justice is also being violated by forms of oppression, both old and new, springing from restriction of the rights of individuals. This is occurring both in the form of repression by the political power and of violence on the part of private reaction, and can reach the extreme of affecting the basic conditions of personal integrity. There are well known cases of torture, especially of political prisoners, who besides are frequently denied due process or who are subjected to arbitrary procedures in their trial. Nor can we pass over the prisoners of war who even after the Geneva Convention are being treated in an inhuman manner.

The fight against legalized abortion and against the imposition of contraceptives and the pressures exerted against war are significant forms of defending the right to life.

Furthermore, contemporary consciousness demands truth in the communications system, including the right to the image offered by the media and the opportunity to correct its manipulation. It must be stressed that the right, especially that of children and the young, to education and to morally correct conditions of life and communications media is once again being threatened in our days. The activity of families in social life is rarely and insufficiently recognized by State institutions. Nor should we forget the growing number of persons who are often abandoned by their families and by the community: the old, orphans, the sick and all kinds of people who are rejected.

The Need for Dialogue

To obtain true unity of purpose, as is demanded by the world society of men, a mediatory role is essential to overcome day by day the opposition, obstacles and ingrained privileges which are to be met with in the advance towards a more human society.

But effective mediation involves the creation of a lasting atmosphere of dialogue. A contribution to the progressive realization of this can be made by men unhampered by geopolitical, ideological or socio-economic conditions or by the generation gap. To restore the meaning of life by adherence to authentic values, the participation and witness of the rising generation of youth is as necessary as communication among peoples.

CHAPTER II

THE GOSPEL MESSAGE AND THE MISSION OF THE CHURCH

In the face of the present-day situation of the world, marked as it is by the grave sin of injustice, we recognize both our responsibility and our inability to overcome it by our strength. Such a situation urges us to listen with a humble and open heart to the word of God, as he shows us new paths towards action in the cause of justice in the world.

The Saving Justice of God Through Christ

In the Old Testament God reveals himself to us as the liberator of the oppressed and the defender of the poor, demanding from man faith in him and justice towards man's neighbour. It is only in the observance of the duties of justice that God is truly recognized as the liberator of the oppressed.

By his action and teaching Christ united in an indivisible way the relationship of man to God and the relationship of man to other men. Christ lived his life in the world as a total giving of himself to God for the salvation and liberation of men. In his preaching he proclaimed the fatherhood of God towards all men and the intervention of God's justice on behalf of the needy and the oppressed (Lk. 6:21–23). In this way he identified himself with his "least brethren," as he stated: "As you did it to one of the least of my brethren, you did it to me" (Mt. 25:40).

From the beginning the Church has lived and understood the Death and Resurrection of Christ as a call by God to conversion in the faith of Christ and in fraternal love, perfected in mutual help even to the point of a voluntary sharing of material goods.

Faith in Christ, the Son of God and the Redeemer, and love of neighbour constitute a fundamental theme of the writers of the New Testament. According to St. Paul, the whole of the Christian life is summed up in faith effecting that love and service of neighbour which involve the fulfillment of the demands of justice. The Christian lives under the interior law of liberty, which is a permanent call to man to turn away from self-sufficiency to confidence in God and from concern for self to a sincere love of neighbour. Thus takes place his genuine liberation and the gift of himself for the freedom of others.

According to the Christian message, therefore, man's relationship to his neighbour is bound up with his relationship to God; his response to the love of God, saving us through Christ, is shown to be effective in his love and service of men. Christian love of neighbour and justice cannot be separated. For love implies an absolute demand for justice, namely a recognition of the dignity and rights of one's neighbour. Justice attains its inner fullness only in love. Because every man is truly a visible image of the invisible God and a brother of Christ, the Christian finds in every man God himself and God's absolute demand for justice and love.

The present situation of the world, seen in the light of faith, calls us back to the very essence of the Christian message, creating in us a deep awareness of its true meaning and of its urgent demands. The mission of preaching the Gospel dictates at the present time that we should dedicate ourselves to the liberation of man even in his present existence in this world. For unless the Christian message of love and justice shows its effectiveness through action in the cause of justice in the world, it will only with difficulty gain credibility with the men of our times.

The Mission of the Church, Hierarchy and Christians

The Church has received from Christ the mission of preaching the Gospel message, which contains a call to man to turn away from sin to the love of the Father, universal brotherhood and a consequent demand for justice in the world. This is the reason why the Church has the right, indeed the duty, to proclaim justice on the social, national and international level, and to denounce instances of injustice, when the fundamental rights of man and his very salvation demand it. The Church, indeed, is not alone responsible for justice in the world; however, she has a proper and specific responsibility which is identified with her mission of giving witness before the world of the need for love and justice contained in the Gospel message, a witness to be carried out in Church institutions themselves and in the lives of Christians.

Of itself it does not belong to the Church, insofar as she is a religious and hierarchial community, to offer concrete solutions in the social, economic and political spheres for justice in the world. Her mission involves defending and promoting the dignity and fundamental rights of the human person.

The members of the Church, as members of society, have the same right and duty to promote the common good as do other citizens. Christians ought to fulfill their temporal obligations with fidelity and competence. They should act as a leaven in the world, in their family, professional, social, cultural and political life. They must accept their responsibilities in this entire area under the influence of the Gospel and the teaching of the Church. In this way they testify to the power of the Holy Spirit through their action in the service of men in those things which are decisive for the existence and the future of humanity. While in such activities they generally act on their own initiative without involving the responsibility of the ecclesiastical hierarchy, in a sense they do involve the responsibility of the Church whose members they are.

CHAPTER III

THE PRACTICE OF JUSTICE

The Church's Witness

Many Christians are drawn to give authentic witness on behalf of justice by various modes of action for justice, action inspired by love in accordance with the grace which they have received from God. For some of them, this action finds its place in the sphere of social and political conflicts in which Christians bear witness to the Gospel by pointing out that in history there are sources of progress other than conflict, namely love and right. This priority of love in history draws other Christians to prefer the way of non-violent action and work in the area of public opinion.

While the Church is bound to give witness to justice, she recognizes that everyone who ventures to speak to people about justice must first be just in their eyes. Hence we must undertake an examination of the modes of acting and of the possessions and life style found within the Church herself.

Within the Church rights must be preserved. No one should be deprived of his ordinary rights because he is associated with the Church in one way or another. Those who serve the Church by their labour, including priests and religious, should receive a sufficient livelihood and enjoy that social security which is customary in their region. Lay people should be given fair wages and a system for promotion. We reiterate the recommendations that lay people should exercise more important functions with regard to Church property and should share in its administration.

We also urge that women should have their own share of responsibility and participation in the community life of society and likewise of the Church.

We propose that this matter be subjected to a serious study employing adequate means: for instance, a mixed commission of men and women, religious and lay people, of differing situations and competence.

The Church recognizes everyone's right to suitable freedom of expression and thought. This includes the right of everyone to be heard in a spirit of dialogue which preserves a legitimate diversity within the Church.

The form of judicial procedure should give the accused the right to know his accusers and also the right to a proper defence. To be complete, justice should include speed in its procedure. This is especially necessary in marriage cases.

Finally, the members of the Church should have some share in the drawing up of decisions, in accordance with the rules given by the Second Vatican Ecumenical Council and the Holy See, for instance with regard to the setting up of councils at all levels.

In regard to temporal possessions, whatever be their use, it must never happen that the evangelical witness which the Church is required to give becomes ambiguous. The preservation of certain positions of privilege must constantly be submitted to the test of this principle. Although in general it is difficult to draw a line between what is needed for right use and what is demanded by prophetic witness, we must certainly keep firmly to this principle: our faith demands of us a certain sparingness in use, and the Church is obliged to live and administer its own goods in such a way that the Gospel is proclaimed to the poor. If instead the Church appears to be among the rich and the powerful of this world its credibility is diminished.

Our examination of conscience now comes to the life style of all: bishops, priests, religious and lay people. In the case of needy peoples it must be asked whether belonging to the Church places people on a rich island within an ambient of poverty. In societies enjoying a higher level of consumer spending, it must be asked whether our life style exemplifies that sparingness with regard to consumption which we preach to others as necessary in order that so many millions of hungry people throughout the world may be fed.

Educating to Justice

Christians' specific contribution to justice is the day-to-day life of the individual believer acting like the leaven of the Gospel in his family, his school, his work and his social and civic life. Included with this are the perspectives and meaning which the faithful can give to human effort. Accordingly, educational method must be such as to teach men to live their lives in its entire reality and in accord with the evangelical principles of personal and social morality which are expressed in the vital Christian witness of one's life.

The obstacles to the progress which we wish for ourselves and for mankind are obvious. The method of education very frequently still in use today encourages narrow individualism. Part of the human family lives immersed in a mentality which exalts possessions. The school and the communications media, which are often obstructed by the established order, allow the formation only of the man desired by that order, that is to say, man in its image, not a new man but a copy of man as he is.

But education demands a renewal of heart, a renewal based on the recognition of sin in its individual and social manifestations. It will also inculcate a truly and entirely human way of life in justice, love and simplicity. It will likewise awaken a critical sense, which will lead us to reflect on the society in which we live and on its values; it will make men ready to renounce these values when they cease to promote justice for all men. In the developing countries, the principal aim of this education for justice consists in an attempt to awaken consciences to a knowledge of the concrete situation and in a call to secure a total improvement; by these means the transformation of the world has already begun.

Since this education makes men decidedly more human, it will help them to be no longer the object of manipulation by communications media or political forces. It will instead enable them to take in hand their own destinies and bring about communities which are truly human.

Accordingly, this education is deservedly called a continuing education, for it concerns every person and every age. It is also a practical education: it comes through action, participation and vital contact with the reality of injustice.

Education for justice is imparted first in the family. We are well aware that not only Church institutions but also other schools, trade unions and political parties are collaborating in this.

The content of this education necessarily involves respect for the person and for his dignity. Since it is world justice which is in question here, the unity of the human family within which, according to God's plan, a human being is born must first of all be seriously affirmed. Christians find a sign of this solidarity in the fact that all human beings are destined to become in Christ sharers in the divine nature.

The basic principles whereby the influence of the Gospel has made itself felt in contemporary social life are to be found in the body of teaching set out in a gradual and timely way from the encyclical *Rerum Novarum* to the letter *Octogesima Adveniens*. As never before, the Church has, through the Second Vatican Council's constitution *Gaudium et Spes*, better understood the situation in the modern world, in which the Christian works out his salvation by deeds of justice. *Pacem in Terris* gave us an authentic charter of human rights. In *Mater et Magistra* international justice begins to take first place; it finds more elaborate expression in *Populorum Progressio*, in the form of a true and suitable treatise on the right to development, and in *Octogesima Adveniens* is found a summary of guidelines for political action.

Like the apostle Paul, we insist, welcome or unwelcome, that the Word of God should be present in the centre of human situations. Our interventions are intended to be an expression of that faith which is today binding on our lives and on the lives of the faithful. We all desire that these interventions should always be in conformity with circumstances of place and time. Our mission demands that we should courageously denounce injustice, with charity, prudence and firmness, in sincere dialogue with all parties concerned. We know that our denunciations can secure assent to the extent that they are an expression of our lives and are manifested in continuous action.

The liturgy, which we preside over and which is the heart of the Church's life, can greatly serve education for justice. For it is a thanksgiving to the Father in Christ, which through its communitarian form places before our eyes the bonds of our brotherhood and again and again reminds us of the Church's mission. The liturgy of the word, catechesis and the celebration of the sacraments have the power to help us to discover the teaching of the prophets, the Lord and the Apostles on the subject of justice. The preparation for baptism is the beginning of the formation of the Christian conscience. The practice of penance should emphasize the social dimension of sin and of the sacrament. Finally, the Eucharist forms the community and places it at the service of men.

Cooperation Between Local Chuches

That the Church may really be the sign of that solidarity which the family of nations desires, it should show in its own life greater cooperation between the Churches of rich and poor regions through spiritual communion and division of human and material resources. The present generous arrangements for assistance between Churches could be made more effective by real coordination (Sacred Congregation for the Evangelization of Peoples and the Pontifical Council "Cor Unum"), through their overall view in regard to the common administration of the gifts of God, and through fraternal solidarity, which would always encourage autonomy and responsibility on the part of the beneficiaries in the determination of criteria and the choice of concrete programmes and their realization.

This planning must in no way be restricted to economic programmes; it should instead stimulate activities capable of developing that human and spiritual formation which will serve as the leaven needed for the integral development of the human being.

Ecumenical Collaboration

Well aware of what has already been done in this field, together with the Second Vatican Ecumenical Council we very highly commend cooperation with our separated Christian brethren for the promotion of justice in the world, for bringing about development of peoples and for establishing peace. This cooperation concerns first and foremost activities for securing human dignity and man's fundamental rights, especially the right to religious liberty. This is the source of our common efforts against discrimination on the grounds of differences of religion, race and colour, culture and the like. Collaboration extends also to the study of the teaching of the Gospel insofar as it is the source of inspiration for all Christian activity. Let the Secretariat for Promoting Christian Unity and the Pontifical Commission Justice and Peace devote themselves in common counsel to developing effectively this ecumenical collaboration.

In the same spirit we likewise commend collaboration with all believers in God in the fostering of social justice, peace and freedom; indeed we commend collaboration also with those who, even though they do not recognize the Author of the world, nevertheless, in their esteem for human values, seek justice sincerely and by honourable means.

International Action

Since the Synod is of a universal character, it is dealing with those questions of justice which directly concern the entire human family. Hence, recognizing the importance of international cooperation for social and economic development, we praise above all else the inestimable work which has been done among the poorer peoples by the local Churches, the missionaries and the organizations supporting them; and we intend to foster those initiatives and institutions which are working for peace, international justice and the development of man. We therefore urge Catholics to consider well the following propositions:

1. Let recognition be given to the fact that international order is rooted in the inalienable rights and dignity of the human being. Let the United Nations Declaration of Human Rights be ratified by all Governments who have not yet adhered to it, and let it be fully observed by all.

2. Let the United Nations—which because of its unique purpose should promote participation by all nations—and international organizations be supported insofar as they are the beginning of a system capable of restraining the armaments race, discouraging trade in weapons, securing disarmament and settling conflicts by peaceful methods of legal action, arbitration and international police action. It is absolutely necessary that international conflicts should not be settled by war, but that other methods better befitting human nature should be found. Let a strategy of non-violence be fostered also, and let conscientious objection be recognized and regulated by law in each nation.

3. Let the aims of the Second Development Decade be fostered. These include the transfer of a precise percentage of the annual income of the richer countries to the developing nations, fairer prices for raw materials, the opening of the markets of the richer nations and, in some fields, preferential treatment for exports of manufactured goods from the developing nations. These aims represent first guidelines for a

graduated taxation of income as well as for an economic and social plan for the entire world. We grieve whenever richer nations turn their backs on this ideal goal of worldwide sharing and responsibility. We hope that no such weakening of international solidarity will take away their force from the trade discussions being prepared by the United Nations Conference on Trade and Development (UNCTAD).

4. The concentration of power which consists in almost total domination of economics, research, investment, freight charges, sea transport and securities should be progressively balanced by institutional arrangements for strengthening power and opportunities with regard to responsible decision by the developing nations and by full and equal participation in international organizations concerned with development. Their recent *de facto* exclusion from discussions on world trade and also the monetary arrangements which vitally affect their destiny are an example of lack of power which is inadmissible in a just and responsible world order.

5. Although we recognize that international agencies can be perfected and strengthened, as can any human instrument, we stress also the importance of the specialized agencies of the United Nations, in particular those directly concerned with the immediate and more acute questions of world poverty in the field of agrarian reform and agricultural development, health, education, employment, housing, and rapidly increasing urbanization. We feel we must point out in a special way the need for some fund to provide sufficient food and protein for the real mental and physical development of children. In the face of the population explosion we repeat the words by which Pope Paul VI defined the functions of public authority in his encyclical *Populorum Progressio:* "There is no doubt that public authorities can intervene, within the limit of their competence, by favoring the availability of appropriate information and by adopting suitable measures, provided that these be in conformity with the moral law and that they absolutely respect the rightful freedom of married couples" (§ 37 A.A.S. 59, 1967, p. 276).

6. Let governments continue with their individual contributions to a development fund, but let them also look for a way whereby most of their endeavours may follow multi-

lateral channels, fully preserving the responsibility of the developing nations, which must be associated in decision-making concerning priorities and investments.

7. We consider that we must also stress the new world-wide preoccupation which will be dealt with for the first time in the conference on the human environment to be held in Stockholm in June 1972. It is impossible to see what right the richer nations have to keep up their claim to increase their own material demands, if the consequence is either that others remain in misery or that the danger of destroying the very physical foundations of life on earth is precipitated. Those who are already rich are bound to accept a less material way of life, with less waste, in order to avoid the destruction of the heritage which they are obliged by absolute justice to share with all other members of the human race.

8. In order that the right to development may be fulfilled by action:

a) people should not be hindered from attaining development in accordance with their own culture;

b) through mutual cooperation, all peoples should be able to become the principal architects of their own economic and social development;

c) every people, as active and responsible members of human society, should be able to cooperate for the attainment of the common good on an equal footing with other peoples.

Recommendations of the Synod

The examination of conscience which we have made together, regarding the Church's involvement in action for justice, will remain ineffective if it is not given flesh in the life of our local Churches at all their levels. We also ask the episcopal conferences to continue to pursue the perspectives which we have had in view during the days of this meeting and to put our recommendations into practice, for instance by setting up centres of social and theological research.

We also ask that there be recommended to the Pontifical Commission Justice and Peace, the Council of the Secretariat of the Synod and to competent authorities, the description, consideration and deeper study of the wishes and desires of our assembly, and that these bodies should bring to a successful conclusion what we have begun.

CHAPTER IV

A WORD OF HOPE

The power of the Spirit, who raised Christ from the dead, is continuously at work in the world. Through the generous sons and daughters of the Church likewise, the People of God is present in the midst of the poor and of those who suffer oppression and persecution; it lives in its own flesh and its own heart the Passion of Christ and bears witness to his resurrection.

The entire creation has been groaning till now in an act of giving birth, as it waits for the glory of the children of God to be revealed (cf. Rom. 8:22). Let Christians therefore be convinced that they will yet find the fruits of their own nature and effort cleansed of all impurities in the new earth which God is now preparing for them, and in which there will be the kingdom of justice and love, a kingdom which will be fully perfected when the Lord will come himself.

Hope in the coming kingdom is already beginning to take root in the hearts of men. The radical transformation of the world in the Paschal Mystery of the Lord gives full meaning to the efforts of men, and in particular of the young, to lessen injustice, violence and hatred and to advance all together in justice, freedom, brotherhood and love.

At the same time as it proclaims the Gospel of the Lord, its Redeemer and Saviour, the Church calls on all, especially the poor, the oppressed and the afflicted, to cooperate with God to bring about liberation from every sin and to build a world which will reach the fullness of creation only when it becomes the work of man for man.

II. United States Documents

INTRODUCTION:
AMERICAN CATHOLICISM AND
SOCIAL RESPONSIBILITY

At the very time the Vatican Council unleashed a searching re-examination of the norms of Christian life and practice, the sociological cement of the Catholic community in the United States was coming unstuck. Throughout its history, the American Church was characterized by four major features: rapid, even spectacular, growth; a foreign, immigrant people and culture; a working-class membership in an upwardly mobile social order; and a profound sense of alienation occasioned both by the hostility of dominant elites and by the interaction of ethnic groups within the Church itself. On each score, the situation has changed drastically in recent years.

The leaders of the Church—bishops, priests, and religious —have always been preoccupied with the demands occasioned by rapid expansion. The small group of assimilated Anglo-Catholics who did so much to shape American Catholic culture were swamped by the first waves of immigrants before the Civil War. During the 1890s, just as a new generation of Irish-American leaders attempted to construct a distinctive American Catholic culture, the Church was once again inundated by waves of newcomers, now from Italy and eastern Europe. Between the two world wars the Catholic population stabilized, growing from seventeen million in 1920 to a little over twenty million by 1940. But then a new period of even more dramatic expansion began, as the American Catholic population almost doubled in the twenty years before the Council, reaching forty million in 1960. An expansion of services accompanied this explosion of population: suburban churches and schools, elaborate seminaries and convents, a vast extension of social and health services, all requiring considerable attention from clergy, religious, and bishops. The confidence of those years, and the bureaucratic structures and attitudes they fostered, are very much a part of the life experience of today's adult Catholics. The days of such unlimited expansion are over; the population has stabilized and demands for services are declining, along with the personnel to provide them. Like the society of which it is a part, American Catholicism subsisted for years on the dream of unending growth, once checked by the Great Depression but rekindled by the concrete experience of personal, institutional, and national advancement in the years following Pearl Harbor. Church and nation alike found questions of community, of the quality of life, of the nature of personal and group relationships relatively easy to avoid amid boom, tougher to face amid decline. Then values and actions long validated by unquestioning assent are challenged, new problems arise which cannot be solved within old assumptions. The allocation of limited resources requires goals, planning, and decisive action, but the Church has not yet developed attitudes or structures appropriate to these needs.

In a very real way there has never been an "American Catholicism." For a variety of reasons the focus of concern of Christians in America has been intensely congregational. Desirous of creating a new center for communal life, immigrant Catholics ignored the broader Catholic culture once their need for a Church, a pastor, and teachers of their own nationality was met. Beyond the parish, French Canadians and Eastern European Catholics were apt to look to the ethnic society more than the diocese. For the nineteenth-century bishop, control of church property and ecclesiastical appointments was essential; once these were guaranteed, he had few demands to make on the parish. In the twentieth century, diocesan bureaus for Catholic charities and education began to encroach on parish life, but they only really blossomed amid the suburban boom of the fifties. A distinctive American Catholic culture, able to integrate Catholic teachings and American values, to exert a liberal influence on the Church

Universal and a Catholic impact on American society, has always been the dream of a small, dedicated elite of Church professionals and intellectuals. It was the driving force of the Americanist movement of the late nineteenth century. Rome, perceiving its tendency to create a powerful, self-conscious, and potentially autonomous American Church, crushed that movement. In the years that followed the condemnation of "Americanism," Rome saw to it that no further national councils were held. The Vatican vigilantly guarded against any assumption of national power by the National Catholic Welfare Conference, and appointed to the major sees of the country men of the mold of William Cardinal O'Connell, in many ways the exemplar of the modern institutional Church. Like the Irish-American community from which he came, he gloried in *Roman* Catholicism and American secular achievement. He created a powerful centralized administration in his diocese, watchfully guarded against innovation or initiative nationally, and faithfully adhered to the Roman line. Critics of the Church he symbolized carried on an underground dream of an American Church, but their power was limited and their influence confined to those few Catholics who, for a variety of reasons, hoped that the parochialism and divisions of the past could be transcended by a new, national, organized and self-confident American Catholic community. Their day came with Vatican II and Pope John, when they gloried in the new sense of possibility, but they gradually realized that very few Catholics really cared about national Church policies.

So the other side of the national parish was not an American Catholicism, but a halfway house which combined Roman orthodoxy and American secular values. If the strength of those two cultural poles erodes, as many feel they have, the resources for renewal may prove difficult to tap. To become Americanized, it turns out, is not necessarily to acquire a sense of confidence and assurance on the basis of which to participate creatively in secular society. Instead the Americanized Catholic has a new set of insecurities— economic, social, and personal—with which to contend. Like his predecessors, his assessment of Church will turn largely upon the local community; if his parish fails to meet his needs, he will drop away; if it is able to meet his needs, he will remain and will even perhaps begin to accept responsibility. But the parochial dimension remains central, because it is built into the very nature of American culture and the necessary role the Church must play in it. In addition, it must be pointed out that many American Catholics remain close to their immigrant roots. Whether revitalized ethnic consciousness can provide the foundation for a renewal of the Catholic sense of mission is an open question, but anyone seriously concerned with the future of American Catholicism must take as careful an account of the problems and needs of those who remain in the ethnic, working-class neighborhoods as of the suburban Catholic constituency.

As late as the 1930s, only Southern Baptists among major American denominations were more apt to be represented among the nation's poor than were Catholics, and less apt to be found amid the higher reaches of business and professional leadership. The prosperity of postwar America and the social revolution facilitated by the GI Bill of Rights brought tremendous changes to American Catholicism. Numerous studies have convincingly demonstrated that Catholics have steadily approached national norms for length of education, entry into the professions, and emergence into leadership roles. That is not to say that Catholics have simply become self-satisfied middle-class people who have "made it"; on the contrary, ethnic stratification remains a marked feature of American economic life and some Catholic groups, most notably Poles and Italians, have had less success than others in breaking into high-status managerial positions. The American Catholic Church now contains a cross section of classes, coming to resemble in its internal class distribution the composition of American society generally. Increasing numbers of well-to-do Catholics are counterbalanced by large numbers of poor newcomers, while Catholics remain highly visible members of the blue-collar sectors so widely discussed in current political and social analysis. This diversification of class composition naturally leads to differing perceptions of the desirable content and style of Church life and poses serious problems for those who hope to develop a sense of social concern which might exert a significant impact on public policy.

For all the variety of ethnic groups in the Church of the past, those who adhered to the Catholic faith shared a common sense of exclusion from the main currents of American life. Even in the postwar years, battles over aid to parochial schools and other divisive issues could rally most Catholics. Minority consciousness took different and highly complex forms, but few Catholics felt fully and completely at home in American society. As a result they tended to accentuate in their religious self-understanding those elements of Catholic belief and practice which distinguished them most sharply from their non-Catholic neighbors. Here again the changes in recent years have been dramatic. The election of John Kennedy, the visit of Pope Paul to the United Nations, the growth of ecumenical understanding, the shared effort of Catholics and Protestants in social action, all have modified the sense of alienation of many middle-class Catholics and lessened the specifically religious dimension of the alienation of minority groups within American society generally. Further, many of the distinguishing characteristics of Catholic culture—the birth-control prohibition, the Friday abstinence, the habit of weekly church attendance, the popularity of massive public demonstrations of faith—have either disappeared or been deprived of legitimation by changing attitudes. The abortion issue remains, but even there studies show a gradual change in Catholic attitudes quite different from the militance of Church leaders. At the very least, the cement of the Catholic community supplied by religious conflict had been sharply reduced while the distinctive standards of Catholic identification are no longer obvious and do not command automatic endorsement.

The heart of the matter, then, is that American Catholicism is becoming an American Church. American ecclesiastical life, in a situation of Church-state separation and religious pluralism, has long been shaped by voluntarism. Historian Sidney Mead once described an American denomination as a voluntary association of like-hearted and like-minded individuals united on the basis of common belief for the purpose of accomplishing tangible and defined objectives. For a century and a half the American Catholic community drew its strength from the social conditions of immigrant communities whose experience reinforced Catholic identification. Responding flexibly to the needs of its diverse people, the hierarchy succeeded in maintaining their allegiance while placing few barriers in the way of their desire both to retain something of their heritage and to participate actively in American life. A broad consensus on doctrine, a widespread acceptance of American secular values, and an openness to a variety of cultural expressions enabled the Church to thrive in the American world.

Only now, as the social cement of the community has come unstuck and theological and devotional consensus has collapsed, do the full implications of voluntarism come home. Religious educators must ask not how to teach but what to teach; social activists must ask not how to win the Catholic community's support for liberal reform but what basic stance Christians should adopt toward American society. At the most fundamental level of the parish, priests and people alike must ask what this community stands for, what functions it fulfills—and should fulfill—in the lives of its members. The renewal of American Catholicism thus takes place amid the collapse of long-taken-for-granted ideals, values, and ways of life. Just as American society generally confronts the traumatic possibility of the end of growth, so Catholics confront the end of that historical self-confidence which supported them in the past. Like their countrymen generally, Catholics must now ask each other what they really believe and what they really want to do. Like other American Churches, Catholicism must find a new enthusiasm of belief and a new sense of purpose if it is to make a vital contribution to the nation and to the Universal Church.

The answer to the question of belief and purpose for the Church may be found in a renewed sense of social and political responsibility. This task is one which involves a clear and self-conscious effort to take seriously the imagery of the Church as "pilgrim" and "servant" made explicit in *Gaudium et Spes* and the social statements of Pope Paul VI. "We are witnesses of the birth of a new humanism, one in which man is defined first of all by his responsibility toward his brothers and toward history," the Council Fathers declared. Christian vocation involves full acceptance of this responsibility in the concrete historical situation in the 1970s. Renewal means something more than adaptation of ecclesiastical practice to the changing needs and aspirations of the Catholic population, important as this may be. Rather than anticipating social trends and accommodating to them, responsible Christians will determine desirable social changes and seek to shape events that will effect these changes.

If the beneficence of American society is now no longer to be taken for granted, then the response to the problem of renewing a sense of belief and purpose becomes more complicated. Uncritical identification with American secular culture, so important a part of the Church's previous outlook, must be replaced by the recovery of a degree of separate Catholic consciousness, on the basis of which to challenge contemporary persons responsibly. Yet authentic prophetic witness must develop within the life of a people. Catholicism cannot entirely detach itself from the national symbols without risking separation as well from the dreams and aspirations to which those symbols point. Of course, Christian participation in the national dialogue will have its greatest value when exercised with fidelity to the Church's particular tradition. But the reverse is also true, for the American vantage point is an important and significant one from which to assess the meaning of that religious tradition. In the 1950s John Cogley wrote of the Catholic attitude toward American society that we are content with standing in moral judgment on it, as if its problems were not our problems, as if its failings were not our own, as if the challenges confronting it were not confronting us. The parochialism of Catholic attitudes in the past should not be replaced with a new parochialism of judgmental self-righteousness but with an attitude of full acceptance of responsibility within a society and culture which is also the inheritance of American Catholics. While listening far more closely than they have in the past to their fellow Catholics in Europe, Africa, Asia, and Latin America, American Catholics must still offer their own, American response, for this is, after all, their land and their people.

These are days of reflection and reassessment for Catholic social action, in part shaped by the inexorable rhythms of American life itself. Nationally, the last decade witnessed a widespread and profound challenge to the social and political goals and methods of New Deal-style liberalism. Poverty and racism called that approach to task on its own grounds of quantitative alleviation of social misery. The atrocity of Vietnam and the bankruptcy of U.S. foreign policy hit liberalism on its exposed flank, while a revival of traditional American moral values threatened to undercut the very foundations of the pluralist, accommodationist politics dominant since the 1930s. These challenges have not been answered; indeed they remain convincing. But the experience of a decade has made many dissenters reluctantly acknowledge that, for all its moral and political weaknesses, the liberal tradition was and remains a remarkably adaptive reflection of the complex realities of American society. As has happened so often in the past, critics have been able to expose weaknesses of moderate liberalism; they have been unable either to renew or replace it.

Catholic social action shares in this mood. For generations, liberal Catholics hoped to facilitate by education and personal witness the participation of Catholics in broad-based American reform efforts. In the 1930s and 1940s such people fought desperately to build bridges between the Catholic population and New Deal reform and CIO unionism. In the 1950s and 1960s they supplemented that effort with an urgent program of promoting Catholic participation in the civil rights movement and combating Catholic nationalism. The Catholic reformer was a mediator who translated the ideals and programs of the American left into language familiar to Catholics, and who at the same time tried to bring some peculiarly Catholic dimension to his own work with reform movements. Today, many of these movements are immobilized; at the same time, the Catholic community is losing much of its coherence and solidarity. The mediating style of the old Catholic social actionist has lost its vitality. It may be that the person who retains the traditional concern with peace and social justice may have to stop waiting for a new mediating situation to arise and instead try to take the lead in shaping a new set of social alternatives for America and building a base for these alternatives in his or her own community.

At one time Catholic social action leaders thought the encyclicals provided both an ethical framework and a theory of social change. On that basis they worked for factory legislation, social insurance, and the development of labor unions. Such goals could be reconciled with a fear of excessive power in the hands of the state and blended easily into a pluralist view of the American social structure and a "countervailing power" theory of the American economy. From the union struggles of the 1930s and 1940s, it was a short step to community organization aimed at aiding the poor to get "a piece of the action," some bargaining power in the multipolar life of the American city. At each stage Catholic social action took the legitimacy and workability of the political and economic system in general for granted. One could serve as an advocate of the poor, confident that, if they could only get on the field with the rules enforced, the game of politics and the discipline of work would bring a result approximating justice. The civil rights crusades of the 1950s and 1960s did not fit so easily into the encyclical/pluralist framework; neither did the Vietnam war. Both raised questions about the legitimacy of the political process, the beneficence of the economy, and the democracy of power relationships, leading many to look for deeper explanations than the "malfunctioning" or "disequilibrium" of the social system. At the very least, they raised questions about the adequacy of the short-run solutions which had long provided the goals of Catholic social action. The result is ambiguity: on the one hand, a radical rhetoric of liberation; on the other, a style of pressure-group conflict and accommodation.

Getting beyond this point is the most important task confronting Catholic social action. For those who believe that the Church exists not for itself but for the world, the fact that the Church's big questions are now the same as the world's should be a source of some hope. Dealing with those questions requires some hard rethinking about the processes of social change, and it will require a good deal of that courage and persistence so marked in people like George Higgins, Paul Hanley Furfey, and Dorothy Day. When one remembers that people like this, and many others less famous, have been living lives for others for up to forty years, the frustra-

tion and disappointments of those who have been on the
scene for a decade may seem less intense. Those trying to
frame the policy for the future can learn from such people
the value of identification with the needs of the Catholic
people, who also have to take control over and responsibility
for their lives. For in the end, it is all the people who must
design and build the city, the nation, and the world they
want for themselves and their children. Catholic reformers
can help make this happen only if they can believe in their
hearts that ordinary people in church, at work, and in their
neighborhoods, communities, and state can control their own
lives, personally and collectively, and can indeed govern
themselves.

The development of a distinctive American Catholic social
theology remains an unfinished task. Yet, the American
Church has produced some remarkable leaders in the postconciliar period, and it has had a few documents which capture the state of transition and change in which the American Church finds itself. The documents in the section that
follow are representative of the best material to issue from
the official teaching Church. As such they deserve study and
critical response. They indicate something of the Church's response in this country to the challenges of Vatican II and the
"signs of the times." They indicate, as well, that much
remains to be done before the American Church will speak
with its own authentic voice to the problems of the day.

HUMAN LIFE IN OUR DAY

When the encyclical *Humanae Vitae* was issued on July 25, 1968, a worldwide explosion immediately followed. The encyclical touched off a crisis of authority, if not a crisis of faith. Many were hoping that the Pope would reverse the traditional Catholic ban on the use of artificial contraception. These hopes were dashed. The hopes had been raised by the formation of a special papal commission which was to examine the tradition to see what the full range of its effects may be. The commission issued both a majority and minority report. The majority report suggested very strongly that the traditional ban on artificial contraception could be reversed; the minority report rejected this and proposed a reaffirmation of the tradition. The Pope followed the minority view, causing a wave of protests the likes of which had not been seen for many centuries. Not only did bishops and theologians protest; many laity as well rejected the encyclical and its consequences. In America the debate focused around a group of younger theologians at Catholic University who issued a proclamation supporting freedom of conscience. This led to a further wave of reprisals by Cardinal O'Boyle of Washington, D.C. Although this specific conflict was eventually resolved, immense harm had been done to the solidarity and legitimacy of the Roman Catholic teaching authority. Recently Father Andrew Greeley and others have suggested that *Humanae Vitae* is the major cause of many people's leaving the Roman Catholic Church (see Andrew M. Greeley, William C. McCready, and Kathleen McCourt, *Catholic Schools in a Declining Church*, Kansas City, Kans.: Sheed and Ward, 1976).

The pastoral letter "Human Life in Our Day" was issued

by the American hierarchy on November 15, 1968, as a commentary and an application of *Humanae Vitae* to the American situation. This was in keeping with the suggestion emerging from Vatican II that local hierarchies should adapt papal teaching to their particular viewpoints. The letter focuses around the theme of the doctrine and defense of human life. Two subthemes within this are the doctrine of the family, with particular reference to the birth-control debate, and peace, with particular reference to the Vietnam war.

The teaching that the letter develops on birth control is placed within the context of the doctrine of the family. Since the family is the place where God's image is reproduced in His creation and is a sign to all of fidelity to life and hope for the future, the Church wishes to emphasize the significance and centrality of family life. The letter states quite clearly that the family now has a prophetic mission, "a witness to the primacy of life and the importance of whatever preserves life." This prophetic mission obliges the family to fidelity to married love and an expression of hope in life, contradicting the forces that seek to prevent or destroy life. Given what the bishops feel is the compromise, the infidelity, and the license of our times, the letter strongly emphasizes the significance of this prophetic mission to oppose the degradation of human life.

After setting this framework, the letter comments on the encyclical. Noting that it is a defense of love and of life, the letter emphasizes the interrelation between the unitive and the procreative meanings of marriage. It reaffirms that these two meanings are impaired and possibly contradicted when acts of intercourse are performed without love or openness to life. The letter states, therefore, that the encyclical is a positive statement which describes the nature of conjugal love and responsible parenthood. It is also an obligatory statement, "interpreting imperatives which are divine rather than ecclesiastical in origin." In response to the critics' argument concerning the primacy of conscience, the bishops refer to their past teaching that conscience is not a law unto itself and that revealed religion has an objective authority. The letter quotes favorable Cardinal Newman's statement that Catholics have a *prima facie* obligation to believe the Pope and to act accordingly. The bishops state that the encyclical sets forth the authentic teaching of the Church, "which Catholics believe interprets the divine law to which conscience should be conformed." The conclusion that the bishops eventually draw is that while circumstances may reduce moral guilt, "no one following the teaching of the Church can deny the objective evil of artificial contraception itself." Thus this pastoral letter sets out and clarifies the authoritative framework in which *Humanae Vitae* must be understood, but offers no critical evaluation of the teaching itself.

The bishops do, however, set out norms for responsible theological dissent. Because there is a place for freedom of inquiry and thought within the Church, it is possible for dissent to occur. This dissent must be set forth with propriety, with regard for the gravity of the matter, and with the deference due to the authority that has pronounced upon the issue at hand. When there is question of dissent from noninfallible doctrine, there is always a presumption in favor of the magisterium. Legitimate dissent is possible only for the most serious and well founded reasons, and then only if the way of raising dissent does not question the authority of the Church and does not give scandal. It is important in this context, the bishops argue, to maintain the proper balance between respect for authority and the duties of conscience. One cannot depreciate the values or rights of either, but neither should one allow either total dominance over the other.

Because of this, it can be argued that there must be an open system in the Church in which diverse factors—the insights of Christians and theologians in new situations which raise new questions—can help clarify the faith and practice of the Church. This allows the possibility of reverent dissent or disobedience in good conscience to a noninfallible teaching of the hierarchy. It is important to remember in this context that many papal teachings have been changed—for instance, on usury, the use of torture, and religious freedom. It is also important to remember that arguments based on natural law or other philosophies are only as strong as their internal consistency. The mere fact that the magisterium of the Church declares a philosophic argument to be correct does not *de facto* make it so. What this points to is the possibility of what could be called a loyal opposition within the Church, not for the purpose of tearing down authority but for the purpose of providing a corrective to it or to open authority to other points of view. Obedience should be neither a rubber stamp nor an easy way to avoid responsible decision-making. Authority and the demands of conscience must be held in tension—but a tension that is creative and conducive to greater development of the good of the whole Church.

The second major theme that this pastoral letter takes up is that of peace. The American bishops recognize that it is particularly important for them to consider this question because their nation contains possibly the largest stockpile of nuclear arms in the world. As a result the bishops join with Vatican II in calling upon American Catholics to evaluate war with "an entirely new attitude." Similarly, the bishops join in the Council's condemnation of wars of aggression and wars fought without limitation. Finally the bishops endorse Vatican II's condemnation of every indiscriminate destruction of whole cities or vast areas with their inhabitants.

The bishops' discussion of the problem of arms control was particularly timely, both because of the escalation of the number of nuclear weapons in most countries and because of the debate that was occurring in the United States. The bishops refer to Vatican II and its condemnation of the *use* of weapons of mass destruction but also note its abstention from condemning the *possession* of such weapons as a deterrent. It is quite clear that neither the Council nor the American bishops wish to condemn the possession of such weapons; however, the Council does state, "The arms race is an utterly treacherous trap for humanity, and one which ensnares the poor to an intolerable degree." The bishops do criticize the arms race in rather strong language and question whether the present national policy of maintaining nuclear superiority is meaningful for security. They clearly recognize that the development of new weapons systems by the United States could incite other nations to increase their offensive nuclear forces, continuing the spiral *ad infinitum*.

In seeking to develop ways of establishing peace, the bishops also call for a total review of the draft system and the establishment of voluntary military service. The bishops recognize that compulsory peacetime military service may really not serve the cause of peace. They also take a strong stand on selective conscientious objection. Although this position quite clearly follows from the traditional just-war theory, Catholics had never before spoken up so strongly in favor of it. The bishops ask that selective objectors be allowed to refuse to serve in wars which they consider unjust or branches of service which would force them to perform actions contrary to their conscience. Since the writing of this pastoral letter, the country has seen the acceptance of a voluntary military service; unfortunately, it has not yet recognized the religious rights of selective objectors.

In discussing the problem of Vietnam, which was the subject of fierce debate at that time, the bishops begin by repeating the judgment that, on balance, the U.S. presence in Vietnam is useful and justified. However, they note that the debate has continued to rage and that a variety of new viewpoints are coming forth. They also recognize that it is the duty of the governed to analyze responsibly the issues of public policy that are involved in such questions. Therefore the bishops, instead of providing such analysis, ask a series of questions by which the individual might analyze the Vietnam situation. These questions focus around an evaluation of the principle of proportionality. The bishops ask how much American resources should be committed to this war. Has the conflict provoked inhuman dimensions of suffering? Would not an untimely withdrawal be equally as disastrous as an untimely prolongation of the war? The bishops conclude by pointing out some moral lessons that are to be derived from American involvement with Vietnam.

Even though this war is now over, these lessons are still applicable. The first is that military power and technology do not suffice to restore order or to accomplish peace. The second is that evils such as "undernutrition, economic frustration, social stagnation, and political injustices may be more readily attacked and corrected through nonmilitary means than by military efforts to counteract the subversive forces bent on their exploitation." Finally, the bishops hope that Americans have learned that violence is not a means of remedying human ills.

Given the state in which we find ourselves today, these lessons should be borne in mind, especially given the problems we have seen in the Mideast and in Latin America. Many of the problems which we are facing today are the result of the social ills to which the bishops refer. Until these ills are corrected by substantive structural change, the problems will remain with us and the solutions will be all the more difficult to achieve. Even though many may have been disappointed by the bishops' reaffirmation of the teaching on birth control and disappointed by the weakness of the statement on Vietnam, nonetheless all must recognize the wisdom of the bishops in pointing to the basic problem of the rejection of a respect for human life that is a major cause of many of our social problems. By seeking to strengthen family life and the causes of peace throughout the world, American Catholics will be making a positive contribution to the development of a true international community.

HUMAN LIFE IN OUR DAY

PASTORAL LETTER OF THE AMERICAN HIERARCHY
ISSUED NOVEMBER 15, 1968

INTRODUCTORY STATEMENT

1. We honor God when we reverence human life. When human life is served, man is enriched and God is acknowledged. When human life is threatened, man is diminished and God is less manifest in our midst.

2. A Christian defense of life should seek to clarify in some way the relationship between the love of life and the worship of God. One cannot love life unless he worships God, at least implicitly, nor worship God unless he loves life.

3. The purpose of this pastoral letter of the United States bishops is precisely the doctrine and defense of life. Our present letter follows the moral principles set forth in the *Pastoral Constitution on the Church in the Modern World* [*Gaudium et Spes*] issued by Vatican Council II. It presupposes the general doctrine of the Church which we explored in our pastoral letter *The Church in Our Day*. It responds to the encyclical *Humanae Vitae* in this same context.

4. We are prompted to speak this year in defense of life for reasons of our pastoral obligation to dialogue within the believing community concerning what faith has to say in response to the threat to life in certain problems of the family and of war and peace.

5. We also choose to speak of life because of the needed dialogue among all men of faith. This is particularly necessary among Christians and all believers in God, and between believers and all who love life if peace is to be secured and life is to be served. There is evidence that many men find difficulty in reconciling their love for life with worship of the Lord of life.

6. On the other hand, it is becoming clear that the believer and the humanist have common concerns for both

life and peace. For example, an agnostic philosopher, much listened to by contemporary students, has this to say:

7. "Why do not those who represent the traditions of religion and humanism speak up and say that there is no deadlier sin than love for death and contempt for life? Why not encourage our best brains—scientists, artists, educators— to make suggestions on how to arouse and stimulate love for life as opposed to love for gadgets? . . . Maybe it is too late. Maybe the neutron bomb which leaves entire cities intact, but without life, is to be the symbol of our civilization" (Erich Fromm, *The Heart of Man: Its Genius for Good and Evil*).

8. The defense of life provides a starting point, then, for positive dialogue between Christians and humanists. Christians bring to the dialogue on the defense of life a further motivation. We are convinced that belief in God is intimately bound up with devotion to life. God is the ultimate source of life, His Son its Redeemer, so that denial of God undermines the sanctity of life itself.

9. Our pastoral letter will emphasize the maturing of life in the family and the development of life in a peaceful world order. Threats to life are most effectively confronted by an appeal to Christian conscience. We pray that our words may join us in common cause with all who reverence life and seek peace. We pray further that our efforts may help join all men in common faith before God Who "gives freely and His gift is eternal life" (Rom. 6, 23).

CHAPTER I

THE CHRISTIAN FAMILY

10. The attitude man adopts toward life helps determine the person he becomes. In the family, man and life are first united. In the family, the person becomes the confident servant of life and life becomes the servant of man. The Church must make good her belief in human life and her commitment to its development by active as well as doctrinal defense

of the family and by practical witness to the values of family life.

11. The Church thinks of herself as a family, the family of God and, so, is the more solicitous for the human family. She sees Christian marriage as a sign of the union between Christ and the Church (cf. Eph. 5, 31–32), a manifestation to history of the "genuine nature of the Church" (*Gaudium et Spes*, 48). Christian married love is "caught up into divine love and is governed and enriched by Christ's redeeming power and the saving activity of the Church" (*Gaudium et Spes*, 48). No institution or community in human history has spoken more insistently and profoundly than the Church of the dignity of marriage.

12. It is in terms of Christ and of salvation history, never of sociology alone, that the Church thinks of marriage. That is the point of her positive teachings on the sanctity, the rights and duties of the married state; it is also the point of her occasional strictures, as when Vatican Council II realistically cautions that "married love is too often profaned by excessive self-love, the worship of pleasure, and illicit practices against human generation" (*Gaudium et Spes*, 47).

13. The family fulfills its promise when it reinforces fidelity to life and hope in its future. The values of fidelity and hope, essential to human life and Christian love, are sometimes weakened even while men continue to think all is well. Such is often the case in our times. Fidelity and hope are especially threatened when the family is considered largely in terms of the pleasures or conveniences it provides for the individual or in terms of its economic or political potential. Christians should be the first to promote material improvement and provide for the family structure, but they must never measure the worth of the family nor the purpose of family life by these standards alone.

14. For the believer, the family is the place where God's image is reproduced in His creation. The family is the community within which the person is realized, the place where all our hopes for the future of the person are nourished. The family is a learning experience in which fidelity is fostered, hope imparted and life honored; it thus increases the moral

resources of our culture and, more importantly, of the person. The family is a sign to all mankind of fidelity to life and of hope in the future which become possible when persons are in communion with one another; it is a sign to believers of the depth of this fidelity and this hope when these center on God; it is a sign to Christians of the fidelity and hope which Christ communicates as the elder brother of the family of the Church for which he died (cf. Eph. 5, 25).

THE FAMILY: A FORCE FOR LIFE

15. It is the unfortunate fact that in all times some men have acted against life. The forms of the threat have varied; some of these endure to this day. Since the family is the source of life, no act against life is more hostile than one which occurs within the family. By such an act, life is cancelled out within that very community whose essential purposes include the gift of life to the world and the service of life in fidelity and hope.

16. For all these reasons, the Christian family is called more now than ever to a prophetic mission, a witness to the primacy of life and the importance of whatever preserves life. The Christian family therefore occupies a preeminent place in our renewed theology, particularly the theology of marriage and of the vocation of the laity. Christian families are called to confront the world with the full reality of human love and proclaim to the world the mystery of divine love as these are revealed through the family.

17. The prophetic mission of the family obliges it to fidelity to conjugal love in the face of the compromises and infidelities condoned in our culture. Its prophetic mission obliges the family to valiant hope in life, contradicting whatever forces seek to prevent, destroy or impair life. In its emphasis on the virtues of fidelity and hope, so essential to the prophetic witness of the family, Christian sexual morality derives therefore not from the inviolability of generative biology, but ultimately from the sanctity of life itself and the nobility of human sexuality.

18. The Christian ascetic of chastity, within and outside marriage, honors the sanctity of life and protects the dignity

of human sexuality. Were there no Revelation nor religion, civilization itself would require rational discipline of the sexual instinct. Revelation, however, inspires chastity with more sublime purposes and creative power. In chaste love, the Christian, whether his vocation be to marriage or to celibacy, expresses love for God Himself. In the case of spouses, marital chastity demands not the contradiction of sexuality but its ordered expression in openness to life and fidelity to love, which means also openness and faithfulness to God.

19. These considerations enter into the definition of responsible parenthood. The decision to give life to another person is the responsibility, under God, of the spouses who, in effect, ask the Creator to commit to their care the formation of a child (cf. *Gaudium et Spes*, 50). The fact that the decision touches upon human life and the human person is an indication of the reverence in which it must be made; the fact that the decision involves openness to God's creative power and providential love demands that it be unselfish, free from all calculation inconsistent with generosity.

20. Responsible parenthood, as the Church understands it, places on the properly formed conscience of spouses all the judgments, options and choices which add up to the awesome decision to give, postpone or decline life. The final decision may sometimes involve medical, economic, sociological or psychological considerations, but in no case can it deliberately choose objective moral disorder. If it is to be responsible, it cannot be the result of mere caprice nor of superficial judgments concerning relative values as between persons and things, between life and its conveniences.

21. Marital love, then, in its deepest meaning relates not only to the birth and rearing of children within the family society, but to the growth and well-being of human society on its every level and in its every aspect. It relates at the same time to the eternal life of those who choose marriage as their way to salvation. It is within this perspective of a total vision of man and not merely of isolated family considerations, narrowly conceived, that Pope Paul, drawing extensively on the content of Vatican Council II, has written his encyclical *Humanae Vitae*.

THE ENCYCLICAL AND ITS CONTENT

22. The *Pastoral Constitution on the Church in the Modern World* provides the theological framework within which Pope Paul works out the teaching set forth in *Humanae Vitae*.

23. "Therefore when there is question of harmonizing conjugal love with the responsible transmission of life, the moral aspect of any procedure does not depend solely on sincere intentions or on an evaluation of motives. It must be determined by objective standards. These, based on the nature of the human person and his acts, preserve the full sense of mutual self-giving and human procreation in the context to true love. Such a goal cannot be achieved unless the virtue of conjugal chastity is sincerely practiced. Relying on these principles, sons of the Church may not undertake methods of regulating procreation which are found blameworthy by the teaching authority of the Church in its unfolding of the divine law.

24. "Everyone should be persuaded that human life and the task of transmitting it are not realities bound up with this world alone. Hence they cannot be measured or perceived only in terms of it, but always have a bearing on the eternal destiny of men" (*Gaudium et Spes*, 51).

25. Pope Paul speaks of conjugal love as "fully human," "a very special form of personal friendship," "faithful and exclusive until death," "a source of profound and lasting happiness." Such love, however, "is not exhausted by the communion between husband and wife, but is destined to continue raising up new lives." There is an "objective moral order established by God" which requires that "each and every marriage act must remain open to the transmission of life."

26. Both conciliar and papal teaching, therefore, emphasize that the interrelation between the unitive meaning and the procreative meaning of marriage is impaired, even contradicted, when acts expressive of marital union are performed without love on the one hand and without openness to life on the other. Consistent with this, the encyclical sees the use of the periodic rhythms of nature, even though such use

avoids rather than prevents conception, as morally imperfect if its motivation is primarily refusal of life rather than the human desire to share love within the spirituality of responsible parenthood.

27. The encyclical *Humanae Vitae* is not a negative proclamation, seeking only to prohibit artificial methods of contraception. In full awareness of population problems and family anxieties, it is a defense of life and of love, a defense which challenges the prevailing spirit of the times. Long-range judgments may well find the moral insights of the encyclical prophetic and its world-view providential. There is already evidence that some peoples in economically underdeveloped areas may sense this more than those conditioned by the affluence of a privileged way of life.

28. The encyclical is a positive statement concerning the nature of conjugal love and responsible parenthood, a statement which derives from a global vision of man, an integral view of marriage, and the first principles, at least, of a sound sexuality. It is an obligatory statement, consistent with moral convictions rooted in the traditions of Eastern and Western Christian faith; it is an authoritative statement solemnly interpreting imperatives which are divine rather than ecclesiastical in origin. It presents without ambiguity, doubt or hesitation the authentic teaching of the Church concerning the objective evil of that contraception which closes the marital act to the transmission of life, deliberately making it unfruitful. United in collegial solidarity with the Successor of Peter, we proclaim this doctrine.

29. The encyclical reminds us that the use of the natural rhythms never involves a direct positive action against the possibility of life; artificial contraception always involves a direct positive action against the possibility of life. Correspondence with the natural system remains essentially attuned to the unitive and procreative intent of the conjugal act even when the spouses are aware of the silence of nature to life.

30. There are certain values which may not oblige us always to act on their behalf, but we are prohibited from ever acting directly against them by positive acts. Truth is such a value; life is surely another. It is one thing to say that an ac-

tion against these values is inculpable, diminished in guilt, or subjectively defensible; it is quite another to defend it as objectively virtuous.

31. The Church's teaching on the moral means to responsible parenthood presupposes certain positive values. One of these is that Christian marriage involves an ever-maturing mutuality between husband and wife, a constantly increasing awareness of the manner in which the total nuptial relationship parallels and symbolizes the love-sharing and life-giving union between Christ and His Church. The unitive and creative values symbolized by sexual expression permeate marriage in its every aspect. This consideration becomes more important as the years of married life go by, especially when changes in society give couples longer years of leisure together after their children begin to live on their own. This explains the importance that couples be united from the beginning of their love by common interests and shared activities which will intensify their nuptial relationship and insure its unity against disruption because of disappointment in one or another of their hopes.

32. No one pretends that responsible parenthood or even fidelity to the unitive love of marriage, as these are understood by the Church, is easy of attainment without prayerful discipline. Recourse to natural rhythms, for example, presents problems which the Holy Father has asked medical science to help solve. Chastity, as other virtues, is not mastered all at once or without sacrifice. It may involve failures and success, declines and growth, regressions in the midst and progress. A hierarchy of values that reflects a conformity to the example of Christ is neither easily achieved nor insured against loss. Moreover, Christians, however many their failures, will neither expect nor wish the Church to obscure the moral ideal in the light of which they press forward to perfection.

33. In the pursuit of the ideal of chastity, again as of every other virtue to which he is bound, the Christian must never lose heart; least of all can he pretend that compromise is conquest. At all times, his mind and heart will echo St. Paul: "Not that I have become perfect yet; I have not yet won, but I am still running, trying to capture the prize for which Christ Jesus captured me" (Phil. 3, 12). In no case does he

suppose that the Church, in proposing such goals, teaches erroneously and needlessly burdens her members.

34. They are quite right who insist that the Church must labor to heal the human condition by more than word and precept alone if she wishes her preaching to be taken seriously. All the moral teaching of the Church proposes objective standards difficult to attain: of honesty, respect for other people's property and lives, social justice, integrity in public office, devotion to learning, to service, to God. These standards demand of those to whom they are preached renunciations, frequently against the grain, but creative in their final effect. They also demand of those who preach these ideals that they, too, play their full part in the struggle against the social evils which obstruct their attainment.

35. We shall consider later in the letter some of our pastoral responsibilities toward the promotion of distributive justice, the rights and stability of the family, and the consequent social climate favorable to marriage morality. In the meantime, the Church, when she fulfills her prophetic role of preaching moral ideals and social reform, must do so with all the patience that the work of teaching requires (cf. 2 Tim. 4, 2).

36. The existence of the Sacrament of Penance in the Church is an indication that Christian ideals are not easy to achieve nor, once achieved, ours forever. The Church cannot, however, compromise the ideal. She is bound to teach it as it is.

THE ENCYCLICAL AND CONSCIENCE

37. Developing last year the teaching of the Council on the nature of the Church, we spoke of the reciprocal claims of conscience and authority in the Christian community as Christ called it into being. We noted that conscience "though it is inviolable is not a law unto itself"; that "the distinction between natural religion and revealed lies in this: that one has a subjective authority, and the other an objective," though both invoke conscience. We recalled that "God does not leave man to himself but has entered history through a Word which is 'the true light that enlightens all

men'; that Word speaks to us and still enlightens us in the Church of Jesus Christ which carries the double burden of human conscience and divine authority."

38. These wider questions of conscience, its nature, witness, aberrations and claims, above all its formation, are presupposed in this encyclical as in any papal or conciliar decisions on moral teaching. We recognize the role of conscience as a "practical dictate," not a teacher of doctrine.

39. Thomas Aquinas describes conscience as the practical judgment or dictate of reason, by which we judge what here and now is to be done as being good, or to be avoided as evil. Vatican Council II says that a man is not to be forced to act in a manner contrary to his conscience (cf. *Declaration on Religious Freedom*, 3). This is certainly true in any conflict between a practical dictate of conscience and a legislative or administrative decree of any superior.

40. However, when it is question of the Pope's teaching, as distinct from a decree or order, on a matter bound up with life and salvation, the question of conscience and its formation takes on quite different perspectives and dimensions. Cardinal Newman puts it in strong terms: ". . . I have to say again, lest I should be misunderstood, that when I speak of conscience, I mean conscience truly so called. When it has the right of opposing the supreme, though not infallible Authority of the Pope, it must be something more than that miserable counterfeit which, as I have said above, now goes by the name. If in a particular case it is to be taken as a sacred and sovereign monitor, its dictate, in order to prevail against the voice of the Pope, must follow upon serious thought, prayer, and all available means of arriving at a right judgment on the matter in question. And further, obedience to the Pope is what is called 'in possession'; that is, the *onus probandi* [burden of proof] of establishing a case against him lies, as in all cases of exception, on the side of conscience. Unless a man is able to say to himself, as in the Presence of God, that he must not, and dare not, act upon the Papal injunction, he is bound to obey it and would commit a great sin in disobeying it. *Prima facie* it is his bounden duty, even from a sentiment of loyalty, to believe the Pope right and to act accordingly . . ." (*A Letter to the Duke of Norfolk*).

41. *Humanae Vitae* does not discuss the question of the good faith of those who make practical decisions in conscience against what the Church considers a divine law and the Will of God. The encyclical does not undertake to judge the consciences of individuals but to set forth the authentic teaching of the Church which Catholics believe interprets the divine law to which conscience should be conformed.

42. *The Pastoral Constitution on the Church in the Modern World* reminds us that "in their manner of acting, spouses should be aware that they cannot proceed arbitrarily. They must always be governed according to a conscience dutifully conformed to the divine law itself, and should be submissive toward the Church's teaching office, which authentically interprets that law in the light of the Gospel. That divine law reveals and protects the integral meaning of conjugal love and impels it toward a truly human fulfillment" (*Gaudium et Spes*, 50). We must not suppose that there is such conflict between authority and freedom, between objective values and subjective fulfillment, that one can only prevail by the elimination of the other.

43. Married couples faced with conflicting duties are often caught in agonizing crises of conscience. For example, at times it proves difficult to harmonize the sexual expression of conjugal love with respect for the life-giving power of sexual union and the demands of responsible parenthood. Pope Paul's encyclical and the commentaries of the international episcopates on it are sensitive as are we to these painful situations. Filled with compassion for the human condition the Holy Father offers counsel which we make our own:

44. "Let married couples, then, face up to the efforts needed, supported by the faith and hope which do not disappoint . . . because God's love has been poured into our hearts through the Holy Spirit, Who has been given to us; let them implore divine assistance by persevering prayer; above all, let them draw from the source of grace and charity in the Eucharist. And if sin should still keep its hold over them, let them not be discouraged, but rather have recourse with humble perseverance to the mercy of God, which is poured forth in the Sacrament of Penance" (*Humanae Vitae*, 25).

45. We feel bound to remind Catholic married couples, when they are subjected to the pressures which prompt the Holy Father's concern, that however circumstances may reduce moral guilt, no one following the teaching of the Church can deny the objective evil of artificial contraception itself. With pastoral solicitude we urge those who have resorted to artificial contraception never to lose heart but to continue to take full advantage of the strength which comes from the Sacrament of Penance and the grace, healing, and peace in the Eucharist. May we all be mindful of the invitation of Jesus: "The man who comes to me I will never turn away" (Jn. 6, 37). Humility, awareness of our pilgrim state, a willingness and determination to grow in the likeness of the Risen Christ will help to restore direction of purpose and spiritual stability.

NEGATIVE REACTIONS TO THE ENCYCLICAL

46. The position taken by the Holy Father in his encyclical troubled many. The reasons for this are numerous. Not a few had been led and had led others to believe that a contrary decision might be anticipated. The mass media which largely shape public opinion have, as the Holy Father himself pointed out, at times amplified the voices which are contrary to the voice of the Church. Then, too, doctrine on this point has its effect not only on the intellects of those who hear it but on their deepest emotions; it is hardly surprising that negative reactions have ranged from sincere anguish to angry hurt or bitter disappointment, even among devout believers. Finally, a decision on a point so long uncontroverted and only recently confronted by new questions was bound to meet with mixed reactions.

47. That tensions such as these should arise within the household of the faith is not surprising and need not be scandalous. The Holy Father frankly confessed that his teaching would not be easily received by all. Some reactions were regrettable, however, in the light of the explicit teaching of Vatican Council II concerning the obligation of Catholics to assent to papal teaching even when it is not presented with the seal of infallibility. The Council declared:

48. "In matters of faith and morals, the bishops speak in the name of Christ and the faithful are to accept their teaching and adhere to it with a religious assent of soul. This religious submission of will and of mind must be shown in a special way to the authentic teaching authority of the Roman Pontiff, even when he is not speaking *ex-cathedra*. That is, it must be shown in such a way that his supreme magisterium is acknowledged with reverence, the judgments made by him are sincerely adhered to, according to his manifest mind and will. His mind and will in the matter may be known chiefly either from the character of the documents, from his frequent repetition of the same doctrine, or from his manner of speaking" (*Lumen Gentium*, 25). Pope Paul has recalled this obligation several times with respect to his encyclical on the regulation of birth, beginning when he exhorted priests "to be the first to give, in the exercise of your ministry, the example of loyal internal and external obedience to the teaching authority of the Church" (*Humanae Vitae*, 28).

NORMS OF LICIT THEOLOGICAL DISSENT

49. There exist in the Church a lawful freedom of inquiry and of thought and also general norms of licit dissent. This is particularly true in the area of legitimate theological speculation and research. When conclusions reached by such professional theological work prompt a scholar to dissent from non-infallible received teaching the norms of licit dissent came into play. They require of him careful respect for the consciences of those who lack his special competence or opportunity for judicious investigation. These norms also require setting forth his dissent with propriety and with regard for the gravity of the matter and the deference due the authority which has pronounced on it.

50. The reverence due all sacred matters, particularly questions which touch on salvation, will not necessarily require the responsible scholar to relinquish his opinion but certainly to propose it with prudence born of intellectual grace and a Christian confidence that the truth is great and will prevail.

51. When there is question of theological dissent from non-infallible doctrine, we must recall that there is always a

presumption in favor of the magisterium. Even non-infallible authentic doctrine, though it may admit of development or call for clarification or revision, remains binding and carries with it a moral certitude, especially when it is addressed to the universal Church, without ambiguity, in response to urgent questions bound up with faith and crucial to morals. The expression of theological dissent from the magisterium is in order only if the reasons are serious and well-founded, if the manner of the dissent does not question or impugn the teaching authority of the Church and is such as not to give scandal.

52. Since our age is characterized by popular interest in theological debate, and given the realities of modern mass media, the ways in which theological dissent may be effectively expressed, in a manner consistent with pastoral solicitude, should become the object of fruitful dialogue between bishops and theologians. These have their diverse ministries in the Church, their distinct responsibilities to the faith and their respective charisms.

53. Even responsible dissent does not excuse one from faithful presentation of the authentic doctrine of the Church when one is performing a pastoral ministry in Her name.

54. We count on priests, the counsellors of persons and families, to heed the appeal of Pope Paul that they "expound the Church's teaching on marriage without ambiguity"; that they "diminish in no way the saving teaching of Christ," but "teach married couples the indispensable way of prayer . . . without ever allowing them to be discouraged by their weakness" (*Humanae Vitae*, 29). We commend to confessors, as does Pope Paul, the example of the Lord Himself, Who was indeed intransigent with evil, but merciful towards individuals.

FAMILY SPIRITUALITY

55. Our concern for family life must extend far beyond the publication of pastoral letters. We pledge ourselves to cooperate in multiplying ways and means toward the renewal of the family and the enhancing of its prestige. Specifically, we shall increase our encouragement in the diocese and the na-

tion of programs undertaken by apostolic groups whose objective is the natural and spiritual strengthening of the Christian family.

56. Because of the primacy of the spiritual in all that makes for renewal, we give top priority to whatever may produce a sound "family spirituality." Family prayer, above all that which derives its content and spirit from the liturgy, and other devotions, particularly the Rosary; family reading of the Scriptures; family attendance at Mass and reception of Communion; family retreats, days of recollection and other special devotions; the observance of occasions of spiritual significance for members of the household—all these will increase the awareness of the family that it is the "Church in miniature."

57. For these reasons, we welcome the work of those theologians who are preparing a modern and valid ascetical theology of marriage. We recall gratefully the spiritual emphasis in many family-life programs, national and local, whose primary focus of concern has been the theology of the Christian family.

58. To prepare future spouses more adequately we recommend specialized team efforts in their behalf on the part of pastors of souls and qualified counsellors, including devout married couples. Such projects will give engaged couples the benefit of human wisdom and of Christian spirituality in the planning of their home, the founding of a family, the education of children, and all that makes for fidelity and hope in their lives together.

59. We endorse the establishment of diocesan family-life centers throughout the country so that Christian couples, physicians, psychologists, sociologists and priests may cooperate in implementing responsible parenthood in accordance with the principles enunciated in *Humanae Vitae*. On the national level, in response to the Holy Father's request for scientific research into effective and moral means of family planning, we bishops in the United States intend to establish an independent, non-denominational, non-profit foundation which will sponsor scientific research resulting in conclusions which will be helpful to doctors, educators and, ultimately, spouses in licit family planning.

60. The responsibility of our Family Life Division to pro-

vide information, educational tools and guidance in the face
of the mounting problems of family life will make it an increasing source of service to diocesan family programs. We
also hope to see established centers of education in family
life under the auspices of local medical schools or doctors'
guilds together with collegiate or adult education programs,
and the chaplains to students or young-adult groups. We
note the Holy Father's tribute to the promising apostolate
which brings together married couples who desire to communicate their experiences to other married couples and thus
become apostles of fidelity to the divine law and guides to
fulfillment in love.

EDUCATION OF CHILDREN IN SEXUALITY

61. In accord with the *Decree on Christian Education* of
Vatican Council II we affirm the value and necessity of
wisely planned education of children in human sexuality,
adapted to the maturity and background of our young people. We are under a grave obligation, in part arising from the
new circumstances of modern culture and communications,
to assist the family in its efforts to provide such training.
This obligation can be met either by systematic provision of
such education in the diocesan school curriculum or by the
inauguration of acceptable educational programs under other
diocesan auspices, including the Confraternity of Christian
Doctrine. Parents are those primarily responsible for imparting to their children an awareness of the sacredness of sexuality; this will ordinarily be best accomplished when both parents discharge this duty in mutual consultation and shared
responsibility. The necessity for greater communication and
cooperation between parents and teachers is highlighted in
this problem; the consequent role of Parent-Teacher Guilds
and similar home-school associations is apparent.

62. Parents are sometimes fearful that their right to teach
the norms of sexual morality to their children may be
usurped or that programs such as we envision may lead to the
sexual misdirection of their children if the teachers involved
are inadequately prepared or emotionally immature. In the
light of such legitimate concerns, the careful selection of in-

structors for these discussions is a serious responsibility to be shared by priests, school authorities and parents, perhaps best under the auspices of parent-teacher associations.

63. The content of these instructions should provide an appreciation of "the true values of life and of the family" (*Humanae Vitae*, 21), in addition to a healthy inculcation, from the earliest years of moral and intellectual formation, of how conjugal love involves a harmonious response from the emotions, the passions, the body and the mind. At the same time, healthy Christian attitudes toward life will be developed in young people if they are given an understanding, consistent with their years, of why the Council insists that those "actions within marriage by which the couple are united intimately and chastely are noble and worthy ones" (*Gaudium et Spes*, 49).

64. During these early years of physical growth and spiritual formation, especially throughout adolescence, our young people and their neighbors should be taught to appreciate the heroic witness to divine life and the unique service to human life given by those who, with love undivided, dedicate to God and their fellow-men the consecration of their celibacy and virginity for the sake of the Kingdom of God. Our priests, religious brothers and sisters have bound themselves to live in persevering single-hearted commitment as intimate collaborators with God Himself, from Whom every family, whether spiritual or natural, takes its name both in heaven and on earth (Eph. 3, 15). Every family is therefore in their debt: the families from which they come, the families to which they bear their special witness of life and love, the national family they strengthen, the family of the Church. No one knows this more than their bishops; no one is more grateful.

THE NEW FAMILY

65. In facing current problems of the American family, we welcome the open approach of the *Pastoral Constitution on the Church in the Modern World* toward marriage and the family. It provides a timely and optimistic overview of the community aspect of marriage, a community that functions

best when all its members understand that freedom is their birthright and a developing sense of responsibility their challenge. It sets up balances which provide for the more perfect personal development of each family member and, at the same time, assures the optimum effect of the family unity in the larger family of man. It recognizes the continual and rapid changes which characterize our times.

66. The style of family living is undoubtedly affected by changing social conditions, yet the family retains a resilience and strength that helps it adapt to change. In fact, the family has always been the witness to change as it passes on the wisdom, successes and accomplishments of one generation to the next as a patrimony for the pursuance of its dreams.

67. Commenting on this adaptability to change that is almost inherent in the family, Pope Paul VI notes that "in a world in the midst of change, it would be useless to want to close one's eyes to the adaptations which even the most stable, most traditional institutions must accept. No matter how great the merits of the family of yesterday may have been, it is the one of today and of tomorrow which must attract the attention of men who are really preoccupied with the welfare of humanity. These 'new families' possess many new characteristics, some of which may certainly give rise to legitimate disquietude. But—we say without fear—the Church looks with pleasure upon many of these innovations: the cessation, for example, of certain social or family restrictions, the freer and more conscious choice of a spouse, the greater stress placed upon the development of husband and wife, the more lively interest in the education of children, and still many other traits which it is not possible to enumerate in detail" (Paul VI to IUFO).

68. One of the best examples of this new type of family structure is the present-day American family. It is a community of individual persons joined by human love, and living a community life that provides for the greatest expression of individualism. At the same time, equalitarian marriage patterns have so developed among Americans as to avoid rigid role assignments within the family and thus make possible a deeper family unity.

69. The family unit develops apart from the parent-

families, yet not totally isolated. In our technological culture, transportation facilities and communications media provide new systems of mobility and yet fortunately allow for a strengthening of human bonds among families, despite the distances in geographical location.

70. The educational attainment of women and new emphasis on legal and social equality between men and women create further tensions but also opportunities for more effective partnership in marriage. This adds a further reason why a Catholic theology of family life must be spelled out to match the changing patterns of the American family. A relevant theology will reinforce the efforts of spouses to achieve conjugal maturity; it will enable them to realize the more profoundly the difference between romance and love and to understand that only gradually will they achieve the harmony between healthy individualism and mutual self-giving in which Christian personalism consists.

NEW TENSIONS, NEW NEEDS

71. Technological and cultural changes bring with them complexities not easily resolved. Some of these set up pressures on the family from outside, some from within. For example, even the family today finds itself under the necessity to develop new channels of "communication"; this seems a formidable word to describe relations within the intimate community that a human family should be. However, the problem is made real by the profoundly changed circumstances under which each family member now seeks to establish an identity while preserving a warm sense of family unity and pride. Family harmony in our day will depend on just such "communication" as parents attempt to solve the authority-obedience dilemma with their growing children. Moreover, reformed "communication" within the family is needed if the manifold educational resources of family life itself are to complement the formal schooling of children.

72. The individual family is now challenged to new responsibilities toward the plurality of families which comprises the nation, the human community and the Church. And so Christian families, conscious of their part in the progress of

the wider human family, will wish to share not only their spiritual heritage with families less privileged but also their material resources. They will seek by their own initiatives to supplement government action, being painfully aware that in our own country many families are victims of poverty, disease and inadequate living standards.

73. Informed social critics are asserting that family instability in the urban areas of America is the result, in part at least, of our national failure to adopt comprehensive and realistic family-centered policies during the course of this century. The breakdown of the family has intrinsic causes, some of them moral, but these have been aggravated by the indifference or neglect of society and by the consequences of poverty and racist attitudes. The object of wise social policy is not only the physical well-being of persons but their emotional stability and moral growth, not as individuals but, whenever possible, within family units.

74. In principle, American social theory has always recognized that the normal family enjoys a real autonomy; only the abnormal inadequacy of a particular family places its members within the competency of our courts. Even then, whenever possible, it is the disposition of our public agencies to supply the defects of nature by providing the neglected, delinquent or homeless child with the nearest possible approach to life and training in a family setting. Americans have tended to prefer, particularly recently, the plan of foster homes where the role of natural parents can be somehow supplied in the development of the person within a human family. Our theory in all these respects has been admirable; its implementation in legislation and in practice has not always kept pace with the problems testing the theory. The present urban crisis is but one evidence of this.

75. Though families, like man himself, do not live on bread alone, without bread they suffer and die. Food programs still need a family orientation. Poor housing, for further example, has an adverse effect on family stability. We urge an expansion of home ownership programs for low- and moderate-income families, especially the larger families frequently neglected in these plans, as well as programs for low-rent housing and housing rehabilitation.

76. Programs devised to assist less advantaged families should at all costs avoid disruption of the family unit. A major disruption occurs when mothers are required to separate themselves from their young children for the sake of added income. Disruption has too often been the result of certain welfare policies which, whether consciously intended or not, have destroyed rather than supported family stability; one such policy we pinpointed in our reference to the "man in the house" rule when we spoke in a recent statement on the national social problem, but others could be documented. Every member of each family has a right to be cared for, not as an isolated person but as a person who belongs with and depends upon a family. We therefore favor the trend to consider social service programs, domestic relations courts and child welfare casework as involving family rather than merely individual dimensions and solutions.

77. Whenever a family is undermined, society suffers the loss. There are no insignificant families, as there is no insignificant person. If families are to function as the good of society requires, each must have income proportionate to its needs.

78. Wages in our country are usually based upon the work done, plus productivity. Little or no consideration is given to the family situation of the individual, his marital status, or the number of children in his home. It should not normally be necessary for the father of a family to "moonlight," seeking employment from more than one source to support his wife and children. Single men and the married men with families receive the same rates of pay for the same work. As a result, one sector of the population bears a disproportionately large share of the financial burden of maintaining the child population, which means the future nation, except for income tax benefits, which may unfortunately be cancelled out by consumer taxes. The effective solution we are urging may well require a family allowance system in the United States similar to those adopted by Canada, many European nations, Australia, New Zealand and some governments of South America. We stand ready to support enlightened legislation in this sense.

79. The challenges and threats to contemporary family life

may often seem insuperable. However, the resources of this nation are more than sufficient to enhance the security and prosperity of our families at home while leaving us free to fulfill our duties in charity and justice abroad. The scientific, educational and financial resources of our nation cannot be better utilized than in defense and development of the family. The future of civilization itself depends upon such creative use of our resources.

80. Our concern with improved social conditions and public policies protective of the family includes recognition of the special merits of some families. We second the tribute of the Council's *Pastoral Constitution* to parents of large families; we add a further tribute to those parents who, in a tradition that has been the strength of American Catholicism, have provided their children, very often at great sacrifice, with educational opportunities under religious auspices from pre-school years to higher education.

81. We are mindful of those families which include disadvantaged children and of families which by adoption assume full responsibility for children not born to them. Adoption corresponds with a deeply human instinct; it gives a home to the homeless and parents to the orphaned while at the same time rewarding the love with which a family welcomes life not originally committed to its keeping.

82. Likewise praiseworthy is the unselfishness which prompts qualified people to become foster parents to children who need material, emotional or spiritual assistance at some point in their lives. Finally, we offer a word of encouragement to our brothers or sisters in Christ who care for children in one-parent families. The sacrifices required to provide for the physical welfare and psychological development of children under these circumstances are sometimes extraordinary. Those who thus spend themselves on behalf of life and love witness to the world and the Church a generosity which cannot fail to inspire others and to sanctify themselves.

FURTHER THREATS TO LIFE

83. At this tense moment in our history when external

wars and internal violence make us so conscious of death, an affirmation of the sanctity of human life by renewed attention to the family is imperative. Let society always be on the side of life. Let it never dictate, directly or indirectly, recourse to the prevention of life or to its destruction in any of its phases; neither let it require as a condition of economic assistance that any family yield conscientious determination of the number of its children to the decision of persons or agencies outside the family.

84. Stepped-up pressures for moral and legal acceptance of directly procured abortion make necessary pointed reference to this threat to the right to life. Reverence for life demands freedom from direct interruption of life once it is conceived. Conception initiates a process whose purpose is the realization of human personality. A human person, nothing more and nothing less, is always at issue once conception has taken place. We expressly repudiate any contradictory suggestion as contrary to Judaeo-Christian traditions inspired by love for life, and Anglo-Saxon legal traditions protective of life and the person.

85. Abortion brings to an end with irreversible finality both the existence and the destiny of the developing human person. Conscious of the inviolability of life, the Second Vatican Council teaches:

86. "God, the Lord of life, has conferred on man the surpassing ministry of safeguarding life, a ministry which must be fulfilled in a manner that is worthy of man. Therefore, from the moment of its conception life must be guarded with the greatest care while abortion and infanticide are unspeakable crimes" (Gaudium et Spes, 51).

87. The judgment of the Church on the evil of terminating life derives from the Christian awareness that men are not the masters but the ministers of life. Hence, the Council declares: ". . . whatever is opposed to life itself, such as any type of murder, genocide, abortion, euthanasia, or willful self-destruction, whatever violates the integrity of the human person . . . all these things and others of their like are infamies indeed. They poison human society but they do more harm to those who practice them than to those who suffer from

the injury. Moreover, they are a supreme dishonor to the Creator" (*Gaudium et Spes*, 27).

A NOTE OF CHRISTIAN OPTIMISM

88. Pressing concerns of the hour have led us to consider with you many of the problems of family life, together with a Christian appraisal of them. The family is, however, much more than the sum of its problems. It is, as we said earlier, the place where the person occurs, where life begins, where fidelity and hope are nourished, where human love reaches its more intense expression. The family is, indeed, that "school of deeper humanity" of which the Vatican Council speaks (*Gaudium et Spes*, 52).

89. The Christian family is an image of God and a sign of the Church. It is the community wherein Christ is most powerfully preached, where Christians first hear the name of God, first learn to pray, and first express their faith. In the words and example of their believing parents, children come to know what faith is and how it must be lived, what life is and how it must be honored. For this reason, a spirituality which is suitable to the contemporary family and which brings all members of the family together in faith and hope is, we repeat, the most urgent need of modern culture.

90. Since the family is the basic unit of human society, it should be the object of civilization's most enlightened concern. Since it is the basic unit of their life, parishes should make the needs of the family and the benefits which the family brings to the parish controlling norms in the planning of parish organizations and activities, liturgical, educational, charitable and social.

91. As bishops of the Catholic Church in the United States, concerned for her present well-being and prospects, our first prayer is for the families who comprise her parishes and dioceses. Our optimism for the future of the Church, the family of God, springs largely from optimism for the future of the family. In turn, our basis for optimism for the future of family life, despite occasional negative signs, rests upon the persevering hope of married couples whose responsibility

to life and vocation to love have been the opening theme of this pastoral letter.

92. As last year we saluted priests, for their special part in the work of God, so this year we salute Christian spouses who "made to the image of the living God and enjoying the authentic dignity of persons, are joined to one another in equal affection, harmony of mind and the work of mutual sanctification. Thus, following Christ Who is the principle of life, by the sacrifices and joys of their vocation and through their faithful love, [they have] become witnesses of the mystery of love which the Lord revealed to the world by His dying and His rising up to live again" (*Gaudium et Spes*, 52).

CHAPTER II

THE FAMILY OF NATIONS

93. We share the deep concern of thoughtful people in our times, a concern voiced by the Vatican Council, that "the whole human family has reached an hour of supreme crisis" (*Gaudium et Spes*, 77). The crisis can ultimately offer great promise for a more abundant human life, but at the moment it portends grave threats to all life. The threats to life depend on urgent and difficult decisions concerning war and peace. In considering these we share the conviction of Vatican Council II that the horror and perversity of technological warfare "compel us to undertake an evaluation of war *with an entirely new attitude*" (§ 80, emphasis added).

94. This compelling obligation is the greater in our case since we are citizens of a nation in many ways the most powerful in the world. The responsibility of moral leadership is the greater in the local Church of a nation whose arsenals contain the greatest nuclear potential for both the harm that we would wish to impede or the help it is our obligation to encourage. We are acutely aware that our moral posture and comportment in this hour of supreme crisis will be assessed by the judgment of history and of God.

95. We renew the affirmation by the Council that "the loftier strivings and aspirations of the human race are in harmony with the message of the Gospel" (§ 77). We speak as witnesses to that Gospel, aware that the issues of war and peace test the relevancy of its message for our generation, particularly in terms of the service of life and its dignity. We seek to speak in the spirit of that Gospel message, which is at heart a doctrine of non-violence rather than violence, of peace understood as Jesus proclaimed it (cf. Jn. 14:27).

96. We call upon American Catholics to evaluate war with that "entirely new attitude" for which the Council appealed and which may rightly be expected of all who, calling themselves Christians, proclaim their identity with the Prince of Peace. We share with all men of good will the conviction that a more humane society will not come "unless each person devotes himself with renewed determination to the cause of peace" (§ 77). We appeal to policy makers and statesmen to reflect soberly on the Council teaching concerning peace and war, and vigorously to pursue the search for means by which at all times to limit and eventually to outlaw the destructiveness of war.

97. The Vatican Council noted that "war continues to produce daily devastation in one or another part of the world" (§ 79). The observation has lost none of its truth in the period since the Council ended; indeed, there have been further grievous outbreaks of war and aggression.

98. Of one mind with the Council, we condemn without qualification wars of aggression however their true character may sometimes be veiled. Whatever case there may have seemed to exist in other times for wars fought for the domination of another nation, such a case can no longer be imagined given the circumstances of modern warfare, the heightened sense of international mutuality and the increasingly available humane means to the realization of that mutuality.

99. We join wholeheartedly in the Council's condemnation of wars fought without limitation. We recognize the right of legitimate self-defense and, in a society still unorganized, the necessity for recourse to armed defense and to collective security action in the absence of a competent au-

thority on the international level and once peaceful means have been exhausted. But we seek to limit warfare and to humanize it, where it remains a last resort, in the maximum degree possible. Most of all, we urge the enlisting of the energies of all men of good will in forging the instruments of peace, to the end that war may at long last be outlawed.

100. Meanwhile, we are gratefully conscious that "those who are pledged to the service of their country as members of its armed forces should regard themselves as agents of security and freedom on behalf of their people. As long as they fulfill this role properly, they are making a genuine contribution to the establishment of peace" (*Gaudium et Spes*, 79).

101. In the Christian message peace is not merely the absence of war. Ultimately, of course, it presupposes that presence within and among men of a positive principle of life and unity which is none other than the divine life to which the Church bears witness, of which Christ in His Church is the source. The soul, then, of a peaceful society is divine charity. But justice, the great concern of the well-ordered state and the justification for its existence, is the foundation of the organized society.

102. Therefore, peace cannot be reduced solely to the maintenance of a balance of power between enemies; nor is it to be brought about by dictatorship, whether this be the imposition of the sheer will of a ruler, a party or even a majority. It is an enterprise of justice and must be built up ceaselessly in seeking to satisfy the all-embracing demands of the common good. This is the point of Pope Paul's positive, dynamic concept of peace: the modern word for peace is development. Peace therefore presupposes the fraternal confidence which manifests itself in a firm determination to respect other persons and peoples, above all their human dignity, and to collaborate with them in the pursuit of the shared hopes of mankind.

ARMS CONTROL

103. It is in nuclear warfare, even in its "cold" phase or form, that mankind confronts the moral issue of modern war

in its extreme case. This has become a situation in which two adversaries possess and deploy weapons which, if used against each other, could annihilate their respective civilizations and even threaten the survival of the human race. Nothing more dramatically suggests the anti-life direction of technological warfare than the neutron bomb; one philosopher declares that the manner in which it would leave entire cities intact, but totally without life, makes it, perhaps, the symbol of our civilization. It would be perverse indeed if the Christian conscience were to be unconcerned or mute in the face of the multiple moral aspects of these awesome prospects.

104. It is now a quarter century since Pope Pius XII summoned that conscience to a "War on War." He pointed out World War II's "unspeakable atrocities," the "image of a hell upon which anyone who nourishes humane sentiments in his heart can have no more ardent wish than to close the door forever." He warned against the further progress of "human inventions . . . directed to destruction," and pleaded that to the recognition of the immorality of wars of aggression there be added "the threat of a judicial intervention of the nations and of a punishment inflicted on the aggressor by the United Nations, so that war may always feel itself proscribed, always under the watchful guard of preventive action." He argued that then "humanity, issuing from the dark night in which it has been submerged for so great a length of time, will be able to greet the dawn of a new and better era in its history" (Christmas broadcast, 1944).

105. The Second Vatican Council, in a solemn declaration, endorsed "the condemnation of total warfare issued by recent popes" and stated: "Every act of war directed to the indiscriminate destruction of whole cities or vast areas with their inhabitants is a crime against God and man which merits firm and unequivocal condemnation" (*Gaudium et Spes*, § 80).

106. The Council explicitly condemned the use of weapons of mass destruction, but abstained from condemning the *possession* of such weapons to deter "possible enemy attack" (§ 81). Though not passing direct judgment on this strategy of deterrence, the Council did declare that "men should

be convinced that the arms race in which so many countries are engaged is not a safe way to preserve a steady peace. Nor is the so-called 'balance' resulting from this race a pure and authentic peace. Rather than being eliminated thereby, the causes of war threaten to grow gradually stronger. . . . Therefore it must be said again: the arms race is an utterly treacherous trap for humanity, and one which ensnares the poor to an intolerable degree" (§ 81).

107. The Council did not call for unilateral disarmament; Christian morality is not lacking in realism. But it did call for reciprocal or collective disarmament "proceeding at an equal pace according to agreement and backed up by authentic and workable safeguards" (§ 82). There are hopeful signs that such a formula may be strengthened by the Partial Test Ban Treaty and that the commitment under the Non-Proliferation Treaty to proceed to a negotiation of balanced reductions of nuclear weapons—at the same time extending the use of nuclear power for peaceful development of the needy nations under adequate inspection safeguards—may provide a positive, sane pattern for the future. We earnestly pray so, commending the furtherance of these hopes to responsible political leaders and to the support of all citizens.

108. Meanwhile, it is greatly to be desired that such prospects not be dashed by irrational resolves to keep ahead in "assured destruction" capability. Rather it is to be hoped that the early ratification by the Senate of the Non-Proliferation Treaty—which in essence is a Treaty between the USSR and the US and other nations—will hasten discussion of across-the-board reductions by the big powers. Despite, and even because of, the provocations in Eastern Europe and elsewhere, the United States should continue steps to create a better climate for these discussions, such as taking the lead in inviting the UN Atomic Energy Commission and other organizations and foreign states to visit its nuclear facilities, and scrupulously reviewing all commitments for the sale, loan or lease of armaments.

109. The Council's position on the arms race was clear. To recall it: "Therefore, we declare once again: the arms race is an utterly treacherous trap for humanity. . . . It is much

to be feared that if this race persists, it will eventually spawn all the lethal ruin whose path it is now making ready" (§ 81).

110. Nonetheless, the nuclear race goes on. The latest act in the continuing nuclear arms race is no doubt the U.S. decision to build a "thin" anti-ballistic missile system to defend against possible nuclear attack by another world power. This decision has been widely interpreted as the prelude to a "thick" ABM system to defend against possible nuclear attack.

111. In themselves, such anti-ballistic missiles are purely defensive, designed to limit the damage to the United States from nuclear attack. Nevertheless by upsetting the present strategic balance, the so-called balance of terror, there is grave danger that a United States ABM system will incite other nations to increase their offensive nuclear forces with the seeming excuse of a need to restore the balance.

112. Despite the danger of triggering an expanded escalation of the arms race the pressures for a "thick" ABM deployment persist.

113. We seriously question whether the present policy of maintaining nuclear superiority is meaningful for security. There is no advantage to be gained by nuclear superiority, however it is computed, when each side is admittedly capable of inflicting overwhelming damage on the other even after being attacked first. Such effective parity has been operative for some years. Any effort to achieve superiority only leads to ever-higher levels of armaments as it forces the side with the lesser capability to seek to maintain its superiority. In the wake of this action-reaction phenomenon comes a decrease in both stability and security.

114. The National Conference of Catholic Bishops pledges its united effort toward forming a climate of public opinion for peace, mindful of the Council's advice that "government officials . . . depend on public opinion and feeling to the greatest possible extent" (§ 82). We will therefore, through existing and improved agencies, support national programs of education for Catholic Americans and for all Americans in collaboration with all religious groups and other organizations.

115. With *Gaudium et Spes,* we commend the arduous and unceasing efforts of statesmen and specialists in the field of arms control and disarmament, and add our own encouragement of systematic studies in this field. As the Council appealed to Catholic scholars throughout the world to participate more fully in such studies, so we call upon intellectuals in the Church in our land to bring scholarly competence and their powers of persuasion to that "war on war" which the modern Popes have without exception pleaded that we wage.

116. We urge Catholics, and indeed all our countrymen, to make a ceaseless vigil of prayers for peace and for all those who are charged with the delicate and difficult negotiations of disarmament. Such prayers provide the most obvious and appropriate occasion for ecumenical services bringing together all in our communities who cherish the blessed vision of peace heralded by the Hebrew prophets and preached by Christ and His Apostles. We cannot but question the depth of the commitment to peace of people of religious background who no longer pray for peace. But those who only pray for peace, leaving to others the arduous work for peace, the dialogue for peace, have a defective theology concerning the relation between human action and the accomplishment of that will of God in which is our peace. So, too, those who, neglectful of the part of prayer, rely only on their own power, or on the pooling of merely human resources of intelligence, energy and even good will, forget the wisdom of Scripture: "If the Lord does not build the house, in vain the masons toil; if the Lord does not guard the city, in vain the sentries watch" (Ps. 127, 1-2).

THE INTERNATIONAL COMMUNITY

117. The Council Fathers recognized that not even ending the nuclear arms race, which itself cannot be accomplished without the full cooperation of the international community, would ensure the permanent removal of the awesome threat of modern war. Nor would disarmament alone, even assuming it to be complete and across the board, remove the causes of war. "This goal undoubtedly requires the establishment of some universal public authority acknowledged as such by

all, and endowed with effective power to safeguard, on the behalf of all, security, regard for justice, and respect for rights" (§ 82).

118. Such an authority, furthermore, is required by the growing, ever more explicit interdependence of all men and nations as a result of which the common good "today takes on an increasingly universal complexion and consequently involves rights and duties with respect to the whole human race" (§ 26).

119. Therefore political leaders should ". . . extend their thoughts and their spirit beyond the confines of their own nation, put aside national selfishness and ambition to dominate other nations, and nourish a profound reverence for the whole of humanity, which is already making its way so laboriously toward greater unity" (§ 82).

120. We commend the efforts of world statesmen, particularly those of our own nation, who seek to extend the spirit and practice of cooperation in international agencies and regional associations of nations, with the object not only of terminating or preventing war, and of building up a body of international law, but also of removing the causes of war through positive programs.

121. Since war remains a melancholy fact of life today, we believe the United States not only should insist on adherence to and the application by all nations of existing international conventions or treaties on the laws of war, such as the revised Geneva Convention relative to the treatment of prisoners of war, but should take the lead in seeking to update them. Certain forms of warfare, new and old, should be outlawed, and practices dealing with civilian populations, prisoners of war and refugees are always in need of review and reform.

122. Here, too, our dependence on responsible writers, informed speakers and competent critics is crucial to the cause of peace. Hence we encourage Catholic scholars to undertake systematic studies of new developments, theories and practices in warfare, including guerrilla warfare, revolution and "wars of liberation." Changing political patterns, improved techniques of communication, new methods of remote controls and of surveillance of individuals and communities alike made possible by science, as well as shifting ethical standards,

make it the vocation of devout intellectuals, both as citizens of their own nations and servants of the common good of mankind, to bring informed competence to the illumination, discussion and resolution of the complex issues, many of them moral, arising from all these.

123. A Catholic position of opposition to compulsory peacetime military service, first formulated on the level of the Holy See by Pope Benedict XV, has had for its premise the fact that such service has been a contributing cause of the breeding of actual wars, a part of the "great armaments" and "armed peace" security concept, and, in the words of Cardinal Gasparri in a letter to Lloyd George, the cause of such great evils for more than a century that the cure of these evils can only be found in the suppression of this system. In the spirit of this position, we welcome the voices lifted up among our political leaders which ask for a total review of the draft system and the establishment of voluntary military service in a professional army with democratic safeguards and for clear purposes of adequate defense. Our call for the end of any draft system at home which, in practice, amounts at times to compulsory peacetime military service is in direct line with previous resolutions of the hierarchy of the United States on compulsory military training (cf. *Our Bishops Speak*, pp. 234, 237).

124. Apart from the question of war itself, we deem it opportune here to reiterate the Council's condemnation of genocide, the methodical extermination of an entire people, nation or ethnic minority for reasons connected with race, religion or status such as that undertaken by the Nazis against the Jews among their own citizens and later against all the Jewish people, as well as so-called "gypsies." We would urge United States ratification of the United Nations Convention on this subject and of every other sound implementing instrument by which the United Nations Declaration of Human Rights can be translated from the level of ideals to that of actuality. Furthermore, we urge increased support by our countrymen and citizens of all nations of all international programs consistent with the protection and promotion of the sanctity of human life and the dignity of the human person in times of war and peace.

125. We earnestly appeal to our own government and to all governments to give the elimination of the present international "war system" a priority consistent with the damaging effect of massive armament programs on all the objectives of the good society to which enlightened governments give priorities: education, public health, a true sense of security, prosperity, maximum liberty, the flourishing of the humane arts and sciences, in a word the service of life itself. Thus can we strive to move away, as reason and religion demand, from the "war system" to an international system in which unilateral recourse to force is increasingly restricted.

126. This will require international peace-making and peace-keeping machinery. To this end we urge all to support efforts for a stronger and more effective United Nations that it may become a true instrument of peace and justice among nations. In this respect the peace motivation of Pope Paul's public support of the United Nations by his moral authority and teaching office at the time of his visit to that body on its anniversary should be normative for Catholics.

127. We would welcome in official pronouncements of our own and other governments, as well as in the increased support given to the United Nations and associated agencies by the citizens of all nations, a greater interest in and direction toward the establishment of that universal public authority which the Council Fathers urged.

128. We recognize that any use of police action by such an international authority, or, in the meantime, by the U.N. as presently constituted, or by duly constituted regional agencies, must be carefully subject to covenants openly arrived at and freely accepted, covenants spelling out clear norms such as that of proportionate force; here, again, the work of qualified conscientious specialists is indispensable.

129. Turning to the more positive aspects of the building of an international community and the duties of us as Americans in this matter, we deplore the lack of a stable, persevering national concern for the promotion of the international common good. This is reflected in the fickleness of public interest in and Congressional support of foreign aid. It is reflected also in a seeming insensitivity to the importance of trade agreements beneficial to developing nations. A like

lack of generosity dangerous to the fully human common good is present in the increasingly bold linking of contraceptive programs, even when superficially voluntary, to needed aid programs. Future aid and trade assistance programs should become increasingly multilateral; they should never merely serve national self-interest except to the extent that national interest is genuinely part and parcel of the general good of the human community.

130. Because of the war in Vietnam, and the growing preoccupation with the social problems of our cities, there is the peril of an upsurge of exaggerated forms of nationalism and isolationism which the teachings of all Churches reprove and the experiences of World War II, had, we hoped, forever discredited.

131. It is the duty of our political leadership, of citizens and especially of believers who acknowledge the brotherhood of man, to promote and develop the spirit of international concern, cooperation and understanding.

132. As the Council noted, ". . . there arises a surpassing need for renewed education of attitudes and for new inspiration in the area of public opinion. Those who are dedicated to the work of education, particularly of the young, or who mold public opinion should regard as their most weighty task the effort to instruct all in fresh sentiments of peace" (§ 82).

133. To assist the agencies and institutions of the Catholic Church in the United States in their response to this "most weighty task," the Catholic Bishops have recently established a Division of World Justice and Peace, corresponding to the newly established Vatican Commission. It is our desire that the Division will stimulate renewed efforts in this field, and coordinate whenever possible such efforts with those of other Christian bodies in an ecumenical framework. We call upon all men of conscience, all public-spirited citizens, to dedicate themselves with fresh energy to this work.

134. We believe that the talents and resources of our land are so abundant that we may promote the common good of nations at no expense to the vitally necessary works of urban and rural reconstruction in our own country. The latter are the first order of domestic policy, just as the former should be the first order of foreign policy. Neither should be neg-

lected, both being equally urgent; in the contemporary and developing world order their fortunes are intertwined.

VIETNAM

135. In a previous statement we ventured a tentative judgment that, on balance, the U.S. presence in Vietnam was useful and justified.

136. Since then American Catholics have entered vigorously into the national debate on this question, which, explicitly or implicitly, is going deeply into the moral aspects of our involvement in Vietnam. In this debate, opinions among Catholics appear as varied as in our society as a whole; one cannot accuse Catholics of either being partisans of any one point of view or of being unconcerned. In our democratic system the fundamental right of political dissent cannot be denied, nor is rational debate on public policy decisions of government in the light of moral and political principles to be discouraged. It is the duty of the governed to analyze responsibly the concrete issues of public policy.

137. In assessing our country's involvement in Vietnam we must ask: Have we already reached, or passed, the point where the principle of proportionality becomes decisive? How much more of our resources in men and money should we commit to this struggle, assuming an acceptable cause or intention? Has the conflict in Vietnam provoked inhuman dimensions of suffering? Would not an untimely withdrawal be equally disastrous?

138. Granted that financial considerations are necessarily subordinate to ethical values in any moral question, nonetheless many wonder if perhaps a measure of the proportions in this, as in any modern war, may be reflected in the amounts inevitably lost to education, poverty-relief and positive works of social justice at home and abroad (including Southeast Asia) as a result of the mounting budgets for this and like military operations. This point has frequently been raised by the Popes, notably by Pope Pius XII, who invoked the principle of proportionality in his analysis of the morality even of defensive wars, particularly when these involve A.B.C. elements (atomic, biological, chemical) and losses dispropor-

tionate to the "injustice tolerated" (Address to Military Doctors, Oct. 19, 1953).

139. While it would be beyond our competence to propose any technical formulas for bringing the Vietnam War to an end, we welcome the bombing halt and pray for the success of the negotiations now underway.

140. Meanwhile there are moral lessons to be learned from our involvement in Vietnam that will apply to future cases. One might be that military power and technology do not suffice, even with the strongest resolve, to restore order or accomplish peace. As a rule, internal political conflicts are too complicated to be solved by the external application of force and technology.

141. Another might be the realization that some evils existing in the world, evils such as undernutrition, economic frustration, social stagnation and political injustices, may be more readily attacked and corrected through non-military means than by military efforts to counteract the subversive forces bent on their exploitation.

142. In addition, may we not hope that violence will be universally discredited as a means of remedying human ills, and that the spirit of love "may overcome the barriers that divide, cherish the bonds of mutual charity, understand others and pardon those who have done them wrong?" (*Pacem in Terris*, Article 171.)

THE ROLE OF CONSCIENCE

143. The war in Vietnam typifies the issues which present and future generations will be less willing to leave entirely to the normal political and bureaucratic processes of national decision-making. It is not surprising that those who are most critical, even intemperate in their discussion of war as an instrument of national policy or as a ready means to the settling even of wrongs, are among the young; the burden of killing and dying falls principally on them.

144. There is sometimes ground for question as to whether the attitudes of some toward military duty do not spring from cowardice. In this problem, as in all crises which test generosity and heroism, cases of moral as well as physical cow-

ardice doubtless occur. But a blanket charge of this kind would be unfair to those young people who are clearly willing to suffer social ostracism and even prison terms because of their opposition to a particular war. One must conclude that for many of our youthful protesters, the motives spring honestly from a principled opposition to a given war as pointless or immoral.

145. Nor can it be said that such conscientious objection to war, as war is waged in our times, is entirely the result of subjective considerations and without reference to the message of the Gospel and the teaching of the Church; quite the contrary, frequently conscientious dissent reflects the influence of the principles which inform modern papal teaching, the Pastoral Constitution and a classical tradition of moral doctrine in the Church, including, in fact, the norms for the moral evaluation of a theoretically just war.

146. The enthusiasm of many young people for new programs of service to fellow humans in need may be proof that some traditional forms of patriotism are in process of being supplemented by a new spirit of dedication to humanity and to the moral prestige of one's own nation. This new spirit must be taken seriously; it may not always match the heroism of the missionaries and the full measure of the life of faith, but it is not contradictory to these and may open up new forms of Christian apostolate.

147. As witnesses to a spiritual tradition which accepts enlightened conscience, even when honestly mistaken, as the immediate arbiter of moral decisions, we can only feel reassured by this evidence of individual responsibility and the decline of uncritical conformism to patterns some of which included strong moral elements, to be sure, but also included political, social, cultural and like controls not necessarily in conformity with the mind and heart of the Church.

148. If war is ever to be outlawed, and replaced by more humane and enlightened institutions to regulate conflicts among nations, institutions rooted in the notion of universal common good, it will be because the citizens of this and other nations have rejected the tenets of exaggerated nationalism and insisted on principles of non-violent political and civic action in both the domestic and international spheres.

149. We therefore join with the Council Fathers in praising "those who renounce the use of violence in the vindication of their rights and who resort to methods of defense which are otherwise available to weaker parties, provided that this can be done without injury to the rights and duties of others or of the community itself" (§ 78).

150. It is in this light that we seek to interpret and apply to our own situation the advice of the Vatican Council on the treatment of conscientious objectors. The Council endorsed laws that "make humane provision for the care of those who for reasons of conscience refuse to bear arms, provided, however, that they accept some other form of service to the human community" (§ 79).

151. The present laws of this country, however, provide only for those whose reasons of conscience are grounded in a total rejection of the use of military force. This form of conscientious objection deserves the legal provision made for it, but we consider that the time has come to urge that similar consideration be given those whose reasons of conscience are more personal and specific.

152. We therefore recommend a modification of the Selective Service Act making it possible, although not easy, for so-called selective conscientious objectors to refuse—without fear of imprisonment or loss of citizenship—to serve in wars which they consider unjust or in branches of service (e.g., the strategic nuclear forces) which would subject them to the performance of actions contrary to deeply held moral convictions about indiscriminate killing. Some other form of service to the human community should be required of those so exempted.

153. Whether or not such modifications in our laws are in fact made, we continue to hope that, in the all-important issue of war and peace, all men will follow their consciences. We can do no better than to recall, as did the Vatican Council, "the permanent binding force of universal natural law and its all-embracing principles," to which "man's conscience itself gives ever more emphatic voice."

154. In calling so persistently in this Pastoral for studies on the application of sound moral principles to new dimensions of changes in the problems of war and peace, we are

mindful of our own responsibility to proclaim the Gospel of peace and to teach the precepts of both natural and revealed divine law concerning the establishing of peace everywhere on earth (§ 79). We therefore make our own the Council's judgment on "the deeper causes of war," sins like envy, mistrust and egoism. We echo the warning given by Pope Paul at the United Nations: "Today as never before, in an era marked by such human progress, there is need for an appeal to the moral conscience of man. For the danger comes not from progress, nor from science—on the contrary, if properly utilized these could resolve many of the grave problems which beset mankind. The real danger comes from man himself, who has at his disposal ever more powerful instruments, which can be used as well for destruction as for the loftiest conquests."

155. The hour has indeed struck for "conversion," for personal transformation, for interior renewal. We must once again begin to think of man in a new way, and of human life with a new appreciation of its worth, its dignity and its call to elevation to the level of the life of God Himself. All this requires that, with refreshed purpose and deepened faith we follow the urging of St. Paul that we "put on the new man, which has been created according to God in justice and holiness of truth" (Eph. 4:23).

Conclusion

156. Christians believe God to be the "source of life" (cf. Jn. 5, 26) and of love since "love comes from God" (cf. 1 Jn. 4, 7). "God is love" (1 Jn. 4, 8) and man has been made in His image and likeness (Genesis 1, 26). Thus, man is most himself when he honors life and lives by love. Then he is most like to God.

157. The doctrine and defense of life require a renewed spirituality in the Church. Such a spirituality will reaffirm the sacred character of married love through which life is begun, the dignity of the family within which love brings life to maturity, and the blessed vision of peace in which life is shared by men and nations in a world community of love.

158. These themes, all of which touch on life, we have ex-

plored in terms of the family, the commonwealth of nations and some of the anti-life forces which threaten these.

159. In her defense of human life the Church in our day makes her own, as did Moses, the words by which God Himself reduces our perplexities to a clear, inescapable choice: "I call heaven and earth to witness against you this day, that I have set before you life and death . . . therefore, choose life that you and your descendants may live . . ." (Deut. 30, 19).

THIS LAND IS HOME TO ME

In many ways the Catholic Church in the United States remained insulated from the experiences which shaped the life of the postwar Church around the world. In Europe the destruction and devastation caused by World War II had forced sensitive Church leaders to re-examine their assumptions and develop a new understanding of the Church and its mission. Beset by great human suffering at home and the presence of significant Communist parties, the Church turned to the people in new ways, to confront the reality that it had become, in the words of Karl Rahner, a church of the *diaspora*, no longer able to claim any particular authority over society, culture, or politics. In other parts of the world the Church shared in the awakening of aspirations associated with the anticolonial revolutions and the even more profound revolution of rising expectations. In Latin America, the Church was gradually forced to deal with the realities of class conflict and polarization; in Africa and Asia, to move beyond the self-understanding of a missionary Church to become more fully a part of the culture of its time and place. In all cases, the result was to force Church leaders, more or less reluctantly, to abandon the triumphalistic theology and social thought of the earlier period and to ask fundamental questions about the nature of the Church and God's purpose for it in the midst of the signs of the times.

One significant response was to begin to recover a sense of the Church as related in a special way to the needs of the poorest and most oppressed of mankind. A more biblical approach to social ethics rekindled a sense of Christian perfectionism, while a growing sense of apartness from the established order of society reinforced an impulse to identify with the outcasts and the poor. Of course, in almost all situations there was an equally powerful desire to retain the privileges and power of the past, so that division became a real characteristic of the Church in most nations of the world. The moderation and balance of Catholic social thought, with its continued reliance upon scholastic categories, often seemed to be torn apart under the combined pressure of moderation and revolution in those areas of the world where social and economic conflict found expression both inside the Church and throughout the communities of which the Church was a part.

The American Church had no experience of wartime devastation. Despite the fears of many in the 1950s, Communism was not a real domestic threat; neither was class conflict and polarization part of the American experience. The sometimes powerful social struggles of the 1930s faded in the glow of postwar prosperity. But the American Church did experience its own changes and it did respond to powerful forces in its own society. The civil rights struggles of black Americans affected the conscience of the Church; so too did the gradual realization that poverty was a part of the American experience. The Church took a strong official stand in favor of civil rights legislation, and many priests and sisters joined in the fight for equal rights for all Americans. This produced conflict in the Church community, particularly when the drive for black freedom and progress reached the heavily Catholic cities of the North and West. The Church also launched its own war on poverty in the mid 1960s; the Campaign for Human Development attempted to raise significant sums of money from churchgoers and make funds available to self-help organizations of the poor. The language of liberation theology began to make itself felt in America, though its applicability was widely debated. Since 1933, the Catholic Worker movement, led by Dorothy Day, had proclaimed a gospel of identification with the poor and the oppressed and had called for voluntary poverty and the practice of the works of mercy, so that the concept of identification with the poor was not unknown to Americans.

Perhaps the most powerful expression of this mood, and certainly the most remarkable document of the postconciliar

American Church, was a pastoral letter published by the bishops of the Appalachian region. The region extended from northern Georgia through western North Carolina, eastern Kentucky and Tennessee, and West Virginia, into western Pennsylvania and included portions of several other states. The Catholic Committee on Appalachia had for years been attempting to sustain and support Catholic pastoral and mission work in the area, where Catholics constituted only a tiny minority of the population. President John F. Kennedy had drawn new attention to the poverty of the region by making the Appalachian Regional Development Act a keystone of his war on poverty. Seeking to relate the Church to the revitalization of the Appalachian people, the Catholic Committee on Appalachia persuaded the bishops of the region to learn more of its needs through a series of dialogues and discussions held throughout the area. After considerable reflection, the bishops issued a pastoral letter expressing their sense of the needs and aspirations of the Appalachian region. Written in a highly innovative, free verse style, the pastoral letter expressed the new sense of identification of the Church with the poor and the oppressed. Its tone sharply defined the struggling people—dignified, strong in faith and with their distinctive culture—over against the corporations who owned much of the resources of the region with little benefit to its people. The scriptural images and the social categories of the third world now were given an Americanized expression. That it was an American document could be seen in the celebration of the people and the modesty of the prescriptions. It acknowledged the economic and political complexities of the situation, and the confidence of the bishops that somehow, if people would only see the suffering of the people of Appalachia and the clear injustices of their situation, solutions could be found.

The Appalachian pastoral constitutes an authentic American response to the documents of the magisterium on social justice and world peace. It relates the categories of those documents and the scriptural language of the emerging social theology to the concrete lives and words of a distinct people. Like the documents of the magisterium, it seeks to highlight a need, touch the conscience, call all persons to action, but not to prescribe a program or a policy. It ends moral passion with intellectual modesty, it leaves to people and democratic processes the solutions that must be found. It is the finest of contemporary American documents on social justice.

THIS LAND IS HOME TO ME

A PASTORAL LETTER ON POWERLESSNESS IN APPALACHIA BY
THE CATHOLIC BISHOPS OF THE REGION

Many of our Catholic people,
especially Church workers,
have asked us to respond
to the cries of powerlessness
from the region called Appalachia.
We have listened to these cries
and now we lend our own voice.

The cries come now from Appalachia,
but they are echoed
—across the land
—across the earth
in the suffering of too many peoples.
Together these many sufferings
form a single cry.

The Living God hears this cry
and he tells us,
what long ago
on a different mountain,
he told his servant Moses that,

—he had heard the cry of his people.
—he would deliver them out of the hands of oppression
—he would give them a rich and broad land.

But before we turn
to this message from the Lord,
we must hear first
the cry of Appalachia's poor.

Their cry is a strong message,
not because we have made it that way,

but because the truth of Appalachia
is harsh.
In repeating this message
we do not put ourselves
in judgment of others.
The truth of Appalachia
is judgment upon us all,
making hard demands on us bishops,
as well as on others.

We know that there will be other opinions,
about the truth of Appalachia,
other views than those of the poor.
But we must remind ourselves
that the poor are special
in the eyes of the Lord,
for he has told us,
in the voice of his Mother,

He has pulled down princes from their thrones,
and exalted the lowly.
The hungry he has filled with good things.
the rich sent empty away. (Luke 1:52–53)

Even so,
we know that our words are not perfect.
For that reason,
this letter is but one part
of an unfinished conversation

—with our people
—with the truth of Appalachia
—with the Living God.

Yet we still dare to speak,
and speak strongly,
first,
because we trust our people
and we know
that those who belong to the Lord
truly wish to do his will;
and second,

because we believe
that the cry of the poor
is also a message of hope,
a promise from the Lord,
that there can be a better way,
for he has told us,
The Truth will make you free.   (John 8:32)

PART I

THE LAND AND ITS PEOPLE

Appalachia makes us think
of people who live in the hills,
who love nature's freedom
and beauty,
who are alive with song
and poetry.
But many of these people are also poor
and suffer oppression.

Once they went to the mountains
fighting to build a dream
different from the injustice
they knew before.
Until this day,
their struggle continues,
a bitter fight
whose sound still rumbles
across the hills.

Yes, the poor of the mountains
have been wounded,
but they are not crushed.
The Spirit still lives.
The sound of music
still ripples through the hills.
Continually the tears of song
burn in outrage,
and outrage lives in struggle.

But the hillfolk of the mountains
are not the only ones who struggle.

Besides the struggle in hollows,
typical of the central region,
there are struggles in industrial centers,
grown gray with smoke and smog,
blaring with the clank and crash
of heavy machinery
and urban congestion,
where working people,
and those who wish there was work,
white and black,
native and immigrant,
speakers of one and many languages,
battle for dignity and security,
for themselves and for their children.

So too there is the struggle in farmland,
typical of rolling hills in the southern sector,
where little farmers and sharecroppers,
day laborers and migrant workers,
who help the earth
yield its food to the hungry,
battle for that same dignity and security,
for themselves and their children.

In all three areas—
—the center
—the north
—the south
in every labor—
—the mine
—the factory
—the farm
the struggle is different,
yet remains the same.
It is at once the struggle
—of all Appalachia
—of the whole nation
—of the whole family.

The Appalachian mountains
form the spiny backbone
of the Eastern United States.
This whole stretch,
which the Federal Government calls
"The Appalachia Region"
runs from Southern New York
to Northern Georgia and Alabama.
It contains 397 counties
in 13 states,
parts of

—Alabama,
—Georgia,
—Kentucky,
—Maryland,
—Mississippi,
—New York,
—North Carolina,
—Ohio,
—Pennsylvania,
—South Carolina,
—Tennessee,
—Virginia,
and all of West Virginia.

In the region there are:

—mountain folk,
—city folk,
—country folk,
—coal miners and steel workers,
—industrial workers and service workers,
—farmers and farm laborers,
—housewives and children,
—teachers and health workers,
—ministers and rabbis and priests,
—artists and poets,
—professionals and technicians,
—lawyers and politicians,

—lobbyists and interest groups,
—executives and managers,
—little business people and big business people,
—coal companies and chemical companies,
—industrialists and bankers.

So, you see,
Appalachia is not a simple place.
There are rich and poor,
big and little,
new and old,
and lots in between.

But somehow,
no matter how confusing it seems,
it's all tied together
by the mountain chain
and by the coal in its center,
producing energy within it.

Of course,
there is more than coal
in the region.
There is

—gas,
—timber,
—oil,
—farms,
—steel mills,
—cheap labor,

but coal is central.

COAL

There is a saying in the region
that coal is king.
That's not exactly right.
The kings are those who control big coal,
and the profit and power

which come with it.
Many of these kings
don't live in the region.

A long time ago in this country
when big industry just got started,
Appalachian coal played a big role.
It fed the furnaces
of our first industrial giants,
like Pittsburgh and Buffalo.
The coal-based industry
created many jobs,
and brought great progress to our country,
but it brought other things, too,
among them
oppression for the mountains.

Soon the mountain people
were dependent on the coal companies
and on the company towns
that came with them.

An old song sings,
*Another day older
and deeper in debt.*
That was life for many people
who lived in the shadow
of the mountain's coal.
Many of our Catholic people
lived under this suffering,
—in the coal mines,
—in the steel mills,
—in the other harsh jobs

that surround coal and steel.

Then came the unions,
as men and women fought hard
to change their lot.
The unions did good work
and for that reason

they were bitterly attacked
by enemies of justice.

But seeds of injustice
were also sown
within the labor movement.

Sometimes criminal forces entered
to crush their democratic structure,
to prevent union growth in other areas,
or to turn contracts
into documents of deceit,
both for labor and management,
thus encouraging their breech
from both sides,
Sometimes workers allowed themselves
to be used for selfish ends,
like keeping out blacks,
or women,
or Indians,
or Spanish-speaking.
Sometimes the labor movement
thought only of workers in the U.S.
and did not take seriously
their membership
in the global human family.
Sometimes, too,
they used the unions
to protect the relative advantages
of a few workers
with little concern for
the great disadvantage of the many.

The real power of the labor movement,
a power which has not been totally crushed,
is the vision that
an injury to one is an injury to all,
whether to white or black,
whether to male or female,
whether to worker or consumer,

whether to union member or non-member,
whether to U.S. citizen or to citizen
of any nation.

But later on for many people,
whose lives were tied to coal,
the unions didn't matter so much any more.
Coal gave way to oil,
and a different suffering
came across the mountains.

The mines in the hills
began to close.
The industrial thunder
of cities near the mines
weakened.
The people from the mountains
fled to the cities
looking for jobs.
But in the cities,
the jobs were few.

It is a strange system
which makes people suffer
both when they have work
and when they don't have work.

THE WIDER PICTURE

The people had to fight one another
for the few jobs:

—mountain people against city people,
—white people against black people,
—Irish people against Polish and Italian people,
—skilled workers against unskilled workers,
—union workers against non-union workers.

As the people were forced
to fight over jobs,
self-defense often became a way of life,

—in wars,
—in sports,
—in movies,
—even sometimes at home.

Our country meanwhile
grew strong and powerful
because of

—exploding war-stimulated technology,
—cheap raw materials from abroad,
—lots of oil,
—and a large work force.

But many people stayed poor,
and suffered attacks on their dignity,
especially

—Indians,
—Blacks,
—Mexican Americans,
—immigrants,
—Puerto Ricans,
—and poor whites, like Appalachians.

Brothers and sisters in suffering,
these people were often forced
to turn against one another,
for some meager piece of a pie,
which, however big
(the biggest the world had ever known),
refused to feed all its children.

As industrial production grew,
it brought blessings to the human family,
but the more it grew
the more some felt
it became like a cancer
eating away its own foundation.

The system produced
for production's sake,

and it tried to train people to consume
for consumption's sake.
The ever growing production and consumption
needed ever more energy,
more than domestic gas
and domestic oil
can supply.

When foreign oil producing nations
suddenly became more demanding
on the world market,
giant U.S. business interests
(who before used to decide prices
of things like oil
on the world market)
got frightened.
They began to plan for
U.S. "energy independence."
One way to do that
was to go back
to a half dead and forgotten past,
to coal.

BACK TO THE MOUNTAINS

So the corporate giants turn their eyes
to the mountains once again.
Slowly, but powerfully
their presence rumbles in,

the heavy trod of
the powerful among the powerful,
those who control:

—finance and credit,
—information systems,
—and energy resources.

Already voices from this camp
have spoken of Appalachia as
an "energy reservation,"

or "giant industrial park."
Appalachia,
a field of powerlessness,
may soon become the seat
of economic power in the United States.

But the new power,
which a return to coal
could bring to Appalachia,
would probably not make its people
any more powerful.
Instead, they would live
a different kind of powerlessness,
one common to the rest of our society—
the powerlessness of isolated little people
in the face of the most powerful corporate giants
on this earth.

THE WORSHIP OF AN IDOL

The way of life
which these corporate giants create
is called by some
"technological rationalization."
Its forces contain the promise
of a world where
—poverty is eliminated
—health cared for
—education available for all
—dignity guaranteed
—and old age secure.
Too often, however,
its forces become perverted,
hostile to the dignity of the earth
and of its people.

Its destructive growth patterns

—pollute the air
—foul the water
—rape the land.

[handwritten margin notes: "Appalachia is symbol of poor around world"; "systemic problem – must look at total system –"]

The driving force
behind this perversion is
"Maximization of Profit,"
a principle which too often converts itself
into an idolatrous power.

This power overwhelms the good intentions
of noble people.
It forces them to compete brutally
with one another.
It pushes people into
"conspicuous consumption"
and "planned obsolescence."
It delivers up control
to a tiny minority
whose values then shape
our social structures.

Of course technological rationalization
and the profit principle
have served important functions
in human development.
It is not they themselves
that form an idol,
but the idol is formed
when they become absolutes
and fail to yield,
when the time has come,
to other principles.

Neither do we believe
that our people
or the people of the nation
have totally fallen prey
to the power of this idol.
But even without that happening,
"Maximization of profit"
in today's world,
has become a crazy death wish,
every day using up more and more
of the earth's riches

and our own dignity.
Like those who write spy thrillers,
its process is fascinated
with everything that can
"self-destruct,"
even if it is ourselves.

Without judging anyone,
it has become clear to us
that the present economic order
does not care for its people.
In fact,
profit and people frequently are contradictory.
Profit over people
is an idol.
And it is not a new idol,
for Jesus long ago warned us,

No one can be the slave of two masters:
either he will hate the first
and love the second,
or treat the first with respect
and the second with scorn.
You cannot be the slave
both of God and money.   (Matthew 6:24)

This is not a problem
only for mountain folk;
it is everybody's problem.

APPALACHIA AS A SYMBOL of entire world-poor all everywhere

In a country whose productive force
is greater than anything the world has ever known,
the destructive idol
shows its ugly face,
in places like Appalachia.

The suffering of Appalachia's poor
is a symbol
of so much other suffering

—in our land
—in our world.
It is also a symbol
of the suffering which awaits
the majority of plain people
in our society
—if they are laid off
—if major illness occurs
—if a wage earner dies
—or if anything else goes wrong.

In this land of ours,
jobs are often scarce.
Too many people are forced
to accept unjust conditions
or else lose their jobs.

Human services for the poor,
and for the almost poor,
are inadequate.
Safety standards
are often too weak,
or ignored.
Workers are injured
unnecessarily.
Legal and medical recourse
for claims against occupational injury
or occupational disease
are often too difficult
or unavailable.
Sometimes
those who should be helping people
in their claims,
seem to stand in the way.
Black lung
and mine accidents
are the most famous examples,
but not the only ones.

On the other hand,
powerful reform movements

are underway
—in the union movement
—in community organizing
—in the consumer movement
—in public interest lobbies
—in religious circles.

To these must be added
even forces from within the
business community:
—managerial personnel who are
  concerned not only with salaries
  and promotion, but also with the
  contribution of the economic order
  to social well being,
  particularly the bringing of jobs
  to poor areas;
—small and medium sized business people
  who wish to operate justly
  but who struggle under the pressure of
  giant economic corporations
  ruthlessly trying to wipe them out;
—stockholders who rebel against
  the impersonal structure of ownership
  and try to make their voices felt
  for justice
  within large corporations.

Together these groups struggle
to achieve what must become
the foundation principle
of our common life,
namely *citizen involvement*
—in our productive base
—in our political institutions
—in our cultural life.
The main task for such citizen involvement
will be to build social structures
which provide full employment
and decent wages
for all people.

Despite abuses,
we feel that a strong and broad
labor movement
is basic,
one which can stabilize the labor market
North and South
East and West
and prevent groups
from playing off different sectors
of working people
against each other.
Even so,
these movements are just beginning
and reach too few people.

We know also
that as they grow stronger,
they will be attacked;
that other forces
will try to crush them.

Unaccountable economic powers
will continue to use
democratic political institutions
for non-democratic purposes.
Sometimes this shows itself brutally,
when policemen act like company enforcers.

At other times, it's more complicated,
when lawyers and legislators
seem to get paid
to keep the people confused,
and to find loop-holes
for the benefit of the rich.

These same massive economic forces,
still accountable to no one,
will even use vehicles of our cultural life,
like communications media and advertising,
and even the educational system,
to justify their ways,
and to pass off their values

as our national values.
This happens
when news that's important to people
can't get time or space,
or when school programs
are designed by experts
without incorporating the voice of the people.

We know that there are many
—sincere business people,
—zealous reporters,
—truthful teachers,
—honest law enforcement officers,
—dedicated public officials,
—hard working lawyers and legislators
who try to do a good job.

But we know too that,
the way things are set up,
it's hard for good people
to do a good job.

It's strange, for instance,
despite earlier reforms,
that a country which took such richness
from Appalachia
left so little for the people.
Great fortunes were built
on the exploitation of
Appalachian workers
and Appalachian resources,
yet the land was left
without revenues
to care for its social needs, like
—education
—welfare
—old age
—and illness.

Some may say
"that's economics"
but we say

that economics is made by people.
Its principles don't fall down from the sky
and remain for all eternity.
Those who claim
they are prisoners of the laws of economics,
only testify
that they are prisoners of the idol.

We make the systems — not in charge of us — can be changed.

The same thing which is so obvious in Appalachia
goes on outside the mountains.
Plain people work hard all their life,
and their parents worked hard before them,
yet they can't make ends meet.

—Food is too expensive.
—Taxes are too high for most.
—(Too low for the rich).
—Sickness puts people into debt.
—College is out of reach for their children.
—Paychecks keep shrinking.

And it's worse still for those who can't work,
especially the elderly.

Meanwhile
corporate profits
for the giant conglomerates,
who control our energy resources,
keep on skyrocketing.

But now there is some promise
of fresh "economic development"
in the Appalachian region,
at least if our industry returns
to a substantial coal base.
From the rest of the world, however,
we know now, after hard experiences,
that "development" often brings little
to the poor,
or to the workers.

Often the reverse.
Yet even if it were to bring prosperity,

there is a question we must ask
about the new energy resources.

It is
"How will we use our energy?"
as well as,
"Where will we get it from?"

If our present system keeps on growing and growing,
it will burn up ourselves
and our world.
The present pattern of energy use,
a great deal of which goes for military production
or else for the production of discardable junk,
is barbaric.

This nation,
containing about 6% of the earth's population,
consumes over 1/3 of the earth's energy
and causes 40% of the earth's industrial pollution.
But even that doesn't tell
the whole truth,
because, at least by 1962 figures,
1.6% of the population of this country
owned 80% of the corporate wealth,
so that averages or per capita statistics
really mislead us
about the ordinary people's situation.
Some talk about a population problem
among the poor.
There's an even bigger consumption problem
among the rich—
consumption not just of luxuries,
but of power,
of the power to shape
—economic structures
—political structures
—cultural structures
all in the service of
—more waste
—more profit

—more power.
Even worse,
U.S. energy consumption is expected
to double in the next decade.
What kind of world would it be,
where "Maximization of Profit":
destroys life
for so many today,
and for future generations?

Ironically,
most people in this country
are not satisfied with the consumer society.
It makes life a rat race,
where nobody feels they belong,
where all are pushed around,
where roots disappear.
With so much busy-ness
and clutter of things,

—things that don't work,
—things you have to keep fixing,
—no time to play or sing
  like folks used to

we get lost in our busy-ness
and grow to hate and abuse
all our things.

Worse still,
swallowing us up in things
is the power of the idol
which eats away at our openness
to the Living God.

But the children of the mountains
have fought for a different way.
Their struggles and their poetry
together keep alive

—a dream
—a tradition

—a longing
—a promise

which is not just their dream,
but the voiceless vision
buried beneath life's bitterness
wherever it is found.

They sing of a life
free and simple,
with time for one another,
and for people's needs,
based on the dignity of the human person,
at one with nature's beauty,
crowned by poetry.
If that dream dies,
all our struggles
die with it.

DEFENDING THE STRUGGLE'S DREAM

Many times before
outside forces
have attacked the mountain's dream.
But never before
was the attack so strong.
Now it comes with

—cable TV,
—satellite communications,
—giant ribbons of highway
   driving into the guts of the land.

The attack wants to teach people
that happiness is what you buy

—in soaps and drinks,
—in gimmicks and gadgets,

and that all of life
is one big commodity market.

It would be bad enough
if the attack only tried
to take the land,
but it wants the soul, too.
When it has its way,
the poet is silent.
Instead comes
noisy blare and din,
the chatter of a language
empty of meaning,
but filled with violence.

This struggle of resistance
is a struggle against violence—
against institutional violence
which sometimes subtly,
sometimes brutally,
attacks human dignity and life.

Therefore,
although the Catholic tradition
fully acknowledges the legitimacy
of self-defense and force
as the final recourse
against injustice,
we must beware of the temptation
of too easy violence—
of a bitterness which can poison
that for which we struggle,
or which,
still worse,

can provoke from forces of injustice
an even more brutal and repressive
institutional violence,
whose first victim
is always the poor.

It is the mountain's spirit of resistance
which must be defended
at any cost,
for at stake is the spirit

of all our humanity.
There are too few spaces of soul
left in our lives.

Once we all
—knew how to dance and sing
—sat in mystery before the poet's spell
—felt our hearts rise to nature's cathedral.
Now an alien culture
battles to shape us
into plastic forms empty of Spirit,
into beasts of burden
without mystery.

If the struggle's dream can be defended,
and we believe it can,
then perhaps the great instruments of attack,
—cable TV,
—satellite communications,
—ribbons of highway,
can become like so many arms,
which instead of crushing life,
reach out to make it fuller,
to bring to others
beyond the mountains,
the promise of their vision.

PART II

THE ANSWER OF THE LORD AND HIS CHURCH

THE GOD OF THE POOR

The living God,
the Lord whom we worship,
is the God of the poor.

In Israel,
he revealed himself to his people
by liberating them from oppression
under the bondage of Egypt:

I have seen the miserable state
of my people in Egypt.
I have heard their appeal to be free
of their slave-drivers . . .
I mean to deliver them
out of the hands of the Egyptians . . .
And now the cry of the sons of Israel
has come to me.

That day, Yahweh rescued Israel
from the Egyptians . . .
and the people venerated Yahweh . . .   (Exodus 3:7-9;
   14:30-31)

Not only in the liberation of his people
does the Lord reveal himself
as the Living God,
but also within Israel
by defending all those
who are victims of injustice.

He will free the poor man who calls on him,
and those who need help,
he will have pity on the poor and feeble . . .
he will redeem their lives
from exploitation and outrage.   (Psalms 72:12-14)

Thus, the God of Israel,
who is also our God,
is the God of the poor,
because he frees the oppressed.

THE MESSIAH AND HIS KINGDOM

But Israel's mission
was to the whole world,
not just to its own nation.
As injustice against Israel
and throughout the world
seemed to mount higher,
the Lord promised
to send a liberator.

He was to be a great King,
whose reign would bring justice.
For his coming,
Israel prayed:

God, give your own justice to the king,
your own righteousness to the royal son,
so that he may rule your people rightly
and your poor with justice . . .
He will defend the poorest,
he will save the children of those in need
and crush their oppressors . . .
He will free the poor man
who calls to him
and those in need;
he will have pity on the poor and the feeble,
and save the lives of those in need.   (Psalm 72:1–4, 12–13)

And there came among us,
a man from Israel,
whom we confess to be
God-with-us,
the messiah long promised.

And when he rose up
to speak in his native Nazareth,
he chose the words
from the prophet Isaiah:

The Spirit of the Lord has been given to me,
for he has anointed me.
He has sent me to bring the good news to the poor,
to proclaim liberty to captives
and to the blind new sight,
to set the downtrodden free,
to proclaim the Lord's year of favour.   (Luke 4:18–19)

And when like Moses of old,
this Jesus climbed a mount
to tell the people his Father's law,
he left no doubt

that he was indeed
the messiah of the poor:

How happy are you who are poor:
yours is the kingdom of God.
Happy you who are hungry now:
you shall be satisfied.

Happy you who weep now:
you shall laugh . . .
But alas for you who are rich:
you are having your consolation now.
Alas for you who have your fill now:
you shall go hungry.
Alas for you who laugh now:
you shall mourn and weep.   (Luke 6:21, 24–25)

The Messiah, his Father and their Spirit
are the Living God.
They are different from the dead idols
which clutter history,
because they,
and not the idols,
act for justice.
The dead idols prove
to be gods of oppression.

I am Yahweh your God who brought you
out of the land of Egypt,
out of the land of slavery.
You shall have no gods except me.   (Exodus 20:1–3)

The choice between the Living God
and inert idols
is not only a choice between justice
and injustice.
It is also a choice
between life
and death:

Today,
I set before you life or death,
blessings or curse.

Choose life, then,
so that you and your descendants may live,
in the love of Yahweh your God,
obeying his voice,
clinging to him;
for in this your life consists,
and on this depends your long stay
in the land which Yahweh
swore to your fathers . . .   (Deuteronomy 30:19–20)

THE CHURCH'S MISSION

Out of faith in the risen Jesus
a new community of people is born,
seeking to be united
in one mind and spirit
with him.
Upon this community
Jesus pours forth his Spirit,
the Spirit of truth,
who teaches us everything
and reminds us of all he said to us.

The whole group of believers was united,
heart and soul;
no one claimed for his own use
anything that he had,
as everything they owned was held in common . . .
None of their members was ever in want,
as all those who owned land or houses
would sell them,
and bring the money from them,
to present it to the apostles;
it was then distributed
to any members who might be in need.   (Acts 4:32–35)

Still the church
is not perfect.
Its early bishop James
had to remind the people:

. . . it was those who are poor
according to the world
that God chose, to be rich in faith
and to be the heir to the kingdom
which he promised to those who love him.
In spite of this,
you have no respect
for anybody who is poor.
Isn't it always the rich who are against you?
Isn't it always their doing
when you are dragged before the court?
Aren't they the ones who insult
the Honorable name to which you have been dedicated?
    (James 2:5–7)

Yet the Church continues, despite its sins,
working for the poor,
insisting on practical love,
and not just prayers
and good intentions:

In this we may distinguish the children of God
from the children of the devil . . .
we are to love one another;
not to be like Cain
who cut his brother's throat . . .

If you refuse to love, you must remain dead;
to hate your brother is to be a murderer, . . .
This had taught us love—
that he gave up his life for us;
and we, too, ought to give up our lives
for our brothers.
If a man who was rich enough in this world's goods
saw that one of his brothers was in need,
but closed his heart to him,
how could the love of God be living in him?
My children,
our love is not to be just words or mere talk,
but something real and active;
only by this can we be certain

that we are children of the truth . . . (1 John 3:10–12,
15–19)

Through the ages,
the church tries to be faithful
to this message.
At times it begins to stray from it,
but always the Spirit is alive within it,
stirring up new voices
to call it back
to its mission for Justice.

THE CHURCH'S SOCIAL TEACHING

For a long time now,
our Church has been restless
with what many call
"The Modern World."
There is much in this modern world
which is good and beautiful:

—the sense of freedom
—the progress of science and technology
—the personal creativity unleashed from
under stifling traditions
—the growing unity of the human family.

The Lord has challenged his people
to take up as his own
whatever is good and beautiful
in the modern world
as in all of his creation.
But he has also challenged us
to resist what is evil,
especially injustice.

Since the industrial age,
we have been active,
speaking and acting
on behalf of the casualties
of the new economic spirit.

At the end of the last Century,
Pope Leo XIII,
wrote a great letter,
ON THE CONDITION OF THE WORKING
   CLASSES.

Our own past brother,
Archbishop Gibbons of Baltimore,
made a great plea that this letter
reflect the views of the common people.
He told the pope,

To lose the heart of the people
would be a misfortune
for which the friendship of the few rich and powerful
would be no compensation.

In the wake of Leo's letter,
as the destructiveness of the new economic order
continued unchecked,
the U.S. Catholic bishops
felt compelled themselves
to draft a letter to their people
on the question of social reconstruction.
While acknowledging that the American people
were not ready for major reconstruction,
and that *the present industrial system is*
destined to last for a long time, . . .
the bishops condemned three grievous abuses:

—*enormous inefficiency and waste*
  in the production and distribution of commodities;
—*insufficient incomes for the great majority*
  of wage earners;
—*and unnecessarily large incomes*
  for a small minority of privileged capitalists.

Further,
they argued for an industrialism
based on cooperation,
rather than on competition:

The majority must somehow become owners,
or at least in part,
of the instruments of production.

Finally, in discussing remedies,
they laid down the following principle:

. . . human beings cannot be trusted
with the immense opportunities for oppression and extortion
that go with the possession of monopoly power.

Still the injustices continued,
so much so that Pope Pius XI felt obliged
to publish another letter,
forty years after Leo's letter,
ON RECONSTRUCTING THE SOCIAL ORDER
AND PERFECTING IT COMFORTABLY
TO THE PRECEPTS OF THE GOSPEL.
Pius XI pointed out how,

. . . in our days not alone is wealth accumulated,
but immense power and despotic economic domination
is concentrated in the hands of a few . . .
This concentration of power has led to
a threefold struggle for domination.
First, . . . the struggle for dictatorship
in the economic sphere itself;
then, the fierce battle to acquire control of the state,
so that its resources and authority
may be abused in the economic struggles.
Finally, the clash between states themselves.

The Catholic bishops of the United States
again responded with their own letter,
THE CHURCH AND SOCIAL ORDER,
in 1940.
They lamented that an unjust society
had caused many working people
to become alienated from religion
and to have lost faith and hope.
Reminding economic powers that
the earth is the Lord's and

the fullness thereof   (Psalm 23:1)
they especially denounced

—*concentration of ownership and control*
—*the anonymous character of economic interests.*

The social system at that time,
at the end of the great depression,
was generating great economic insecurity
for many people.

The bishops judged then that,

an important factor making for insecurity
is the immense power and despotic domination
which is concentrated in the hands of those few
who frequently are not the owners,
but only the trustees and directors
of invested funds.

They single out one group
in this attack:

Those who, because they hold and
control money,
are able also to govern credit
and determine its allotment,
for that reason supplying,
so to speak,
the life-blood to the entire economy,
and grasping as it were in their hands
the very soul of production.

They called for a more just social order,
where property would be broadly distributed
and people would be truly responsible for one another.

Now, closer to our own day,
the popes have continued to speak
on the social question,
Many will remember the warm letters
of Pope John XXIII,
PEACE ON EARTH, and MOTHER AND TEACHER
and Pope Paul's letters

ON THE DEVELOPMENT OF PEOPLES
and A CALL TO ACTION.
In a more contemporary context,
with a view to the poor across the globe,
the popes have called us back
to the message of Jesus
and to Yahweh the God of JUSTICE.

We bishops have not been silent either.
At the Vatican Council
we spoke strongly for justice and the poor
in THE PASTORAL CONSTITUTION ON THE
   CHURCH
IN THE MODERN WORLD.

The joys and the hopes,
the griefs and the anxieties . . .
of this age,
especially those who are poor
or in any way afflicted.

And finally,
when we gathered in Synod just a few years ago
with all our fellow bishops of the world,
scrutinizing the signs of the times
and listening to the Word of God,
we were

able to perceive the serious injustices
which are building around the world
a network of domination, oppression, and abuses . . .

But we also noted,

a new awareness which shakes (people)
out of any fatalistic resignation
and which spurs them on to liberate themselves . . .
Action on behalf of justice
and participation in the transformation of the world
fully appear to us
as a constitutive *dimension*
of the preaching of the Gospel,
or, in other words,

of the Church's mission
for the redemption of the human race
and its liberation from every oppressive situation.

Thus,
there must be no doubt,
that we, who must speak the message
of Him who summoned Moses
and who opened his mouth
in Jesus of Nazareth,
and who keeps the Spirit alive
on behalf of justice
for so many centuries,
can only become
advocates of the poor.

This is not to be simplistic,
to see all in black and white,
to be ignorant of economics
and the contributions of other human sciences,
but in a profound sense
the choices are simple
and stark:

—death or life;
—injustice or justice;
—idolatry or the Living God.

We must choose life.
We must choose justice.
We must choose the Living God.

PART III

FACING THE FUTURE

A PROCESS OF DIALOGUE AND TESTING

More and more people recognize
that a new social order is being born.
Indeed,

the Spirit of God
presses us to this recognition.
We do not understand it all,
but we know we are part of it,

—in Appalachia,
—in our nation,
—across the world.

In what follows,
we hope to give some guidance
to our Catholic people
for sharing in that birth struggle.

We have no easy answers,
so this is but a first step.
It must not be the last step.
Hopefully, this letter,
itself a product of dialogue,
will start a process,
wherein the Catholic community
can join together with all people of good will
throughout the region
to reflect on and for
a more just society.

While we have no answers,
we have some principles
to guide the process.
our searching must carefully balance
the following three elements:

1. closeness to the people;
2. careful use of scientific resources;
3. a steeping in the presence of the Spirit.

In regard to the first element, we must
continually take time and invest creativity
into listening to our people,
especially the poor.
For it is they who,
out of their frustrations, dreams, and struggles,
must lead the way for all of us.

Next we must listen to the vast majority
of plain people
who would not be called poor,
but who are not rich,
and who increasingly share
in the powerlessness of the poor.
Finally, strange as it may seem,
we must also challenge the rich.
For although the Lord himself
has told us that

It is easier for a camel to pass through
the eye of a needle,
than for a rich man
to enter the kingdom of heaven,   (Matthew 19:24)

although one rich young man
went away sad,

for he was a man of great wealth,   (Matthew 19:22)

there is also
the story of Zacchaeus
who accepted the demands of justice,
who returned his property to the poor
and paid back four fold
whatever was stolen.
That day salvation came to his house.

The Son of Man has come
to seek out and save what was lost.   (Luke 19:10)

Throughout this whole process
of listening to the people,
the goal which underlies our concern
is fundamental in the justice struggle,
namely, citizen control,
or community control,
The people themselves
must shape their own destiny.
Despite the theme of powerlessness,
we know that Appalachia

is already rich here
in the cooperative power
of its own people.

In regard to the second element,
we must be careful with science,
because scientific models are not value free.
So much of science has been used,
in the contemporary world,
to oppress rather than liberate,
but science is not itself evil.

Rather it is our task to take it up,
and to infuse it with wisdom and humility,
in the service of justice.

In regard to the third,
we note with joy
the renewed zeal
for the presence of the Spirit
in prayer and meditation
among our Catholic people.
We know that if this renewed presence
can mature into a convergence
with the thirst for justice,
a new Pentecost will truly be upon us.

To begin this process
of dialogue and testing
we invite
the Catholic Committee of Appalachia
to draft
for us and with us,
as well as for and with
all people of good will,
a *comprehensive plan of action*.
Together we may begin to test it
throughout the region.

This plan would constitute
our first tool which
hopefully, each year

could be brought up to date,
in the light of fresh experience.

There are several specific points
which now we would like to recommend
for inclusion in the action plan.

First, and most important,
in accord with our recommendation
from the Synod document,
JUSTICE IN THE WORLD,
we would like to
commend where they exist
and recommend where they do not,
Centers of Reflection and Prayer,
in the service of action,
throughout the region.

Such centers could
integrate the analytical social science skills
and the profound spirituality
necessary for persevering creativity
in the struggle for justice.

They could also link fragmented struggles
from different parts of the region,
and even outside the region,
thus supporting healthy localism
with the richness of a wider national
and international network.

In addition,
we would like to know in what way
the Church might cooperate
with *other major institutions*
of the region,
provided they are open
to the voice of the poor.
Especially we welcome
the opportunity to share with

—university people,
—people skilled in economic life, ·

—artists and poets,
—government people.

Also,
as suggested by the letter of Paul VI,
A CALL TO ACTION,
we commend where they exist,
and recommend where they do not,
Centers of Popular Culture
in every parish,
or in areas where there are no parishes,
as a sign of the Church's concern,
linked to the broader action centers
places where the poor feel welcome,
spaces for people to come and share
at all levels,
so that if a new society is to be born,
it will emerge from the grass roots.

Especially we stress
emphasis on the *economic questions,*
for these are the first and most basic
questions for all people.
We call attention
to the presence of powerful
multinational corporations
now within our region.
The fate and role of these institutions
is a major question
not only for Appalachia,
but for the whole world.
Pope Paul VI has warned us that:

The multinational enterprises . . .
largely independent of the national political powers
and therefore not subject to control
from the viewpoint of the common good . . .
can lead to a new and abusive form
of economic domination of the social, cultural,
and even political level.
The excessive concentration of means and powers

that Pope Piux XI already condemned
on the fortieth anniversary of RERUM NOVARUM
is taking on a new and very real image.

As a counter-force
to the unaccountable power
of these multinational corporations,
there must arise a corresponding
multinational labor movement,
rooted in a vision of justice,
rising above corruption
and narrowness,
with a universal concern
—for all workers
—for all consumers
—for all people.

We are happy to note
that some voices at least
are raising up such a vision
within the ranks of labor.

Finally,
there are a number of issues
which we hope the Committee
will take up in its investigations.
We simply list them here,
knowing that there may be many more:

—role of coal in the life of the region & nation;
—energy consumption patterns and life style;
—land acquisition;
—retribution, and redistribution;
—tourism and recreation industries;
—exploitation of cheap labor;
—occupational health and safety;
—union reform and extension;
—community unions;
—community organizing and citizen control;
—public voice in local, state and national politics,
—church investments as seed money;
—cooperatives

—education;
—health systems;
—family life;
—the elderly;
—arts and crafts;
—music and poetry;
—prayer.

CONCLUSION

As this letter closes, sisters and brothers,
we wish you
and all people throughout the region
the gift of peace in the Lord.
We know that all those who love the Lord
will struggle to follow his path,
no matter how confusing that may be
during these times.

We ask you to weigh seriously with the Spirit
the matters we have put before you,

—in your own silence;
—in your families;
—in your work;
—in your parishes.

We ask you to share
in dialogue and testing
with the leaders of your local church
and with us bishops
what we have presented here.
There will be different views,
but let us test them together

—with the people,
—with one another,
—and with the Spirit.

We wish to thank
the many Spirit-filled and dedicated
people of our Church,

who all along have been struggling
in hidden or dramatic ways,
for justice and unity among people.
We thank the youth
who have not given up hope,
and who continue to believe in freshness
in human experience.
We thank parents,
whose lives have been such
that our youth have reason to hope.
We thank the elderly,
who despite great hardship,
continue to survive
with spirit and grace,
and whose quiet wisdom
inspires us all.

We thank the volunteers,
not of this region,
the countless Sisters, Brothers,
Priests and lay people,
who have come to work at our side.
We especially thank
women in the region,
for we cannot but note the great role
women have played here
in the struggle for justice.
In the contemporary mission of the Church,
the voice and action of women
bring a special charism to the struggle
for justice.

Dear sisters and brothers,
we urge all of you
not to stop living,
to be a part of the rebirth of utopias,
to recover and defend the struggling dream
of Appalachia itself.
For it is the weak things of this world,
which seem like folly,
that the Spirit takes up

and makes its own.
The dream of the mountains' struggle,
the dream of simplicity
and of justice,
like so many other repressed visions,
is, we believe,
the voice of the Lord among us.

In taking them up,
hopefully the Church
might once again
be known as

—a center of the Spirit,
—a place where poetry dares to speak,
—where the song reigns unchallenged,
—where art flourishes,
—where nature is welcome,
—where little people and little needs
   come first,
—where justice speaks loudly,
—where in a wilderness of idolatrous destruction
   the great voice of God still cries out
   for life.

AMERICAN CATHOLIC
SOCIAL THOUGHT:
TWO DOCUMENTS

In the wake of the Vatican Council, the American bishops reorganized their national office, creating a National Conference of Catholic Bishops and a secretariat, the United States Catholic Conference, replacing the older National Catholic Welfare Conference. Within the United States Catholic Conference, a new Department of Social Development and World Peace was established in response to the call for national offices of justice and peace to work with the pontifical office established by mandate of Vatican II. The Department of Social Development expanded gradually in the years following the Council, assisting the bishops to deal with such difficult questions as the Vietnam war, political oppression and torture in Latin America, world hunger, and domestic social policy. Each year many documents emerge from the national episcopal conference, some directed at the Congress, others at the American Catholic people. Two of those documents are offered here as a sample of the quality of these statements and the kinds of concerns which occupy the bishops at a national level.

The first statement, "The Economy: Human Dimensions," was the bishops' response to the economic difficulties which plagued America in the middle seventies—particularly rising unemployment and inflation. The bishops attempted in this document to apply basic moral teachings to economic policies, and make some concrete recommendations for action in the public arena.

In February 1976 the bishops issued a statement on "Political Responsibility" to guide the faithful during the national election. Without attempting to dictate public policy or assume a moralistic stance, the bishops did insist on their right and responsibility to participate in the national debate on goals and policy. They proceeded to outline eight areas of public policy on which they had already spoken, and they called on the faithful to give close attention to these issues in evaluating political candidates.

In both these statements the influence of contemporary social teachings can be found. The American bishops have tried to apply these teachings to concrete issues of policy and to influence both government and their own followers to go through the same process of moral evaluation and concrete action. While the influence of Church leaders on Congress seems more limited than in the past, and while the faithful do not blindly follow episcopal leadership on these or other issues, the statements do point to the directions in which the American hierarchy can be expected to move in the years ahead.

THE ECONOMY: HUMAN DIMENSIONS

A STATEMENT OF THE CATHOLIC BISHOPS OF
THE UNITED STATES
NOVEMBER 20, 1975

> This unemployment returning again to plague us after so many
> repetitions during the century past is a sign of deep failure in this
> country. Unemployment is the great peacetime physical tragedy of
> the nineteenth and twentieth centuries, and both in its cause and
> in the imprint it leaves upon those who inflict it, those who per-
> mit it, and those who are its victims, it is one of the great moral
> tragedies of our time.

> The Bishops of the United States,
> *Unemployment*, 1930.

1. This was the judgment of our predecessors as they responded to the economic crisis of 1930. As pastors, teachers
and leaders, we recall and emphasize their words as our country faces important economic, social and moral decisions in
the midst of the highest unemployment since the 1930s.

I. THE CHURCH'S CONCERN

2. Despite recent hopeful signs, the economy is only slowly
and painfully recovering from the recent recession, the worst
since World War II. We are deeply concerned that this recovery may lack the strength or duration to alleviate the
suffering of many of the victims of the recession, especially
the unemployed. It is the moral, human and social consequences of our troubled economy which concern us and their
impact on families, the elderly and children. We hope in
these limited reflections to give voice to some of the concerns
of the poor and working people of our land.

3. We are keenly aware of the worldwide dimensions of
the problem and the complexity of these issues of economic

policy. Our concern, however, is not with technical fiscal matters, particular economic theories or political programs, but rather the moral aspects of economic policy and the impact of these policies on people. Our economic life must reflect broad values of social justice and human rights.

II. The Church's Teaching

4. Our own rich heritage of Catholic teaching offers important direction and insight. Most importantly, we are guided by the concern for the poor and afflicted shown by Jesus, who came to "bring good news to the poor, to proclaim liberty to captives, new sight to the blind, and to set the downtrodden free" (Luke 4:18). In addition, the social encyclicals of the Popes and documents of the Second Vatican Council and the Synod of Bishops defend the basic human right to useful employment, just wages and decent working conditions as well as the right of workers to organize and bargain collectively. They condemn unemployment, maldistribution of resources and other forms of economic injustice and call for the creation of useful work experiences and new forms of industrial organization enabling workers to share in decision-making, increased production, and even ownership. Again and again they point out the interrelation of economics and ethics, urging that economic activity be guided by social morality.

5. Catholic teaching on economic issues flows from the Church's commitment to human rights and human dignity. This living tradition articulates a number of principles which are useful in evaluating our current economic situation. Without attempting to set down an all-inclusive list, we draw the following principles from the social teachings of the Church and ask that policy-makers and citizens ponder their implications.

a. Economic activity should be governed by justice and be carried out within the limits of morality. It must serve people's needs.[1]

b. The right to have a share of earthly goods sufficient for oneself and one's family belongs to everyone.[2]

c. Economic prosperity is to be assessed not so much

from the sum total of goods and wealth possessed as from the distribution of goods according to norms of justice.[3]

d. Opportunities to work must be provided for those who are able and willing to work. Every person has the right to useful employment, to just wages, and to adequate assistance in case of real need.[4]

e. Economic development must not be left to the sole judgment of a few persons or groups possessing excessive economic power, or to the political community alone. On the contrary, at every level the largest possible number of people should have an active share in directing that development.[5]

f. A just and equitable system of taxation requires assessment according to ability to pay.[6]

g. Government must play a role in the economic activity of its citizens. Indeed, it should promote in a suitable manner the production of a sufficient supply of material goods. Moreover, it should safeguard the rights of all citizens, and help them find opportunities for employment.[7]

6. These are not new principles. They are drawn directly from the teachings of the Church, but they have critical relevance at this time of economic distress. Under current conditions, many of these principles are being consistently violated.

III. Dimensions of the Economic Situation

7. In these reflections we wish to examine briefly the dimensions of our economic problems in three areas: unemployment, inflation and distribution of wealth and income.

A. UNEMPLOYMENT

8. In October, government figures show eight million persons were unemployed, representing 8.6% of the work force.[8] Millions of other persons have given up seeking work out of discouragement or are in part-time jobs although they desire full-time work. Taking this into account, the actual level of unemployment in our country is over 12%. It is estimated

that 20 million people will be jobless at some time this year, and that one-third of all Americans will suffer the traumatic experience of unemployment within their families.

9. The official unemployment rate does more than underestimate the true extent of joblessness. It also masks the inequitable distribution of unemployment. The figures for October indicate that minorities, blue collar workers, young people and women bear a disproportionate share of the burdens of joblessness.[9]

10. These realities clearly indicate that the nation's commitment to genuine full employment has been seriously eroded, if not abandoned. Since World War II, unemployment has been substantial, persistent and drifting upward. In fact, when joblessness rose dramatically during the latest recession, it took the form of an acute and visible crisis, superimposed on a long-term unemployment problem which has persisted for decades.

11. The costs of this tragic under-utilization of our country's human resources are enormous. In economic terms, these high levels of unemployment cost literally hundreds of billions of dollars in lost productivity and tens of billions of dollars in lost revenue and increased expenses for all levels of government.

12. As lamentable as these financial costs are, the social and human impact is far more deplorable. In our society, persons without a job lose a key measure of their place in society and a source of individual fulfillment; they often feel that there is no productive role for them. Many minority youth may grow up without meaningful job experiences and come to accept a life of dependency. Unemployment frequently leads to higher rates of crime, drug addiction, and alcoholism. It is reflected in higher rates of mental illness as well as rising social tensions. The idleness, fear and financial insecurity resulting from unemployment can undermine confidence, erode family relationships, dull the spirit and destroy dreams and hopes. One can hardly bear to contemplate the disappointment of a family which has made the slow and painful climb up the economic ladder and has been pushed down once again into poverty and dependence by the loss of a job.

13. The current levels of unemployment are unacceptable

and their tremendous human costs are intolerable. Unemployment represents a vast and tragic waste of our human and material resources. We are disturbed not only by the present levels of joblessness, but also by official government projections of massive unemployment for the rest of this decade. We sincerely hope that these figures do not represent resignation to the human and economic waste implied in these rates of unemployment. As a society, we cannot accept the notion that some will have jobs and income while others will be told to wait a few years and to subsist on welfare in the interim. For work is more than a way to earn a living. It represents a deep human need, desired not only for income but also for the sense of worth which it provides the individual.

B. INFLATION

14. There are those who insist that we must tolerate high levels of unemployment for some, in order to avoid ruinous inflation for all. Although we are deeply concerned about inflation, we reject such a policy as not grounded in justice. In recent years, our country has experienced very high levels of inflation. During this past year, there has been some reduction in inflation, but there are already signs of its renewal, spurred by large increases in food and fuel prices.

15. Inflation weakens the economic stability of our society and erodes the economic security of our citizens. Its impact is most severe on those who live on fixed incomes and the very poor. The double distress of inflation and recession has led to a painful decline in real income for large numbers of people in recent years. Clearly, steps must be taken to limit inflation and its impact.

16. However, low unemployment and high inflation are not inevitable partners, as history and the experience of other industrialized countries bear out. Policy-makers should seek and use measures to combat inflation which do not rely upon high rates of joblessness. For many of our fellow citizens, the major protection against inflation is a decent job at decent wages.

C. DISTRIBUTION OF INCOME AND WEALTH

17. Within our country, vast disparities of income and wealth remain. The richest 20% of our people receive more income than the bottom 60% combined. In the area of ownership, the disparities are even more apparent. The top one-fifth of all families own more than three-fourths of all the privately held wealth in the United States while over one-half of our families control less than 7% of the wealth.

18. The distribution of income and wealth are important since they influence and even determine our society's distribution of economic power. Catholic social teaching has condemned gross inequality in the distribution of material goods. Our country cannot continue to ignore this important measure of economic justice.

IV. POLICY DIRECTIONS

19. Fundamentally, our nation must provide jobs for those who can and should work and a decent income for those who cannot. An effective national commitment to full employment is needed to protect the basic human right to useful employment for all Americans. It ought to guarantee, through appropriate mechanisms, that no one seeking work would be denied an opportunity to earn a livelihood. Full employment is the foundation of a just economic policy; it should not be sacrificed for other political and economic goals. We would support sound and creative programs of public service employment to relieve joblessness and to meet the vital social needs of our people (housing, transportation, education, health care, recreation, etc.).

20. The burden and hardship of these difficult times must not fall most heavily on the most vulnerable: the poor, the elderly, the unemployed, young people and workers of modest income. We support efforts to improve our unemployment compensation system and to provide adequate assistance to the victims of the recession. Efforts to eliminate or curtail needed services and help must be strongly opposed.

21. We continue to support a decent income policy for those who are unable to work because of sickness, age, disability or other good reason. Our present welfare system should be reformed to serve our country and those in need more effectively.

22. Renewed efforts are required to reform our economic life. We ask the private and public sectors to join together to plan and provide better for our future, to promote fairness in taxation, to halt the destructive impact of inflation and to distribute more evenly the burdens and opportunities of our society. We also ask that consideration be given to a more efficacious use of the land, the nation's primary resource in order to provide gainful employment for more people. We should also explore the impact of technology and endeavor to preserve the small family farm and other approaches to economic life which provide substantial and productive employment for people. It is not enough to point up the issues in our economy and to propose solutions to our national problems while accepting uncritically the presupposition of an economic system based in large part upon unlimited and unrestrained profit.

23. We pledge our best efforts in support of these goals. We call on local parishes, dioceses, Catholic institutions and organizations to undertake education and action programs on issues of economic justice. We renew our commitment to assist the needy and victims of economic turmoil through programs of financial assistance and active participation in the dialogue over the formulation and implementation of just economic policies. We call on our people to pray for our country in this time of need and to participate in the difficult decisions which can still fulfill the promise of our land.

24. Working together with renewed vision and commitment, our country has the productive capacity and human and material resources to provide adequately for the needs of our people. We take this opportunity to renew the challenge of our fellow Bishops of 45 years ago:

> Our country needs, now and permanently, such a change of heart as will, intelligently and with determination, so organize and distribute our work and wealth that no one need lack for any long

time the security of being able to earn an adequate living for himself and for those dependent upon him.

The Bishops of the United States,
Unemployment, 1930.

APPENDIX

In adopting this resolution, the Bishops sought to link this effort to a major statement issued in 1919 on similar matters. Entitled "The Bishops' Program for Social Reconstruction," the statement called for: minimum wage legislation; unemployment insurance and protection against sickness and old age; minimum age limit for working children; legal enforcement of the right of labor to organize; a national employment service; public housing; and a long term program of increasing wages.

It also urged: prevention of excessive profits and incomes through regulation of public utilities and progressive taxes on inheritance, income, and excess profits; participation of labor in management; a wider distribution of ownership through cooperative enterprises and worker ownership in the stock of corporations; and effective control of monopolies even by the method of government competition if that should prove necessary.

Most of these proposals have been enacted. Partial progress has been made toward others. The 1919 statement provides a historical framework for the current resolution and evidences a long-standing concern for economic justice on the part of the Catholic community in this country.

NOTES

1. Vatican II, *The Church in the Modern World*, 64; John XXIII, *Mater et Magistra*, 38–39.
2. Vatican II, *The Church in the Modern World*, 69.
3. John XXIII, *Mater et Magistra*, 74.
4. Pius XI, *On the Reconstruction of the Social Order*, 74; John XXIII, *Pacem in Terris*, 11, 18; Vatican II, *The Church in the Modern World*, 67; Paul VI, *A Call to Action*, 6.

5. Vatican II, *The Church in the Modern World*, 65.

6. John XXIII, *Mater et Magistra*, 132.

7. John XXIII, *Mater et Magistra*, 20; Vatican II, *The Church in the Modern World*, 67, 70.

8. The Employment Situation: October 1975; U. S. Department of Labor, Bureau of Labor Statistics; November 7, 1975.

9. Department of Labor figures for October 1975 indicate:

> One out of five teenagers was jobless.
> Over 11% of all blue collar workers were out of work.
> 14.2% of all minority persons were unemployed.
> Nearly 40% of all minority teenagers were jobless.
> 134 of our 150 major urban areas were officially listed as areas of substantial subemployment.

POLITICAL RESPONSIBILITY:
REFLECTIONS ON AN ELECTION YEAR

A STATEMENT OF THE ADMINISTRATIVE BOARD
OF THE UNITED STATES CATHOLIC CONFERENCE
FEBRUARY 12, 1976

This year marks the two hundredth anniversary of the founding of our republic with its remarkable system of representative democracy. It is also a year that will test the workings of this democracy. A national election is a time for decisions regarding the future of our nation and the selection of our representatives and political leaders. As pastors and teachers, we address this statement on political responsibility to all Americans in hopes that the upcoming elections will provide an opportunity for thoughtful and lively debate on the issues and challenges that face our country as well as decisions on the candidates who seek to lead us.

I. PUBLIC RESPONSIBILITY AND THE ELECTORAL PROCESS

We call this year a test of our democratic institutions because increasing numbers of our fellow citizens regard our political institutions and electoral processes with indifference and even distrust. Two years ago only 36% of those eligible voted in the national Congressional elections; in contrast, 46% voted in 1962. In 1972 only half of the eligible citizens exercised their right to vote, down from a peak of 63% in 1960. This trend—and the alienation, disenchantment and indifference it represents—must be reversed if our government is to truly reflect the "consent of the governed."

Abuses of power and a lack of governmental accountability have contributed to declining public confidence, despite significant efforts to uncover and redress these problems. Equally important, government has sometimes failed to deal effectively with critical issues which affect the daily lives of its citizens. As a result, many persons caught in the web of poverty and injustice have little confidence in the responsiveness of our political institutions. This discouragement and feelings of powerlessness are not limited to the poor who feel these most intensely, but affect many social groups, most alarmingly the young and the elderly. This leads to a loss of human resources, talent and idealism which could be harnessed in the work of social and national progress.[1]

However, we believe that the abandonment of political participation is neither an effective nor a responsible approach to the solution of these problems. We need a committed, informed, and involved citizenry to revitalize our political life, to require accountability from our political leaders and governmental institutions and to achieve the common good. We echo the words of Pope Paul VI who declared: "The Christian has the duty to take part in the organization and life of political society."[2] Accordingly, we would urge all citizens to register to vote, to become informed on the relevant issues, to become involved in the party or campaign of their choice, to vote freely according to their conscience, in a word, to participate fully in this critical arena of politics where national decisions are made.

Certain methods used in political campaigns sometimes have intensified this disaffection. We call on those seeking public office to concentrate on demonstrating their personal integrity, their specific views on issues and their experience in public service. We urge a positive presentation of their programs and leadership abilities. In this way they can contribute to a campaign based on vital issues, personal competence and real choices which will help to restore confidence in our electoral process.

II. The Church and the Political Order

It is appropriate in this context to offer our own reflections on the role of the Church in the political order. Christians believe that Jesus' commandment to love one's neighbor should extend beyond individual relationships to infuse and transform all human relations from the family to the entire human community. Jesus came to "bring good news to the poor, to proclaim liberty to captives, new sight to the blind and to set the downtrodden free." (Luke 4:18.) He called us to feed the hungry, clothe the naked, care for the sick and afflicted and to comfort the victims of injustice. (Matt. 25.) His example and words require individual acts of charity and concern from each of us. Yet they also require understanding and action upon the broader dimensions of poverty, hunger and injustice which necessarily involve the institutions and structures of economy, society and politics.

The Church, the People of God, is itself an expression of this love, and is required by the Gospel and its long tradition to promote and defend human rights and human dignity.[3] The 1971 Synod of Bishops declared that action on behalf of justice is a "constitutive dimension" of the Church's ministry and that, "the Church has the right, indeed the duty, to proclaim justice on the social, national and international level, and to denounce instances of injustice, when the fundamental rights of man and his very salvation demand it."[4] This view of the Church's ministry and mission requires it to relate positively to the political order, since social injustice and the denial of human rights can often be remedied only through governmental action. In today's world concern for social justice and human development necessarily require persons and organizations to participate in the political process in accordance with their own responsibilities and roles.

The Church's responsibility in the area of human rights includes two complementary pastoral actions: the affirmation and promotion of human rights and the denunciation and condemnation of violations of these rights. In addition, it is the Church's role to call attention to the moral and religious dimensions of secular issues, to keep alive the values of the Gospel as a norm for social and political life, and to point out the demands of the Christian faith for a just transformation of society.[5] Such a ministry on the part of every Christian and the Church inevitably involves political consequences and touches upon public affairs.

Christian social teaching demands that citizens and public officials alike give serious consideration in all matters to the common good, to the welfare of society as a whole, which must be protected and promoted if individual rights are to be encouraged and upheld.

In order to be credible and faithful to the Gospel and to our tradition, the Church's concern for human rights and social justice should be comprehensive and consistent. It must be formulated with competence and an awareness of the complexity of issues. It should also be developed in dialogue with other concerned persons and respectful of the rights of all.[6]

The Church's role in the political order includes the following:

education regarding the teachings of the Church and the responsibilities of the faithful;

analysis of issues for their social and moral dimensions;

measuring public policy against Gospel values;

participating with other concerned parties in debate over public policy;

speaking out with courage, skill and concern on public issues involving human rights, social justice and the life of the Church in society.

Unfortunately, our efforts in this area are sometimes misunderstood. The Church's participation in public affairs is not a threat to the political process or to genuine pluralism, but an affirmation of their importance. The Church recognizes the legitimate autonomy of government and the right of all, including the Church itself, to be heard in the formulation of public policy. As Vatican II declared:

By preaching the truth of the Gospel and shedding light on all areas of human activity through her teaching and the example of the faithful, she [the Church] shows respect for the political freedom and responsibility of citizens and fosters these values. . . . She also has the right to pass moral judgments, even on matters touching the political order, whenever basic personal rights or the salvation of souls make such judgments necessary.[7]

A proper understanding of the role of the Church will not confuse its mission with that of government, but rather see its ministry as advocating the critical values of human rights and social justice.

It is the role of Christian communities to analyze the situation in their own country, to reflect upon the meaning of the Gospel, and to draw norms of judgment and plans of action from the teaching of the Church and their own experience.[8] In carrying out this pastoral activity in the social arena we are confronted with complexity. As the 1971 Synod of Bishops pointed out: "It does not belong to the Church, *insofar as she is a religious and hierarchical community,* to offer concrete solutions in the social, economic and political spheres for justice in the world."[9] (Emphasis added.) At the same time, it is essential to recall the words of Pope John XXIII:

> It must not be forgotten that the Church has the right and duty not only to safeguard the principles of ethics and religion, but also to intervene authoritatively with her children in the temporal sphere when there is a question of judging the application of these principles of concrete cases.[10]

The application of Gospel values to real situations is an essential work of the Christian community. Christians believe the Gospel is the measure of human realities. However, specific political proposals do not in themselves constitute the Gospel. Christians and Christian organizations must certainly participate in public debate over alternative policies and legislative proposals, yet it is critical that the nature of their participation not be misunderstood.

We specifically do not seek the formation of a religious voting bloc; nor do we wish to instruct persons on how they should vote by endorsing candidates. We urge citizens to avoid choosing candidates simply on the personal basis of self-interest. Rather, we hope that voters will examine the positions of candidates on the full range of issues as well as the person's integrity, philosophy and performance. We seek to promote a greater understanding of the important link between faith and politics and to express our belief that our nation is enriched when its citizens and social groups approach public affairs from positions grounded in moral conviction and religious belief. Our view is expressed very well by Pope Paul VI when he said:

> While recognizing the autonomy of the reality of politics, Christians who are invited to take up political activity should try to make their choices consistent with the Gospel and, in the frame-

work of a legitimate plurality, to give both personal and collective witness to the seriousness of their faith by effective and disinterested service of men.[11]

The Church's responsibility in this area falls on all its members. As citizens we are all called to become informed, active and responsible participants in the political process. The hierarchy has a responsibility as teachers and pastors to educate the faithful, support efforts to gain greater peace and justice and provide guidance and even leadership on occasion where human rights are in jeopardy. The laity has major responsibility for the renewal of the temporal order. Drawing on their own experience and exercising their distinctive roles within the Christian community, bishops, clergy, religious and laity should join together in common witness and effective action to bring about Pope John's vision of a well ordered society based on truth, justice, charity and freedom.[12]

As religious leaders and pastors, our intention is to reflect our concern that politics—the forum for the achievement of the common good—receive its rightful importance and attention. For, as Pope Paul VI said, "politics are a demanding manner—but not the only one—of living the Christian commitment to the service of others."[13]

III. ISSUES

Without reference to political candidates, parties or platforms, we wish to offer a listing of some issues which we believe are central to the national debate this year. These brief summaries are not intended to indicate in any depth the details of our positions in these matters. We wish to refer the reader to fuller discussions of our point of view in the documents listed in the summary which appears below. We wish to point out that these issues are not the concerns of Catholics alone; in every case we have joined with others to advocate these concerns. They represent a broad range of topics on which the Bishops of the United States have already expressed themselves and are recalled here in alphabetical order to emphasize their relevance in a period of national debate and decision.

A. ABORTION

The right to life is a basic human right which should have the protection of law. Abortion is the deliberate destruction of an unborn human being and therefore violates this right. We reject the 1973 Supreme Court decisions on abortion which refuse appropriate legal protection to the unborn child. We support the passage of a constitutional amendment to restore the basic constitutional protection of the right to life for the unborn child. (*Documentation on the Right to Life and Abortion*, 1974; *Pastoral Plan on Pro-Life Activities*, 1975.)

B. THE ECONOMY

Our national economic life must reflect broad values of social justice and human rights. Current levels of unemployment are unacceptable and their tremendous human costs are intolerable. We support an effective national commitment to genuine full employment. Our strong support of this human right to meaningful employment is based not only on the income it provides, but also on the sense of worth and creativity a useful job provides for the individual. We also call for a decent income policy for those who cannot work and adequate assistance to those in need. Efforts to eliminate or curtail needed services and help in these difficult economic times must be strongly opposed. (*The Economy: Human Dimensions*, 1975.)

C. EDUCATION

All persons of whatever race, condition, or age, by virtue of their dignity as human beings, have an inalienable right to education.

We advocate:

1. Sufficient public and private funding to make an adequate education available for all citizens and residents of the

United States of America and to provide assistance for education in our nation's program of foreign aid.

2. Governmental and voluntary action to reduce inequalities of educational opportunity by improving the opportunities available to economically disadvantaged persons.

3. Orderly compliance with legal requirements for racially integrated schools.

4. Voluntary efforts to increase racial and ethnic integration in public and nonpublic schools.

5. Equitable tax support for the education of pupils in public and nonpublic schools to implement parental freedom in the education of their children. (*To Teach as Jesus Did,* Nov. 1972.)

D. FOOD POLICY

The "right to eat" is directly linked with the right to life. This right to eat is denied to countless numbers of people in the world. We support a national policy in which:

U.S. world food aid seriously combats hunger and malnutrition on a global basis, separates food aid from other considerations, gives priority to the poorest nations, and joins in a global grain reserve.

U.S. domestic food programs meet the needs of hungry and malnourished people here in America, provide strong support for food stamps to assist the needy, the unemployed, the elderly and the working poor, and strive to improve and to extend child nutrition programs.

U.S. agricultural policy promotes full production and an adequate and just return for farmers. (*Food Policy and the Church: Specific Proposals,* 1975.)

E. HOUSING

Decent housing is a basic human right. A greater commitment of will and resources is required to meet our national housing goal of a decent home for every American family. Housing policy must better meet the needs of low and middle income families, the elderly, rural areas and minorities. It should also promote reinvestment in central cities and equal housing opportunity. Preservation of existing housing stock and a renewed concern for neighborhoods are required. (*The Right to a Decent Home*, 1975.)

F. HUMAN RIGHTS AND U.S. FOREIGN POLICY

Human dignity requires the defense and promotion of human rights. Many regimes, including communist countries and some U.S. allies, violate or deny their citizens' human and civil rights, as well as religious liberty. Internationally, the pervasive presence of American power creates a responsibility to use that power in the service of human rights. In the face of regimes which use torture or detain political prisoners without legal recourse, we support a policy which gives greater weight to the protection of human rights in the conduct of U.S. affairs. (*Resolution on the 25th Anniversary of the U.N. Universal Declaration of Human Rights*, 1973.)

G. MASS MEDIA

We are concerned that the communications media be truly responsive to the public interest. We strongly oppose government control over television programming policy, but we deplore unilateral decision-making by networks. We urge that broadcasters, government, private business, and representatives of the viewing public seek effective ways to ensure accountability in the formulation and implementation of broadcast policy. We recommend exploring ways to reduce the commercial orientation of the broadcasting industry to better serve the public. (*Statement on the Family Viewing Policy*, 1975.)

H. MILITARY EXPENDITURES

The arms race continues to threaten humanity with universal destruction. It is especially destructive because it violates the rights of the world's poor who are thereby deprived of essential needs and it creates the illusion of protecting human life and fostering peace. We support a policy of arms limitation as a necessary step to general disarmament which is a prerequisite to international peace and justice. (*U.S. Bishops on the Arms Race*, 1971 Synod.)

This is not an exclusive listing of issues of concern to us. We are also concerned about issues involving the civil and political rights of racial and ethnic groups, women, the elderly and working families. We support measures to provide health care for all of our citizens and the reform of our criminal justice system. We are concerned about protection of the land and the environment as well as the monumental question of peace in the world.

IV. Conclusion

In summary, we believe the Church has a proper role and responsibility in public affairs flowing from its Gospel mandate and its concern for the human person and his or her rights. We hope these reflections will contribute to a renewed sense of political vitality in our land, both in terms of citizen participation in the electoral process and the integrity and accountability of those who hold and seek public office.

We pray that Christians will follow the call of Jesus to provide the "leaven" for society (Matt. 13:34; Luke 13:20), and heed the appeal of the Second Vatican Council:

To enlighten one another through honest discussion, preserving mutual charity and caring above all for the common good . . . to be witnesses to Christ in all things in the midst of human society.[14]

NOTES

1. Joint Economic Committee Hearings, October 20, 1975; *New York Times*, February 1, 1976; *Wall Street Journal*, February 2, 1976.

2. *A Call to Action*, Pope Paul VI, 24, 1971.

3. *Human Rights and Reconciliation*, Synod of Bishops, 1974.

4. *Justice in the World*, Synod of Bishops, 1971.

5. *Justice in the World*, ibid.

6. *A Call to Action*, op. cit., 4, 50. *The Church in the Modern World*, Second Vatican Council, 43, 1965.

7. *The Church in the Modern World*, op. cit., 76.

8. *A Call to Action*, op. cit.

9. *Justice in the World*, op. cit.

10. *Pacem in Terris*, Pope John XXIII, 160, 1963.

11. *A Call to Action*, op. cit., 46.

12. *Pacem in Terris*, Pope John XXIII, 35, 1963.

13. *A Call to Action*, op. cit.

14. *The Church in the Modern World*, op. cit., 43.

III. Latin American Documents

admits to mistake of Church in obedience to rich - Committ to poor

Importance of Base Communita which means import. of lay communities - Puebla - 1979 Decided to reaffirm base Comm. as these dynamism of church even tho a few of them becoming a splittry factor. People come & read Scripture and understand it in their own lives. can see where Scripture gives hope to poor & say they can overcome - Becomes dangerous to people from a political view - Considered subversive. Look few what happens out of base community.

INTRODUCTION:
LIBERATION THEOLOGY

Within the history of Catholic Christianity, there have been a variety of ways of doing theology. The Church Fathers, for example, developed a theology of wisdom. This was basically a thematic reflection upon the Bible, with the primary emphasis on developing one's religious life. Although a variety of philosophic concepts were used, there was no major attempt made to create a synthesis; rather the emphasis was on the development of theology to promote a rich Christian understanding of life. This theology was also characterized by a de-emphasis of the world and an emphasis on the salvation of the individual. Consequently, this theology did not seek to understand the structures of the world in which Christianity was lived; the center of attention was the individual and how he or she might bring to perfection the gift of salvation received in baptism. As the situation of Christianity changed, theology began to be developed as rational knowledge. Here theology was seen as an intellectual discipline which was born of the meeting of faith and reason. This style of theology was brought to its high point in the synthesis forged by Thomas Aquinas, who used the newly discovered Aristotelian philosophy as a means of articulating the truths of Christianity. In this framework, theology had a variety of purposes. First it was to define, explain, and present for the understanding of all the truths that were revealed by God. Second, it was to examine doctrine to separate true teaching from false teaching. Finally, through this process of definition and examination, theology would teach revealed truth authoritatively. Although in this style of theology, the relationship between the Church and the world was recognized, the major emphasis was on constructing a system which could be used to defend and explain the truths of Christianity both to its members and to those who wished to be converted. As such, this style of theology is primarily an in-house exercise.

In recent times, two new styles of theology have emerged which have influenced a great number of people. The first of these is political theology, which has been developed in Germany under the leadership of Johannes-Baptist Metz. The purpose of political theology is to determine anew the relationship between religion and society, in particular under the conditions of our modern society. It has as its principle task the deprivatization of theology to help Christians understand the social, public, and communal nature of the gospel message. This style of theology has been influenced tremendously by the developments of Vatican II and the urgency of the situation in which Christians find themselves with respect to the problems of the modern world. As such, it is an attempt to articulate, primarily from a European point of view, how religion and society may be related so that religion may become a vital part of the process of living within the world. The second development in theology is theology as a critical reflection on praxis (action), or liberation theology. Praxis or action means a re-emphasis on charity as the center of Christian life, with particular reference to how one lives out one's Christian life in the world. The critical dimension implies an analysis of both persons and social structures and their principles of operation. This is an attempt to interpret historical events to help reveal and proclaim their meaning and significance for the life of the community.

There are a variety of reasons for such developments in theological methodologies. The first of these is the basic choice of the purpose of religion. If religion is to save one from the world, then a theology such as that of early Christianity is appropriate. If, on the other hand, theology is seen as a way of helping to save the world, then one can understand why political or liberation theology is very appropriate. Also, a variety of secular pressures come to bear on the understanding of religion and its place in the world. For example, the Enlightenment shattered the unity of religion and society and reduced Christianity to a particular phenomenon within a pluralistic milieu. Consequently, religion lost most of the critical edge that it had enjoyed in past centuries. The philosophies of French personalism and existentialism set a context in which the practice of faith was understood as an individual event; therefore private virtue and I-Thou encounters, which are apolitical, were emphasized. Finally the very experience of one's life situation helps one determine what religion is to mean. If there is a great harmony between religion and the society in which it exists, religion will tend to confirm the values of the status quo. On the other hand, if people are oppressed or if religion is oppressed, then religion tends to be critical and attempts to change the values of the society in which it exists.

Liberation theology has arisen out of the experience of Christians in Latin America and is a way of articulating the purpose of the Church within Latin America. It is primarily an attempt to develop the theology proper to the Latin American situation rather than to try to adapt European theology to the situation of Latin America. It is also an examination of a variety of ways in which the Church might use the influence it has within Latin America.

One of the elements of liberation theology is its critique of development. Development is typically seen in terms of economic growth, as exemplified by the use of the rise of gross national product and the per capita income as indexes of growth. Development also tries to postulate a total social program. That is, it tries to articulate the interrelations between economics, politics, culture, and the social structures of the society. It is thus an attempt to allow humans to control their own destiny. Liberation theology, however, sees development as linked to the international organizations which are closely connected to governments which control the world economy. Thus the changes which a philosophy of development would encourage would occur always within the formal structures of the existing economic/political structures of these governments; i.e., the development model is premised upon the status quo. Thus, liberation theology, on the one hand, sees development as a way of ensuring that some money is redistributed or recycled to the developing nations, but, on the other hand, realizes that such an arrangement will never allow the developing nations to step outside the situation of neocolonialism in which they presently exist.

In general, we may say that liberation theology is based on a dynamic concept of the person, creatively oriented toward a social future, acting in the present for the sake of the future. Liberation theology does not see history as a development of the potentials pre-existent in the person in society; rather, it seeks qualitatively different ways of being a person in order to achieve an ever more total and complete fulfillment of the person in solidarity with all others. Thus it is oriented toward what may be, rather than toward what is. Specifically, liberation theology hopes to eliminate oppressive human relations, structures, and social systems. To do this, it calls for the removal of inequalities between social classes. It hopes to remove the exploitative uses of power that now exist. Following from this is a rejection of institutional violence that characterizes so many social systems. Finally, liberation theology hopes to remove the oppressive forms of international dependency that now exist. Positively, liberation theology hopes to enable persons to become subjects of their own self-determination so that they can help in their own transformation and in the transformation of the social, economic, and political structures in which they live. Thereby it hopes to effect positive change in the social, economic, and political realms. It also hopes for the creation of a new person and a new sense of social solidarity. The condition for these positive changes is an attempt to free persons from sin and to bring them to solidarity with God.

One specific problem that liberation theology addresses is that of the relationship between the Church and society. The perception of early Christianity was that temporal realities, such as social structures, do not have an authenic existence for they belong to an age that is passing away. Also history had no meaning other than as an insignificant prelude to the coming of the eschatological age that Jesus would initiate upon his return. Therefore early Christianity did not attempt to articulate any positive relation between the Church and the state; rather, it existed within its own sphere having as little to do with the state as possible. In the Thomistic synthesis, an attempt was made to build a society based on Christian principles and on a Christian understanding of values such as justice, human dignity, and social solidarity. From this perspective, the individual was to join Christian groups and societies and was indirectly to initiate changes in the social structure. In this model of indirect modification of existing social structures, the Church had two missions: preaching the gospel and providing the right ideas and motives to help the laity direct the restructuring of the social sphere. In the Thomistic model, the Church takes society seriously, but attempts to restructure it on Christian principles and a Christian vision of society; it also seeks to effect these changes indirectly through its proclamation of correct ideas and the positive influence of Christian laity in social structures.

Liberation theology suggests that new social elements are coming into being which force a new understanding of the relation of the Church and society. Persons are more conscious of being active subjects of history rather than passive objects as they have been traditionally understood. Human reason has also become political reason. That is, reason now analyzes political power to effect the conditions that are necessary for a full human life. Also we now have an increasing sophistication in our means of evaluating social policy and actions. We have a better understanding of the causes, goals, and motivations that go into effecting change within the social system. Finally, the rise of secularization has forced a number of issues to be re-evaluated. Secularization in general is a breaking away from the domination by religion of individuals and the world. This implies a transformation of the self-understanding of the person. It suggests that the individual may be much more of a creative subject than had been previously recognized. It also emphasizes, in conjunction with this, that the self is an active agent of history. Secularization further implies that the world must be defined in its own terms rather than in reference to religion. In this perspective, the world is seen as a self-contained unit. Therefore secularization affirms a freedom from all ideologies which reinforce the status quo. Included among these, of course, would be religion, which it can be demonstrated, historically has often supported the status quo.

Religion is responding to these pressures in a variety of ways. One of these is a growing rejection of a world of pure nature to which was added a world of pure supernature with no intrinsic connection with the natural. Consequently, there is a growing acceptance of a vision of one world with one common destiny, the unity of all people with God. This implies a rejection of dualism with its suggestion that a person has two lives which are not closely connected, one Godly and the other worldly. This reorientation also suggests the affirmation of the category of history in that one's total personhood—self, society, and the attainment of the common good—are to be fulfilled in an evolutionary manner. This is seen not as a living out of the potentialities of the past, but rather an actualization of the promises of the future. Therefore the Church is not seen *per se* as an ultimate social structure. The Church is an institution which has as its purpose the creation of a new community in which all individuals stand in solidarity. As a result of this, the Church has the task of what can be called critical negativity: evaluating what *is*, in the light of the gospel promise of what is to be, and indicating the changes necessary to close this gap. Thus liberation theology sees the Church as involved in politics not as an outsider but from within. Because of this the Church may no longer occupy the privileged position, but must enter into the process of creating the new community promised by Jesus and must help provide concrete means of freeing the community to be able to articulate this in the political and social structures in which it lives.

only 3 of 14 doc.

THE MEDELLÍN CONFERENCE
DOCUMENTS

The documents from the Second General Conference of
Latin American Bishops, held at Medellín, Colombia,
August 24–September 6, 1968, are a concrete example of an
application of many of the themes of liberation theology.
These documents provide an examination of the relationship
of the Church to Latin America. They also indicate the possibilities of the present moment, and the steps necessary to
actualize these possibilities. These documents also remain
within the mainstream of Catholic social teaching, especially
the themes of *Populorum Progressio*, but adapt them to the
specific situation of Latin America.

The two major themes that the Conference addresses are
those of justice and peace. The document on justice suggests
a variety of programs and changes that will be needed to
change the structures that are causing the present injustice in
Latin American countries. The first part of the document
suggests a variety of directions for social change that must
occur within institutions like families, the economy, organizations of workers, the conditions of rural life, and the problems connected with the increasing industrialization of Latin
America. Next, the document analyzes some elements of political reform which must be initiated to bring about greater
justice. The main suggestion here is a call both for representation of the people and for their participation within political processes. The document also calls for decisions to be
made on the basis of the common good rather than on the
good of privileged groups. The third theme is *concientización*
—the formation of a social conscience and an understanding
of the political problems of the community and its social

structures. The document expresses the hope that social conscience will be awakened within many different groups of people and that such a reorientation of political perceptions will help bring about a re-emphasizing of religious values and a beginning of social harmony within the peoples of Latin America.

The document on peace focuses on the unjust situations which promote tensions that inhibit the development of peace. One aspect of this is the tensions that exist between social classes and what the document calls internal colonialism, that is, the keeping of certain groups under continual domination. Another aspect is the relationship between international tensions and external neocolonialism. This implies that the problems that occur between the major nations also have an impact upon how these nations' economic decisions will affect the developing nations that stand in a dependent relationship to them. The final dimension of tension is that which exists within the countries of Latin America themselves. Two specific problems that are dealt with here concern excessive nationalism and armaments. The document points up the moral scandal of people starving while money is being spent on arms.

These documents are both a reflection upon specific problems facing the Latin American Church and an example of how liberation theology suggests that religion and political analysis might be blended. The documents state clearly their religious premises, and equally clearly show how these religious principles are to play a part in political analysis. Thus, on one level, the documents present us with an excellent example of a new theological method. But on another, more important level, they indicate clearly the changed position of the Church within Latin America, the new agenda facing the Church, and the urgency of the situation within which the Church finds itself.

JUSTICE

I. Pertinent Facts

1. There are in existence many studies of the Latin American people.[1] The misery that besets large masses of human beings in all of our countries is described in all of these studies. That misery, as a collective fact, expresses itself as injustice which cries to the heavens.[2]

But what perhaps has not been sufficiently said is that in general the efforts which have been made have not been capable of assuring that justice be honored and realized in every sector of the respective national communities. Often families do not find concrete possibilities for the education of their children. The young demand their right to enter universities or centers of higher learning for both intellectual and technical training; the women, their right to a legitimate equality with men; the peasants, better conditions of life; or if they are workers, better prices and security in buying and selling; the growing middle class feels frustrated by the lack of expectations. There has begun an exodus of professionals and technicians to more developed countries; the small businessmen and industrialists are pressed by greater interests and not a few large Latin American industrialists are gradually coming to be dependent on the international business enterprises. We cannot ignore the phenomenon of this almost universal frustration of legitimate aspirations which creates the climate of collective anguish in which we are already living.

2. The lack of socio-cultural integration, in the majority of our countries, has given rise to the superimposition of cultures. In the economic sphere systems flourished which consider solely the potential of groups with great earning power. This lack of adaptation to the characteristics and to the potentials of all our people, in turn, gives rise to frequent political instability and the consolidation of purely formal institutions. To all of this must be added the lack of solidarity which, on the individual and social levels, leads to the com-

mitting of serious sins, evident in the unjust structures which characterize the Latin American situation.

II. DOCTRINAL BASES

3. The Latin American Church has a message for all men on this continent who "hunger and thirst after justice." The very God who creates men in his image and likeness, creates the "earth and all that is in it for the use of all men and all nations, in such a way that created goods can reach all in a more just manner,"[3] and gives them power to transform and perfect the world in solidarity.[4] It is the same God who, in the fullness of time, sends his Son in the flesh, so that He might come to liberate all men from the slavery to which sin has subjected them[5]: hunger, misery, oppression and ignorance, in a word, that injustice and hatred which have their origin in human selfishness.

Thus, for our authentic liberation, all of us need a profound conversion so that "the kingdom of justice, love and peace" might come to us. The origin of all disdain for mankind, of all injustice, should be sought in the internal imbalance of human liberty, which will always need to be rectified in history. The uniqueness of the Christian message does not so much consist in the affirmation of the necessity for structural change, as it does in the insistence on the conversion of men which will in turn bring about this change. We will not have a new continent without new and reformed structures, but, above all, there will be no new continent without new men, who know how to be truly free and responsible according to light of the Gospel.

4. Only by the light of Christ is the mystery of man made clear. In the economy of salvation the divine work is an action of integral human development and liberation, which has love for its sole motive. Man is "created in Christ Jesus,"[6] fashioned in Him as a "new creature."[7] By faith and baptism he is transformed, filled with the gift of the Spirit, with a new dynamism, not of selfishness, but of love which compels him to seek out a new, more profound relationship with God, his fellow man, and created things.

Love, "the fundamental law of human perfection, and

therefore of the transformation of the world,"[8] is not only the greatest commandment of the Lord; it is also the dynamism which ought to motivate Christians to realize justice in the world, having truth as a foundation and liberty as their sign.

5. This is how the Church desires to serve the world, radiating over it a light and life which heals and elevates the dignity of the human person,[9] which consolidates the unity of society[10] and gives a more profound reason and meaning to all human activity.

Doubtless, for the Church, the fullness and perfection of the human vocation will be accomplished with the definitive inclusion of each man in the Passover or Triumph of Christ, but the hope of such a definitive realization, rather than lull, ought to "vivify the concern to perfect this earth. For here grows the body of the new human family, a body which even now is able to give some kind of foreshadowing of the new age."[11] We do not confuse temporal progress and the Kingdom of Christ; nevertheless, the former, "to the extent that it can contribute to the better ordering of human society, is of vital concern to the Kingdom of God."[12]

The Christian quest for justice is a demand arising from biblical teaching. All men are merely humble stewards of material goods. In the search for salvation we must avoid the dualism which separates temporal tasks from the work of sanctification. Although we are encompassed with imperfections, we are men of hope. We have faith that our love for Christ and our brethren will not only be the great force liberating us from injustice and oppression, but also the inspiration for social justice, understood as a whole of life and as an impulse toward the integral growth of our countries.

III. Projections for Social Pastoral Planning

6. Our pastoral mission is essentially a service of encouraging and educating the conscience of believers, to help them to perceive the responsibilities of their faith in their personal life and in their social life. This Second Episcopal Conference wishes to point out the most important demands, taking into account the value judgment which the latest Documents

of the Magisterium of the Church have already made concerning the economic and social situation of the world today and which applies fully to the Latin American continent.

DIRECTION OF SOCIAL CHANGE

7. The Latin American Church encourages the formation of national communities that reflect a global organization, where all of the peoples but more especially the lower classes have, by means of territorial and functional structures, an active and receptive, creative and decisive participation in the construction of a new society. Those intermediary structures —between the person and the state—should be freely organized, without any unwarranted interference from authority or from dominant groups, in view of their development and concrete participation in the accomplishment of the total common good. They constitute the vital network of society. They are also the true expression of the citizens' liberty and unity.

a) The Family

8. Without ignoring the unique character of the family as the natural unit of society, we are considering it here as an intermediary structure, inasmuch as the families as a group ought to take up their function in the process of social change. Latin American families ought to organize their economic and cultural potential so that their legitimate needs and hopes be taken into account, on the levels where fundamental decisions are made, which can help or hinder them. In this way they will assume a role of effective representation and participation in the life of the total community.

Besides the dynamism which is generated in each country by the union of families, it is necessary that governments draw up legislation and a healthy and up-to-date policy governing the family.

b) Professional Organization

9. The Second Latin American Episcopal Conference addressed itself to all those who, with daily effort, create the goods and services which favor the existence and develop-

ment of human life. We refer especially to the millions of Latin American men and women who make up the peasant and working class. They, for the most part, suffer, long for and struggle for a change that will humanize and dignify their work. Without ignoring the totality of the significance of human work, here we refer to it as an intermediary structure, inasmuch as it constitutes the function which gives rise to professional organization in the field of production.

c) Business Enterprises and the Economy

10. In today's world, production finds its concrete expression in business enterprises, the industrial as well as the rural; they constitute the dynamic and fundamental base of the integral economic process. The system of Latin American business enterprises, and through it the current economy, responds to an erroneous conception concerning the right of ownership of the means of production and the very goals of the economy. A business, in an authentically human economy, does not identify itself with the owners of capital, because it is fundamentally a community of persons and a unit of work, which is in need of capital to produce goods. A person or a group of persons cannot be the property of an individual, of a society, or of the state.

The system of liberal capitalism and the temptation of the Marxist system would appear to exhaust the possibilities of transforming the economic structures of our continent. Both systems militate against the dignity of the human person. One takes for granted the primacy of capital, its power and its discriminatory ultilization in the function of profit-making. The other, although it ideologically supports a kind of humanism, is more concerned with collective man, and in practice becomes a totalitarian concentration of state power. We must denounce the fact that Latin America sees itself caught between these two options and remains dependent on one or other of the centers of power which control its economy.

Therefore, on behalf of Latin America, we make an urgent appeal to the businessmen, to their organizations and to the political authorities, so that they might radically modify the evaluation, the attitudes and the means regarding the goal, organization and functioning of business. All those financiers deserve encouragement who, individually or through their organizations, make an effort to conduct their business according to the guidelines supplied by the social teaching of the Church. That the social and economic change in Latin America be channeled towards a truly human economy will depend fundamentally on this.

11. On the other hand this change will be essential in order to liberate the authentic process of Latin American development and integration. Many of our workers, although they gradually become conscious of the necessity for this change, simultaneously experience a situation of dependence on inhuman economic systems and institutions: a situation which, for many of them, borders on slavery, not only physical but also professional, cultural, civic and spiritual.

With the clarity which arises from the knowledge of man and of his hopes, we must reiterate that neither the combined value of capital nor the establishment of the most modern techniques of production, nor economic plans will serve man efficiently if the workers, the "necessary unity of direction" having been safeguarded, are not incorporated with all of the thrust of their humanity, by means of "the active participation of all in the running of the enterprise, according to ways which will have to be determined with care and on a macro-economic level, decisive nationally and internationally."[13]

d) Organization of the Workers

12. Therefore, in the intermediary professional structure the peasants' and workers' unions, to which the workers have a right, should acquire sufficient strength and power. Their associations will have a unified and responsible strength, to exercise the right of representation and participation on the levels of production and of national, continental and international trade. They ought to exercise their right of being represented, also on the social, economic and political levels, where decisions are made which touch upon the common good. Therefore, the unions ought to use every means at their disposal to train those who are to carry out these re-

sponsibilities in moral, economic, and especially in technical matters.

e) Unity of Action

13. Socialization understood as a socio-cultural process of personalization and communal growth, leads us to think that all of the sectors of society, but in this case, principally the social-economic sphere, should, because of justice and brotherhood, transcend antagonisms in order to become agents of national and continental development. Without this unity, Latin America will not be able to succeed in liberating itself from the neo-colonialism to which it is bound, nor will Latin America be able to realize itself in freedom, with its own cultural, socio-political and economic characteristics.

f) Rural Transformation

14. The Second Episcopal Conference wishes to voice its pastoral concern for the extensive peasant class, which, although included in the above remarks, deserves urgent attention because of its special characteristics. If it is true that one ought to consider the diversity of circumstances and resources in the different countries, there is no doubt that there is a common denominator in all of them: the need for the human promotion of the peasants and Indians. This uplifting will not be viable without an authentic and urgent reform of agrarian structures and policies. This structural change and its political implications go beyond a simple distribution of land. It is indispensable to make an adjudication of such lands, under detailed conditions which legitimize their occupation and insure their productivity for the benefit of the families and the national economy. This will entail, aside from juridical and technical aspects not within our competence, the organization of the peasants into effective intermediate structures, principally in the form of cooperatives; and motivation towards the creation of urban centers in rural areas, which would afford the peasant population the benefits of culture, health, recreation, spiritual growth, participation in local decisions, and in those which have to do with the economy and national politics. This uplifting of the rural

areas will contribute to the necessary process of industrialization and to participation in the advantages of urban civilization.

g) Industrialization

15. There is no doubt that the process of industrialization is irreversible and is a necessary preparation for an independent economy and integration into the modern worldwide economy. Industrialization will be a decisive factor in raising the standard of living of our countries and affording them better conditions for an integral development. Therefore it is indispensable to revise plans and reorganize national macro-economies, preserving the legitimate autonomy of our nation, and allowing for just grievances of the poorer nations respecting always the inalienable rights of the person and of intermediary structures, as protagonists of this process.

POLITICAL REFORM

16. Faced with the need for a total change of Latin American structures, we believe that change has political reform as its prerequisite.

The exercise of political authority and its decisions have as their only end the common good. In Latin America such authority and decision-making frequently seem to support systems which militate against the common good or which favor privileged groups. By means of legal norms, authority ought effectively and permanently to assure the rights and inalienable liberties of the citizens and the free functioning of intermediary structures.

Public authority has the duty of facilitating and supporting the creation of means of participation and legitimate representation of the people, or if necessary the creation of new ways to achieve it. We want to insist on the necessity of vitalizing and strengthening the municipal and communal organization, as a beginning of organizational efforts at the departmental, provincial, regional and national levels.

The lack of political consciousness in our countries makes the educational activity of the Church absolutely essential, for the purpose of bringing Christians to consider their participation in the political life of the nation as a matter of conscience and as the practice of charity in its most noble and meaningful sense for the life of the community.

INFORMATION AND "CONCIENTIZACIÓN"

17. We wish to affirm that it is indispensable to form a social conscience and a realistic perception of the problems of the community and of social structures. We must awaken the social conscience and communal customs in all strata of society and professional groups regarding such values as dialogue and community living within the same group and relations with wider social groups (workers, peasants, professionals, clergy, religious, administrators, etc.)

This task of "*concientización*" and social education ought to be integrated into joint pastoral action at various levels.

18. The sense of service and realism demands of today's hierarchy a greater social sensitivity and objective. In that regard there is a need for direct contact with the different social-professional groups in meetings which provide all with a more complete vision of social dynamics. Such encounters are to be regarded as instruments which can facilitate a collegial action on the part of the bishops, guaranteeing harmony of thought and activities in the midst of a changing society.

The National Episcopal Conference will implement the organization of courses, meetings, etc., as a means of integrating those responsible for social activities related to pastoral plans. Besides priests and interested religious and laymen, invitations could be extended to heads of national and international development programs within the country. In like manner the institutes organize to prepare foreign apostolic personnel will coordinate their activities of a pastoral-social nature with the corresponding national groups; moreover, opportunities will be sought for promoting study weeks devoted to social issues in order to articulate social doctrine applying to our problems. This will allow us to affect public opinion.

19. "Key men" deserve special attention; we refer to those persons at a decision-making level whose actions effect

changes in the basic structures of national and international life. The Episcopal Conference, therefore, through its Commission on Social Action or Pastoral Service, will support, together with other interested groups, the organization of courses of study for technicians, politicians, labor leaders, peasants, managers and educated men of all levels of society.

20. It is necessary that small basic communities be developed in order to establish a balance with minority groups, which are the groups in power. This is only possible through vitalization of these very communities by means of the natural innate elements in their environment.

The Church—the People of God—will lend its support to the downtrodden of every social class so that they might come to know their rights and how to make use of them. To this end the Church will utilize its moral strength and will seek to collaborate with competent professionals and institutions.

21. The Commission of Justice and Peace should be supported in all our countries at least at the national level. It should be composed of persons of high moral caliber, professionally qualified and representative of different social classes; it should be capable of establishing an effective dialogue with persons and institutions more directly responsible for the decisions which favor the common good and detect everything that can wound justice and endanger the internal and external peace of the national and international communities; it should help to find concrete means to obtain adequate solutions for each situation.

22. For the implementation of their pastoral mission, the Episcopal Conferences will create Commissions of Social Action or Pastoral Service to develop doctrine and to take the initiative, presenting the Church as a catalyst in the temporal realm in an authentic attitude of service. The same applies to the diocesan level.

Furthermore, the Episcopal Conferences and Catholic organizations will encourage collaboration on the national and continental scene with non-Catholic Christian Churches and institutions, dedicated to the task of restoring justice in human relations.

"Cáritas," which is a Church organization[14] integrated in

the joint Pastoral Plan, *will not be* solely a welfare institution, but rather will *become operational* in the developmental process of Latin America, as an institution authentically dedicated to its growth.

23. The Church recognizes that these institutions of temporal activity correspond to the specific sphere of civic society, even though they are established and stimulated by Christians. In actual concrete situations this Second General Conference of Latin American Bishops feels it its duty to offer special encouragement to those organizations which have as their purpose human development and the carrying out of justice. The moral force of the Church will be consecrated, above all, to stimulate them, not acting except in a supplementary capacity and in situations that admit no delay.

Finally, this Second Conference is fully aware that the process of socialization, hastened by the techniques and media of mass communication, makes these means a necessary and proper instrument for social education and for *"concientización"* ordered to changing the structures and the observance of justice. For the same reason this Conference urges all, but especially laymen, to make full use of mass media in their work of human promotion.

NOTES

1. Cf. Synthesis of this situation in the *Work Paper* of the Second Conference of Latin American Bishops, Nos. 1–9.

2. Cf. PAUL VI, Enc. *Populorum Progressio*, No. 30.

3. Cf. Vatican Council II, pastoral constitution *Gaudium et Spes*, No. 69.

4. Cf. Gn. 1, 26; Vatican Council II, pastoral constitution *Gaudium et Spes*, No. 34.

5. Cf. Jn. 8, 32–35.

6. Cf. Eph. 2, 10.

7. Cf. 2 Cor. 5, 17.

8. Cf. Vatican Council II, pastoral constitution *Gaudium et Spes*, No. 38.

9. Cf. Vatican Council II, pastoral constitution *Gaudium et Spes*, No. 41.

10. Cf. Vatican Council II, pastoral constitution *Gaudium et Spes*, No. 42.

11. Cf. Vatican Council II, pastoral constitution *Gaudium et Spes*, No. 39.

12. Cf. Vatican Council II, pastoral constitution *Gaudium et Spes*, Ibid.

13. Cf. Vatican Council II, pastoral constitution *Gaudium et Spes*, No. 68.

14. Cf. Paul VI, Enc. *Populorum Progressio*, No. 46.

Institutional injustice is a violence and engenders a response of violence.

Spiral of violence — 1st level —

Institutionalized — 2nd the response

revolt 3rd response from state which is to counter violence, becomes repression. Invites more violence from people.

Speaks of conversion — Not to Catholic faith but conversion to ones personal faith. Change eye & understanding of faith. A change of perspective of what is going on, often in case of Latin American Bishops.

PEACE

I. The Latin American Situation and Peace

1. "If development is the new name for peace,"[1] Latin American under development with its own characteristics in the different countries is an unjust situation which promotes tensions that conspire against peace.

We can divide these tensions into three major groups, selecting, in each of these, those variables which constitute a positive menace to the peace of our countries by manifesting an unjust situation.

When speaking of injustice, we refer to those realities that constitute a sinful situation; this does not mean, however, that we are overlooking the fact that at times the misery in our countries can have natural causes which are difficult to overcome.

In making this analysis, we do not ignore or fail to give credit to the positive efforts made at every level to build a more just society. We do not include this here because our purpose is to call attention to those aspects which constitute a menace or negation of peace.

TENSIONS BETWEEN CLASSES AND INTERNAL COLONIALISM

2. *Different forms of marginality:* Socio-economic, cultural, political, racial, religious, in urban as well as rural sectors;

3. *Extreme inequality among social classes:* Especially, though not exclusively, in those countries which are characterized by a marked bi-classism, where a few have much (culture, wealth, power, prestige) while the majority has very little. The Holy Father describes this situation when directing himself to the Colombian rural workers: ". . . social and economic development has not been equitable in the great continent of Latin America; and while it has favored those who helped establish it in the beginning, it has neglected the

masses of native population, which are almost always left at a subsistence level and at times are mistreated and exploited harshly."[2]

4. *Growing frustrations*: The universal phenomenon of rising expectations assumes a particularly aggressive dimension in Latin America. The reason is obvious: excessive inequalities systematically prevent the satisfaction of the legitimate aspirations of the ignored sectors, and breed increasing frustrations.

The same low morale is obtained in those middle classes which, when confronting grave crises, enter into a process of disintegration and proletarization.

5. *Forms of oppression of dominant groups and sectors*: Without excluding the eventuality of willful oppression, these forms manifest themselves most frequently in a lamentable insensitivity of the privileged sectors to the misery of the marginated sectors. Thus the words of the Pope to the leaders: "That your ears and heart be sensitive to the voices of those who ask for bread, concern, justice. . . ."[3]

It is not unusual to find that these groups, with the exception of some enlightened minorities, characterize as subversive activities all attempts to change the social system which favors the permanence of their privileges.

6. *Power unjustly exercised by certain dominant sectors*. As a natural consequence of the above-mentioned attitudes, some members of the dominant sectors occasionally resort to the use of force to repress drastically any attempt at opposition. It is easy for them to find apparent ideological justifications (anti-communism) or practical ones (keeping "order") to give their action an honest appearance.

7. *Growing awareness of the oppressed sectors*. All the above results are even more intolerable as the oppressed sectors become increasingly aware of their situation. The Holy Father referred to them when he said to the rural workers: "But today the problem has worsened because you have become more aware of your needs and suffering, and you cannot tolerate the persistence of these conditions without applying a careful remedy."[4]

The static picture described in the above paragraphs is worsened when it is projected into the future: basic education will increase awareness, and the demographic explosion will multiply problems and tensions. One must not forget the existence of movements of all types interested in taking advantage of and irritating these tensions. Therefore, if today peace seems seriously endangered, the automatic aggravation of the problems will produce explosive consequences.

INTERNATIONAL TENSIONS AND EXTERNAL NEOCOLONIALISM

8. We refer here, particularly, to the implications for our countries of dependence on a center of economic power, around which they gravitate. For this reason, our nations frequently do not own their goods, or have a say in economic decisions affecting them. It is obvious that this will not fail to have political consequences given the interdependence of these two fields.

We are interested in emphasizing two aspects of this phenomenon.

9. *Economic aspect.* We only analyze those factors having greater influence on the global and relative impoverishment of our countries, and which constitute a source of internal and external tensions.

a) *Growing distortion of international commerce.* Because of the relative depreciation of the terms of exchange, the value of raw materials is increasingly less in relation to the cost of manufactured products. This means that the countries which produce raw materials—especially if they are dependent upon one major export—always remain poor, while the industrialized countries enrich themselves. This injustice clearly denounced by *Populorum Progressio*,[5] nullifies the eventual positive effect of external aid and constitutes a permanent menace against peace, because our countries sense that "one hand takes away what the other hand gives."[6]

b) *Rapid flight of economic and human capital.* The search for security and individual gain leads many members of the more comfortable sectors of our countries to invest their money in foreign countries. The injustice of such procedures has already been denounced categorically by the encyclical *Populorum Progressio*.[7] To this can be added the loss of technicians and competent personnel, which is at least as serious and perhaps more so than the loss of capital, because of the high cost of training these people and because of their ability to teach others.

c) *Tax evasion and loss of gains and dividends.* Some foreign companies working in our country (also some national firms) often evade the established tax system by subterfuge. We are also aware that at times they send their profits and dividends abroad, without contributing adequate reinvestments to the progressive development of our countries.

d) *Progressive debt.* It is not surprising to find that in the system of international credits, the true needs and capabilities of our countries are not taken into account. We thus run the risk of encumbering ourselves with debts whose payment absorbs the greater part of our profits.[8]

c) *International monopolies and international imperialism of money.* We wish to emphasize that the principal guilt for economic dependence of our countries rests with powers, inspired by uncontrolled desire for gain, which leads to economic dictatorship and the "international imperialism of money"[9] condemned by Pope Pius XI in *Quadragesimo Anno* and by Pope Paul VI in *Populorum Progressio.*

10. *Political Aspect.* We here denounce the imperialism of any ideological bias that is exercised in Latin America either indirectly or through direct intervention.

TENSIONS AMONG THE COUNTRIES OF LATIN AMERICA

11. We here denounce the particular phenomenon of historico-political origin that continues to disturb cordial relations among some countries and impedes truly constructive collaboration. Nevertheless, the integration process, well understood, presents itself as a commanding necessity for Latin America. Without pretending to set norms of a truly complex, technical nature, governing integration, we deem it opportune to point out its multi-dimensional character. Integration, in effect, is not solely an economic process; it has a broader dimension reflected in the way in which it embraces

man in his total situation: social, political, cultural, religious, racial.

Among the factors that increase the tensions among our countries we underline:

12. *An exacerbated nationalism* in some countries. The Holy Father[10] has already denounced the unwholesomeness of this attitude, especially on a matter where the weakness of the national economics requires a union of efforts.

13. *Armaments.* In certain countries an arms race is under way that surpasses the limits of reason. It frequently stems from a fictitious need to respond to diverse interests rather than to a true need of the national community. In that respect, a phrase of *Populorum Progressio* is particularly pertinent: "When so many communities are hungry, when so many homes suffer misery, when so many men live submerged in ignorance . . . any arms race becomes an intolerable scandal."[11]

II. DOCTRINAL REFLEXION

CHRISTIAN VIEW OF PEACE

14. The above mentioned Christian viewpoint on peace adds up to a negation of peace such as Christian tradition understands it.

Three factors characterize the Christian concept of peace:

a) Peace is, above all, a work of justice.[12] It presupposes and requires the establishment of a just order[13] in which men can fulfill themselves as men, where their dignity is respected, their legitimate aspirations satisfied, their access to truth recognized, their personal freedom guaranteed; an order where man is not an object, but an agent of his own history. Therefore, there will be attempts against peace where unjust inequalities among men and nations prevail.[14]

Peace in Latin America, therefore, is not the simple absence of violence and bloodshed. Oppression by the power groups may give the impression of maintaining peace and order, but in truth it is nothing but the "continuous and inevitable seed of rebellion and war."[15]

"Peace can only be obtained by creating a new order which carries with it a more perfect justice among men."[16] It is in this sense that the integral development of a man, the path to more human conditions, becomes the symbol of peace.

b) Secondly, peace is a permanent task.[17] A community becomes a reality in time and is subject to a movement that implies constant change in structures, transformation of attitudes, and conversion of hearts.

The "tranquility of order," according to the Augustinian definition of peace, is neither passivity nor conformity. It is not something that is acquired once and for all. It is the result of continuous effort and adaptation to new circumstances, to new demands and challenges of a changing history. A static and apparent peace may be obtained with the use of force; an authentic peace implies struggle, creative abilities and permanent conquest.[18]

Peace is not found, it is built. The Christian man is the artisan of peace.[19] This task, given the above circumstances, has a special character in our continent; thus, the People of God in Latin America, following the example of Christ, must resist personal and collective injustice with unselfish courage and fearlessness.

c) Finally, peace is the fruit of love.[20] It is the expression of true fraternity among men, a fraternity given by Christ, Prince of Peace, in reconciling all men with the Father. Human solidarity cannot truly take effect unless it is done in Christ, who gives Peace that the world cannot give.[21] Love is the soul of justice. The Christian who works for social justice should always cultivate peace and love in his heart.

Peace with God is the basic foundation of internal and social peace. Therefore, where this social peace does not exist there will we find social, political, economic and cultural inequalities, there will we find the rejection of the peace of the Lord, and a rejection of the Lord Himself.[22]

THE PROBLEM OF VIOLENCE IN LATIN AMERICA

15. Violence constitutes one of the gravest problems in Latin America. A decision on which the future of the countries of the continent will depend should not be left to the

impulses of emotion and passion. We would be failing in our pastoral duty if we were not to remind the conscience, caught in this dramatic dilemma, of the criteria derived from the Christian doctrine of evangelical love.

No one should be surprised if we forcefully re-affirm our faith in the productiveness of peace. This is our Christian ideal. "Violence is neither Christian nor evangelical."[23] The Christian man is peaceful and not ashamed of it. He is not simply a pacifist, for he can fight,[24] but he prefers peace to war. He knows that "violent changes in structures would be fallacious, ineffectual in themselves and not conforming to the dignity of man, which demands that the necessary changes take place from within, that is to say, through a fitting awakening of conscience, adequate preparation and effective participation of all, which the ignorance and often inhuman conditions of life make it impossible to assure at this time."[25]

16. As the Christian believes in the productiveness of peace in order to achieve justice, he also believes that justice is a prerequisite for peace. He recognizes that in many instances Latin America finds itself faced with a situation of injustice that can be called institutionalized violence, when, because of a structural deficiency of industry and agriculture, of national and international economy, of cultural and political life, "whole towns lack necessities, live in such dependence as hinders all initiative and responsibility as well as every possibility for cultural promotion and participation in social and political life,"[26] thus violating fundamental rights. This situation demands all-embracing, courageous, urgent and profoundly renovating transformations. We should not be surprised therefore, that the "temptation to violence" is surfacing in Latin America. One should not abuse the patience of a people that for years has borne a situation that would not be acceptable to anyone with any degree of awareness of human rights.

Facing a situation which works so seriously against the dignity of man and against peace, we address ourselves, as pastors, to all the members of the Christian community, asking them to assume their responsibility in the promotion of peace in Latin America.

17. We would like to direct our call in the first place to those who have a greater share of wealth, culture and power. We know that there are leaders in Latin America who are sensitive to the needs of the people and try to remedy them. They recognize that the privileged many times join together, and with all the means at their disposal pressure those who govern, thus obstructing necessary changes. In some instances, this pressure takes on drastic proportions which result in the destruction of life and property.

Therefore, we urge them not to take advantage of the pacifist position of the Church in order to oppose, either actively or passively, the profound transformations that are so necessary. If they jealously retain their privileges and defend them through violence they are responsible to history for provoking "explosive revolutions of despair."[27] The peaceful future of the countries of Latin America depends to a large extent on their attitude.

18. Also responsible for injustice are those who remain passive for fear of the sacrifice and personal risk implied by any courageous and effective action. Justice, and therefore peace, conquer by means of a dynamic action of awakening (concientización) and organization of the popular sectors, which are capable of pressing public officials who are often impotent in their social projects without popular support.

19. We address ourselves finally to those who, in the face of injustice and illegitimate resistance to change, put their hopes in violence. With Paul VI we realize that their attitude "frequently finds its ultimate motivation in noble impulses of justice and solidarity."[28] Let us not speak here of empty words which do not imply personal responsibility and which isolate from the fruitful non-violent actions that are immediately possible.

If it is true that revolutionary insurrection can be legitimate in the case of evident and prolonged "tyranny that seriously works against the fundamental rights of man, and which damages the common good of the country,"[29] whether it proceeds from one person or from clearly unjust structures, it is also certain that violence or "armed revolution" generally "generates new injustices, introduces new imbalances and causes new disasters; one cannot combat a real evil at the price of a greater evil."[30]

If we consider then, the totality of the circumstances of our countries, and if we take into account the Christian preference for peace, the enormous difficulty of a civil war, the logic of violence, the atrocities it engenders, the risk of provoking foreign intervention, illegitimate as it may be, the difficulty of building a regime of justice and freedom while participating in a process of violence, we earnestly desire that the dynamism of the awakened and organized community be put to the service of justice and peace.

Finally, we would like to make ours the words of our Holy Father to the newly ordained priests and deacons in Bogotá, when he referred to all the suffering and said to them: "We will be able to understand their afflictions and change them, not into hate and violence, but into the strong and peaceful energy of constructive works."[31]

III. PASTORAL CONCLUSIONS

20. In the face of the tensions which conspire against peace, and even present the temptation of violence; in the face of the Christian concept of peace which has been described, we believe that the Latin American Episcopate cannot avoid assuming very concrete responsibilities; because to create a just social order, without which peace is illusory, is an eminently Christian task.

To us, the Pastors of the Church, belongs the duty to educate the Christian conscience, to inspire, stimulate and help orient all of the initiatives that contribute to the formation of man. It is also up to us to denounce everything which, opposing justice, destroys peace.

In this spirit we feel it opportune to bring up the following pastoral points:

21. To awaken in individuals and communities, principally through mass media, a living awareness of justice, infusing in them a dynamic sense of responsibility and solidarity.

22. To defend the rights of the poor and oppressed according to the Gospel commandment, urging our governments

and upper classes to eliminate anything which might destroy social peace: injustice, inertia, venality, insensibility.

23. To favor integration, energetically denouncing the abuses and unjust consequences of the excessive inequalities between poor and rich, weak and powerful.

24. To be certain that our preaching, liturgy and catechesis take into account the social and community dimensions of Christianity, forming men committed to world peace.

25. To achieve in our schools, seminaries and universities a healthy critical sense of the social situation and foster the vocation of service. We also consider very efficacious the diocesan and national campaigns that mobilize the faithful and social organizations, leading them to a similar reflection.

26. To invite various Christian and non-Christian communities to collaborate in this fundamental task of our times.

27. To encourage and favor the efforts of the people to create and develop their own grass-roots organizations for the redress and consolidation of their rights and the search for true justice.

28. To request the perfecting of the administration of justice, whose deficiencies often cause serious ills.

29. To urge a halt and revision in many of our countries of the arms race that at times constitutes a burden excessively disproportionate to the legitimate demands of the common good, to the detriment of desperate social necessities. The struggle against misery is the true war that our nations should face.

30. To invite the bishops, the leaders of different churches and all men of good will of the developed nations to promote in their respective spheres of influence, especially among the political and financial leaders, a consciousness of greater solidarity facing our underdeveloped nations, obtaining among other things, just prices for our raw materials.

31. On the occasion of the twentieth anniversary of the solemn declaration of Human Rights, to interest universities in Latin America to undertake investigations to verify the degree of its implementation in our countries.

32. To denounce the unjust action of world powers that works against self-determination of weaker nations who must

suffer the bloody consequences of war and invasion, and to ask competent international organizations for effective and decisive procedures.

33. To encourage and praise the initiatives and works of all those who in the diverse areas of action contribute to the creation of a new order which will assure peace in our midst.

NOTES

1. Cf. PAUL VI, Enc. *Populorum progressio*, No. 87.

2. Cf. PAUL VI, *Address to the Peasants*, Mosquera, Colombia, 23 August, 1968.

3. Cf. PAUL VI, *Homily of the Mass on Development Day*, Bogotá, 23 August, 1968.

4. Cf. PAUL VI, *Address to the Peasants*, Mosquera, Colombia, 23 August, 1968.

5. Cf. PAUL VI, Enc. *Populorum progressio*, Nos. 56–61.

6. Cf. Ibid., No. 56.

7. Cf. Ibid., No. 24.

8. Cf. Ibid., No. 54.

9. Cf. Ibid., No. 26.

10. Cf. Ibid., No. 62.

11. Cf. Ibid., No. 53.

12. Cf. Vatican Council II, pastoral constitution *Gaudium et Spes*, No. 78.

13. Cf. JOHN XXIII, Enc. *Pacem in terris*, No. 167 and PAUL VI, enc. *Populorum progressio*, No. 76.

14. Cf. PAUL VI, *Message of January 1st*, 1968.

15. Cf. PAUL VI, *Message of January 1st*, 1968.

16. Cf. PAUL VI, Enc. *Populorum progressio*, No. 76.

17. Cf. Vatican Council II, pastoral constitution *Gaudium et Spes*, No. 78.

18. Cf. PAUL VI, *Christmas Message*, 1967.

19. Cf. Mt. 5, 9.

20. Cf. Vatican Council II, pastoral constitution *Gaudium et Spes*, No. 78.

21. Cf. Jn. 14, 27.

22. Cf. Mt. 25, 31–46.

23. Cf. PAUL VI, *Homily of the Mass on Development Day*, Bogotá, 23 August, 1968; Cf. PAUL VI, *Opening address at the Second General Conference of Latin American Bishops*, Bogotá, 24 August, 1968.

24. Cf. PAUL VI, *Message of January 1st*, 1968.

25. Cf. PAUL VI, *Homily of the Mass on Development Day*,

Bogotá, 23 August, 1968.

26. Cf. PAUL VI, Enc. *Populorum progressio*, No. 30.

27. Cf. PAUL VI, *Homily of the Mass on Development Day*, Bogotá, 23 August, 1968.

28. Cf. PAUL VI, *Ibid*.

29. Cf. PAUL VI, Enc. *Populorum progressio*, No. 31.

30. Cf. PAUL VI, Enc. *Populorum progressio*, No. 31.

31. Cf. PAUL VI, *Address to new priests and deacons*, Bogotá, 22 August, 1968.

MESSAGE TO THE PEOPLES
OF LATIN AMERICA

OUR WORD, A SIGN OF COMMITMENT

The Second General Conference of the Latin American Episcopate to the peoples of Latin America: "Grace and peace from God, our Father, and from the Lord Jesus Christ."[1]

Upon finishing the work of this Second General Conference we wish to direct a message to the peoples of our continent.

We want our word as pastors to be a sign of commitment.

As Latin American men we share the history of our people. The past definitively identifies us as Latin Americans; the present places us in a decisive crossroads, and the future requires of us a creative labor in the process of development.

LATIN AMERICA, A COMMUNITY IN TRANSFORMATION

Latin America, in addition to being a geographical reality, is a community of peoples with its own history, with specific values and with similar problems. The confrontation and the solutions must acknowledge this history, these values and these problems.

The continent harbors very different situations, but requires solidarity. Latin America must be one and many, rich in variety and strong in its unity.

Our countries have preserved a basic cultural richness, born from ethnic and religious values that have flourished in a common conscience and have borne fruit in concrete efforts toward integration.

Its human potential, more valuable than the riches hidden in its soil, makes of Latin America a promising reality brimming with hope. Its agonizing problems mark it with signs of injustice that wound the Christian conscience.

The multiplicity and complexity of its problems overflow this message.

Latin America appears to live beneath the tragic sign of underdevelopment that not only separates our brothers from the enjoyment of material goods, but from their proper human fulfillment. In spite of the efforts being made, there is the compounding of hunger and misery, of illness of a massive nature and infant mortality, of illiteracy and marginality, of profound inequality of income, and tensions between the social classes, of outbreaks of violence and rare participation of the people in decisions affecting the common good.

THE CHURCH, THE HISTORY OF LATIN AMERICA AND OUR CONTRIBUTION

As Christians we believe that this historical stage of Latin America is intimately linked to the history of salvation.

As pastors, with a common responsibility, we wish to unite ourselves with the life of all of our peoples in the painful search for adequate solutions to their multiple problems. Our mission is to contribute to the integral advancement of man and of human communities of the continent.

We believe that we are in a new historical era. This era requires clarity in order to see, lucidity in order to diagnose, and solidarity in order to act.

In the light of the faith that we profess as believers, we have undertaken to discover a plan of God in the "signs of the times." We interpret the aspirations and clamors of Latin America as signs that reveal the direction of the divine plan operating in the redeeming love of Christ which bases these aspirations on an awareness of fraternal solidarity.

Faithful to this divine plan, and in order to respond to the hopes placed in the Church, we wish to offer that which we hold as most appropriate: a global vision of man and humanity, and the integral vision of Latin American man in development.

Thus we experience solidarity with the responsibilities that have arisen at this stage of the transformation of Latin America.

The Church, as part of the essence of Latin America, despite its limitations, has lived with our peoples the process of colonization, liberation and organization.

Our contribution does not pretend to compete with the attempts for solution made by other national, Latin American and world bodies; much less do we disregard or refuse to recognize them. Our purpose is to encourage these efforts, accelerate their results, deepen their content, and permeate all the process of change with the values of the Gospel. We would like to offer the collaboration of all Christians, compelled by their baptismal responsibilities and by the gravity of this moment. It is our responsibility to dramatize the strength of the Gospel which is the power of God.[2]

We do not have technical solutions or infallible remedies. We wish to feel the problems, perceive the demands, share the agonies, discover the ways and cooperate in the solutions.

The new image of the Latin American man requires a creative effort: public authorities, promoting with energy the supreme requirements of the common good; technicians, planning concrete means; families and educators, awakening and orienting responsibility, the people incorporating themselves in the efforts for fulfillment; the spirit of the Gospel, giving life with the dynamism of a transforming and personalizing love.

THE CHALLENGE OF THE PRESENT MOMENT: POSSIBILITIES, VALUES, CONDITIONS

Our peoples seek their liberation and their growth in humanity, through the incorporation and participation of everyone in the very conduct of the personalizing process.

For this reason, no sector should reserve to itself exclusively the carrying out of political, cultural, economic or spiritual matters. Those who possess the power of decision-making must exercise it in communion with the desires and options of the community. In order that this integration respond to the nature of the Latin American peoples, it must incorporate the values that are appropriate to all and everyone, without exception. The imposition of foreign values and criteria would constitute a new and grave alienation.

We count upon elements and criteria that are profoundly

human and essentially Christian, an innate sense of the dignity of all, a predilection to fraternity and hospitality, a recognition of woman and her irreplaceable function in the society, a wise sense of life and of death, the certainty of a common Father in the transcendental destiny of all.

This process requires of all of our nations the surmounting of mistrust, the purification of exaggerated nationalism and the solution of their conflicts.

We consider it irreconcilable with our developing situation to invest resources in the arms race, excessive bureaucracy, luxury and ostentation, or the deficient administration of the community.

The firm denunciation of those realities in Latin America which constitute an affront to the spirit of the Gospel also forms part of our mission.

It is also our duty to give recognition to and to stimulate every profound and positive attempt to vanquish the existing great difficulties.

YOUTH

In this transformation, Latin American youth constitute the most numerous group in the population and show themselves to be a new social body with their own ideas and values desiring to create a more just society.

This youthful presence is a positive contribution that must be incorporated into the society and the Church.

COMMITMENTS OF THE LATIN AMERICAN CHURCH

During these days we have gathered in the city of Medellín, moved by the spirit of the Lord, in order to orient once again the labors of the Church in a spirit of eagerness for conversion and service.

We have seen that our most urgent commitment must be to purify ourselves, all of the members and institutions of the Catholic Church, in the spirit of the Gospel. It is necessary to end the separation between faith and life, "because in Christ Jesus . . . only faith working through love avails."[3]

This commitment requires us to live a true scriptural poverty expressed in authentic manifestations that may be clear signs for our peoples. Only poverty of this quality will show forth Christ, Saviour of men, and disclose Christ, the Lord of history.[4]

Our reflections have clarified the dimensions of other commitments, which, allowing for modifications, shall be assumed by all the People God:

To inspire, encourage and press for a new order of justice that incorporates all men in the decision-making of their own communities;

To promote the constitution and the efficacy of the family, not only as a human sacramental community, but also as an intermediate structure in function of social change;

To make education dynamic in order to accelerate the training of mature men in their current responsibilities;

To encourage the professional organizations of workers, which are decisive elements in socio-economic transformation;

To promote a new evangelization and intensive catechesis that reach the elite and the masses in order to achieve a lucid and committed faith;

To renew and create new structures in the Church that institutionalize dialogue and channel collaboration between bishops, priests, religious and laity;

To cooperate with other Christian confessions, and with all men of good will who are committed to authentic peace rooted in justice and love.

The concrete results of these deliberations and commitments we give to you in detailed and hopeful form in the Final Documents which follow this Message.

A FINAL CALL

We call to all men of good will that they cooperate in truth, justice, love and liberty, in this transforming labor of our peoples, the dawn of a new era.

In a special way we direct ourselves to the Church and Christian communities that share our same faith in Jesus

Christ. During this Conference our brothers of these Christian confessions have been taking part in our work and in our hopes. Together with them we shall be witnesses of this spirit of cooperation.

We wish also to caution, as a duty of our conscience, as we face the present and future of our continent, those who direct the destinies of public order. In their hands is the possibility of an administrative conduct that liberates from injustice and acts as a guide to an order having for its end the common good, that can lead to the creation of a climate of confidence and action that Latin American men need for the full development of their lives.

By its own vocation, Latin America will undertake its liberation at the cost of whatever sacrifice, not in order to seal itself off but in order to open itself to union with the rest of the world, giving and receiving in a spirit of solidarity.

We find dialogue with our brothers of other continents who find themselves in a similar situation to ours to be most important for our work. United in difficulties and hopes, we can make our presence in the world a force for peace.

We remind other peoples who have overcome the obstacles we encounter today, that peace is based on the respect of international justice, justice which has its own foundation and expression in the recognition of the political, economic and cultural autonomy of our peoples.

Finally, we have hope that the love of God the Father, who manifests Himself in the Son, and who is spread abroad in our hearts by the Holy Spirit, will unite us and always inspire our actions for the common good.[5]

Thus we hope to be faithful to the commitments that we have made in these days of reflection and common prayer, in order to contribute to the full and effective cooperation of the Church in the process of transformation that is being lived in our America.

We hope also to be heard with understanding and good will by all men with whom we commune in the same destiny and the same aspiration.

All our work and this same hope we place under the protection of Mary, Mother of the Church and Patroness of the

Americas, in order that the reign of God may be realized among us.

We have faith:

> in God
> in men
> in values
> and the future of Latin America.

"The grace of Our Lord Jesus Christ, the charity of God and the fellowship of the Holy Spirit be with you all."[6]

Medellín, 6 September, 1968

NOTES

1. Cf. 1 Cor. 1, 3.
2. Cf. Rom. 1, 16.
3. Cf. Gal. 5, 6.
4. Cf. 2 Cor. 8, 9.
5. Cf. Rom. 5, 5.
6. Cor. 13, 13.

APPENDIX

THE CALL TO ACTION

In celebration of the American national bicentennial, the National Conference of Catholic Bishops organized a massive program of discussion and consultation on the theme of justice in the world. This program, under the motto "Liberty and Justice for All," featured a yearlong program of hearings and parish discussion in which Catholics were invited to present to the bishops their views regarding the outstanding issues of justice confronting the Church and society. In six major regional hearings and an extraordinary international convocation, bishops heard testimony from experts and rank and file Catholics alike on topics ranging from parish renewal to world peace. More than half the nation's dioceses organized parish programs, many leading to diocesan conventions called to examine and revise the priorities of the local Church. As the climax of this program, the first national assembly of the American Catholic Church took place in Detroit October 21–23, 1976.

Representing almost all the nation's dioceses and some eighty national organizations, 1,351 voting delegates participated in the Call to Action Conference, as the assembly was called. The basis of their work was provided by eight working papers prepared by committees of scholars, bishops, and persons active in the ministries of the Church. Each of the eight reports—on the topics of church, ethnicity and race, family, humankind, nationhood, neighborhood, personhood, and work—summarized the results of the nationwide consultation and offered several proposals for action. The delegates debated, revised, and amended these proposals and ultimately passed some thirty lengthy resolutions containing more than three hundred specific items for action. These resolutions then were sent to the National Conference of Catholic Bishops, which would consider them at their 1977 spring meeting. On the basis of the advice received through this unique program, the bishops had promised to prepare a five-year pastoral plan on justice.

While the bishops decided on the theme of justice for their bicentennial celebration, in direct response to Pope Paul VI's call for action for justice and the 1971 Synod's urging of concrete efforts to bring action for justice into the mainstream of church life, the process of listening and speaking ensured that a wide range of issues within the Church would share attention with problems of social justice. Participants emphasized the need for the Church to provide a fitting witness for justice in its own life. Accordingly they devoted considerable attention at every level to the human needs of church members, families, ethnic and cultural groups, and the alienated. A great many resolutions, therefore, dealt with issues of pastoral care, church organization and finances, and services to the spiritual needs of distinct groups. Many others dealt with the ministry, education, and women in the Church.

Yet, the Call to Action Conference also gave considerable attention to social, political, and economic questions. In the parish program, participants had defined these issues in personal terms and focused on the local community. Thus they emphasized the need to share resources with the poor, to live simply, to resist the materialism of society and the violence of the media. They urged more effective and understanding leadership from the clergy to help members assess their social, political, and civic responsibilities. Action proposals often centered on family and neighborhood programs of outreach to persons in need or on local community organization. While the tone of the local discussions supported the thrust of church leadership on issues of public policy, many participants showed a lack of familiarity with the social teachings of the modern Church or with the positions taken on public issues by the American hierarchy. On the other hand, their emphasis on education for justice and on more relevant homilies indicated their awareness of the need to know more. Finally, the participants at the grass roots were generous and compassionate in their response to issues of war, hunger, and human rights in the international arena, but their views were seldom specific.

The Call to Action delegates seemed generally more aware of public issues, so that while they did not abandon the pastoral tone of the preliminary recommendations, they tended to sharpen their focus and become more specific in demanding action. The resolutions cover such an enormous range of problems and needs that little time was left to the delegates to establish priorities among them. The bishops are left, then, with a huge agenda which they must try carefully to translate into a program for action that responds to the human needs revealed through the process and at the same time has a realistic base in the limited resources of the Church.

The bishops could take satisfaction in the resolutions on issues of justice and peace, for, with few exceptions, they were enthusiastically supportive of episcopal initiatives in these areas. The delegates called on the bishops to try more vigorously to implement such statements as those on "The Economy: Human Dimensions" and "Political Responsibility." They asked for a national commission to formulate an action plan to bring the Church's commitment to full employment and adequate income to the parishes and dioceses of the country and for parish political-responsibility committees to provide forums for the study of political programs and awaken to a greater sensitivity to Christian responsibility in the political order. Resolutions on public policy, too, gave strong support to positions which the bishops had taken in support of a program of national health care, adequate housing, and equal educational and employment opportunity and in opposition to abortion. Only in strongly urging passage of the Equal Rights Amendment to the Constitution did the delegates go far beyond the bishops in dealing with domestic issues.

The delegates registered similar support for episcopal leadership on international issues, particularly those dealing with human rights and world hunger. Here, again, they noted the significance of the issues and urged their Church to speak out; but, like most Americans, they were unable to formulate clear

action proposals for changes. Only on disarmament did the
delegates move in a radical direction. Here they unequivocally
condemned the arms race and urged the church to take the
leadership in opposing the possession and threatened use of
nuclear weapons—a direct rejection of deterrence policy. They
linked this plea to proposals for peace education, legislative
action to protect the rights of selective conscientious objectors, and liturgical events to mark repentance for the sins
of nuclear arms policy past and present.

In short, the Call to Action Conference supported the
basic thrust of recent Catholic teachings on social justice and
world peace and called upon the American bishops to take
decisive action to make these teachings better known and
to implement their own statements at the local level. Diocesan offices of justice and peace, community action, and political responsibility were proposed as vehicles for education
and action. Such offices, to be coordinated through the bishops' national secretariat, were envisioned as a network of support for a vigorous Catholic participation in national debates
on economic priorities, social justice, and public policy. The
bishops received this advice and were to act upon it at their
annual meeting of May 1977.

Copies of the Call to Action resolutions can be obtained
from the Department of Social Development, United States
Catholic Conference, 1312 Massachusetts Avenue, N.W.,
Washington, D.C. 20005. An inexpensive newsprint edition,
with background information, can be obtained from the
Quixote Center, Room 301, 3311 Chauncey Place, Mount
Rainier, Maryland 20822.

INDEX